Dark Days

Dark Days
A Memoir

D. RANDALL BLYTHE

DA CAPO PRESS
A Member of the Perseus Books Group

Set in 11 point Giovanni

Cataloging-in-Publication data for this book is available from the Library of Congress.
ISBN: 978-0-306-82314-5 (hardcover)
ISBN: 978-0-306-82315-2 (e-book)

First Da Capo Press edition 2015
Published by Da Capo Press
A Member of the Perseus Books Group
www.dacapopress.com

Da Capo Press books are available at special discounts for bulk purchases in the U.S. by corporations, institutions, and other organizations. For more information, please contact the Special Markets Department at the Perseus Books Group, 2300 Chestnut Street, Suite 200, Philadelphia, PA 19103, or call (800) 810-4145, ext. 5000, or e-mail special.markets@perseusbooks.com.

10 9 8 7 6 5 4

This book is dedicated to anyone who tries to do the right thing. There are those who talk a lot of talk, and then there are those who walk the walk. To the ones who still put in the hard yards, even when it's scary: I salute you.

This is also for anyone struggling with alcohol or drug addiction. There is a better way, trust me—you don't have to live that way anymore if you don't want to.

Contents

part 1

PRAGUE

—

MILITARY HOSPITAL IN PRAGUE. ALL
THIS FROM A SHOW THAT HAD HAPPENED
TWO YEARS AGO. I HAD ABSOLUTELY
NO IDEA THIS HAD OCCURED, WAS
COMPLETELY SHOCKED, AND WE ALL STOOD AROUND
FOR A SECOND TRYING TO FIGURE IT OUT.
I READ PART OF IT ALOUD & MARK LOOKED
AT ME & SAID "OH, SOMEONE DIED AT THE
SHOW" IN HIS SERIOUS VOICE. IT WAS ALL
QUITE SURREAL, SO I QUICKLY TRIED TO
GATHER MY THINGS (GRABBING AN EXTRA
PACK OF SMOKES) THAT THEY WOULD LET ME
TAKE — I WAS TRYING TO FIND MY PHONE
CHARGER, OR BOTH OF THEM, & WAS GETTING
FRUSTRATED AS THE MAIN POLICEMAN KEPT
SAYING IN HIS THICK ACCENT "OK, IT'S
TIME TO GO" SO FUCK IT — OFF I WENT —
SOMEONE FROM MY CREW SAID I MIGHT
WANT TO THINK ABOUT CALLING MY EMBASSY,
AND THE MEN WALKED ME THROUGH THE AIRPORT,
NO CUSTOMS, WITH THE HEAD COP
(WE'LL CALL HIM MIKHAIL FOR NOW —

chapter one

$\mathcal{U}$ ntil the handcuffs snapped around my wrists, I still thought I might be dreaming. Ratchet-arm teeth clicking into a receiving pawl make a very distinct sound. Like a pump-action twelve gauge being racked outside your back door, or a tree limb cracking beneath your weight, it is a sound that swiftly wakes you up to the reality of your situation. It is a sound that says:

You're screwed.

This was not the first time I'd heard that particular noise, but it was the first time in my forty-one years that I had ever been truly scared by it. The rest were mere speed bumps on the way to my next drink. Laughing with a bunch of filthy punk rockers as we were hauled out of a squat into the rainy San Francisco night, a fine spray of mace shutting us up as it filled the back of the paddy wagon on the way to the station. Dropping my scooter in front of a police station then slurring insults at an officer as he cuffed me three blocks from my house, my jacket full of punctured cans spraying cheap lager like a human beer fountain. Good-natured ribbing with a cop as he waited for my girlfriend to return with a carton of Marlboros before taking me off to Richmond City Jail after failing to do sixty-five community service hours for taking a leak in an alley.

A night or two in jail, then back to the bar with a colorful story to tell and a little more street cred to hang on my spiked leather jacket. Another load of 100 percent pure uncut punk rock John Wayne horseshit.

Taking three boxes of over-the-counter sleeping pills and drinking a bottle of cheap wedding champagne in an ill-informed attempt to kill myself after the girlfriend had left me for another man yet again. Waking up insanely wasted because I didn't know over-the-counter pills won't do the trick, then stacking all the furniture in the house on the stove and catching the house on fire. Laughing maniacally and swinging from a tree in the back yard like a clumsy chimp as the house billowed smoke and the police and fire department arrived. Spitting in the cop's face and calling him a pig as he slams me onto the brick sidewalk and starts in on me with the stick before my neighbor runs out and stops him. Laughing and laughing and laughing on the way to the mental ward to have my stomach pumped because I knew the joke was on him—he couldn't hurt a dead man.

Laughter and hate and pure joy when your booze-and-drug-addled brain is convinced you are finally leaving this terrible life. Free at last, free at last; no more of this bullshit world with its bullshit people who make you drink so much. Click, click, click. Off you go to the cell or the loony bin, but you are too wasted to care. Sometimes it's really funny. Sometimes it's a relief.

This time was very, very different than those others. This was scary. I was almost two years sober, far from depressed, and I certainly wasn't laughing or even cursing. Cussing out the officer cuffing me would have been futile. He didn't speak English. I wasn't even on my home continent.

Our plane had touched down at Prague Ruzyne International Airport about five minutes before the cuffs encircled my wrists, and I was positively ebullient. It was the rare time when my band and crew did not pile into the tour bus for yet another long, cramped drive—instead we had flown to the Czech Republic from Norway. This meant we had what was left of the day to roam Prague, a rare luxury I planned on making the most of. Touring bands grinding out the European summer festival circuit don't see much except for one muddy backstage parking lot after the other.

The rest of the time is spent driving from one country to the next, making mostly futile mental notes to come back one day and actually visit some of the beautiful countryside that's glimpsed through the dust-coated windows of a rented night liner as it ferries you to the next show. Being a tourist doesn't pay too well, but you can make decent scratch driving through all that gorgeous scenery if there's a 40,000-person gig at the end of the day's road. European travel for most professional bands isn't full of sight seeing, it's full of actual *travel*. Overnight drives, gigs during the day, and on "days off," really long drives. There are worse ways to make a living though, and every now and then, like this particular day, you luck out and get to actually explore a bit.

As is the custom on the continent, before the plane had even come to a complete stop overhead bins were opened and people were grabbing their bags. Passengers poured over each other and into the aisles to begin the rugby-like skirmish that is European plane deboarding. No matter how many times I fly in Europe, this ridiculous display of self-important savagery never fails to piss me off, and often my bandmates, crew members, and myself will bring the stampeding herd to a complete and extremely aggravated stop. Ignoring what is undoubtedly furious, unintelligible cursing from the people behind us, one or more of us will strike a linebacker's pose, blocking the aisle while we politely defer to the elderly people, children, pregnant women, and anyone else who wishes to get off the plane unmolested and needs help with their baggage. Call me provincial, an uncultured American, or even a redneck, but Southern manners were a big part of my upbringing.

But today, June 27, 2012, I didn't care. Let them pummel each other to death in their senseless rush for the door. The long tour was just four days from being over, and a real day off awaited. As I gathered my things, I took the opportunity to snap a photo of our monitor tech, Brian, asleep across the aisle from me with his mouth wide open. I put my camera away and entered the fray. When an overweight balding Italian man nearly knocked me over in his charge down the aisle for the door, I just laughed. *Ciao, bello!* It was going to take a lot more than briefly being a pin for a human bowling ball to ruin my mood.

Dark history beckoned to me from just a few kilometers away in Prague, and I looked forward to seeing it with relish.

———

*N*othing fascinates me more than visiting sites where tragedies, biblical in their scope, unfolded, and I was excited to continue on with the Nazi Death Trip that had held me in its iron grip as this tour's theme, starting with a solo photography expedition to Auschwitz One and Birkenau a few weeks earlier. As I walked alone through the sodden killing grounds, a small knot of Hasidic Jews, who stared silently at the ruins of the crematoriums, trailed me. In the darkened bathroom corral, I heard them mutter in Hebrew as they gazed at the remnants of the communal toilet, a long and rough concrete plank with holes punched in it at one-foot intervals for defecation. I turned and took a picture of them walking beneath the infamous wrought iron gate that reads *Arbeit Mach Frei*, entering Auschwitz One of their own volition as raindrops dripped from their wide brimmed hats onto their beards, their heads craned skyward to see the words that spelled doom for so many. The sky wept with the Jews that day, and it had been a cold, wet, and emotionally exhausting journey. But my great uncle had died in a snowy French forest fighting the men that had built this place, and I wanted to *feel* why the blood that runs through my veins had been spilled in the Ardennes.

During the German occupation of Prague, the river Vltava had literally run red. Snaking through the city, the Vltava was stained crimson with the blood of Czechoslovaks as the haughty Reinhard Heydrich, known as the Butcher of Prague, the main architect of the Final Solution, brutally annihilated the Czech resistance during the Reich's reign of terror. Heydrich's well-known hubris was his undoing, for he hadn't completely crushed the

Czechs' will, and died at the hands of two young Czechoslovakian paratroopers trained as assassins by the British. But the Butcher had lived up to his namesake before fragments from a grenade had poisoned his mad blood.

I wanted to wander Prague's dark and winding streets after the sun had set, listening for the echoes of jackboots on the Charles Bridge, the screams of *Sieg Heil* in Old Town Square, and perhaps even a whisper of resistance on the wind, the sharp ghost reports from a contraband revolver as a long dead fiery young Hasid took a few pot shots at Nazi stormtroopers clearing the Jewish Quarter. As the Jews were being shipped off to Terezin internment camp to await eventual extermination, Hitler was said to have ordered the Jewish ghetto left intact, planning for it to be a future "Museum of an Extinct Race." Prague was a treasure trove of tragedy indeed.

Some people avoid these places, the Auschwitz's and Choeung Ek's and Wounded Knee's of the world, saying they do not wish to think of such things. I am drawn to them, not as some morbid casualty vampire, but to bear witness with a respectful curiosity. I feel a deep need to listen to the remnants of history's saddest songs, to keep their mournful melody alive on my lips and in my heart. My psyche craves the lessons humanity's blood-rusted fissures have to carve into my soul, and maybe, just maybe, if I soak up enough of them, one day I will begin to make sense of today's ongoing global hostilities.

So it was with a cheerful eye towards catastrophe that I finally stumbled off the plane, hauling my camera gear and dragging behind my rolling laptop case that bulged with my requisite ridiculously excessive amount of books. About midway up the glass-and-steel exit ramp, a blond woman with some sort of badge on her blue uniform asked to see my passport, inspected it carefully, and motioned me onwards. Normally any sort of passport check occurs at customs, located within the confines of an airport building itself, not on a moveable jet bridge. I didn't pay too much attention to this mildly curious event, figuring it for some sort of random check.

I beelined towards the jetway's exit doors, eager to get through customs and out of the airport for a cigarette. Arriving at the top of the jetway, a nervous-looking man in uniform gestured me towards a small glass enclosed room. I saw all the other passengers walking in the opposite direction and out into the concourse. Perhaps they were all EU citizens and went a different way than us Americans. I shrugged and walked into the room, seeing my bass player, John, already inside and looking pretty freaked out. The blond woman who had inspected my passport reappeared beside me and asked for my passport again, keeping it this time. John looked even more worried.

John is always happy to research the worst aspects of any given country we are traveling to, and then inform us that in all probability we will be kidnapped by drug cartels for ransom money or decapitated by fundamentalist religious nuts soon after landing in said country. But perhaps this time he had a right to be a tad bit nervous. In the room with us were three heavily muscled plainclothes officers with badges slung around thick necks holding up their severe Eastern Bloc–style haircuts. Behind them were five even larger, very heavily armed men decked out in SWAT-style tactical gear: Black combat fatigues. Body armor. Loaded submachine guns. Pistols and large, pointy knives that obviously weren't designed for the dinner table strapped to their waists and legs. They had black ski masks pulled over their heads, only cold eyes and pursed lips visible through holes in the fabric.

They appeared to be on some sort of mission to apprehend and execute a highly sought after international terrorist right on the spot.

I saw this fierce display of force, laughed out loud, and began to sing the beginning verse of "Celebration" by the almighty Kool and the Gang. *There's a party going on right here . . .*

I didn't know what was going on, but whatever it was I knew it couldn't have anything to do with me or my band. Who the hell would send an anti-terrorism squad loaded for bear after five smelly rock-n-roll long hairs from a small Virginia city?

"No, there is definitely no party here," John said. "This is something serious."

The tone of his voice wiped the grin right off my face. My mind cranked into overdrive, old behaviors from my drinking days immediately rising to the surface as I furiously searched for someone to blame for this delay. Which idiotic band or crew member had some illegal "dry goods" in their luggage? For once, I knew it wasn't me—my days of smuggling drugs over international borders had long been over. Maybe someone had stupidly accepted something *bad* in the guise of a gift in the Norwegian airport, something you never do in any airport. Or perhaps our manager or the promoter of the next day's show hadn't remembered to fill out some form and our work visas were not in order. Yes, that was probably it—thanks to someone's foolish oversight, we were going to be denied entry into the Czech Republic. The guns and masks seemed a bit heavy handed, but maybe they took deportation seriously in the former Eastern Bloc. My anger intensified thinking about the hole I was going to chew in whoever's ass had screwed this up so badly, costing us time, money, a show, and a day off.

I suddenly realized I was letting that cunning old anger monkey back into my mind, the one I fed with booze for so long until he shrieked so hard it nearly tore my head off and killed me. I calmed myself and began to look on the bright side. Oh, well. Norway was a great place for a night off, and the flight back to Scandinavia was fairly short. I began to wonder if Hitler had ever visited Oslo.

Within two minutes of deboarding, my entire band and crew had joined John and me in the room with the cops. As we stood there asking each other what was going on, the woman who held my passport walked up to me and in heavily accented English said my name.

"David Blight?" (No one ever says my last name, Blythe, correctly. The *the* is silent, so it's pronounced *BLĪ*, like "fly" with a *b* instead of an *f*.)

"That's me," I answered.

"This is for you," she said, handing me a few sheets of official-looking paper bound together with red, white, and blue twine, "You will come with us for some questions. Please gather any medicines you may need in the next few hours."

I looked at the paper. In convoluted, very poorly written English, it read that I was responsible for the death of young man whose name I'd never heard of before this instant, apparently a fan of my band who attended the one concert we had played in Prague two years previously. From what I could gather, the paper said that I had knowingly and with harmful intent assaulted this young man, somehow throwing him from "the podium" (which I took to mean "stage"), after which he had sustained a head injury, gone into a coma, and died a few weeks later in a military hospital in Prague. I was to be charged in court with killing this young man.

Time slowed to a surreal pace as I tried to process this unexpected information. *This obviously isn't reality. I have never killed anyone in my life*, I thought, *this is some sort of crazy mistake. I must be dreaming.*

As my band and crew gathered around me, my guitarist Mark snatched the papers from my hands and read them.

"Ooooooooh. Someone must have died at the show," Mark said, looking up from the papers and handing them back to me. His soft voice seemed to echo a bit and then begin to slip away, like a fader being slowly pulled down on a soundboard's vocal track. As I took the papers, it felt as if a strange distance suddenly grew between us, imposed by these large war-like policemen and this bizarre situation.

"It is time to leave now. We must go," said the largest of the plainclothes officers, his Czech accent forcing the words into an unfamiliar cadence.

"Gimme a second," I replied. I bent down and unzipped my computer bag, looking for my cell phone charger and bottle of Lexapro, a mild anti-depressant I had been prescribed for the last year or so. Through the weirdness of the moment, other, more practical, behaviors from the drinking days arose as I rummaged for as many extra packs of cigarettes as I could find. In some corner of my mind it was dimly registering that I was probably going to be locked up for a few days. Cigarettes are valuable currency in jail, but apparently I had left my extra packs in my checked luggage. I had seven Marlboros in the pack in my pocket.

"We must go now. You must hurry," the big cop said again.

"Hold your horses. I'm almost ready," I said. I was getting annoyed by this pushy cop, and I was ready to wake up as well. I had had enough of this particular dream. I closed my bag and straightened up.

"Call my wife and let her know I've been arrested," I told Mark as the over-anxious cop and another of the plainclothes officers gripped my biceps tightly and began leading me away from my band and crew.

"You might want to get some representation, and call the embassy," one of my crew called to me as I walked away. This struck me as a particularly ludicrous thing to say. Might? *Might?*

As we walked from the small room and into the airport proper, my mind shifted gears from disbelief to a hyper-focused awareness of my surroundings. Self-preservation ripped away the gossamer haze that had coated reality just seconds before, and everything became bright and crystalline. As I was led past curious onlookers through Ruzyne International, flanked by eight heavily armed men, I had a very clear thought, simultaneously pragmatic and bizarre:

Focus. Pay attention to everything happening around you right now. Choose every word you say very carefully. This is immensely important to your well being, perhaps even your survival. Do not let your attention waver or wander. Focus. This is going to make a great book one day. Focus.

It seemed very strange, even inappropriate, to be thinking about writing a book at a moment like this, and I wondered what was wrong with my brain; but even as I thought this, my eyes began scanning my surroundings and I heard clicking sounds in my mind, like my Canon's shutter button being depressed in rapid fire mode. As strange as it was, I knew I was capturing images and filing them away for later use.

The two officers on either side of me were almost dragging me through the airport, their steps hurried and their hands clamped hard on my arms. They seemed strangely nervous to me. What did they have to worry about?

"Relax, okay?" I said to them. "I'm not going anywhere. You guys have a bunch of guns, remember?" The cops eased up a bit, and we walked out through the sliding doors of the airport entrance, and towards a red-colored unmarked car in the taxi lane. The five SWAT team cops walked away from us without a word as soon as we were out of the airport. I supposed they were there in case my band and crew had tried to fight the police and resist my arrest. Now that it was just me, apparently machine guns and face masks were no longer necessary. I wasn't sad to see them go.

One of the cops told me to face the car and put my hands on its roof, and as I did so I spread my feet apart automatically. I knew the drill, and had no desire to piss them off—that had never worked in my favor before, despite a few valiant efforts. The cop did the standard pat down that always precedes a ride in a police vehicle, emptying all the pockets of my cut-off camo BDUs and placing the contents in a clear plastic bag. As I took my hands off the roof of the car, a last-ditch thought came to me once again that maybe I was dreaming. I pinched my forearm, hard. Regrettably, I seemed to be awake. The cop asked me if I had any drugs or weapons hidden on my person.

"Nope. But could I smoke a cigarette before we go downtown?"

The cop looked confused.

"We are not going downtown. We are going to the police station," he said "and you can have a cigarette later. Put your hands together."

Click, click, click. This was definitely real. At least they weren't assholes about it and didn't cuff me too tight. Some cops will do that, especially if you have had a little too much of the jerk juice. They opened the car door and carefully guided me into the back seat, making sure I didn't bump my head on the way in. They closed the door, and I heard one laugh as they spoke briefly in Czech outside the closed doors. They got into the car, and we pulled away from the airport. No one said a word.

Focus, focus, focus.

chapter two

$\mathcal{I}$t's hard for me to explain how uncomfortable I feel when someone describes me as a *rockstar*. A while ago, I was the only member of my band asked to do an interview for a well-known hard rock magazine's one hundredth issue, the theme of which was "The 100 Greatest Living Rockstars." All members of my band are paid the same as equal business partners, there are very few individual writing credits on our records, we all go on the same tours riding the same bus. There is no "leader" of the band. And as far as I know none of my guys lives a more exotic or glamorous lifestyle than any of the others, including me. I suppose I was selected to represent my band simply by virtue of being its front man, a job that admittedly seems to require a somewhat larger-than-life personality by its very nature, at least if you want to be effective at it. Regrettably, often this personality manifests its worst aspects via the full-blown cases of egomania-cloaked insecurity known in our business as L.S.D. (lead singer's disease). Musicians afflicted with L.S.D. are easy to spot, especially for another musician—they are constantly in the press blabbering on about absolutely nothing, even when they are not promoting an upcoming release or in the midst of a touring cycle (about eighteen months on average, by the way), tend to have no interests outside of promoting their band (and thus, themselves, since they have no real sense of identity or self-worth), and behind the sacred veil of the backstage door are the most demanding, needy, flat-out-annoying jackasses you will ever have the misfortune of rubbing shoulders with. And while lead singers are certainly not the only breed of musician to contract L.S.D. (in fact some of the most hideous cases I have witnessed were in players who would be too terrified to squeak a single note into a microphone in a room full of deaf people), it *is* called lead singer's disease, not rhythm guitarist's disease, for a reason. As my wife likes to not-so-gently remind me at times, I do have a rather, um, *loud* personality, but on the whole I think I do a pretty good job of keeping my L.S.D. in check.

While I rarely enjoy doing interviews, this particular magazine has done a great deal to advance my band's career (thanks, guys—you know who you are), so I agreed. I obviously enjoy expressing myself publicly with words, otherwise I wouldn't sing in a band (and you wouldn't be reading this book), but not through the often-distorting filter of a journalist's written lens. Regardless, when I did the interview, I expressed the fact that I didn't really consider myself a rockstar and wasn't comfortable with being labeled as such, and to the magazine's credit they included that in the full-page spread they gave me. When the issue came out, I read it, but it still just felt weird to be included.

On the magazine's cover, I was drawn in caricature along with twenty or so other musicians. Virtually all of the cartoon dudes adorning the magazine's cover fall under what I believe most folks' definition of a rockstar would be, and their bands are light years beyond mine in popularity. Some of them are even household names across the globe. I know about half of these men personally, and several are dear friends, whom I always try to crush in one of my over-exuberant bear hugs whenever we meet in person. But even on the cover of the magazine the illustrator captured my impostor complex pretty well: the cartoon version of me lurks to the side of all the real rockstars, a rueful sideways grimace on my penciled face that says *What in the hell am I doing here? I better split before I knock something over and they realize I snuck in through the back door with the help.*

Strange or not, after almost twenty years in this business I am finally starting to accept the fact (no matter how distasteful and bizarre I may find it) that some people do indeed consider me a rockstar. And although I never dreamed of or planned on becoming a rockstar, I also never dreamed of or planned on becoming a rampaging alcoholic hell-bent on destroying everything good in my life, repeatedly breaking the hearts of those who loved me most in the process. But somehow both things seem to have occurred, both are fairly public knowledge, and since I've been sober a few years now and have returned to what little senses I have left, I might as well face the music (as it were) and make the best out of both situations. For those of you unfamiliar with who I am, my band, and/or my reputation, I better qualify myself and explain a little about my life. I'll address the rockstar stuff first and get it out of the way upfront, because while it is pretty interesting at times, its impact on my life is inconsequential compared to my alcoholism. For me, being considered a rockstar is just fancy window dressing, a really nice paint job on a worn out sports car in need of constant, daily maintenance. It may look really cool, but underneath the shine a turd is a turd, even if you gold plate it.

———

My name is David Randall Blythe. I reside in Richmond, Virginia, United States of America. On the records my band releases (and on the cover of this book) I am credited as D. Randall Blythe. This is because my father told me once when I was younger that one day, whenever I (hopefully) figured out what I was going to do for a living, that "D. Randall Blythe will look *really* sharp" (his exact words) as my professional name. I tend to agree, and although neither of us ever imagined that I would wind up playing heavy metal for a living (not exactly a realistic or stable career choice in the average parent's eyes), and my choice of profession has caused him just a wee bit of consternation a time or two (and that's putting it mildly—I think he's still waiting for me to "grow out of it"—sorry Pops), I have always remembered his advice. I love and respect the old goat, so D. Randall it is. Thanks, Dad.

Most everyone just calls me Randy though.

The band I sing for, lamb of god, has sold over two million records world wide. The music we make is not exactly what you would call "radio friendly," but our last four albums have been released on a major label. We have been nominated for the biggest prize the music industry gives, a Grammy award, on four separate occasions, handily losing all four times, might I add (some of my bandmates have been to the Grammy ceremonies a few times, and good for them—they seem to have had a good time walking the red carpet and raging the after parties, but that scene is simply not for me. If I were to attend, it would only result in broken glass, disgrace for my family, and a furtive flight out of Tinseltown). On tour with lamb of god, I have flown literally around the world several times, playing in front of large crowds numbering anywhere from 1,500 to over 100,000 people. On tour and off, fans regularly ask for my autograph and/or to take a picture with me, some of the younger ones' hands shaking so hard with nervousness at meeting me that I gently grab their camera phones from them and take the damn photo myself after a few blurry attempts. People tattoo my signature, the lyrics I write, and sometimes even my portrait indelibly into their flesh. More than once, fans (mostly female, but there has been a dude or two) have cried when they met me or my bandmates. Lamb of god has been hand-picked to open up for the biggest names in the heavy metal business. Incredibly, people actually tell me that they consider it an honor to meet me.

Whenever I sit and take stock of my professional life, often a part of me says, "Huh? Wait a minute, you do *what* for a living? Nooooo . . . stop pulling my leg!"

It makes me happy inside that all of these things continue to astound me on a daily basis, that I'm not so jaded and bitter by two decades in this wacky, often ugly, business that I don't remember how blessed I am to do what I do. I'm so grateful for the unique experiences and opportunities that my job has provided me, and it honestly touches me deeply when someone says, "Hey man, I just want you to know that your music has helped me get through a really difficult period in my life." This is the greatest compliment a fan can give me, as I feel like I have done my job. Forget the recognition, forget the travel, and especially forget the money—other people's music has helped me to get through some really hard times, times I was so low that I honestly believe that a song alone kept breath in my lungs. So if a person, even just one person, can use music I helped create to keep their head up in a rough spot, then I feel like I have in some small way repaid a debt to all those who put their blood, sweat, and tears into the tunes that kept me going when I wanted to just crawl into a hole and die.

But no matter how many people say those sweet words to me, the ones that mean so much and make my heart want to burst out of my chest with joy, no matter how many times I hear a few thousand fans boomeranging the words I wrote in some cheap spiral bound notebook back at me, singing so loudly they almost drown out the PA, a part of me is (and always will be, I think) convinced that one day *they will find out*, and then it will all be over quicker than a duck on a june bug. Who *they* are and exactly *what* it is *they* will find out, I have no clue. But as sure as the sun will rise, I just know *they* are gonna show up one day, and when that day comes . . . it's back to sweating in a restaurant kitchen or on a roofing crew for me. Oh well—it was a nice ride while it lasted.

So while some folks do consider me a bonafide rockstar, and all heartwarming artistic rewards and paranoid insecurity aside (obviously symptomatic of my L.S.D.), I still look at things a little differently. Maybe because I don't enjoy the *rockstar* label, particularly not when it is thrown in my face, and especially not when it's slurred out after one too many beers by acquaintances or fans who think they are being cute (you're not cute, you're *drunk*) or are trying to look "cool." If you say anything remotely resembling the following words to *any* professional musician, you look the antithesis of cool; in fact, you mostly resemble a dirty convenience store microwave overheating at the tail end of a three-day bender:

"Heeeeeeeey, Mister Rockstar, how's the big time treatin' ya? Must be nice to be you, not having to work and all that, cruising around the world in that tour bus and just partying all day and night!"

Give me a break. Anyone carrying these idealized pipe dreams around in their witless noggin of what being a professional musician is has no conception based in any sort of reality of what it actually is we do for a living, or what it requires. There are plenty of jobs that are a lot, lot harder than mine. I know this, because from the time I was twelve until I was thirty-three years old, I worked those kinds of jobs, and not a single one of them involved sitting down in an air conditioned office, or sitting down *period* until I slumped onto a barstool after busting my hump all day in a kitchen, someone's yard, or on a roof. The majority of my adult life I worked a regular job *and* did the band. I know what back-breaking physical labor is, and I know what it means to wonder if you are going to make the rent, and I know the hollow dread that fills you as you try not to cry, looking in your empty wallet and thinking, *How in God's name am I supposed to feed myself and my family like this? How are we going to make it through this month?* I lived that way for a long time; in other words, I know what work is. While I wouldn't trade my job for any other you could offer me, being in a band is *work*. And if you are crazy enough to try and do it for a living, it is hard work. Very hard.

Another thing that gets my goat to chewing a ball of tin foil is when younger guys or girls who want to do the band thing come to me and say something like this:

"I love your music! Man, you guys are so lucky! You get to just play music to all your fans for a living! I really wish my band could go tour the world like yours! We aren't that lucky—maybe one day though . . . "

I have some bad news for you, pal—you will never be as lucky as us. Not as long as you think that way, because for the most part it's not luck, it's work. For some odd reason, tons of otherwise intelligent people seem to hold a weird belief that luck is a major factor involved in "getting a career" as a professional musician, especially in this day of idiotic reality TV "talent" competition shows. The pervasive cultural myth of the *lucky break* has only gotten stronger with the advent of these mawkish clown-shoe battle royales, and young players hang their career hopes on getting accepted into some ridiculous contest, not on skilled hands calloused from playing guitar in empty dive bar after empty dive bar for years on end. You don't hatch out of some rockstar egg, you work and *hone your craft.*

Just for kicks, I would love to meet an actual brain surgeon at a cocktail party (or wherever it is brain surgeons kick it). I just want to see the look on their face when I hit 'em with this gem: "You are a *brain surgeon?* Wow, that's so cool—you are so lucky! You get to crack open skulls, dick around with medulla oblongatas, and save lives all day long—plus you get *paid!* I always wanted to take a whack with a scalpel through someone's dome, but I'm not that lucky. Maybe one day they will let me into the ER, though! I just gotta meet the right hospital administrator . . . "

Admittedly becoming a brain surgeon requires more work (and a truck load more education) than becoming a heavy metal singer (and is certainly a much more important job), but the principle is the same. In the real world, no one is going to "discover" you. Especially if you're too busy smoking joints and playing video games on your couch to actually play music in front of real, live, breathing human beings. The Internet will not get you a record deal, no matter how many "friends" your band has on all the social media sites. There have been a few lucky exceptions, but there's that *luck* word again. Just go play the lottery if you want to try to *win* something. Your odds are probably better. Plus, even if you *won* a record deal, that in no way guarantees you a *career*. If you're curious and need a more in-depth explanation, there are plenty of ex-professional musicians in New York City and Los Angeles who will gladly tell you all about it, assuming they have a spare moment between delivering you your burrito and running table eight their enchiladas supreme.

There is also the matter of *talent*. Yes, being a professional musician requires some innate talent, I believe—not tons, as Top-40 radio clearly illustrates, but there has to be *something* there. I hate to further crush anyone's dreams, but not everyone has musical talent. There, I said it—yes, I'm a big meanie. No matter how many drum lessons you take, no matter how many feel-good "you can do anything if you set your mind to it" self-help books you read (and I own a shelf full—I never finish them for some reason; maybe because I know that reading that stuff doesn't get the new record written), no matter how many times you do the visualization exercises you read in one of those wastes of paper, imagining yourself on stage in front of thousands of adoring fans and saying into the mirror "I am a rock God, I am a rock God, I am a rock God"—you cannot cultivate musical talent where there is none. If you have no musical talent, just give up and find something you are good at. It's okay—not everyone is meant to do this. How will you know if you have no talent? Get out and play in front of as many people as you can (no, your girlfriend doesn't count), as often as you can, anywhere you can. Trust me, sooner or later, someone will let you know, either gently or not-so-gently with the time honored "don't quit your day job." When you hear that more than "I really enjoyed your set," it's time to hang it up and take up knitting or something. Sorry.

But beyond the modicum of talent required (if it exists, it can be nurtured with practice) to get your foot into the door of this dirty game, the bottom line here, like most anywhere else, is work. There are many, many talented musicians out there just waiting to be discovered; thousands of players with far more natural musical talent in their pinky fingers than me or any of my band members. But the overwhelmingly vast majority of them will never even come minutely close to being professional musicians for a few simple reasons (and right about now some people are going to start to really hate me as they read this, but it is the indisputable truth):

Most wannabe pro-musicians are simply not strong enough to put up with all the sniping bullshit that is thrown at you when you have the audacity to publicly perform music you wrote yourself, much less even attempt to make a living from it (or any sort of art for that matter, as some reviews of this book will surely attest). They do not possess a thick enough skin to handle the constant rejection, criticism, and never-ending underhanded attempts by everyone and their crooked uncle to rip off what little bit of money they do manage to make. They do not have the will to stand up for themselves and ignore those who cry "greedy wanna-be rockstar pig!" when they ask for enough money to at least fill the van's gas tank to get to the next town; because unlike the fantasy land that the current generation of spoiled brat Internet critics seem to live in ("Music should be freeeeee, maaaaaaan!"), for those of us living in the real world and not at Mom's house, gasoline, equipment, and uhm, food actually costs *money*. And even if they happen to have the cojones to deal with all the creeps, critics, jerks (and of course the *worst* of them all, the family members) who have never picked up an instrument but are all too happy to tell you how you are wasting your time, most folks simply are not willing to suffer long enough, not ready to be broke for the years and years it takes 99 percent of us to finally be able to support ourselves at a mere sustenance level. I don't blame them. Who in their right mind would waste years of their lives on a ridiculous dream with no immediate returns, ending in decades long bouts of self-loathing, financial disgrace, and smug familial I-told-you-so's for the overwhelming majority of those who are foolhardy enough to try and pursue that dream? Many times over the years I have wondered, *What in the hell am I doing? This will never work! I must be crazy.*

You can't sit around and dream your way into a career in the music business, anymore than I can dream my way into being a professional skateboarder. If that worked, I would have been a highly paid world record holding pro-skater at age fourteen, surrounded constantly by a bevy of adoring Hawaiian Tropic bikini models. Instead, I'm a forty-something dude who still likes riding around on my skateboard for fun; in fact I *love* it. Always have. But even as a kid I didn't love it *enough* to do what it took to get really, really good. I know a few who did though—some of them have skeletons made mostly out of metal and weird synthetics now.

As Marilyn Monroe reportedly once said—"I wasn't the prettiest, I wasn't the most talented. I simply wanted it more than anyone else."

Suppose you do want it badly enough, then what? It's time to start living the dream, right? The reality for most people who pay the bills with music is not what you see on television. I make a more than comfortable living, and I haven't worried about where my next meal is going to come from in a long time, but MTV won't be calling me to show off my two bedroom house on *Cribs* anytime soon, that's for sure. I have never owned a brand-new car in my life (I have owned four total, and three of them were beaters that I drove until they just wouldn't drive anymore. Currently, I'm quite happy with my used Toyota truck, thank you very much. There is no Ferrari in my nonexistent garage), and most of the clothes I buy come from the Army Navy surplus store on the south side of Richmond. The cost of living in Richmond is quite reasonable compared to cities like NYC or LA, where famous musicians are supposed to go live their fabulous lives in opulent splendor amongst the beautiful people. My overhead is relatively low, I save my money, and my band is established well enough, with a large enough and dedicated long-term fan base, that I'm not particularly worried about getting on decent tours and selling enough t-shirts to make the mortgage payment (by the way, that is where most of your revenue lies—merchandise. Virtually no one makes money from record sales, because they don't really exist anymore. Just a fact). I don't work a straight job anymore, and if I'm smart, I won't have to. I am the happy exception to the rule, though. Many of my friends in established bands with fairly large fan bases are what I call "semi-professional" musicians, because when they aren't on the road, they are slinging drinks at the local watering hole to make that rent check. Signing autographs one week, the next carrying out the bar trash at the end of their ten-hour shift. This is reality.

There is no retirement plan in this business, no 401(k) waiting for you when you finally can't drag your not-so-cute-anymore aching frame onto the stage. There is no company health insurance (most of my professional musician friends can't afford health insurance, but hey—that's America, right?). There are no paid vacations, and when you're touring (once again, where you make that rent money from merch sales), there are no personal leave or sick days. No one cares if you feel terrible. No one cares if you have strep throat. No one cares if your migraine is killing you. No one cares that you are losing your mind because your wife has just left you via text message for Clarence, the thirty-eight-year-old bag boy at the grocery store who "understands her" (yes, this happened. Not to me, but it happened. Clarence, you motherfucker). *No one cares.*

The promoter has given your booking agent (who takes a percentage of every show you play, by the way) an advance and doesn't want to go broke over one canceled show. Your crew, who works twice as hard as you for none of the glory, needs to get paid, and paid on time because they have rent and child support and hospital bills and their daughter needs to get glasses. Gas has to be put into whatever vehicle you are carrying your dog-and-pony show around the country in, and since the teleporter doesn't exist yet, your driver needs some moolah. Your fans have waited months to see you do your thing, paid their hard-earned money for a ticket, and they expect to be entertained. They deserve it, too, because as I said, we are very, very blessed to be doing this for a living.

Without the fans, I would still make music. I did it long before anyone but my friends and family knew my name, and if no one ever heard another song I wrote ever again, I would still be kicking out the jams, because that is what I love to do. It is as much a part of my life as reading books, which I simply cannot live without. So I would still be writing songs, but I would be writing when and if I had the spare time and energy to do so at the end of a long day working my straight job, and my focus on the music would not, by circumstance, be so absolute. I believe my art would suffer. My fans have allowed me to live a life I never dreamed of as a younger man, and for that I owe them. So when you're on tour and you don't feel so hot, if you have any sort of integrity or respect for the people who got you to where you are, you do your damn job. Shut up, rub some dirt on it, get your ass onstage, and give the people what they paid for. No excuses. No one cares.

Most band guys I know suffer from a variety of ailments and/or chronic pain of some sort, generally due to repetitive motion injuries and bad decisions made while exhausted and/or intoxicated. Compressed vertebrae, pinched nerves, bone spurs, tendinitis, hair-line fractures, weird skin conditions from being immersed in the rolling germ factory that is a tour bus—it's endless. Spend enough time around a few touring musicians and sooner or later you will hear the creaks and groans as they sit down to compare their list of bodily complaints and swap remedies. It's like sitting with a group of twenty-to-forty-somethings who have been zapped prematurely into a backstage senior citizen's home for aging rockers.

It takes a different breed of human to try to do this stuff for a living (and by different, I mean completely lacking in common sense). You have to be a little cracked to even try to make it in the high weirdness that is the music business. It gets even weirder once you attain a little popularity, and people start assuming they *know you.* Suddenly there is a multitude of mewling milk-toothed experts holding forth on all sorts of things about you, your personality, and your personal life; things these people who have never met you have no way of knowing besides what they can gather from that hallowed and infallible source of all information in this "information" age, the Internet. Thousands of them will anonymously either praise or condemn you, depending on what the almighty hive mind has pronounced within the last five minutes.

If this being a professional musician thing is so darn hellish and impossible to attain, as I may be leading you to believe with all this talk of doom and gloom, then why in the world did I bother to try in the first place? Why do I still do it now?

Because I love it.

And I love it because truth be told, at its absolute best it *is* a dream come true. There is nothing in the world like the feeling of listening to a song, a song you spent weeks and weeks writing and arguing with your bandmates over, finally recording it and getting it just right after three weeks of ripping your vocal chords apart, then hearing that song blasting out through a PA louder than a 747 jet engine, hearing that song that you know in your guts *kicks ass* rip in perfect time out of you and your bandmates, watching it smack the waiting audience in the face, and then hearing that song roar back at you on the voices of a few thousand people who have taken that song, that thing you created, and loved it enough to take it into their heart and soul and make it a part of their own lives, giving that damn song a whole new meaning and a life of its own.

It's a massive energy exchange, an amazing, sublime, and holy experience of pure communication. When it's happening, you can feel every single molecule in your body vibrating in perfect harmony with the universe. I wish that every single person on this planet could have that experience. If everyone could feel it, just once, I think the world would be a better place, and we would understand that everyone in fact is the same, equal in the eyes of God, and that every voice on this planet deserves to be heard, that everyone's song deserves to be sung. I wish this could happen for everyone, because I truly do believe in the intrinsically equal value of every human life on this whirling green and blue spaceship we travel through the cosmos in.

But all hippy-dippy crap aside, almost none of the thousands upon thousands of kids with an instrument and a dream will ever make it out of the basement and onto a stage in a professional capacity to attain that feeling. Because they aren't strong enough in their convictions, don't have enough will power to follow those convictions, and most importantly, aren't willing to suffer long enough and work hard enough until the process of living those convictions finally, finally pays off. They just don't want it badly enough. The numbers never lie. Sorry, kid.

Somewhere though, through the magic of time and space travel that the holy act of writing and reading provides, I can actually feel the burning eyes of a few kids on this page, eyes that blaze with malice and determination, eyes trying their best to sear a hole through this page and into my head for daring to try to tell them that they have no hope of living this dream I've done my best to write out of their hands. When they are done reading this and cursing me for being a patronizing rockstar son of a bitch, they will throw this book across the room and into the poster covered practice space wall, they will pick up their instrument or their notebook and pen, and they will get to work. They will not listen to any of the voices that tell them they can't do it, least of all my sardonic croaking. Not *ever*.

These are the ones I will see down the line somewhere, on tour, and they will rock my socks completely off. They can even tell me to kiss it, because I obviously didn't know who I was dealing with. I know they are out there, and I can feel them coming my way even as I write this. I know this because I was one of them. We can smell our own kind.

I'm looking forward to it, kid. Now get back to work.

————

*B*ut I was explaining my dubious status as a rockstar, and its effect on my life. I previously mentioned one of the greatest gifts and curses of our current age, the Internet, specifically its hive mind aspect. The hive mind is a vast and interconnected global game of *he said/she said*, with virtually no rules of accountability, no reliable yardstick by which the truth may be measured, not to mention any sort of arbiter of good taste.

Following my arrest and eventual release, I cracked open my laptop and read a large amount of incorrect information concerning myself and my situation, information that spread at the speed of wifi on wings of speculation. I didn't really bother to try to correct the many falsehoods concerning my legal situation that peppered the Internet, because to do so would have been an exercise in futility. The hive mind is much too big and far too stupid to take correction. Its very nature prevents the existence of veracity on a global scale within its confines. Too many screaming chefs, not enough sweaty line cooks. But this is my book, not the Internet, so I can speak factually here, with no one contradicting me or adding their two unsolicited counterfeit cents; at least not until some asshole with no writing talent of their own "remixes" it. Here are a few facts about me, ones you may take to the bank, no matter what anyone else says. If you bother reading the rest of this book, you'll know a few more as well, because I am writing this, *me*, good ol' Uncle Randy, not a ghost writer, not a co-author, and certainly not a giant digital conglomeration of slobbering critics and jabbering pundits. Just *me*, and I reckon I should know a few things about *me* after more than forty years of being *me*, so here they are:

1. I was born February 21, 1971, in Fort Meade, Maryland, United States of America.

2. Except for the first two years of my existence, I have lived in the Southeastern United States of America (AKA *Dixie*), primarily in Virginia and North Carolina.

3. I am happily married to an awesome woman as of this writing (assuming the wife doesn't get fed up and split before this goes to print).

4. My band, lamb of god, formed in the winter of 1994 in Richmond, VA. I joined the band in the late summer of 1995, and since 2004 lamb of god has been my primary source of income, and for the most part I love my job.

5. I am a rampaging alcoholic who drank insane, mind-blowing amounts of booze for twenty-two years until I sobered up at the youthful age of thirty-nine in 2010.

Those things are facts, but all they really let you know is that I'm a married Southerner with a cool job and a drinking problem that should have killed me but didn't. At the base of it, that's all there truly is to know about me, but I guess that wouldn't make for a very interesting book (and my publishers would probably be a little pissed if I submitted a one sentence manuscript). How did I get to where I am today in my field? Besides the obvious stuff I've already laid out (being stubborn/foolish enough to stick with this band thing until it actual worked), why do I get to travel the world and play music for a living when almost everybody else who wants to doesn't? Since false modesty is almost as great a sin as hubris to me, and many times more annoying, I'll lay it out right now—there *are* a couple of things that I am very, very good at. In fact, I'm one of the best in the business. My unique proficiencies?

1. I'm really good at screaming rhythmically like some sort of terribly wounded, very angry mountain ape, *and* I can do this night after night without losing my voice.

2. I'm extremely good at convincing large crowds of sweaty, hairy people who are packed in some dingy venue like furry sardines in a concrete tin, to do things that most normal folks find distasteful, such as flinging their bodies around in an extremely violent-looking manner, wrecking into each other for a solid hour so hard that it hurts to move the next day and their bodies are covered in bruises, all the while screaming at them in the above mentioned mountain ape voice.

Not a very impressive skill set I know; in fact it seems ludicrous even by my low standards, but I actually make decent money doing these things. I travel the world, getting paid to go jump around and holler like a buffoon in exotic places most folks will only dream of ever seeing. It's really quite astounding to me, every single time I think about it. I still can't believe people all over the globe look forward to me and my band coming to their countries and doing our ridiculous hirsute song and dance. Amazing.

But I still don't consider myself a rockstar, at least not a *real* rockstar. *Real* rockstars are filthy rich, have legions of beautiful women or men (or both) throwing themselves at them, and can't walk down the street without getting hassled to death. *Real* rockstars get invited to weird stuff like fashion week parties in Milan and the White House. Neither the President nor anyone with a last name like Gaultier has called yet, so while I am quite well-known in the genre of music I play, I am not a *real* rockstar.

I prefer the term *budget rockstar*. A budget rockstar resembles a real rockstar in many superficial ways, and many budget rockstars try their best to maintain the appearance that they swim in the same pool as the big boys and girls, but there are some very big, often insurmountable differences. A budget rockstar cannot afford to blow his extra cash on diamond-plated teeth, a garage full of Porches and Lamborghinis (we would never even qualify for financing for a set of tires), or obscure impressionist art from Micronesia. A budget rockstar will probably never meet, and definitely will never date, a super model. A budget rockstar will never own a private jet or yacht, nor be accepted into some weird club for enthusiasts of said luxury vehicles. A budget rockstar will never utter the words "Hold on a sec, Preston—my house keeper in Malibu is on the other line."

As I said before, I know some real rockstars, and count a few as good friends—they are all amazing and humble people who have worked very hard to get where they are. But they exist in a different realm than me and guys in bands like mine, having a different species of renown that comes with its own set of problems. I am absolutely fine with that—the amount of fame I have obtained as a musician makes me uncomfortable at times, and it's low grade compared to the level of public recognition these dudes have. Maybe one day I will become that famous, but I seriously doubt it, and it's certainly no goal of mine. Unless they are stupid with their money (and many have been—not my friends, but more than one rockstar, real or budget, has gone bankrupt), real rockstars don't have to tour for months on end, playing five to six nights a week in order to maintain their lifestyle (although some do, because they love to be on the road). My band does, and that's okay. We make good money, live comfortably, and can support our families from our music alone. It's a really good life, and I am happy with our level of success. Sure, some fame has come with that success, but I can still go to the coffee shop or bookstore without being mobbed.

In summary, I am a semi-famous guy in a pretty well-known heavy metal band who makes a very respectable living touring the world as a glorified t-shirt salesman. I worked really hard to get where I am, I have a large fan base who loves my band's music, and a few really famous friends who respect what I do. I pay my bills doing something I love, I own my home, I have a beautiful wife, and my family loves me. I am a happy guy most of the time, and that's the truth—who in their right mind wouldn't be if they were in my position? My life is really neat.

But (and there is *always* a "but"), there is a dark side to this way of life. And if you are already predisposed to certain less-than-wholesome things, it can and will suck you in as you walk this path, dragging you down into places you thought you would never go in your worst dreams . . .

ANYONE READING THIS - IF YOU ARE
EVEN ARRESTED UNDER SUSPICION OF
ANY CRIME, DON'T SAY A FUCKING
WORD EXCEPT "I WANT TO TALK TO A
LAWYER". IT'S THE ONLY WAY TO GO,
AS ANYTHING YOU SAY THE COPS WILL
TRY & USE AGAINST YOU. I HAD MY
SUNGLASSES ON, AS I HAD LEFT MY
REGULAR GLASSES IN OUR ROADCASE
IN FUCKING MILAN.

chapter three

rom the back seat of the station-wagon-style police car, I could see the driver periodically eyeballing me in his rearview mirror. The cop beside me stared straight ahead silently through dark sunglasses; the two men in front were no louder. As we pulled out of the airport complex and into the mid-afternoon sun, the driver turned on the radio. Pop music filled the car, at once both foreign and horrid in its familiarity, the Czech singer's phrasing perched somewhat awkwardly atop the standard Top 40 formulae that sedates radio listeners the world over with its repetitious banality. We pulled onto the highway and sped into the passing lane, blowing past car after car with the disregard for speed limits that is the privilege of police everywhere. Aside from being very sober, very frightened, very confused as to why I had been arrested, and traveling in a grocery getter cop car through a foreign country (as the screeching Czech vocals in my ears painfully reminded me), this ride felt oddly familiar. The highway scenery had the homogenous look of roads surrounding airports the world over—utilitarian business hotels, a few depressing-looking houses, and large empty spaces broken up only by metal towers carrying power lines. I looked down at my cuffed wrists, sighed, then stared out the window, trying to calm my racing mind.

Within the span of approximately five minutes, I had gone from being on tour, where I was cheered enthusiastically by thousands of fans on an almost daily basis, to being arrested in an airport and told that I had killed another human being. I began thinking about the sailboat I had been on almost exactly twenty-four hours ago, cutting briskly through a fjord by the small Norwegian holiday town of Arendal. The organizers of the show we were playing had arranged us very special transport to the festival grounds on Tromøy, an island of staggering natural beauty that sat in the clean water of the fjord like an emerald on a beautiful Nordic woman's heaving bosom. We would travel to Tromøy just as the Vikings had hundreds of years ago, in a wooden boat. The sailboat, a dignified and immaculately preserved craft built by hand in 1931, was captained by a young Norwegian music fan in exchange for free tickets to the festival, and his two-person crew included a young blond woman of classic Scandinavian beauty. I had sat on the polished wooden stern with our guitarist Mark, snapping pictures of the many picturesque islands in the clear water we navigated. *Who gets to do this kind of stuff?* I looked over to Mark and grinned, grateful and overwhelmed by the experience.

"Sometimes our lives are pretty damn amazing, aren't they?" I said.

Mark, not exactly fond of touring and much preferring to stay at home with his family, guitars, and race cars in various states of repair, sat with back against the ancient mast, looking perfectly content. How could he not?

"Yes, they are," he replied with a wide grin of his own.

I shook my head, focusing myself and banishing daydreams of friends on sailboats, majestic fjords, and hot Norwegian women, because none of those things were doing me any good at this particular second. I was under arrest; in cuffs like the proverbial common criminal. I needed to remember that, and act accordingly at all times. The party was over. Now it was time to figure out what in the hell was happening to me.

As the driver of the police wagon suddenly swerved with a curse, switching lanes to go around a geriatric driver who was creeping along in the fast lane, the cop beside him who had been in such a hurry at the airport turned around in the front passenger seat and looked at me. "So, you do remembering anything at all about what happened?" he asked me over his shoulder in a sympathetic sounding voice, forming the words with difficulty.

"You know, I'm not really sure what's happening *right now*, so before I say anything I think I would like to see a lawyer," I replied.

"Nothings at all? No memory of two years ago happenings?" he said, as if he hadn't heard me and were asking how the tour had been going.

"I'm not saying anything until I get a lawyer," I said more firmly, "and I'll be needing to speak to someone at the American embassy."

He grunted his assent and fell silent again. As terrified as I was, a part of me began laughing hysterically inside. These men would have to rustle up someone who spoke much better English if they were going to try to play the standard cop mind games with me. With the exception of this man, who seemed to have about a second grader's comprehension of my native language, I had only heard them speak briefly in Czech, which I had no hope of deciphering. This was all just normal background noise to me, as I am used to being surrounded by people speaking in foreign tongues for much of the year during a touring cycle. Without the intimidating spectacle of the machine gun toting masked men surrounding him, my fear of this man started to recede a bit, and I began to think of him as a kind of dolt. Not because of his lack of ability to speak my language well, which is certainly no measure of intelligence in a world with thousands of different languages in existence, but because he had been foolish enough to try to pry information out of me in a buddy-buddy voice when he had to know damn well his English language chops weren't exactly stellar. While I'm no police psychologist, a ride to the police station seemed a bit early in the game to me to start the ham-handed good cop routine. The silent routine along with the wretched Czech pop tunes was far more effective at unnerving me. Weren't they supposed to let me marinate in this fear and bewilderment, maybe sweat a little before they started trying to get me to slip up and say something that would indict myself?

The whole situation began to feel ludicrous to me. I had never even *attempted* to kill anyone, much less succeeded, in my entire life. This had to be a mistake. Sure, I had had encounters with people running on stage over the years, usually resulting in them being removed from the stage by security or our crew. The aggressive nature of my band's music and our physically rowdy fan base had resulted in audience members sustaining injuries before—at each other's hands though, in the audience area, never on stage, and for the most part unintentionally. The people who come to our shows generally don't wish to hurt each other anymore than people playing a game of sandlot football do—they are just blowing off steam. Nobody wants to *harm* anyone. My band has stopped shows before when we knew someone had been hurt in the audience, or even if we had thought that the crowd was getting a little too crazy—we don't wish to be the soundtrack to injury. I sat trying to recall the one show we had played in Prague—I remembered it had been a wild and exasperating one, with no security that I could recall and fans jumping on and off the stage all night. I remembered one drunken boy I had finally wrestled to the ground on stage and held down for a while, never stopping singing, until he got the point that I didn't want him there. But I had never attacked him—I had been joking just the previous day with a crew member about how I hoped this show would be better than the last time we had been in Prague, because it had been a nightmare of drunken audience members repeatedly charging the stage, especially this one kid I had put on his back like a misbehaving puppy. To my knowledge, no one in lamb of god had assaulted an audience member that night or any other. If someone had been hurt and then died two years ago, even by accident, obviously we would have been made aware of it by now. Wouldn't we?

Surely this would all be cleared up at the police station in relatively short order, perhaps with the help of someone from my embassy, and I would be on my way in a day or two. In the meantime, I was pretty sure I was going to spend my first night in a Czech jail. This didn't particularly frighten me. Once you've tasted the hospitality of the 9th Street Hotel a few times (as Richmond City lock up is fondly known to some of us) spending a drunken night in a holding cell with scowling black drug dealers who act offended by your pale skin tone, a seemingly suicidal redneck who throws the word *nigger* around the cell like confetti at a New Year's Eve party, and an angry, crack-crazed transvestite hooker who looks like Mr. Universe in dime store drag, other jails just seem bland in comparison. How bad could it be? I just hoped they would let me smoke in there, because the nicotine beast was starting to rear its ugly head pretty hard.

Buildings alongside the highway began to appear with greater frequency, and soon we were driving into the bewildering maze that is Prague. Prague is a city of internationally renowned beauty, but my attention was solely focused on myself and the three men in the car with me. Everything outside the vehicle went past in a blur, a technicolor smear of European city dwellers and tourists wandering their natural habitat of majestic buildings, souvenir shops, and sidewalk cafes. We pulled up to a large, grim, off-white building with communist-era architectural features, drove around back, into a dimly lit basement level car park, and stopped in front of a large plain metal door. This place definitely had a cell waiting for me inside.

The officers walked me to the door and rang a buzzer. It opened, and we walked into a dimly lit plain hallway with a heavy barred door five feet away. A graying police officer with a large ring of keys stepped out of the gloom and unlocked the door, exchanging Czech greetings with the men who had arrested me as he let us into the building. We walked to the end of the hall, went up a flight of stairs, and stopped in front of a large cinderblock walled holding cell. One of the officers opened the barred door, and motioned me inside. I sat down on the metal bench running the length of the room. Previous occupants had scratched their names in the flaking yellow paint that covered the bench, the letters adorned with unfamiliar accent marks. Two officers left, shutting the cell door and leaving me with my English-speaking friend, who stood leaning against the opposite wall, staring at me like he was sorry to see me in such a sad predicament. There was an empty ashtray sitting on the bench beside me, looking prettier than any tourist trap in all of Europe.

"Excuse me, what's your name?" I asked him.

"My name?" he replied, seemingly amused at the question. "Alex."

"Well, Alex, can I have one of my cigarettes now?"

Alex sighed heavily, shook his head like he really shouldn't be letting me smoke, reached in the plastic bag of my stuff and pulled out the crumpled box of Marlboros, looked inside it to make sure there was no contraband, and gave it to me. I picked one of the seven cigarettes out of the pack and asked him if I could have my lighter, too. This evoked another deep sigh, like I was some troublesome distant relative asking him for a large loan he couldn't afford. He handed over my orange Bic. I lit the cigarette, took a deep drag, leaned back against the cinderblocks, and exhaled. The nicotine hit my bloodstream, danced its vicious and seductive ballet on my synapses, and much needed endorphins flooded my brain. *Okay*, I thought, *now we can think*. Alex pulled out an unfamiliar looking pack of his own, Czech I assumed, and lit up, leaning back against the wall.

"You like to smoke?" he asked.

"Way too much. You smoke, too, I see." He nodded. This conversation was getting deep. "Uhm, I need to call my embassy."

"Someone has called them. We do this when foreigner is arrested. Protocol."

"Thank you," I replied, not sure whether to believe him. "When will I see someone from the embassy?"

Alex shrugged. "They will call."

"Okay. What about a lawyer? I need to talk to a lawyer."

"Yes, yes. You will have advocate," he said as if this was a silly request "We will help to find. It is required for us to help."

For some reason I immediately believed he would help me find an advocate—someone I assumed, by his odd yet confident and rapid pronunciation, must be a lawyer. Alex leaned against the wall smoking, looking at me with bored eyes. He stepped toward me, stubbed out his half-smoked cigarette in the ashtray, and then turned to walk away, scratching his head like he was trying to recall something.

"So, that day . . . nothing do you remember? Nothing at all?"

I have very little legal advice for the reader, as I am a musician, not an attorney. But I will provide what meager knowledge I possess now as a public service announcement, just in case anyone has been living under a rock or is simply not smart enough to deduce these things for themselves. These are sound instructions, ones that have served me well over the checkered course of both my drinking and musical career, and I learned them early on simply by watching fairly one-dimensional police and court TV shows as a child. Television is for the most part a vast and vacuous flickering cathode/digital wasteland, designed to annihilate critical thought and sedate you into a drooling somnambulant state of consumerist zombiedom, but you may take these tid-bits as gospel truth. Just trust me on this.

1. Never, ever, ever sign any sort of business contract without having a competent lawyer (who specializes in the sort of business the contract concerns) thoroughly review it *first.*

2. Never, ever, ever believe anything any police officer tells you if you are placed under arrest, other than the fact that you are, indeed, under arrest. This includes but is not limited to: *Your friends have all already confessed, If you help us we will help you, We have several witnesses ready to testify against you,* and especially *This is going to go a lot smoother for you if you just go ahead and tell us what happened.*

3. Never, ever, EVER provide answers to ANY questions an officer asks if you are placed under arrest (other than your name, rank, and serial number) until you have consulted with a lawyer first. Just politely state that you will need to speak with an attorney before you say anything, stay quiet, and wait until the cavalry arrives.

Once again, I followed the rules of the game and restated my need for a lawyer. Alex shot me a not unfriendly look that said *You are really starting to be a royal pain in my ass, you know that, right, bro?,* lit a smoke with yet another dramatic sigh, and disengaged from the situation and into his flip phone. His cigarette instantly set the nicotine monkey in my head to screeching and I burned another of my rapidly dwindling supply to shut him up. Five left. Damn.

After ten or so minutes the woman who had handed me the warrant for my arrest walked briskly into the cell with the other two detectives, looked at me, and said something in Czech to Alex. He approached me, fished around in his pocket and found a ring of keys, then began to unlock my handcuffs. The cuffs weren't biting into my wrists and weren't uncomfortable, but it was going to be nice to have them off.

Except that Alex couldn't seem to figure out how to unlock them, bless his heart. As he fiddled with them for a minute or two, muttering under his breath, I began to wonder, *Has this man ever cuffed anyone before? Is this his first day on the job or something? Is he even really a cop?* The standard lock truly seemed to perplex him, and I honestly wanted to tell him to fetch me my wallet from the plastic bag across the room so I could get out my handcuff key and show him how to get these damn things off. (Like I said, I hadn't been in trouble in a long time, but before I was thrown out of the Boy Scouts I learned to take their motto "Be prepared" pretty seriously.) Eventually the curly haired detective who had driven us to the police station walked over, took the key, and in a matter of seconds my wrists were free. Alex scowled at the cuffs like it was their fault (they did look a little old and scratched up—maybe they were training cuffs) and put them back in the holster on his belt. The blond woman looked at me and spoke.

"Do you understand why you are here?" she asked. Her English was clear and her blue eyes were level. I could feel the fear snaking into my body again, my autonomic nervous system triggering its stress response activity. My heart was racing and my palms began to sweat.

"Not really," I said.

"There has been an investigation. Witnesses say you pushed this young man off of the podium. He hit his head. He is dead. Do you understand this?"

"I did not know that any sort of investigation happened, or that anyone thinks I am responsible for any sort of crime in this country or anywhere else. This is all news to me."

Stay calm. Stay calm.

"I believe that," she continued in a flat voice. "Tomorrow you will be interrogated. Your friends will come here in the morning to answers questions as well." This woman wasn't trying to intimidate me. She did not have to.

"Where are my friends? Are they under arrest, too?"

"No, they are not under arrest. They are at a hotel. In Prague."

"So I am spending the night here, correct?"

She nodded.

"When will I be released?"

She shrugged.

"What is your name?" I asked.

Like Alex, she looked slightly amused that I would bother to ask her this question.

"Lucie."

"So, Lucie, am I being charged with murder?"

"No, you are not being charged with murder."

"Do you know the word *manslaughter*?" I asked her.

"Yes. Yes, I do. It is something like this."

"Okay," I said quietly. There was not much else to talk about until I saw a lawyer. This was pretty bad. This was *very* bad.

Lucie stood over me looking down. She stared into my eyes for a second and then spoke softly.

"Would you like to know the penalty for this crime?" she asked.

"Sure," I said. Time slowed down again as I stared right back in her eyes.

Stay calm. Stay calm. Stay calm.

"Five to ten years," she said through a slight smile, then turned and walked out of the cell.

It was the first hint of emotion I had seen her display.

Fuck.

chapter four

As I sit here at my writing desk in my rented house by the sea, remembering the sad chain of events that led me to write this book, I can look out the window on a clear day and catch a glimpse of the Atlantic Ocean that I love so much. Literally as far back as my memory goes, I have cherished my time near her, and longed to navigate her currents and ride her waves when I am away. Two islands over from the one I sit on writing this, I saw the ocean for the first time as a very young child. My family went there after church one Sunday, and my mother says that as soon as I laid my four-year-old eyes on the huge swelling blue landscape in front of me, I charged fearlessly toward it, still in my tiny polyester church clothes, and crashed laughing into the waves. Nothing has changed in my forty-two years; I always feel the most serene by the shore, for the ocean is the eternal healer to me. I love to walk the beach at night, alone or with family or friends, especially my mother, who loves it as much or more than I do. We walk and listen to the tides, discuss our lives, look at the stars and wonder at the immensity of the heavens, and breathe the salt air, grateful to live near nature's most magnificent creation. The ocean is life itself, and to lay footprints in its sands is an act of prayer.

The last few days have been very foggy here. Even when I step onto my front porch, I can see nothing but the low white mist that covers this island. The row of houses across the street is partially obscured by a diaphanous shroud, and the immense sea a block beyond them has completely disappeared into solid fog, like a dove folded beneath a magician's handkerchief. On my porch in my rusted thrift store rocking chair, I can still hear the waves rolling as the tide goes out, and if I sniff the air I can smell the salt on the winds of a nor'easter as they blow against my skin. I can smell the rich loam of the salt marsh behind my house where I throw my cast net for bait fish and shrimp to put food in my belly. I am surrounded on all sides by water, water that soothes my soul, water that can provide me with all I need. I can hear it, feel it, smell it, and if I cook the shrimp waiting in an iced bucket in my refrigerator, I will taste it. But today I cannot see it at all—it might as well not be there, unless I get up from this chair, leave this house, and walk to it. My ocean is a vanished lover, hiding through the fog just two blocks away, calling to me to walk to her for relief, even as I sit here in sadness and write.

For many, many years, my life as an active alcoholic was just like today. I was surrounded by life, things and people that could have brought me great joy, grand opportunities I wasted because I sat in a haze of alcohol, drugs, and sadness. I simply would not and could not get up and walk a few blocks through the fog back to freedom and life. Often when I meet people for the first time today, they tell me how glad they are I am finally free and clear after all my experiences in the Czech Republic. They usually say something along the lines of "Thank God you are done with all that. That must have been hell, man." These experiences humble me, and I feel a great swell of love for these people. I am grateful for their kindness, but I often want to tell them:

"That was nothing. I have been to hell before. I kept an apartment there for a few decades. Getting arrested, going to prison, the trial—all of it—was like a vacation compared to a couple of other things I've lived through."

That may sound overly dramatic, but I mean those words with every fiber of my being. I've been through two particular circles of hell before, and while I didn't emerge unscathed, I'm still here to tell the tale, so I think I will just in case my experience can somehow help someone roasting in my old subterranean stomping grounds have a little hope to get out. The first circle of my hell is my alcoholism, or as I like to oh-so-delicately call it when I personify it, *The Motherfucker*. Let's have a gander at that charming bastard, shall we?

As I wrote earlier, my alcoholism is a far more important part of my life than my occupation. My alcoholism defines me in a way my job could never even hope to. My job is not *me*, despite what a lot of people seem to think. I can, and one day probably will, walk away from my job when it's run its course to a happy, dignified end. Or, like a very loud, very hairy, *very* unsexy group marriage gone terribly awry, when I decide I can no longer tolerate being married to four other men whom I love but can't be with anymore because I am planning to smother them all in their sleep. Then I will storm out after one final epic fire-breathing conniption fit, the likes of which hasn't been seen since the fall of Sodom and Gomorrah. Either way, once I'm done with my band, whether it be amiable (and I hope it is) or during one of our famously turbulent moments, I will no longer be the singer of lamb of god. I will do something else; re-invent myself in whatever image I wish, hopefully something a whole lot quieter and a great deal more peaceful.

I can't wait for the day when a long-haired kid in a black t-shirt with some band's name printed on an illegible font on it comes up to me and says, "DUDE! Aren't you Randy from lamb of god? Holy fuck, it *is* you! I freakin' *love* 'Sacrament,' why don't you guys write more songs like 'Redne-'"

"I'm sorry, my son, but you are mistaken," I will gently interrupt with a far away look in my eyes, stroking my greying beard in a soothing manner, "It is true, I was once that man, but that was many moons ago. Now I am but a simple fisherman, quietly living out the last of his days by the sea, listening for the wisdom the trade winds whisper to those with open ears. Now I must bid you adieu, but here—have a tomato from my garden. Go in peace, my son, and make your own metal, for I am no longer of that realm." Then I will turn, gather up my robe (because every wise old man wears a robe) and hobble slowly away down the beach, leaning heavily on my extremely ornate driftwood walking stick. That will be nice. *So nice.*

Regrettably, I can't just gently inform my alcoholism that I am no longer an alcoholic, hand it a ripe tomato, and walk away down the beach. I can't break up with my alcoholism when the romance is over—that died ages ago, and it will never sign the divorce papers. I can't even get all pissed off at it and say, "Look here, *you motherfucker,* listen up: I've had enough of your bullshit, I'm done with it; so adios, you soul-crushing, pernicious sumbitch!", flick it the bird, then ride off into the sunset in my truck, blasting Black Flag's *My War* and feeling pretty damn awesome. I *never* get to be a "not-an-alcoholic." I will always be an alcoholic. *Always.* I view everything through its bloodshot eyes. *Everything.* My alcoholism will be with me until the day I die, and it will go to the grave with me. My band, my friends, my family, my wife—none of them will be there, peering up at the coffin lid, waiting for the worm party to begin, but my alcoholism will be, finally asleep forever just like me, resting in my pickled bones. I haven't had a drink in a hot minute, but if I do not keep my alcoholism in remission, simply by abstaining, it will put me in that grave a whole lot sooner than I wish. It will kill me—of this I am absolutely certain. I am not certain I will remain sober the rest of my life, because my alcoholism is a sneaky bastard, but I am certain that if I drink, I will die.

My health, even while I was drinking, has always been pretty robust. I have a rather large tolerance for pain. This is a blessing and curse. Because it wasn't until I was in so much pain it was either kill myself or go on drinking to my death that I finally got sober. It took me twenty-two years of drinking and drugging to finally get enough of that pain. Twenty-two years of fighting a nebulous foe that I just couldn't beat. I drank a lot. A whole lot.

But that is not what makes me an alcoholic, I believe. What makes me an alcoholic is the fact that when I take a drink, just one drink, I have absolutely zero idea of what is going to happen next, except that I am going to drink more, and I am going to drink until I'm done. Anything else I may or may not do is a mystery to everyone, especially me. Some people have very fond memories of partying with me, because I could be a whole lot of fun to drink with at times. I could be pleasant and funny. I could be very charming and generous, generally to a fault. I could certainly make a lot of people laugh, both with and at me. Or, alternately, I could suddenly decide that someone was looking at me funny, and decide to punch them in the face. I could suddenly become argumentative over apparently nothing. I could decide that it was a good idea to steal something for some odd reason. I could decide to start breaking things. I could decide that I could jump from some insane height and be okay. I could decide that even though I was seeing three of everything, I was fine to get behind the wheel of a car and endanger my life, the life of anyone stupid/drunk enough to get in the car with me, and the lives of anyone unlucky enough to be on the roads near me at that time. I could decide to become suddenly very cruel, emotionally and even physically abusive, treating you lower than whale shit, *especially* if I love you, romantically or otherwise.

I could decide to do all of these things, and in fact I have, over and over again. I am not proud of many, many things I have done. I do not deny them, but I sure as hell do not sit on my weeping ass in a useless ball of self-loathing remorse anymore, either. Why? Because I cannot help anyone else with this same problem that almost killed me if I am consumed by guilt over my past, the key word being *my*. How egotistical and self-absorbed! To not help others who are lost and suffering, because I am too busy wallowing in shame over the past like a pig in shit inside a filthy pen with an open door. The past is the past, and what's done is done. I can't change that, but I *can* try to help someone else like me, and part of helping that person is letting them know *I understand them*, because I *do*—I understand every single alcoholic and drug addict that has ever walked the face of the earth, no matter what their circumstances are, because in our particular illness, we are all the exact same. I understand them in a way that the smartest addiction expert with a million Ivy League degrees hanging on his office wall will *never know*, if he is not of my tribe. I know the alcoholic and the addict like I know myself. To help them (because we are a very closed-off bunch), I have to let them know that I was just like them or worse. I must never forget or deny where I come from.

So I remember, and I talk about it to people like myself.

Always waking up with a terrible hangover and dread, a horrid feeling of impending doom hovering like a kamikaze pilot circling over my head. After a certain point in my drinking career I knew something was wrong, that I was not living correctly, yet I continued to drag myself into the worst places and create the worst situations I could. I had no real regard for anyone's wants or needs but my own dark impulses. And I fulfilled those impulses, even though I hated myself for doing so and hurting the people who cared the most about me. I did these things over and over, and I hated myself for years because of it. Why in God's name would any intelligent person in their right mind do these things? Or even a complete idiot who was relatively sane?

The fact of the matter is that when I drink, I am 100 percent certifiably insane. Hopelessly, utterly, undeniably bat shit *crazy*. I do things that are abhorrent to me; anathema to my nature, my morals, and my upbringing. And once I start, I cannot stop the craziness. It just spirals on and on, ever downward, until I die or hit rock bottom. And even at rock bottom, despite all evidence that I should stop, I will grab a cold beer and a pick ax and keep digging deeper. It's insane. The only way I know to not be crazy is just not to drink. It's amazingly simple, yet it is something I must remind myself of on a daily basis. I don't like the person I became; I don't ever want to be that man again. And I don't have to.

My alcoholism is no way any sort of excuse for any of my past behaviors. Just because I quit drinking, my life was not suddenly transformed into a tabula rasa—if I have wronged someone, drunk or not, then the responsibility for this lies squarely with me. And I must do my best to set things square with that person. Sometimes that means never contacting that person again. Some people just don't ever need to hear from me again. I do not blame them. I was an asshole sometimes, there's no two ways around it.

And just because I am sober now does not mean anyone else should care. I do not deserve a cookie for finally trying to act like a decent human being. I have been very lucky that most people I have talked to have just said "We are just happy you are okay now, man. Just don't drink, okay?" I have been told by these people that even in the midst of my craziness, they could see a good person hiding inside me, being beaten down by the booze monster, but struggling to stay alive. I don't know if that's the case or if I just picked very kind and forgiving people as friends. Regardless, today I accept responsibility for my actions. *All of my actions*, past and present. If I hide from this responsibility, then I am being dishonest with myself. And if I can convince myself that I am not to be held accountable for my actions, then it's just a hop, skip, and a jump to convincing myself that I can take maybe just one drink.

Then, from there, after doing as much damage as possible to everything and everyone around me, I will die.

Today, I do not want to die.

———

It has been one of the greatest unexpected joys of my life as a sober man to talk about my past life to friends I have made in sobriety, like I did with my dear buddy Bubble not long ago. I loved hearing him say, "You know, people have told me all these crazy stories about you for years, about what a lunatic you were when you were drinking. I just can't imagine you being that way. I know you were, but I just can't see it. I only know you this way, as good old Randy." I have heard similar words a few times, and while I don't run away from my past or people in it, it's nice to start off a friendship without the other person wondering if I am going to do something abominably insane at any second and try to drag them along with me for the ride.

I am not unique in my alcoholism. No one is. It's all the same, and I am a garden variety drunk. If you have no understanding of alcoholism or addiction, then you cannot even begin to understand the level at which that all of us are crazy. Absolutely out-to-lunch, call-the-men-in-the-white-coats *crazy*. If you are unlucky enough to have an active alcoholic or drug addict in your life, you probably don't understand why your husband or wife or father or neighbor or whoever will not just stop drinking. Or taking pills. Or snorting cocaine. Or shooting dope. Or doing whatever substance it is they are doing that is killing them and killing you, that has changed them into this awful person, that makes them do such strange, self-destructive things. I can tell you why—they are insane. One hundred percent certifiable. And their addiction's need for drink and/or drugs has twisted their perceptions to the point where they do not even know that they are unhinged, that the problem (if they even recognize that they have one) is their addiction. They may even pay it lip service, but they don't truly know yet, know it in their soul—because if they knew, they would stop. I didn't know, as ridiculous as it seems. I always used to laugh, "Oh yeah, I am an alcoholic, big surprise—look at what I do for a living, hahaha." Everyone around wasn't laughing after a while, though. I was pathetic, just like all the rest of the drunks and addicts. I made it out, but many, many, many of them won't, and they will die. It happens every hour. That is just a fact.

I made it out because I finally accepted help when it was offered. I had been offered help before, but I didn't deign to take it, for I had not had enough pain yet. Pain is the great motivator for me, and I've learned all the important lessons in life the hard way. This is because I am bullheaded, and want to do everything on my own. But someone reached out when I was finally hurting bad enough to listen, and I slowly got better with their and many others' help. I could not get sober on my own, I *had* to have help, as most of us do. But I had to go through an immense amount of pain first. I'm pretty tough physically and mentally, and I fought a long and bloody battle, but in the end the alcohol beat me like a rented mule. It beat me until I cried out to the universe for mercy with every atom in my being. Then I started to get better.

I do not know why I was finally able to reach a level of pain that allowed me to quit drinking before I died, yet people I love are still killing themselves all around me. In the last few years I have lost many friends, the majority of whom were in my business, from drinking and drugs. All of them were very nice people. Why did they have to die while I stay alive? Why couldn't they get the chance to understand what I understand now? Many of them were as smart or smarter than me—couldn't they see what they were doing to themselves? Probably not. They were crazy, but I was just as crazy—I don't know why I'm still alive. I should be dead a thousand times over. All I know is that I am here now, so I had better make the most of it and be ready to help my friends when and if they want to get sober. And if not, I will be there to bury them and try to be of some small comfort to their loved ones. Many more people I know will die from drug and alcohol abuse. I know this to be true, because I know a lot of alcoholics and drug addicts, and their odds are not good. I also must help any person that I can who is willing to accept help that I am capable of giving, because people who had never heard my name, who didn't know me as some rockstar, just as a drunk in pain, helped me to get and stay sober. I owe those people, and I will pay it forward. Otherwise I would be just another self-centered asshole, and I might as well go get drunk and try to forget everything until I kill myself.

I don't have the foggiest idea why I'm an alcoholic. To tell you the truth, I don't really care—it's not important to me in the slightest. Knowing what has made me this way has absolutely zero practical application in my immediate life. If I walked outside and one of the Eastern Diamondback rattlesnakes that live around here lit me up, I wouldn't stand around moping and staring at the snake for one damn millisecond, wondering, "Why has this happened? Could I have prevented this? Why, oh God, why me?"—my ass would be gone faster than a toupee in a hurricane and on my way to a hospital. Maybe I should have been more careful, but it's a little bit late for that now, isn't it? I can't undo that snake bite anymore than I can undo my alcoholism, but I can treat both, survive, and live to be happy if I catch it in time. Booze in my bloodstream is just as deadly to me as Diamondback venom—it just takes longer, hurts more people, and makes me act a whole lot weirder. There has been a long-running nature vs. nurture debate on the topic of alcoholism and addiction; while that ever shifting dialogue may be of interest to scientists and sociologists (of which I am neither), it's not much help in keeping me sober right in this very instant. Since my life has seemed to consist of one long connected chain of this-very-instants, many of them extremely drunken this-very-instants, I don't have time to worry about the hows and whys of my alcoholism—I have to live in the present moment and think about what I'm actually going to *do* about my alcoholism. Besides, the academics haven't been able to come up with a proven answer to the cause of alcoholism for as long as there has been alcohol, which is longer than we have had written language (what scientists and archeologists *have* proved is that mankind was fermenting alcoholic beverages as far back as the Stone Age). Maybe one day they will know why some people become slobbering belligerent Cro-Magnons after they drink while others can take it or leave it, but to my knowledge it's still got them stumped. If the highly trained brainiacs busting up the human genetic code under their zillion-dollar terminator microscopes haven't been able to figure it out, then why should I bother taxing what few brain cells I have left rolling around in my knotty head in a futile quest for the answer *why?*

Of course I have wondered about it from time to time, but I don't have any alcoholism that I know of in my immediate family, excluding my great-grandfather who blew his brains out on his front porch with a shotgun. I have been there myself, in fact have pointed a loaded twelve gauge at my head at time or two. I suppose I didn't have the guts to do it, or some small sane part my sodden brain reached out through the madness and reminded me that someone would have to clean up the mess I had made. Perhaps some malevolent gene with a fondness for alcohol and firearms came down from my Irish great-grandfather, perhaps not. My brothers don't seem to have a problem with booze.

If it's genetics, then I suppose I won the lottery. I was not abused as a child, I did not grow up in an alcoholic home, and although I have suffered some pretty extreme trauma in my life, I was already drinking alcoholically before the heavy-duty shit really hit the fan. Plus, I know people who were severely abused as children, did have alcoholic parents, grew up in an insane environment, and have gone through things far worse than I did before they ever hit puberty . . . yet they can enjoy a drink without becoming a menace to themselves and others. They can take it or leave it. They can drink just one or two beers, then walk away with an enjoyable feeling and not need *more*.

I do not understand this way of thinking or being. Not at all.

I always need more.

Always.

Admittedly, the business I am in is very conducive to nurturing a good case of alcoholism. Booze and drugs are plentiful and often free. And fans often want to buy you a drink, or give you drugs, so that they may experience your company for a while. While the vast majority of these fans are just cool people who want to show you their appreciation for your music with a cold drink, maybe a joint or a bump of the old booger sugar, some are psychic vampires who will do anything to say they hung out with you, to try and worm their way into your life. They do not care about you, if you live or die—they just want to live vicariously through you for a bit. These are the worst sort for an alcoholic or drug addict musician, because you will do anything to get what your addiction wants, including letting these people into your life. These are not your friends, these are not your true fans, they are cancer to people like me.

So the music industry has a lot of partying, easily accessed free drugs and booze, and very little restraints on behavior, and almost no level of accountability to any sort of boss. As long as you can get on stage or into the studio and still do your job, no one in the business really cares. You are a cash cow. Milk 'em 'til their dead, cut 'em up, grill the remains on a barbecue of re-releases, and move on to the next young calf. So party 'til you drop, right?

If the music industry is such a bad environment, then why isn't everyone who ever stepped on a stage a rampaging drug addict or drunk? Because despite the fact that this book is being written by an alcoholic musician, and despite the fact that many books written by my musician friends deal with alcoholism and addiction, not every musician is a booze-soaked drug addled mess. I know many folks who do this for a living who can drink normally, and I don't think there is a single thing wrong with drinking if you can do it normally and in moderation. Hell, I don't think there is anything wrong with getting rip-roaring drunk and making a jackass out of yourself every now and then, as long as you don't drive or hurt anyone else while you're doing it. Sometimes a proper, good-old-skull-splitting-dry-heaving-oh-god-I-swear-I'll-never-drink-again-if-you-just-make-this-stop hangover is actually beneficial to normal folks—they get painfully reminded why they can't party like that every night, they feel like crap for a couple of days, so they do the logical thing and take a break until next year's National Amateur Hour rolls around (St. Paddy's Day, Cinco de Mayo, New Years Eve, etc.) and maybe, *maybe* they cut loose again. That sort of drinking behavior (moderately sensible) sounds pretty painless compared to the way I guzzled almost daily. But since the laws of good literature require a story to have some sort of conflict, and I suppose since we have become a society of casualty vampires who love nothing more than watching a good train wreck, no one is interested in reading a book by a musician who writes "I have two beers every three days or so on average. I don't wreck my car, get arrested, or try to catch my girlfriend's house on fire at least once a year. I'm a mellow, well-adjusted guy."

Boring. But these guys do exist. Lots of them. I know plenty of them, and they do the same thing I do for a living. There is a world of other people in occupations far more stressful than mine who can drink normally too. But some people who will never have to work a day in their life, who grew up lacking nothing, are just as crazy and miserable on the polished teak deck of their yacht once they climb into a thousand dollar bottle of Merlot as the dirtiest bum sipping a pint of Thunderbird in a piss-stained trench coat under a bridge. They are one and the same, and they are just like me. Alcoholism does not discriminate due to race, color, creed, religion, economic status, age, sex, sexual preference, political inclination, spiritual beliefs, upbringing, morality—none of it. Alcoholism descends on murderous black wings upon whomever it so chooses. It's a mystery.

So, if I can't blame my genetics, my parents, my job, my wife, or even God (yes, I believe in God, for lack of a better term; but the God I believe in doesn't want me to kill myself with booze) for my alcoholism, then who do I blame?

No one. It just is. I can't even sink into a good session of self-loathing and blame myself, because I don't believe I made myself this way. I certainly drank myself to a point where I was completely out of control, and I have no one to blame for that *but* myself. But I would have stopped far before I did if I could have— God knows I tried and failed for years. *Years.* As a child, I never said, "I want to be an alcoholic and fuck my life all to hell when I grow up." I never wanted to be this way—but I am.

We do the best we can with the cards we're dealt. I got cut a bad hand with a pickled joker in it, and I held onto him for way too long. I finally folded, cut my losses, and left the table. But the deadly game goes on, and it's a game I can't win, so I better not gamble anymore, not if I want to live. I told my wife the other day that if I ever start drinking again, she should leave me as fast as she can, and don't ever look back. I also told her that if I die from drinking, I want her to tell anyone that asks what happened to me this:

"He was a drunk. He used to be sober, but he decided to screw it up, so it killed him. He knew better."

That's how I want it to go down if things go South. That's the uncut shit right there, the raw truth, and now y'all know it, too. Today though, I don't think I'll die. Today, I think I'll live.

How about you?

QUICKLY — AS ALL OF THIS WAS GOING
I COULD TELL MIKHAIL WANTED THINGS TO
HURRY, BUT HE WAS FAIR, LET ME USE
MY PHONE (ONLY TO TALK TO JEFF), ~~BECAUSE~~
IT WAS PUSHIN MIDNIGHT — THEY SAID I
<u>HAD</u> TO HAVE A LAWYER BY 8 AM OR
THE COURT WOULD APPOINT ME ONE (WTF?)
FINALLY I ~~TOLD~~ COHEN GOT MARTEN RADVAN
ON THE PHONE (WHO WAS AT DINNER) WHO
SAID HE WOULD CALL BACK — I TOLD
~~THE~~ MIKHAIL I HAD A LAWYER WHO
WOULD BE THERE AT 7:30 — THEY
TOOK ME DOWNSTAIRS, FINGERPRINTED ME +
TOOK PHOTOS (INCLUDING TATTOOS)
THEN TOOK ME DOWNSTAIRS TO A CELL —
WAS MADE TO STRIP BY ENTERING CELL,
HAD TO SQUAT — THEN INTO THE CELL
LED BY A YOUNG MAN — ~~WHO~~ HE GAVE
ME SOME BREAD WITH CHEESE(?) JUST,
WAS CHILLIN' WHEN THE LIGHT WENT ON
+ KID CAME BACK + ASKED FOR AUTOGRAPH
THEN G'NIGHT.

chapter five

As soon as Lucie, the blond-haired police woman, was out the door I lit another cigarette and started doing the doomsday math. *Five to ten years.* I was forty-one years old. Assuming the worst happened and I wound up serving ten whole years of my life, I would probably be fifty-two by the time I got out of prison—I tacked on a year for the time it would take for this thing to get through trial. Fifty-two years old—I could do that. I could do ten years in prison. I know men who have done a lot longer, and have a good life now. Assuming I survived prison, I wouldn't be a senior citizen by the time I got out of jail. I could write in prison, the endless touring cycle would be over for a while, I would have plenty of time to churn out a few books. I could do this. I was tough enough.

I began to think about what my life would be like as a fifty-two-year-old ex-con, freshly released from a Czech prison. Would I have sketchy tattoos, maybe a knife scar down the side of my face? Would I have somehow developed a limp or a bad Czech accent? Would my singing voice still be there, beaten to hell no doubt by ten years of hand rolled Czech cigarettes, but serviceable enough to do a reunion tour and make a little cash to start my life over with? Would my band still be in any shape to play, much less interested? What in the hell would the music climate be like in ten years anyway? Would our fans still even care enough to show up to see a bunch of old men with a freaked out jail bird front man wheeze through a set? What about my mind? Would being institutionalized that long break me? Would I walk out of prison a shattered, bitter man, unfit for society? I had just started to become a whole human being in the last two years—what would prison do to that man? What about my wife? Oh, God, *my wife.* Ten long years waiting on a husband in a prison on the other side of the Atlantic. I couldn't ask her to do that, no way. She was still in her thirties, she could meet someone else, and maybe they could build a new life together and have children. I didn't want her to turn into a lonely resentful woman after all the hell I had already put her through with my drinking. I wanted her to be happy, she didn't deserve anymore pain because of me, I would have to let her go, it was the only right thing to do . . .

After a minute I realized that I was doing exactly what I wasn't supposed to be doing in my current situation—freaking out. I have a terrible tendency to awfulize things. My mind loves to pre-dict horrific outcomes to events that have yet to happen, and in reality will almost certainly never occur, at least not in the or-der of the ludicrously self-centered chain of events that unfold so rapidly in my head. Almost anything can set my mind racing towards an ego-riddled doomsday. Within a matter of seconds, I can mentally chart a progression starting with me neglecting to cut my front lawn and ending in global nuclear catastrophe—and I do mean within *seconds.* Having a highly active imagination is not always a blessing, I assure you. Despite the fact that there was some very real, very heavy-duty negative stimulus at the moment, I knew that if I let it run the show in my head I was done for. It would only be a matter of time before I would say or do some-thing stupid and my prophecies would become self-fulfilling. I quieted the doom monkeys in my head by silently saying the words I would repeat more times than I cared to remember in the course of the next year:

You better square yourself away, and you better do it PDQ, soldier. People have been through a lot worse than this and come out okay, so stop whining, shut up, pay attention, be patient, and we'll see what your next move will be.

I took my own advice and looked over at Alex. My face must have betrayed the shit show running through my head, because a sly smile painted his lips. So far the Czechs didn't seem too big on displays of emotion, but his tiny smirking grin was enough to light a fire under my ass. Fuck him—he wouldn't see me freak out again, no way.

"Hey, chief, I need to call my lawyer. Can I have my cell phone for a minute?" I said.

"Chief? That is not my name," he said, looking confused and slightly annoyed.

"I know that. I just need my cellphone, if that's okay. I need to call my lawyer back home."

Alex sighed and handed me my phone.

"Thanks, chief." I was gratified to see his puzzled scowl return.

I hit the power button on my phone and looked at its screen. My battery was almost dead, showing a 10-percent charge. Crap. This was going to have to be fast and efficient. I opened my address book and dialed my band's lawyer, Jeff Cohen. Jeff is an entertainment lawyer who has been with us for most of our career. He is not a criminal attorney, but he is an extraordinarily smart man and I knew he would set the ball in motion to get me competent representation. Jeff picked up on the first ring and I heard his rapid voice come blasting through the phone.

"Okay, Randy, what the fuck is going on over there? Are you all right?"

"Hi, Jeff. I'm fine, but I'm in jail in Prague, and from what I can gather, they are going to charge me with manslaughter. I need a lawyer, and I need one now."

"I've already called the embassy, they gave me a list of names, and I'm working on getting you an attorney right now. I'll call you back in five minutes," Jeff said, "Don't say *anything.*"

"I won't, bro. Call me."

I hung up the phone. Thank God someone else was trying to do something, because at the moment all I could do was sit there with Alex staring at me while I smoked my last few cigarettes. I looked at him.

"Well, my lawyer in America is making some calls to lawyers here—he's trying to contact them right now. He will call me right back." I said.

"This advocate, he speaks Czech?" Alex asked.

"No, but he will find a lawyer who speaks English."

"Czech is very difficult language. Perhaps you should let soud give you advocate."

"Soud? What is a soud?" A suspicion rose inside me—whatever a soud was, it probably wasn't my best source for an attorney referral.

"The soud. The people who will hear what you will say about this incident," he said, mimicking a person sitting behind a desk and banging a gavel.

I did laugh in his face this time—I just couldn't stop myself. My pal Alex wanted me to accept a court appointed lawyer. For a manslaughter trial. In a foreign country. Every time this cop spoke, I felt better and better about the situation, because he provided soothing, if unintended, comedic relief.

"A *court-appointed* lawyer? For this? No thanks. I'll wait for my attorney back home to hire me one."

"You must have advocate by 8:00 tomorrow morning, or soud will give you one."

Being unfamiliar with the Czech legal process, I could only assume that Alex was telling me the truth, and that I had better get my own lawyer asap or else God only knew what kind of attorney I would wind up with. I looked at my phone and its rapidly shrinking battery indicator. Jeff had better get back to me soon.

"My American lawyer will have someone for me by 7:30, no problem. He's making the calls right now," I assured a skeptical-looking Alex.

"This will be difficult, very difficult; but it is your time. You are supposed to be in Germany for concert in two days I hear. To not have an advocate . . . this could make this impossible, I think. The soud will give you advocate very quick. It will be very good advocate. Then you can go to Germany," he replied.

"Yes, you're right; it *is* my time, and I think I will wait until I get my own lawyer. And I don't believe I'll be going to Germany anyway, so let's just forget about that."

Soon an officer came into the holding cell with a cordless phone in his hand, and gave it to me. It was a man from the American embassy.

"Hello, David, how are you doing?" he asked.

"Not so great. I'm in jail and I'm not really sure what's going on. Are y'all going to send someone over here?" I asked. That seemed to be what always happened in the movies—some sort of representative from the embassy eventually arrived to visit the frightened Yank who happened to wind up in some dingy Third World cell, either by accident or due to getting busted at the airport after foolishly taping a few kilos of high-quality, low-cost, locally produced narcotics to their belly. The embassy person always reassured the imprisoned American that they would have them out of there quickly, as soon as the appropriate palms were greased or whatever. I wondered what my embassy guy would look like.

"Well, the consulate is kinda closed for the night and the officer has left for the day, so nobody will be able to see you this evening. I'll leave a note for the morning officer, who gets here at 8:30, to run over and see you. Right now there's really nothing we can do for you—they arrested you legally. It is just our policy to call and make sure you are being treated humanely. Are they feeding you?" he asked.

"Hey, Alex, are y'all gonna give me any food?" I asked him. He nodded yes. "Yeah, I guess they will feed me."

"They aren't torturing you or anything, are they? Because if they are, we can go a different route, and things will change very quickly, I can promise you that."

"No, they have been pretty polite so far. I just need to get a lawyer—I think the guy who arrested me is trying to get me to take a court-appointed one."

"Look, we aren't allowed to give you any legal advice, but we gave your lawyer, Mr. Cohen, a list of names of Czech attorneys who have worked with Americans before."

"Yeah, I heard. He's trying to contact them now."

"Well, just hang tight, David. I know this isn't fun. I've left a note on the desk of the officer coming in in the morning—we'll have someone over to visit you first thing tomorrow, I promise."

I hung up and handed the phone back to Alex.

"I hope your embassy will help you? It is their job, I think."

"I suppose so. They said they will send someone tomorrow morning."

"But you must have advocate by 8:00. Or the sou-"

"Yes, yes; I know. The soud will give me one."

"Yes. By 8:00. I think the soud is good for you."

"Maybe so, but I think I'll wait and get my own."

Alex looked away, shook his head, and went back to playing with his phone. The news from the embassy had not been encouraging. They couldn't give me any legal advice, it probably wasn't even dark yet and they were already closed, and a note had been left for some nebulous person to come see me in the morning.

A note. *A note?!* Shouldn't there be some sort of high-tech alert ripping down the cyber-wires? Shouldn't some brainy communications tech with a sexy-looking headset be leaping up from in front of a giant electronic map of Prague right about now, pointing at the frantically blinking red dot indicating my exact position in the jail, and tersely speaking to the commander in the underground command room (because there *had* to be an underground command room commanded by a commander in a former Eastern Bloc American embassy):

"Sir, they have another one. He's one of ours—David Blythe—a musician from Richmond, VA. And they're trying the old soud advocate trick again."

"DAMMIT!" the steely-eyed commander would curse, a thin cigar clenched between his gritted teeth. "Mobilize A Squad— we're going in. Tell my wife I won't be home for dinner—this could take a while. Damn Czechs!"

Isn't that what happened in the movies? When I talked to the embassy, I should have heard assault rifle bolts being slammed home, body armor being strapped on, scrambled signal headset communication devices being fired up—where were my heavily armed guys? The Czechs had certainly brought all their scary stuff to the airport—we had to have that kind of artillery for sure. At the very least, someone in a trench coat, a fedora, and leather gloves should be passing a large envelope full of unmarked bills to a shadowy figure in some foggy back alley right about now. Instead, they left a note—a note!—(probably on an old stickie with failing glue) on some doubtlessly over-crowded desk. A scrap of paper that probably said something like, "Hey, you might want to swing by the city jail—there's some redneck from Virginia locked up down there."

This obviously wasn't the movies, and my status had been reduced to a note, like the honey-do lists my wife leaves me every now and then ("Hey, babe—please don't forget to take out the re-cycling when you get home"). What if the office cleaning lady accidentally threw it away? In my mind, some old and very underpaid Czech woman of Mexican descent, (although I had never seen a single Latino in all of Europe to my knowledge, much less a Czexi-can. By the way, this is why I refuse to eat Mexican food in Europe— there are no Mexicans there to make it, or at least properly train the Euros how to assemble happiness in a tortilla, AKA the bur-rito) wearily trudged the embassy office, emptying trash cans full of State secrets bound for the incinerator and vacuuming the floors. One wrong bump of a Hoover handle and the note would fall into a waste basket. My government would never know I had been im-prisoned, and I would be sent off to make Czech license plates for the next fifty years until a black t-shirt wearing, long-haired grass-roots campaign to free me finally reached the ears of a powerfu-

"I am going to get a coffee. Would you like one?" Alex asked, interrupting my reverie.

"Yes!" I almost screamed. Coffee, the black stuff of life that coursed through my alcoholic veins like blood does in normal humans, was exactly what I needed right now. All sober alcoholics consume way too much caffeine. It is a requirement—just ask one of us. I couldn't even remember if I had a cup today, other than the instant I had made in my Norwegian hotel room that morning, which might as well have been a hundred years ago. Things were looking pretty grim, but I still had a couple of cigarettes, and soon I would have coffee. At least I wasn't being held hostage by some savage rainforest tribe—thank God the Czechs possessed the accoutrements of a civilized nation.

Alex left, locking me in the cell, and returned briefly with two mugs of instant coffee. The Nescafe was strong and sweet, and I was extremely grateful for it, even though it was instant. Alex and I drank our coffee and smoked silently, until he began clearing his throat and furrowing his brow. I could see he was searching deeply into his mind, trying to find the correct terminology to convey whatever it was he was about to say.

"Maybe is bad . . . " He struggled mightily to find the words, then continued, "No, maybe is . . . good for big heavy metal star to . . . to . . . taste Czech prison." He finished with a smirk, as if I had never considered the horrors of incarceration.

Holy CRAP—Alex was trying to play good cop/bad cop with me. All by himself.

The faux concern for my touring commitments. The extolling of the virtues of the soud's advocates. The coffee. And now, the threat of prison. This was freaking *amazing*. Was it really possible that Alex *did not know* that you needed at least two cops to play good cop/bad cop? What kind of police training did this man actually have? Didn't he know that by embarking on a solo broken English good cop/bad cop mission, he had just reinvented himself in the image of a huge, cigarette smoking, mildly schizophrenic kindergartener who had gotten a late start learning to speak? Since *bad Alex* had momentarily wrestled the psychic reigns from *good Alex*, I saw no reason not to smirk back at him.

"No, I don't think that would be so good for me. In fact, I don't think that will be happening—sorry, I'm not so interested in 'tasting prison.' Yes, I think I'll be skipping that."

Alex seemed a bit surprised by my confidence, raising an eyebrow above his coffee mug, but didn't say anything else. I wondered if the mental exertion it had taken to be two different officers in a day had taken its toll. He finished his coffee, told me he was going to make a phone call, and left me locked in the cell. Exhaustion set in and I lay down on the long metal bench, threw my arm over my face to block out the sickly glow of the flickering fluorescent tubes closed my eyes, and fell into an uneasy sleep . . .

———

I awoke from my nap to the cell door opening and Alex walking towards me with a phone. "It is advocate," he said as I took the phone, shaking my head to try to wake up. A polite man on the other end informed me in a Czech accent that he was a lawyer, that Jeff had contacted him, but that he lived a few hours away from Prague and mostly dealt with cases of fraud. He also wasn't listed as a lawyer by the Czech bar association, which would be a necessary qualification to take on a case like mine. I told him I could see where that could present a small hurdle to our attorney/client relationship. He told me he was sorry he couldn't help me, but that he would try to give Jeff the names of some qualified attorneys. I thanked him and hung up.

This was getting more bizarre by the second. An out of town fraud lawyer with no legal credentials? It was nice of him to call, but I wasn't charged with swindling old ladies out of their retirement checks. Plus, even if I had been, could a lawyer who wasn't really a lawyer help me out there anyway? Apparently things worked differently in the Czech Republic—I mean, so far I had been under the watchful smoking eye of Alex, a cop who didn't seem to know how to be a cop. I hoped the fraud attorney (or whatever he was) would give Jeff a name or two of someone who at the very least had passed their bar exam. I sighed and handed the phone back to Alex, who could tell the conversation hadn't gone well and mercifully didn't ask me any questions.

Soon my cell phone screen lit up displaying Jeff's number. "Tell me something good, Jeffrey," I said.

"Okay, kiddo," he answered with one of his patented catchphrases, "I got a hold of one guy but he's two hundred kilometers outside of Prague and mostly deals with white collar crime, not this kind of stuff."

"Yup, he called."

"Lovely fellow, certainly not our man though. But I do have some names for you—do you have a pen and paper?"

I made a frantic writing motion in Alex's direction, the universal sign for *Hey, I need a pen and I need it yesterday.* He gave me a pen and I began writing down the strange Slavic names Jeff spelled out for me on the back of my arrest papers.

"These are all attorneys, recommended by the State Department, who have represented Americans before. I'm still calling around trying to reach them. I'll ring you back in five minutes," Jeff said, "Remember, don't say *anything.*"

"I don't know what I would say other than I need a lawyer, and that I'm about to run out of cigarettes. That's about the extent of my situation here."

"We'll have you an attorney soon."

I hung up and noticed Alex looking at me questioningly. "May I see paper?" he asked.

I saw no reason not to let him read the list, and handed it to him. Very quickly, I saw his eyes widen as he read the list. He pointed at the very first name on the paper, said something to himself in Czech that sounded like he wasn't very happy, and then spoke to me.

"Ah, Jiri Teryngel! Very big, very important advocate in Czech Republic. He will call Jiri Teryngel?"

"I'm sure he will. I want the best lawyer possible," I replied.

"This Jiri Teryngel, he is very expensive advocate," Alex said, shaking his head slowly.

"That's okay. I'm sure we can make it work," I said, smiling inside.

Right at that moment, my phone lit up—it was Jeff so I answered.

"What's going on now?" he asked me.

"Nothing. The officer who arrested me seemed pretty impressed by the first name on the list though, Jiri Teryngel," I said, mangling the pronunciation. "He says he's some sort of big shot, high dollar lawyer here."

"Haha!" Jeff laughed quickly, "Good! Fuck him! Let him sweat. I told you I wou-"

"Jeff, my battery is dying so we need to make this quick, " I cut in. I love Jeff and he's never let me down, but he can be rather loquacious and time was of essence here. "Have you found me a lawyer or not? The cops say I have to have one by 8:00 a.m. or they are going to appoint me one."

"Listen, can anyone hear us talking?" he said.

"No, I think we're good. English isn't exactly this guy's forte, if you get my drift." I said.

"Okay, good. Look, just keep telling them you will have one soon. I've called a bunch of people, but it's late over there and most law offices are already closed. I have a Czech friend I knew from law school who is making some calls as well. Don't worry. I'll keep trying until someone picks up. Will they let you use a phone to call a Czech number? You should try to call some of those numbers, too, to see if you can get ahold of anyone" he said.

"I don't know. I'll try. Just get me a lawyer as soon as you can, bro," I said.

"I will. Don't worry—I got this. Has the embassy called or sent anyone yet? We've already been on the horn with them."

"Yup, they called. There's nothing they can do for me right now. Look, I gotta go—my battery is really dying quick. Call me back when you have a lawyer for me, okay?" I said.

"I will. Hold tight," Jeff said, and hung up.

Alex had been watching me closely as soon as I said Jiri Teryngel's name again, and looked expectantly at me.

"So, you will have Jiri Teryngel as your advocate?" he asked.

"I think so. My lawyer is trying to contact him. Can I make a few calls to try and contact these other advocates from a phone here?"

"I will try to have called some names for you," he said, and I handed him the list. Alex called to someone in the hall, and they took the list and walked away. He turned to me.

"It is very late. Many advocates will be at home now, not working. I am thinking it is better for you if to you let soud give advocate. I am worried you will not make your concert if you do not have advocate in time," Alex said, sounding concerned again.

"I don't think we have to worry about me getting to any concert anytime soon," I said.

"It is your choice." He shrugged, and began playing with his phone again.

Alex seemed to be suffering the delusion that he had given me a parking ticket, not arrested me for manslaughter. It was becoming more and more apparent that I wasn't going anywhere anytime soon. I just hoped that if Jeff couldn't find me a lawyer by 8:00 a.m. that they would let me switch to one of my choice once one did become available. I got the distinct feeling that Alex was ready to wrap up the evening's festivities and go home for a cold beer and a nap. I didn't think he really cared who represented me in court; he just wanted to clock out and leave the police station. I couldn't really blame him. By this time it had to have been hours since I had been arrested, and we had been in this cell for several of them. The place sucked, and I bet he wanted to leave it almost as badly as I did. I tried to fall back to sleep, but couldn't get comfortable on the metal bench. My cell phone began to vibrate.

"Tell me you have me a lawyer, Jeff," I answered.

"Yes! He is at dinner with his wife right now, but will call you shortly. His name is Martin Radvan, he speaks English, and he practiced in America for several years," Jeff said.

"Sounds great. But is he a licensed member of the bar association here? The fraud guy wasn't. I need a real lawyer."

"Yes, he is—he's on the list the people from the embassy gave me."

"Wonderful. I hope he has the number at the jail, because my cell phone is going to die any second."

"No worries. Hang in there, kiddo—he'll call soon."

"Thanks, Jeff," I said, and hung up. Immediately the screen on my phone went blank as the battery died. I was now cut off completely from the outside world. Hopefully this Radvan guy would actually call. I handed the dead phone to Alex.

"Well, that's the end of that. She's kaput. But my Czech lawyer will be calling the jail soon," I said.

"Yes, phone is kaput. I take it now to remove SIM card for records," he said.

"Excuse me? You are going to read my SIM card? Is that what you are saying?" I asked.

"Yes," he replied, and walked away, leaving me fuming in the locked cell. If this had been in America, I would have started raising hell, yelling about invasion of privacy, guilty until proven innocent, habeas corpus, four score and seven years, Rodney King, Waco, and a bunch of other inapplicable stuff. If that didn't work, I would have quoted some imaginary obscure legal precedent that ended with a phone-snooping officer doing life in prison in order to make Alex at least question the wisdom of digging through my data. But this was the Czech Republic, I had no idea of the legality of this act (actually, I had no idea about its legality in the States, but that's beside the point—it just seemed awful Orwellian to me), and I wasn't about to give Alex the satisfaction of knowing that he had rattled my cage. Besides, I didn't have anything in my phone that could indict me of a crime that, to my knowledge, I didn't commit. I figured the worst-case scenario would be me having to explain to some of my more famous friends why some crazed Czech police officer was calling them in the middle of the night to tell them how much they loved their new album (metal fans are everywhere). Still, it reminded me of exactly how little control I had over anything that was happening to me in this foreign country. I could only control myself, so I tried (unsuccessfully) to not smoke my remaining cigarettes. Dammit.

After a while (I have no idea of how long, for the police had taken my watch when I was first arrested), Alex returned to the cell with the cordless phone again, handing it to me with what looked like relief on his face as he said, "It is Czech advocate." Thank God.

"Hello? Is this Mr. Radvan?" I asked.

"Yes, this is Martin Radvan. What can I do for you today, sir?" a pleasant-sounding voice said, as if he was a waiter asking what I would like for dinner. Mr. Radvan's lightly Czech-accented English was clear, and he spoke with an ease that revealed his familiarity with my language. I felt a rush of relief flow through me.

"And you are an attorney? A member of the Czech bar? Who can handle a criminal case in court? In Prague?" I asked, just make sure he wasn't another out of town non-licensed fraud specialist.

"Yes, I am a lawyer here in Prague. That is why I have called you. Now how may I help you, Mr. Blythe?" he replied in his even voice, probably wondering why in the hell this American idiot was asking him such ludicrous questions.

"Well, you can come get me out of here," I said, and explained my predicament briefly, starting with my arrest and ending with my current residence at the jail. Martin assured me he would be there by 7:30 a.m., thus relieving my court appointed lawyer anxiety. I hung up the phone and told Alex I had retained a lawyer who would be there bright and early, so he could forget all that soud advocate stuff. Alex grinned as if to say *Hey—you can't blame a man for trying!* He led me down some stairs into a room where I was fingerprinted and had my mug shot taken.

I have been fingerprinted several times before, almost always drunk. One of my favorite games to play with the police back in my drinking days was "Let's see how bad I can piss off the cops during fingerprinting before they kick my ass," which entails swaying a lot, "accidentally" knocking over the ink pad they use for the prints, moving my hand just a fraction of an inch or so as they roll your inked up fingers onto the paper, or having a violent coughing fit as the press your palm onto the print paper. Needless to say, what is normally a five-minute process could stretch out to ten or even fifteen minutes, contingent upon a complex and ever-shifting algorithm consisting of a) how wasted I was, b) how belligerent I was feeling that evening, and c) how patient the cops were. I'm surprised I never had my anarchic phalanges broken by some night shift cop who wasn't amused by my drunken she-nanigans, but I honestly really did look forward to fingerprinting every time I went to the drunk tank.

But tonight I was hungry, tired, scared, (and for a change) so-ber, so I was in no mood to play the fingerprint game with the Czechs. They were very, very thorough, inking prints on areas of my hands that I didn't even know had prints. Then it was time to get my mug shot.

If you've never been arrested, then you probably think the mug shot process is just a classic headshot, taken with a camera with a big flash bulb on it, old school like in the movies. We've all seen the photos in newspapers or online of scowling gangsters against the backdrop of a white wall with height measurements painted on it, or—even better—freshly arrested drunk celebrities, hair in crazy disarray, eyes pointing in two different directions like a cou-ple of inebriated goldfish desperately trying to escape the toxic bowl of their head. These pictures look like the beautiful people have been propped up against the wall just long enough for the photo to be snapped before they collapse into a puddle of pills, booze, and hubris on the station floor. We look at these off-kilter head shots and laugh smugly to ourselves, thinking: *Well, you don't look so fancy now, do you, Mr. Big Shot? About time someone took you down a notch or two.*

What a sad bunch of voyeuristic assholes we are.

When you have tattoos, weird birthmarks, and distinguishing scars (all of which I possess in abundance) the mug shot process doesn't stop with the classic frontal and profile headshot I just mentioned. It involves stripping down to your skivvies and having the cops photograph just about every inch of your body, from different angles, while they critique your ink. The Czechs in the booking room were doing this, pointing at my tattoos and talking amongst themselves, when I began to get impatient and started to drop my boxer shorts so they could snap a picture of my ass—the alarmed photographer shook his head no and picked up the speed with which he was photographing me.

When the photo session was finally over, I put my clothes back on and Alex led me out and down even more stairs to a room where a young guard in his early twenties sat behind a counter. There was some paperwork to sign, the exact nature of which I'm not positive, but I believe it was a list of my belongings that were to be kept until my release. I was weighed and measured like you would be at a doctor's appointment, then told to strip down to my underwear. I handed my clothes to the guard; then Alex, the guard, and I went into a room where my clothes were put on a hanger, covered with a (I shit you not) burlap sack, and hung up on a rack. Then I was told to take off my boxers, squat, and cough. After they were sure I hadn't smuggled in anything up the old poop chute, the guard told me in fairly good English that I could take a shower if I wished. He gestured toward a rickety shower setup in the corner of the room and handed me a bar of soap. Alex said he would see me tomorrow, and he and the young guard left the room, locking the door behind them.

I was grateful that the water was hot and the pressure was decent. I scrubbed my body the best I could with the small bar of soap and stood there with the hot water beating on my back. Little did I know that this would be the cleanest and last solo shower I would have for over a month. I turned off the water and grabbed the towels the guard had left for me beside the shower. They were not cloth, but two gigantic blue paper towels that didn't allow me to dry myself completely, but I was clean. I stood there in my underwear for a second, then knocked on the door.

The guard reappeared by himself and opened the door. He handed me a pair of threadbare and ill-fitting faded blue prison fatigues and some slippers, which I put on, and told me to follow him. As we were walking I suddenly realized how hungry I was—I hadn't eaten a thing that day, and although I generally do not draw comfort from food in stressful situations, I knew I would need some fuel if I were to think clearly in the morning. The guard told me I had missed dinner, but he rummaged around in a cabinet beside his desk for a minute, found a piece of bread with a thin slice of some sort of sandwich meat in it. Handing it to me, he said, "I saw you on television today."

"The news?" I replied.

"Yes. You are very famous in Czech Republic now," he said, not unkindly, and gestured me to follow him down a dim hall toward a row of cell doors.

Great. Just what I always wanted to be known for abroad—manslaughter.

As we were walking, I couldn't help noticing how young this guy looked. I assumed he had to be at least twenty-one to be a guard at the city jail, but he could have passed for seventeen. He wasn't a big man, and he didn't have a gun. All I could see in the way of a weapon was a nightstick. My animal brain, the primitive part of me concerned with fight and flight, began to quickly assess the situation in that dark hallway. It was screaming at me that I could overpower this young man, that I could throttle him to death with his own nightstick very easily, and then I would be free. He looked soft, I was behind him, no one else was around, and I would move swiftly and without mercy. It would be over in seconds.

Free.

Then the part of me that lived in the twenty-first century, not the Middle Ages, took over and let me know that it would be both wrong and pointless. He seemed like a very nice young man who was just doing his job. I had no real desire to hurt him. I don't like violence, but it lives within me, as it does within every human. I believe we would have perished as a species long ago if we were not born with this fighting instinct, the burning inner directive of kill or be killed. Within the constraints of a civilized social order, this brutal survival instinct is not necessary most of the time. The need to implement it almost never arises. But I was alone in a foreign jail, not an over-priced spa/meditation retreat with a few hundred other rich Americans with nothing better to do with their time and money. My lizard brain was automatically erecting the defenses that survival in captivity necessitates. The trick in jail is to know when to use the beast, and when to subdue it. I hoped I wouldn't have to use it at all, but I knew I would be ready.

Always ready.

We stopped in front of a battered looking door with multiple heavy locks and a small eye-level hatch. I looked at the number painted on the scratched steel door and smiled.

Thirteen. My lucky number. This was a good sign.

I walked into the cell and the guard shut and locked the door behind me. I heard his footsteps echoing as he walked away down the hallway. By the light of single dim bulb set into a metal cage-like socket covering in the ceiling, I could see two metal slabs bolted to the floor and opposite walls, a thin plastic mattress on each one. There was a metal commode with a metal sink bolted to the wall next to it in front of one of the beds. A small barred window sat high in the wall opposite the entryway. I stood on one of the beds and looked out the window, only to see a cinder-block wall a few feet away. I was alone in the small room.

I sat on one of the beds and ate my sandwich, then lay back on the plastic mattress, trying my best to cover up with the thin blanket that had been provided with my bed. Despite my mind attempting to race in circles fast enough to keep me awake, my exhaustion overtook me, and I quickly began to fall asleep. Right as I was on the edge of a deep slumber, I heard a knock on the door. I bolted upright, immediately thinking that perhaps the Czechs had come to their senses and decided it was a mix-up and would let me go. I sprinted the few feet toward the door as the guard opened the small door set in the hatch cut into the steel. He handed me a piece of paper and a pen.

"May I have your autograph?" he asked.

Lord have mercy. Here we go.

THURS JUNE 28th

WOKE UP - BREAKFAST OF SOME SORT - SURE IT WAS AHEAD.
MISSED PART FROM YESTERDAY WHERE MIKHAIL MADE ME TWO
INSTANT COFFEES - THEY WERE GOOD & SWEET TOO - MIGHT HAVE BEEN TODAY
THOUGH. ANYWAY, AFTER BREAKFAST SOMEONE FROM EMBASSY SHOWED UP - WOMAN, W/A
CZECH WOMAN. SHE JUST CAME TO SAY HI BASICALLY & TO ASK HOW I WAS, ALSO TO
HAVE ME SIGN SOME STUFF ABOUT WHO THEY COULD RELEASE INFORMATION TO. NOT
MUCH HELP THERE. THEN IN CAME MARTIN RADVAN, MY LAWYER, & HIS KINDA
METAL HEAD LOOKING ASSISTANT TOMAS. - OOPS, MAYBE IT WAS VLADIMIR -
I RUINO. WE TALKED - I THINK IST WAS WITH TOMAS FIRST, THEN LATER
WITH VLADIMIR. TOMAS SHARED SOME SMOKES WITH ME. THEN BACK TO THE
HOLE. I BELIEVE I HAD A CZECH ROOMIE, A YOUNG MAN W/ DARK HAIR
THAT CAME IN THAT NIGHT LATE. BED WAS MORE COMFORTABLE THAN MY
EURO BUNK, HAHA. I HAD A SHOWER EITHER THAT NIGHT OR THE NEXT -
TOWEL WAS DISPOSABLE PAPER THINGY.

FRI JUNE 29th   THE HOLE IS ROOM 13

WOKE UP IN THE HOLE, HAD BREAKFAST. SLEPT A LOT. / BACK TRACK TO
YESTERDAY - WENT WITH CRAPPY ASS TRANSLATOR, TOMAS, RADVAN, &
AMBASSADOR OFFICERS TO GIVE STATEMENT TO CZECH POLICEWOMAN (FIND
OUT HER NAME LATER) - I GAVE A LONG STATEMENT - I DIDN'T LIKE THE WAY
THE TRANSLATOR WOULD SAY AT CERTAIN TIMES "THAT'S NOT IMPORTANT,
SHE SAYS, NOT SO IMPORTANT". YES IT FUKKIN IS IMPORTANT IF I
SAY IT IS - REGRETABLY THEY DON'T SEEM TO THINK SO, HA!

chapter six

The first morning you wake up in jail after being arrested is always a) very, very disorienting, and b) very, very, disappointing. Your eyes crack open, the ugly paint job of your new home (always a bland institutional color, normally some atrocious shade of pink, yellow, or green some shrink somewhere determined was "calming") hits your bloodshot peepers like a bucket of vomit tossed in your face, and you think to yourself: *Where in the fuck AM I?* Then you realize that you are back in jail, and try to remember the day before, up to the point where the details get fuzzy and finally lost (*Okay, so I left the bar to go get a pack of cigarettes, and then I . . . then . . . well, then I guess something must have happened*); or, if you weren't completely hammered, it all comes flooding back in a painful wave of recall (*You IDIOT—why, why, why did you do that?*), and then the usual anger and shame swiftly sets in. I am by no means a hardened career criminal. But I have been arrested enough times, almost always over some alcohol-related incident, that I when I used to wake up in jail, I didn't panic. I'm wasn't scared, and I didn't start freaking out, thinking *OH MY GOD! I am in JAIL! What have I done to deserve this, this place is not for me, please God, get me out of here!* I would sit up, look around, shake my head, and say to myself:

Well Einstein, looks like you've done it again. Good job, dummy—I hope you enjoyed yourself.

My first morning incarcerated in Prague was very different than those cheery rise-and-shines as a guest of the fine gentlemen of Richmond's Fraternal Order of Police. First of all, my cell was dark, still only lit by the single bulb in my room. The American city jails I had been in before were always obnoxiously lit by 6:00 a.m., all the better to highlight their vomit-hued paint scheme. My cell was so dim I couldn't make out what shade of puke the jail's interior decorator had chosen; this was pretty unsettling. It felt like a medieval dungeon, or at the very least a communist gulag (after all, I was in the former Eastern Bloc), not that I had done any time in either. I was alone in a dark, locked, subterranean cubicle in a foreign country—I might as well have been at the bottom of an abandoned well or remote ghost town mineshaft, unable to climb out with no one around to throw me a rope. It was a hole, and that is what I began to think of it as: the hole.

Second, I wasn't hungover and I wasn't filled with anger and shame—I remembered everything about the previous day in great detail, and to my knowledge I still hadn't done anything wrong.

Third, I was pretty damn scared. Although I have had brief moments of panic and dread after waking up in an American jail, wondering if I had accidentally (or not-so-accidentally) killed anyone the night before, it was never long before I figured out that I had merely gotten drunk and had done something that was, to some varying degree, shameful. While that certainly isn't the greatest feeling to greet the new day with, I'm sure it's a truckload better than waking up and realizing you are a newly minted murderer. Plus, once I sussed out that I hadn't killed or injured anyone *too* badly, I knew I would be able to get out on bail or my personal recognizance within a day or two at the most. On this morning, I had no idea what had happened, or what was going to happen, other than the overwhelming feeling that I was in some deep doo-doo.

Four, while I was indeed rather terrified, I wasn't thinking *Good Christ, I need a drink,* which was always my first thought after I had sorted out why I was in jail in the first place. During my previous arrests, that was the thought that stayed with me from the moment I woke up in the clink until the second I bellied up to the bar and slugged down a cold one. The nearest bar was, of course, always my very first port of call upon sailing out of the drunk tank I had blown into the night before on the fetid beer-breathed winds of my alcoholism. (See, I told you us drunks are crazy— sane people try to avoid repeatedly taking wrong turns that wind them up in bad neighborhoods where they could possibly be severely beaten up, robbed, raped, or killed—which is exactly what Richmond City Jail is, a bad neighborhood on steroids. Drinking for me was like losing my road map and saying, "Screw it! Let's ride!"—I never knew where I would wind up, but surprise, surprise, a time or two it was in lockup.)

Luckily a drink was the last the thing on my mind this particular morning. And as long as I am not thinking about taking a drink, I can actually *think*, so I realized I was starting to freak out, and centered myself the best way I know how—I said a quick prayer. I asked the being I refer to as God to give me the strength to handle whatever was going to come my way that day, good or bad. I didn't ask for a specific outcome, I just asked for some extra-juice to help me act like a dignified man. Praying calmed me down, and soon a guard brought me breakfast.

As I've previously stated, I believe in a God—don't worry, I'm not going to get all nutty and religious on you, I'm not on a mission to "save" anyone, and actually I could care less whether or not you believe in God—it's really none of my business, just like my spiritual beliefs are none of yours. I normally don't discuss my relationship with the divine with strangers (I find it gauche to run around professing my deepest personal beliefs to any who would listen, plus my God doesn't need me to convince others to believe in him/her/it), but since I am writing a book about how I got through all this stuff, about how I tried to maintain a positive mental attitude in the face of adversity—well, what I consider to be God was a huge part of that.

I can't recall exactly what they gave me for breakfast that morning, but I would bet good money that it consisted mostly of a white, semi-sweet, knot roll-like piece of bread, because that's what they gave me almost every morning for the next thirty-six days, with slight variations. It sure as hell wasn't Eggs Benedict, smoked salmon, and crispy bacon on a fine china plate; nor was it that far simpler, but most divine of all breakfast foods—grits with cheese, salt, pepper, and Texas Pete hot sauce—but it was better than nothing. After I ate and brushed my teeth with the flimsy toothbrush I had been issued with my clothes the night before, the door opened, Alex appeared, and we went back upstairs to the holding cell from the day before. I was out of cigarettes, so I asked Alex if he would bum me one, and he did, even making me a coffee. Despite his clumsy and bizarrely schizophrenic attempt at good cop/bad cop the day before, I could tell Alex wasn't a bad guy; just like everyone else I dealt with in the Czech Republic legal system (with a few glaring exceptions), he was just trying to do his job the best he could, and I can't fault anyone for that.

I asked Alex if he could give me one of my antidepressant pills, and he hesitated, saying that a doctor needed to look at the medicine to make sure it wasn't some sort of narcotic. Apparently none of the Czech police could read the label on my pill bottle, or would to do a simple Google search. Alex must have seen that this made me slightly nervous and felt sorry for me, because he got me a Lexapro and told me I could have just one for now until a doctor figured out what kind of pills they were. I thanked him and told him I only took one a day anyway. Technically, Alex probably shouldn't have given me that pill, but he could easily see I wasn't behaving like a drug addict in withdrawal (as a policeman, I have no doubt that he had arrested more than one dope sick junkie and watched them kick in a cell—it's not a pretty sight; one I would witness shortly) and was probably telling him the truth. Plus, as I said, he seemed like a pretty decent guy overall.

Soon after taking my pill, two neatly dressed women were led into the holding cell, one an attractive young blond and the other a middle aged lady with a kind face and salt-and-pepper hair. I stood up from the bench I was seated on and shook both their hands, and the blond introduced herself as being an officer from the American Embassy with the perfectly astonishing name of Sonnet Frisbie. *This* was my embassy guy? Sonnet didn't look a thing like the middle-aged, harried, chain-smoking, probably alcoholic, prematurely graying-from-too-much-clandestine-activity embassy guys in the movies. She didn't have bags under her eyes, and she didn't appear particularly rattled by much of anything, including my current predicament. Wasn't she supposed to at least be sweating a little, like the embassy guy in *Midnight Express?* (I know in retrospect that in a situation like mine, the *very last* thing you want is some nervous-looking, slightly disheveled man in a suit smelling of the local gin and Pall Malls as he rolls up into the jail as your embassy's representative—you want someone cool as cucumber, and Sonnet was just that.) Oh, well—at least she had an awesome name.

Sonnet Frisbie—that's the type of moniker I would give a *femme fatale* character were I writing some sort of hard-boiled spy novel, or bestow my child if I were a more poetic, less talented, metal version of Frank Zappa. What a *great* name, and I didn't even have to think it up for this book! If I ever meet Sonnet's parents, I'll thank them for doing the heavy lifting for me here. Anyway, Sonnet and her companion Hana (whom I believe was a Czech national acting as a translator between her and the Czech authorities) were there to check on me, make sure the cops weren't torturing me, and have me sign some paperwork concerning what information could be released by my embassy to the press.

I thought about the press and my situation for a moment, then put down the names of my family, my attorney, and my band's manager. I would try to contain as much information about my arrest as I could for as long as I could, for I guessed that the Internet, particularly the heavy metal news sites and message boards, was already ablaze with wild rumors. Undoubtedly, some of the more troglodyte-like dwellers of these virtual gathering places, having already tried, convicted, and hung me in their tiny little pinheads, would be pressing the return button on their generic "Fuck that murdering asshole, I hope he gets raped in prison (plus lamb of god sucks)" posts as fast as their fat little pizza-stained fingers would allow (I was, of course, correct). I didn't want to give these assholes anymore fuel than they already had to post speculation that could possibly confuse or cause concern for anyone who cared for me—family, friends, fans, and well-meaning strangers. Besides, these mouth breathers would undoubtedly write what- ever "news" they wanted anyway, accurate or not. For me, the truth is not malleable. If I don't know the whole truth of a story, even mine, *especially* mine, I won't tell any of it until I know what the hell I'm talking about. This one was still unfolding, it was my tale, and I decided that I would be the one to tell the whole story, and not until I was damn well ready. Let the rumors fly, but I wouldn't add to them if I could help it.

Sonnet understood my concerns and seemed to agree that for the moment, this was probably for the best. She also informed me that she had been in contact with my family and would keep them apprised of any developments with my situation as they oc- curred. She also confirmed what the consular officer had told me on the phone the day before—my embassy could not provide me with any legal advice, a policy I still have a hard time wrapping my head around to this day. I was in some serious legal trouble in a foreign country—obviously, competent legal counsel was the thing I needed most at that point. I had always operated under the assumption that the job of a foreign embassy, besides main- taining diplomatic relations with the nation it was placed in, was to ensure the well being of its citizens in that country. Perhaps I'm a bit of an idealist, or just ignorant of the vagaries of interna- tional relations; but having on hand some sort of ambassadorial attorney familiar with the judicial system of the country in which it operates, just in case a tourist gets into a sticky situation, seems like something an embassy would cover. I wasn't being held captive by a Pushtan tribal warlord in the mountains of Afghanistan, and I wasn't expecting them to send in SEAL Team Six, but a visit from a lawyer to explain what the hell was going on would have been nice. Regardless, Ms. Frisbie was very pleasant, and I knew she didn't make the rules, just abided by them. She gave me a list of attorneys that had worked with Americans in the Czech Republic before, and I was gratified to see Martin Radvan's name on the list. Before she left, she promised once more that she would stay in touch with my family, and as I later found out, she kept her word. I will always be grateful to her for that, because I was far more worried about them than myself most of the time.

After Sonnet and Hana left, I asked Alex if he could take me to the bathroom. In the hall I saw our merch guy, Steve Stephens walking toward me. Steve is a lovely man from Birmingham, England, who travels with us on European tours selling our T-shirts and other wares. I think very highly of Steve, and we've had several great talks about music, books, and life over a good meal and coffee or just sitting on the tour bus as we rumbled through the night to the next gig. Our eyes met, and I could tell it pained him deeply to see me in such a bad situation. My band carries a road crew of seven to eight people when we tour, and without them we wouldn't be able to put on the shows that we do. They are employees, but they are also our friends, and over years they have become like family to us—Steve even flew to America for his first time once during a tour just to ride the bus and hang out with us for a week. I was happy to see Steve's face, but it really bothered me to see the upset in his eyes when he looked at me, so I gave him a smile and a nod, hoping he could tell I was okay. His dark eyes shot to the ground and he walked out a doorway. His would be the last familiar face I would see for quite a while.

After draining the lizard, it was back to the holding cell, and soon my lawyer arrived with a colleague. Martin Radvan was a casually dressed bespectacled man with a well-groomed mustache in his fifties. He limped into the cell and introduced himself in the pleasant and even voice I had heard on the phone, then introduced his associate. Tomas Morysek was a tall, slenderly built, young man in his twenties with a beard and long hair pulled back into a pony tail that hung down his back. Had he not been wearing a suit and tie, he could have very easily passed for a member of my band. I stood, shook both their hands, then we sat down and I noticed the source of Mr. Radvan's limp.

Martin's right foot was wrapped in a blood-spotted bandage and contained in an open-toed brace. A few of his toes and some of the flesh surrounding them poked out from beneath the bandage—what I could see of the foot was bright red, very swollen, and rather angry in appearance. It looked like an extremely infuriated fat man put on a forced diet, bloody nosed after being repeatedly, viciously, slapped with a large book of dessert recipes. Martin's foot was *gnarly*, in the same way those of us who skateboard describe a particularly heinous slam onto concrete.

"Excuse me, Mr. Radvan," I inquired, "but what happened to your foot? Are you okay?"

"Oh this," he chuckled, waving in dismissal at the bleeding, moribund appearing appendage, "I must go to the hospital later today. They have to cut some small part of it off—it has happened before. It is nothing."

It sure didn't look like nothing to me; in fact it looked pretty damn serious from where I sat. *Cut some part of it off? It's happened before?* I thought. *If it looks that bad and they couldn't whack off enough of it the first go around, will he stomp in on a peg leg when it's time for court? Good Lord, what kind of savage country have I landed in? I need to get out of here right now.*

"Well, I hope the doctors can . . . fix it." I grimaced, and we began discussing my case. Martin and Tomas informed me that they were there to be present during my interrogation that day, since according to Czech law a suspect has the right to have a lawyer present during any questioning by the police, just as we do in America, as long as the suspect isn't a complete moron and doesn't waive that right. I had been under the mistaken impression that I would be seeing a judge that day, perhaps to set bail, and that is why Alex had been insisting that I have an attorney by 8:00 AM. Martin and Tomas told me that I would be interrogated for quite a while, so I should be prepared to answer many questions. The interrogation would take longer than normal as well, since by law all questions had to be asked and answered in the Czech language; this would require a licensed translator, which the state would provide. I told Martin and Tomas what I could remember of the day in question, and then an officer came to lead us to the interrogation.

———

Since I had been arrested, my mind had been turning and searching frantically for a clear picture of May 24, 2010, more than two years before the day I was taken into custody. As I sat in the holding cell, over and over I read and re-read the poorly translated English warrant for my arrest, hoping for clues that would explain what had led me to this strange and frightening place. The warrant stated that on that day at our show in Club Abaton, I had made some sort of gesture that a young man named Daniel had apparently interpreted as an invitation to join me on the stage. Daniel had climbed up onto the three-foot-high stage, whereupon I had then allegedly pushed him with both hands into his chest, causing him to fly from the stage, landing on the concrete floor of the club. Daniel sustained an injury to the back of his head as a result of this fall, and had been taken to a hospital, where he died thirty days later. The warrant said that I acted with intent to hurt Daniel—since I had to have been aware of the height of the stage, I had to have been aware of the potentially deadly nature of pushing someone from it, therefore I was responsible for killing this young man. I was to be charged with intentionally causing the young man bodily harm that resulted in his death (manslaughter of a sort). As I read this paper and tried to come to grips with what was happening to me, I was really only certain of two things: a) that I had never meant to hurt, much less kill anyone that day; and b) that I had not been drinking before our performance in Prague on May 24, 2010. These were the only two things that allowed me to fight for my freedom over the coming months. Without both of these things being certain, I would have had no choice but to plead guilty. I would be in prison right now, as my conscience would not allow me to defend myself if I felt there was a possibility that either by intent or a drunken mistake I had ended this young man's life.

What I remembered of May 24, 2010 was (and is to this day) exactly this: I woke up on our tour bus in Prague, either as we were pulling through the city to the venue or already at the venue. I tend to believe that we were near the venue, as I had vague memories of seeing a river passing by from a window of our bus, but this could have been during a cab ride later in the day. Regardless, I woke up, more than likely made a coffee in the front lounge of the bus as is my habit, and walked off the bus, which was parked next to the club on a small cobblestone street that ran behind the venue. It was a cloudy day, and I walked around the building to the street in front of the club to see if there was anything interesting near the venue. There didn't appear to be anything appealing that I recall, just an empty street, which is rather standard for the areas surrounding rock clubs—these venues are often on the outskirts of whatever town they are in, many times in an industrial area so there aren't any real neighbors to complain about the loud music and drunken patrons that emerge at late hours from these places. I then walked back around the block to my bus and saw a member of our crew unloading gear from the truck we rented to carry it. I'm not 100 percent certain which crewmember it was—I believe it was our lighting tech at the time, Jay—but I do remember very vividly what that person said to me:

"Don't even bother going into the club. It's a fucking dump—we're already having problems getting the gear in there."

On tour, I generally spend as little time as possible at the venues we play. Once you've seen the inside of one dirty rock bar, you've seen them all. A dark, graffiti covered rectagonal room that reeks of stale beer, piss, and vomit is not where I want to spend my time, and that's just the dressing rooms—the concert area is usually worse. Some venues and their backstage areas are actually quite nice, but all the members of my crew have been in enough shit holes to know one when they see it, so I took my guy's advice, grabbed my book and journal from the bus, and settled down outside to sit and read and write for a bit. I must not have had to take a poop, otherwise I would have gone in and used the bathroom in the club—no number two is allowed on most tour buses, as their chemical toilets are not equipped with grinders to chop up all the collected shit and paper fine enough for it to shoot out the pipe that empties the septic tank. Plus, a bus toilet smells bad enough when there's a bunch of guys just pissing in it—thirteen dudes dropping deuces after nights of drinking way too much beer and eating truck stop food would be truly horrific, so pooping outside the bus is the way to go.

Regardless, I don't remember going into the club for any significant amount of time that day until right before we played—I vaguely recall at some point walking up the stairs to the entrance of the Abaton, poking my head into the venue briefly, seeing a mess of equipment crammed into an obviously insufficient amount of space and some very unhappy looking crewmembers, then turning around immediately and walking back downstairs to resume reading. We pay our crew to make our show run smoothly, and I very rarely talk to them much before a show if they are on stage setting up or working on our gear. They don't need me clowning around, getting in their way, asking them a million useless questions—generally being an annoying nuisance. I am expert at all of these things, especially if there is nothing to do nearby and I've had a bunch of coffee, which is, of course, almost always the case within an hour or so of me waking up on tour. When the crew looks less than content, as they did that day, I stay far, far away until it's time for me to do my thing on stage. Except for the first day of tour, when our sound and monitor engineers need to dial in my stage sound, I don't even go to sound check—it's not like I'm Pavarotti.

I clearly remember that at one point as I sat there reading and writing, it began to rain, so I moved into the open doorway of the club entrance and sat there smoking cigarettes and looking out on the rain. I do not remember how long it rained, only that I didn't wish to go back on the bus to read, where I couldn't smoke and the television was guaranteed to be on and blaring, so I did my reading and writing elsewhere that day, as I do most days.

The next thing I remember is my drummer Chris walking up to me at some point in the afternoon. The rain must have stopped, because he said, "Hey, me and Steve Stephens are going to take a cab into the city center in a bit if you wanna pitch in and catch a ride with us." The next thing I remember is being in a taxi on the way to the center of Prague with Chris and Steve, both guys who like to do a bit of exploring, just like myself. I was looking forward to seeing the architecture, perhaps the old Jewish Quarter, and hopefully a few of the gorgeous Czech women I had heard about from friends who had lived in Prague since the fall of the Iron Curtain (it is true—there are many, many women of great Slavic beauty in that city). We were dropped off not too far from Old Town Square, and began walking toward it down a broad avenue, soon cutting off onto one of the countless winding cobblestone side streets that snake crazily through Prague and make it such a bewildering place for a newcomer to navigate. Right at the end of the street as it emptied into Old Town Square sat a Starbuck's coffee shop, and I quickly ran inside to grab an iced mocha, for it was a warm and (now) sunny summer day and perfect for some chilled caffeine. (I would become a daily visitor to that very same coffee shop over two years later when I returned to stand trial.) I then rejoined my friends on the edge of a very crowded Old Town Square.

There was some sort of celebration in the square that day, because there were literally thousands of cheering people packed into its sizable confines, waving Czech flags and applauding as men in what appeared to be a sports team's jerseys took turns yelling into a microphone from a platform erected in front of the large monument to Jan Hus (a vocal critic of the Catholic Church who was excommunicated and burned at the stake for his "heretical" views, sparking the Hussite Wars) in the middle of the square. I was sure this gathering had to be something to do with soccer, but after asking a stranger what was going on, my hunch was proven wrong—the Czech national hockey team had just won the world hockey championship, and the victory had driven the normally publicly taciturn Czechs to a huge and rare display of red-faced, screaming, public exuberance.

I was happy for the Czechs, and they all seemed to be in a really great mood, but all you could see of the square was hooting, beer drinking, hockey fans. Very large public gatherings of intoxicated sports enthusiasts has never been my thing (I have seen them turn ugly very quickly more than once), so we pressed on in search of more viewable sites.

Leaving Old Town Square, we proceeded through the narrow streets and walked across the famous Charles Bridge that spans the Vltava, heading towards Prague Castle. I remember being impressed by the view from the bridge, and enjoyed seeing all the musicians busking and the artists set up the entire length of the bridge, selling their paintings and photographs and handmade jewelry. I am always happy to see street musicians playing and artists out in public hawking their wares, and I often give them change or buy some small piece of art if it catches my eye. I am glad to see them even if they are terrible players or their art is atrocious, because they are displaying belief in themselves and their ability to create something worthwhile, even if only for themselves. That takes *guts*, and guts are something I quite admire. A city's artists and musicians are the living, breathing chroniclers of its soul, and there were plenty out in the sun that day in Prague. I remember thinking on the bridge how much more I enjoyed the urban outdoor culture of Europe than that of most cities back home, which are (with a few notable exceptions, such as New York City, still undeniably the greatest metropolis on earth) becoming increasingly sanitized, resembling more and more the deathly strip mall environs of those cities' suburbs as chain stores pop up like cancerous polyps invading once healthy tissue. As I walked smugly towards the bridge's end, feeling oh-so-cultured and well traveled, a sharp and overpowering odor hit my nose, reminding me of one of Europe's distinctive shortcomings.

In any major European city on a hot enough summer day, the smell of the piss of a thousand years wafts through the air depending on how close you are to a sewer grate. Some are worse than others, but I have yet to find a European city that has somehow managed to renovate their ancient sewer systems thoroughly enough that the urine of antiquity has finally been flushed away. Prague was nowhere near as bad as Rome (as the reigning champion in the pee smell department, Rome completely baffles me with its terrible plumbing. I mean, didn't the Romans *invent* indoor plumbing?), but the *eau de wee-wee* was strong enough for me to comment on it to Steve and Chris as we walked off the bridge and headed up the hill towards Prague Castle.

I remember walking for a long while uphill, climbing many steps that ran beside a stone wall, which I believe was the outer wall of the castle. As we reached the summit, we saw a group of four or five young people standing there, and they called out to Chris and me. They were lamb of god fans, and had traveled from somewhere outside of Prague to see the show that night. We signed some autographs for them and took a few pictures. One of them I remember very clearly had long blond dreadlocks.

They were very polite fans, not pushy or invasive of our space, nor taking up too much of our time—polite fans are a joy to meet, and unless I have something urgent to do (like getting on stage or going to the bathroom) I almost never mind taking the time to take a photo or sign something for well-mannered people. They told us they were looking forward to the show, then we said our goodbyes.

Here my memory fails me, because I don't know whether or not we even looked inside the castle courtyard; but I do know that if we did, it would have been no more than a glimpse. We certainly didn't have time to take a tour of such a large structure, so shortly upon reaching the top of the hill we had climbed we caught a taxi back to the venue.

We arrived back at the club just before our set. I recall walking quickly up the stairs and remembering there was one way in and out of the club. The only way to win in a single-entrance club situation is to go undetected, so on that night I was swift and stealthy, never even looking up from the floor as I wove my way uninterrupted through the crowd to the dressing room. The dressing room was a small room through a short hall crammed with equipment beside stage right (the left side of the stage from the audience's perspective). I put on my monkey suit (the stinking pair of shorts, dirty t-shirt, and smelly shoes I wear every night so my regular clothes won't get sweaty), did my vocal warm up, and walked onto the stage from stage right. I had walk carefully through the back line of amplifiers, guitar cabinets, and crawl over Chris's drum set until I reached stage left, where my guitarist Mark and I are stationed before a show and during our few short breaks. I remember it being a particularly difficult trip to stage left; there were piles of cables and guitars and pieces of drum hardware in my way. I could see why our crew had been so grouchy looking earlier in the day. The stage was tiny, and getting all that stuff up there and working had to have been quite a chore. It was extremely cramped, and as I heard our intro track begin to roll,

Mark's guitar tech Drew told me "Be careful—it's a small stage and it's really tight." I handed Drew my glasses for safe keeping, Chris counted in the first song, Mark walked on stage, and I followed shortly, just as I have on countless other nights.

What do I remember about the set we played that night? Not much. It was just a show like any of the hundreds of other shows my band has played in its career. It was loud. It was hot. I dumped a lot of water over my head to cool off. There were a lot of people dressed in black with long hair smashing into each other. We seemed to go over okay with the crowd. Nothing particularly spectacular or horrible occurred to my remembrance. Only a few things stood out when I searched my brain for any sort of clue.

I remember that right from the beginning of our set, there seemed to be a lot of people onstage. People who did not belong. People who were not in our band, crew or working as security. As a matter of fact, I don't remember there being security of any sort present in the area near the stage, because people kept on hopping up, bumping into me as they ran across the already crowded platform and leaping into the crowd. At every show my band plays, there is a signed contract with the promoter of the gig that states what lamb of god as an organization requires in order to put on a show. One of these requirements is trained security and a reliable barricade placed properly in front of the stage, both measures meant to ensure that audience members do not jump onstage and that both the band and audience are safe. Sometimes certain things are struck from a contract or rider depending on the promoter's budget for the show, but never, ever security or a barricade. Lamb of god draws a rowdy crowd, to put it mildly; if there was no security at our shows, then more than likely our equipment would get knocked over every night, we would get knocked off stage, and eventually someone (probably several someones) would get seriously hurt. On this night, not only was there seemingly no security present, but no real barricade. If there was one, it was flimsy and pushed up flush with the stage, because fans were leaning on the stage, and kept hitting my feet whenever I would prop one up on a monitor, irking me quite a bit and causing me to back away the two or three feet I had into Chris's drum kit. I began to wonder where in the hell security was, and couldn't wait for the gig to be over. This show was a disaster—the club sucked, my crew was pissed off, the stage was tiny and crowded with our equipment. A crowded stage is a dangerous stage for me, because I hop all over the place constantly when we play, despite not seeing well because of my lack of glasses and the stage lights that constantly glare into your eyes. The fans punching my feet and running around on stage made it even worse, and as the non-existent security did absolutely nothing to stop them, I began to get very annoyed.

I was particularly annoyed with one young blond haired fan who jumped onto the stage again and again, trying to put his arms around me as I tried to sing. I watched him fly into the audience at one point and hit the floor pretty hard, only to re-appear on stage not too long after. He had already made two appearances prior to this instance, and despite my pointing at him, shaking my head to communicate my displeasure, here he was again. I decided at this point I had had about enough of his shenanigans, figured that he was drunk or crazy, and decided to teach him a lesson. As he came toward me, I reached out with my left arm around his neck, slipped my hip behind his, and took us both to the ground. Once we were on the ground, I wrapped one of his legs with my left leg in what my middle school wrestling coach would have called a half-grapevine, then straightened up a bit and grabbed him around his throat with my left hand. I didn't choke him, but applied enough pressure to let him know I meant business, and in between singing lyrics into the mic I had kept in my right the hand whole time, I began to yell something to effect of "No! No more, you asshole!" into his face. I suppose the best analogy of this whole physical confrontation would be that of a mother dog when she puts one of her pups on its back with her mouth and growls at it—*Hey, knock it off kid. I'm serious.*

This young man apparently didn't think I was serious, because he began to grin and raise his hands at me in the horns (the clenched thumb and raised index and pinky finger salute you see audience members doing at all rock concerts now), almost giggling beneath me. I must admit, this slightly pissed me off—I was trying to work, he seemed to think that it was his right to come up and drunkenly disrupt our performance, and now the little shit seemed to be smirking at me. I held my temper in check though, didn't throttle the grin off his lips, and just continued singing and yelling "No more!" in his face until he decided he had had about enough of being on his back and tried to get up.

Oh, no. That wasn't about to happen. *You wanted to be up here so badly, you little fucker,* I thought, *and now here you are. With ME. You'll leave when I decide it's time for you to leave.* He began to look a bit panicked, and started to struggle some more to get up, so I took my hand off his throat, wrapped my left arm around his neck and pressed my whole body down on him. I gave up yelling "No" at him, and pressed the microphone into his face as I kept screaming the lyrics into it. This really seemed to freak him out—he couldn't move and I was screaming into his face from just inches away. I held him there until he looked truly shook up, then I let him go. I figured I had made my point and he would not be returning to the stage. I do not remember him leaving the stage, but I do remember my bassist John looking at me and saying, "That was fucking *awesome.*"

That is the last truly clear memory I have from the stage that night. My next recollection is hazy, and doubtlessly colored by repeated viewings of video of the show that night, countless rereading of the specific wording of the charge laid against me, and examining in great detail the many conflicting testimonials witnesses gave concerning that evening's events. I remember someone I believed to be my friend whom I had just so sternly warned

against coming onstage, a young male with blond hair, flying off
the stage in front of me, disappearing into the crowd, then getting
up holding their head like it hurt. I believe, but am in no way
100 percent certain, that I pushed this person from the stage, and
that it would have been from about the middle of the stage. I remember this person getting up looking shaken and me looking
into the audience to see if he was okay. I remember several audience members giving me the thumbs up sign, as if to say, "He's
fine, keep going." I remember this young man shaking his head
briefly as if he was not okay, then proceeding to briefly head bang
again as if nothing had happened before wandering back into the
crowd. This gave me a moment's concern, but I supposed that he
was fine, and we continued to play. No one told us otherwise.

I don't remember the end of the show, but I do remember
very clearly what happened next. I walked off stage and into the
dressing room, and my cell phone began to ring almost immediately. I looked and saw it was lamb of god's publicist, Maria
Ferrero, ringing me. I didn't answer, because after paying a few
mammoth phone bills as the result of Euro touring, I had learned
my very costly lesson. I remember wondering what Maria was doing calling, as she never does when we are overseas—she knows
better. The phone rang again—it was Maria once again. This time
I answered, because I figured it was something important if she
was repeatedly calling me in Europe.

"Hey Maria, what's up?" I asked.

"Randy, Paul's dead," she said.

"What?" I asked. "Paul who?"

"Paul Gray. Paul from Slipknot."

"Fuck. In De Moines?" I asked.

"That's what I'm hearing. I just didn't want you to have to find
out by reading about it on the Internet."

"Thanks, Maria. I gotta make some calls. Bye."

Paul Gray was a friend of mine from Iowa who played bass
in the multiple-platinum selling nine-member band of masked

lunatics, Slipknot. Lamb of god had toured with Slipknot a few times, starting in 2004 on Ozzfest, a roving multiple-band package ordeal that travels around the United States in the summertime spreading mayhem everywhere it touches down. Paul and I had met before at a club gig lamb of god did in Iowa, but we really bonded the summer of 2004, stealing golf carts from the venues we played, joking around, and talking about punk rock bands. We went on to have our fair share of good times in the years after that, from raging nightly backstage during a nine-week tour our bands did together, to bumping into each other at different festival gigs throughout the world. The last time I saw him alive, he had come to see us in Des Moines, despite the fact that he had a flight in a few hours to Europe to start a tour. He was a big-hearted man; once I stayed at his house in Des Moines with my other band at the time, Halo of Locusts, when we played a gig in his home city. Paul wasn't even in Des Moines at the time, he was on tour, but when I called to see if he was in town, he insisted that we stay at his house and called a friend with keys to his house and had her open it up for us. Paul and I had talked several times about a musical project we wanted to do, and had figured out a few people we would cherry pick from other bands to make something unique and entirely different from Slipknot and lamb of god. I still have the musical ideas in my head, but I haven't been able to think of anyone that could fill his shoes. Maybe I never will, because he was a special guy. I miss him dearly.

After I hung up with Maria, I told my bandmates and crew about Paul, and spent the rest of the evening mostly out by our bus texting with various friends back home about his death. I decided to take my first drink of the day and did a shot or two of Jagermeister in his honor (because what makes more sense to an already depressed alcoholic when someone dies than to ingest a depressant?), then went to bed. We left sometime around three or four a.m.

The next day was spent riding the bus to Poland. I got stinking drunk and cried, listening to Slipknot on my iPod and writing bad lyrics in a notebook. I was trying to hear Paul's voice one last time in his bass lines, but all that was left was his music. I was so sad that he was dead, that I would never get to speak to my friend again in this life; even as I sped toward my own doom in a shot glass full of black German cough syrup.

That is truly all I remember of May 24, 2010. I only remember that much because it was our first time in Prague, security was so bad I had to wrestle some kid to the ground on stage, and Paul Gray died. It was a bad day, but I wish I could remember more of it. I wish I could remember every second. Then maybe I would have had some real answers to all the impossible questions that were about to be asked of me.

I GAVE MY STATEMENT, THEN THE LADY COP ASKED SOME QUESTIONS, THEN RADVANA TOMAS & EVEN THE TRANSLATOR THREW IN A FEW QUESTIONS. OR HE SEEMED TO HAVE A GOOD HEART, BUT HIS TRANSLATING SKILLS WERE NOT THAT HOT. ANY WAY, AFTER STATEMENT I WENT BACK TO THE HOLE. A DEFINITE MISS FROM YESTERDAY: AFTER WAKING UP, MIKHAIL GAVE ME ONE OF MY LEXAPRO'S. HE SAID IT WAS OK, EVEN THOUGH THE CZECH POLICE DIDN'T RECOGNIZE IT. THIS TURNED INTO A CAR TRIP ACROSS PRAGUE W/ THE BARNESTON DUDES FROM AIRPORT TO A DR. WE GOT THERE & SHE DIDN'T KNOW ENGLISH, SO SHE REFUSED TO GIVE THEM ANY CLEARANCE TO GIVE ME MY MEDS ANY FURTHUR. SHE SAID WE HAD TO HAVE A TRANSLATOR. SO THAT RESULTED IN THE DRIVER OF THE CAR GETTING VERY PISSED & DRIVING LIKE FUCKING CRAZY BACK TO THE JAIL — HE WAS SCREAMING TEARS & CUSSIN IN CZECH & YELLING ABOUT THE DR. IN CZECH. CRAZY FUCK. WE GOT BACK TO JAIL & THEY MADE SOME CALLS SO WE GOT BACK IN THE CAR & WENT BACK TO THE DR — I FASTENED MY SEAT BELT EVEN W/ MY CUFFS ON & MIKHAIL SAID "DON'T WORRY, DON'T BE AFRAID — MY COMRADE IS A VERY CALM DRIVER" HAHAHA! I DON'T KNOW IF HE WAS JOKING OR GOT THE WORDS WRONG, BUT FUCKIN' A THAT DUDE HAULED ASS. SO WE GOT THERE & MY TRANSLATOR WAS ... A FEMALE DWARF! NO FUCKING WAY! SHE TRANSLATED IT REAL QUICK & OFF WE WENT — AT THE ROUNDABOUT NEAR THE JAIL I GOT THE COP TO TRY & DRIFT AGAIN & HE LAUGHED & SQUEALED HIS TIRES. YEE-HAW! HE SEEMED TO BE A BIT CALMER THEN AFTER WE

chapter seven

There was crap everywhere in the interrogation room—papers stacked high on a cheap-looking desk, books with titles I couldn't read, a dirty antique computer monitor. The place reminded me of a young, unhappy, English professor's office; a shambolic cubicle to pay dues in until either tenure or that first book contract arrives (I've sat in a few of these offices). Behind the desk sat Lucie. In front of the desk stood a tall thin man in his mid-forties who introduced himself in passable English as my translator. In order to protect his identity, I'll call him Antonio. Lucie said a few sentences in Czech to him, then he turned to me and asked me my name, date of birth, occupation, what I had done for employment for the last two years (which I thought I had just answered), my level of education (about five years total years of college, but she just typed down high school. Oh well. It's not like a BA in English would have done me any good here anyway), my social status (um, sorta popular now, but not at all in high school?), my net monthly income (none of your damn business), and whether I had been the subject of any investigation for criminal activity in the Czech Republic or any other country. I answered her questions honestly, including the criminal activity—I told her I had been arrested before while drunk, but no, to my knowledge I had never been "under investigation" (which sounded awfully serious to me) for criminal activities. I wasn't some kind of king pin; amazingly, even my driving record is pretty spotless, bar the occasional speeding or parking ticket, and I hadn't had one of those for a few years. To my knowledge my record was pretty clean, and all of my charges, even the more unsavory ones, had been dismissed.

Then Lucie read me my rights, which Antonio haltingly translated. I don't remember exactly what they were, but none of them seemed to be the right to remain silent. Or maybe it was, but that didn't seem like such a hot idea—I had my attorney present, who nodded to me to answer these questions. I had to trust in his judgment—what other choice did I have? Lucie asked if I was currently dependent on alcohol or drugs or had been in the past. I replied no, I was not currently using drugs (other than my antidepressant, caffeine, and nicotine) or alcohol, in fact hadn't a drink for almost two years, but that I used to drink on tour. She wanted to know if I drank beer or hard liquor (I suppose I didn't exactly look like a wine aficionado), and how much of it. I told her mostly beer, and remembering back to the time of that tour, which was towards the end of my drinking, I told her on average five or six beers a day, which was the truth. I didn't mention the fact that as a person in the advanced stages of alcoholism, at that point sometimes I would be drunk after three beers or that conversely sometimes I could drink eighteen beers and feel sober as a judge—this is one of the most baffling aspects of a drunk's life, when the human body stops processing alcohol in any sort of predictable manner. It didn't seem like the best time to bring up what a terrible mess I used to be, though. Small beers or large beers, she wanted to know. This was getting complex. Regular, I guessed? I wasn't slugging forty ouncers of malt liquor in the alley, just drinking five or six regular beers, you know? Small or large beers, she repeated. Okay, small it is. (I later found out that in the Czech Republic a small beer is approximately ten fluid ounces, almost the size of a regular twelve ounce can of beer in the States. They also have large *and* double large beer sizes—a double large weighs in at about a liter. The Czechs take their beer very seriously, and brew some of the world's best.)

Then she asked me if I had anything I wished to say regarding my person or character, to explain what kind of man I was. I told her that I sang for lamb of god, restated that I hadn't had anything to drink or taken any drugs in almost two years, that I was not a crude or savage person, and that I have done volunteer work, donated cash, and raised funds for various charitable organizations, most recently a breast cancer research organization. All of these things were 100 percent true (well, I can be both crude and savage depending if the situation warrants such behavior, but for the most part I'm a relatively articulate and well-mannered man). I did say that I had never received psychiatric treatment, which was the only lie I had told since my arrest. I informed her I was taking a low dose of Lexapro for mild depression, which in itself necessitates a visit to a psychiatrist to obtain a prescription, but I did not think it would do me any good to relay the story of my ridiculous attempt to kill myself over a woman in my twenties and winding up in the looney bin back home for a couple of days. For some reason, my gut instinct told me to keep that dusty old cuckoo in the clock. I didn't like lying, but I really didn't want them to place me in some sort of padded cell because I was an idiot once almost two decades ago. I didn't think it would bode well for my case if these strange people thought I was mentally unstable. As I tried to convey the image of a calm, compassionate, sane man, I got the feeling that no matter what I said, the Czech authorities would think I was a little "off" in some way. This was a valid assumption, as I would later learn. When I was done attempting to paint a reasonable picture of my self, Antonio spoke again.

"She will hear your statement now. Please go slowly. Speak as plainly as you can, as I will be translating and she will be typing it out."

Uhm, my "statement"? What in the hell did that mean? Should I yell, "Not guilty!"? That's all I really wanted to state at that moment.

"She wants you to tell her about the day of the incident."

So I did. I recounted everything that I could remember of May 24, 2010 in as great detail as possible, which wasn't that much when it comes down to it. This still took quite a while, as Antonio keep interrupting me to clarify what I meant by a simple sentence, or for the definition of some (what I took to be) fairly rudimentary word. This was not encouraging to me. I knew going into the interrogation that I would have to choose my words very careful, but Antonio wasn't instilling much confidence in me that what I was saying was what Lucie was recording on her computer screen. Mr. Radvan had instructed me to just tell the truth, which was what I already intended to do. This wasn't a very tall order since I had nothing to hide and didn't remember much anyway; but I knew how the police worked, how they would try to find holes and inconsistencies in everything I said, how any single word or phrase could be turned against me. It was critical to my freedom that I explain without ambiguity what I recalled of that day, and the fact that my translator was obviously unqualified to teach even a group of fifth graders beginning English made me very, very nervous. Martin could see this, and he leaned over from his chair beside a me a few times, patted me on the knee, and softly said, "It's okay—just tell her what you can remember." He was a comforting presence that I would come to like greatly over the course of the next year.

It's impossible for me to accurately express how incredibly unnerving it was to be asked to suddenly recall a fairly nondescript day on tour from more than two years ago, shortly after being informed I had killed a fan of my band, while knowing my bare-bones recollection could have an immensely significant impact on whether or not I would be spending the next ten years of my life behind bars in a foreign country.

Looking at the copy of my testimony now, well over a year and a half after it was given, I see I did a pretty good job of laying out exactly what I remembered in a chronological order. I didn't jump all over the place, and I was precise. I told the truth. I also stressed what I instinctively knew would be a few critical details—that the stage was small and that until we were playing, I had not been on or near it. That there was no security to my knowledge on or in front of the stage, and that this was highly irregular. That I had removed my glasses and thus my vision was impaired. That I had made it clear that audience members were not allowed on stage, yet one in particular repeatedly ignored that fact. That until two days before, neither myself nor my band had been made aware that an audience member had been injured, much less died. I also explained what stage diving was, because I assumed (correctly) that the authorities would have absolutely zero understanding of what happens at a metal concert, including the seemingly senseless act of flinging one's body through the air in the hope that a bunch of sweaty strangers will be kind enough to break your fall. Reading this takes me back to that disheveled room, and I can see myself sitting in front of that chintzy cluttered desk, trying to speak evenly through the sweating trepidation, over the heart that was doing its best to beat itself right out of my chest. Reading this shows me that I was doing the best that I could in that moment. Reading this, I know now I didn't let myself down.

Reading this I also now *definitely* know that poor Antonio is not destined to go down in history as the hero of future translator lore, the paradigm all men and women in the multi-lingual clarification biz aspire to. I do not wish the reader to think I disliked Antonio; in fact I felt quite the opposite (hence his pseudonym—I'd hate to damage his reputation). He was the very model of *bonhomie* who seemed to honestly feel sorry for me. But . . . let's just say that if this book ever gets translated into Czech, I hope he's not the one who gets the gig.

Perhaps I am being a bit hard on Antonio, as I am currently reading the copy of my interrogation statement (bear with me—this gets a little convoluted) that the superlative translator I hired during my court case, Rudy (who also happens to be an attorney and a hell of a nice guy), translated from the Czech version of my statement that Lucie typed up however she saw fit based on whatever Antonio managed to intermittently translate in real time from my nervous but plainly spoken layman's English. There were far too many moving parts to this equation, and it makes my temples throb just remembering the fear and fierce frustration I felt as I swiftly realized that my future status as a free man was riding on what was, in essence, a high-stakes Slavic game of Chinese whispers. My transcript of the whole interrogation shows a pretty mangled transmogrification of the words I actually spoke, which would be pretty damn funny except for the fact that a single lost or mistranslated word could have (and did in some places) have a very large impact on what I was trying to convey—the truth, which I was certain held the key to my innocence. The fact that the subtle nuances of tone and inflection of the English language simply do not translate into the corresponding but even subtler nuances of tone and inflection of the fiendishly difficult Czech language did nothing to further my cause as well. Regardless of the whos, hows, and whys of the whole thing, I could see that I was going to go through some linguistically hard times for however long it took to see my legal problem to its end.

After I had said my piece (it must have taken me somewhere between an hour and an hour and a half to relate what I could have told a native English speaker in fifteen or twenty minutes), Antonio began translating questions; first eleven queries from Lucie, then three by Mr. Radvan, then finally a round of alternating final questions from both of them. I felt like a pawn on a verbal chess board; but one being used by both opponents in a bizarre and chaotic Czech version of the game I could only guess the rules of. Lucie asked me what time we had played, how long our set was, if we had taken any breaks during the performance, and how many people were in attendance at the gig. I answered the best I could by approximating times and the amount of people at the gig, numbers that change every night and from tour to tour in varying amounts. After relaying in one of my answers how bad my band and crew had thought the club sucked, she wanted to know why we thought it was such a bad club, making me wonder if she was offended by my judgment of Czech rock venues. She asked if I had drank any alcohol during or right before our performance. I replied honestly that if I had had anything to drink, it would have been a single beer during our performance, as I would be too busy singing to drink much more. I also informed her that I mostly drink water onstage, and half the time I just dump it over my head to cool myself off, which makes the stage pretty slick and dangerous sometimes (incredibly enough, the fact that I move a lot and rapidly, sweat profusely, and douse myself with water to cool off onstage would repeatedly come up in witnesses' testimonies as evidence that I was acting extremely strange, even *evil*, thus indicating that I was obviously on drugs of some sort—I suppose the Czechs, being a land-locked people, consider public wetness unseemly?). Martin asked me if I did any body building exercises (while I realize my hulking physique could easily lead someone to believe I am a Mr. Universe contestant, I am just way too slack to lift weights with any sort of regularity), if people are normally allowed to get on stage (absolutely not), and if anyone had approached me after the concert with any sort of health complaint (nope). About midway through the questioning, Lucie asked me about the young man that I pinned down onstage, and a thorough dissection of this incident began.

There is a scientific hypothesis known as the Ebbinghaus Forgetting Curve that deals with the exponential decay of human memory over time. The forgetting curve illustrates that information that is not consciously reviewed through active recall, thereby strengthening its retention, is lost very rapidly. (This is why we have to study for exams instead of just reading a textbook through once, then acing a final without breaking a sweat.) The strength of a memory depends on several factors, one of which is its importance to an individual; for example most people of this era will certainly remember where they were when they first heard news of the World Trade Center being hit by terrorist-hijacked planes on September 11, 2001. That was a *big* event, and the surroundings of a person as they learned of it are more than likely seared into their memories along with the awful images of the towers collapsing—I know I remember exactly where I was when I heard the news (walking into a restaurant kitchen to start work). But where I was the previous day at 3:00 p.m. (the time I showed up for my shift on 9/11—I slept late that day), I have absolutely no clue—maybe at work? Maybe at the river fishing? Maybe at the bar having a drink? To my knowledge, nothing unusual or important happened that day. My memory of September 10, 2001, is lost.

My memory of the show we played on May 24, 2010 was slightly better than my recollection of 3:00 p.m. on September 10, 2001, but not by much. The only reason I remembered any details at all of that show, or the day surrounding it, was because it was my first time in the Czech Republic. I always remember my first time in a new country. My friend Paul died that day as well—obviously most people will remember where they were when they hear a friend or relative has passed away. I probably would have forgotten the annoying young man I had to wrestle to the ground if it wasn't for those two things; it was just another day at work. That day wasn't the first time in the history of rock-n-roll someone had stormed the stage and proceeded to act like a jackass; on tour I deal with jackasses on a daily basis. As well, neither myself nor any member of my band had witnessed anyone getting seriously injured. We would have remembered that. Once after a particularly rowdy show, I saw a man backstage with a broken femur, a splinter of bone protruding through his ripped red flesh like a snapped celery stalk poking out of a freshly quartered venison tenderloin that had been wrapped in bloody denim. He had just returned from serving a tour of combat duty in Iraq, and I can still hear him screaming about how he had finally made it home alive and had just wanted to have a good time at a show as he lay bleeding on a medic's gurney backstage. I do not forget it when I see fans get injured. I can't. It's too important and it's too traumatic.

Back to Lucie's line of questioning: Without prior knowledge of anyone being hurt, much less attempting to injure them, it was pretty hard for me to recall hurting anyone, to which I felt she was trying to get me to admit. I was extremely careful in choosing my words, as I knew in my bones that this would be the part of my testimony reviewed with the greatest scrutiny. In the last chapter, I talked about the final time the fan who kept jumping on stage had joined us once again, about how he had flown from the stage, and how I didn't know whether or not for sure I had pushed him. In my initial statement to Lucie however, I stated that when I saw this man coming onstage for the final time, I pushed him away from me, and I remembered him falling into the crowd and standing up. This was not strictly true, as I did not (nor do I to this day) truly remember pushing him at all. I know what I believed happened, and I feel deep down in my gut that this is the truth. In reality, I cannot say what actually occurred based upon any sort of memory that I would consider in the slightest bit reliable. What I believe today happened that night was slowly, painfully, formulated over the next months leading up to and through my trial, and is based on countless hours of searching my mind, reading witness testimonies, looking at videos of the show, and even the opinion of the Czech Republic's sole legally certified expert in the science of biomechanics, the only man allowed to speak as an authority in that field in any court of law in the entire country. The truth that sits inside my soul, aching quietly like a father who has discovered he has passed on some terminal genetic defect to his offspring, is not what I spoke that day under questioning. Why? Because I did not know it yet. Why would I not just say then that I had no true recollection of pushing anyone at all? Once again, it comes down to the unreliability of human memory. I was under a lot of stress. I was exhausted, confused, and very, very frightened. I also had some new information I had read over and over during the last twenty-four hours. Here it is:

"On 24.5.2010 in the time period between 21:30–22:45 in the club Abaton, street Na Koince 8, Prague 8 during a musical performance of the band Lamb of God (USA), where he is a singer, after unclear instructions given by him to the audience, which were interpreted as invitation to the podium, the damaged Daniel ___, born _._.1991 climbed up on the podium. The damaged Daniel ___ was intentionally thrown off the 98cm high podium by the accused David Randall Blythe who unexpectedly approached the damaged /___/ and pushed him by both of his hands into the chest so the damaged fell over the metal barrier (131 cm high fence) and fell by the back of his head on the floor under the podium which caused him bleeding into the brain, brain contusion and brain swell. As a consequence he lost consciousness and, despite all medical care provided, he died on 23. 6. 2010 in the ___ Hospital. The accused must have been aware of the fact that the podium is elevated and fenced off by railing. With regard to the circumstances, the accused must have been aware that the necessary consequence of a backward fall on one's back is impact of head against the floor.

Therefore the accused intentionally caused bodily injury to another person and this act led to the death."

That is exactly what the warrant for my arrest sitting beside me on my desk right now reads (with the exclusion of Daniel's last name, date of birth, and the name of the hospital he died in). Since I had been arrested, I must have read the warrant at least forty or fifty times, trying desperately to make sure I understood exactly what it said, and to remember or at least make sense of the events described in the charge against me. There was also a page and a half worth of other data concerning the case—a restatement and explanation of the charge, justification of the charge, the fact that my government had refused to cooperate in prosecuting me, the names of witnesses interviewed, and a more technical medical explanation of the cause of Daniel's death after his injury. Finally, the paper read that if I did not chose a defense attorney within one hour of receiving the warrant (and Lucie had handed me the paper the second I was arrested), then an attorney would be appointed to me at my cost, unless a request for free or reduced price defense was granted under some paragraph in the Czech legal code. (Reading this again as I write this, I realize now that good old Alex had been taking it easy on me—he could have slapped me with the soud's finest within thirty minutes of getting to the jail, as it took us half an hour to get there from the airport through traffic. An hour to find an attorney? Holy moly.)

There was a ton of brand-new and very upsetting stuff rolling around in my noodle; and despite my best efforts to remain calm and level-headed, I was not in the clearest state of mind during the interrogation. Not by a long shot. After constant review of the only information I had at the time (the arrest warrant), disturbing imagery began to arise in my head; a hazy, hesitant, picture of pushing this annoying young man off the stage. I began to wonder if what the paper said was true. If it was true, I had to find out. What if I had killed him? This slowly started to seem feasible. I began to accept that I might have to accept the consequences of actions I did not clearly remember committing. Whether or not my memory of how events had occurred was accurate had no bearing on the fact that a young man was dead, and I was possibly to blame. Indeed, if I was to blame, if this tragedy was truly my fault, I knew that no matter how frightening, I could not run from a just and deserved punishment. Not if I wanted to still call myself a *real man*.

I decided I would rather die in prison (always a distinct possibility in the penal system) as a real man than live free as a coward because I was too damned scared to face an uncertain future in an effort to find out the truth. If warranted, I would pay the price for a deadly crime I might have committed, and do so without complaint. I still believe in (and try to live by) a concept that is sadly almost lost, even ridiculed at times as anachronistic, in our western society: honor. To me, to not at least attempt to find out the truth, by any means necessary, would be *dishonorable.* A man or woman stripped of their honor is not a man or woman at all to me. Only one person can take your honor away: yourself. I would not dishonor myself or my family name by failing to do everything in my power to face the truth. I realize those are very strong words; words some people might even laugh at. But my actions over the next year would back them up, and that is an irrefutable fact. Just like my honor, no one else can take that truth from me. It's okay to have strong convictions, and to act on them no matter how frightening that may be at times. And people, I'm here to tell you: you'd better believe I was scared shitless. I say this without a shred of embarrassment—I'm not some stoic hard-ass. I was terrified. However, I would be so deeply ashamed if I hadn't pushed through the fear and tried to do the right thing, I don't think I would have ever been able to look in a mirror again. During my drinking days, I had done the wrong thing so many times out of fear. I categorically refuse live that way anymore. *Ever.*

As I contemplated my future with a growing sense of dread, I began to see the blond headed young man on stage for the final time more clearly. I started to envision him in front of me, yet again waving his hands stupidly around, and he bounded toward me. I saw myself pushing him from the stage, and him hitting the floor hard in front of me; only to rise, hold his head briefly, then begin to bang his foolish head and rock out again. As what I thought I might be starting to remember faded away, I imagined him walking away and out onto the street behind the club, then falling down and losing consciousness. I saw him being taken to a hospital, then dying as his family sat beside his hospital bed in tears.

Dear God, please forgive me. I think I may have killed a man.

The vague memory of pushing that particular young man was 100 percent false. That person is alive and healthy, and walks the earth today. I know this because I have met him, and he seems like a fine and moral man, despite his foolish actions that night. When photographs of him and me wrestling on stage would surface in newspapers and on websites later, he would do me a greater service than he will ever know by coming forward of his own free will and explaining that he was not Daniel. Sadly, Daniel is, in fact dead, but I have no memory of ever seeing his face, much less pushing him to his death. I only have what I have come to believe happened between him and me.

Lucie and Martin began to pepper me with questions about this young man. Was he the only one who had come onstage? ("No, definitely not.") At what point in the concert did you have physical contact with this person? ("The middle? Towards the end? I don't know really.") How many people did you push on stage or push off the stage at the Prague concert in 2010? ("Only one, if that occurred at all.") How did you and with what force did you push this person? (My statement reads: "I pushed him in the chest, at least I think I did, and I think it was with both arms and open hands. I pushed him with some force, enough to keep him away from me. I certainly didn't take a running start to tackle him like you would in football. There wasn't enough room onstage for that, anyway.") How did this person respond to being pushed? Did he step back, climb down, fall off stage etc.? ("I don't know how he got back to the auditorium, whether he climbed, jumped, or fell. Because I don't see very well without my glasses, all of these are possible.") Did you ask the person you pushed if he was okay? ("I didn't ask him anything—the people around him gestured that he was okay.") Were you angry with this person that was repeatedly getting onstage and were you planning on fighting him back? ("No. I was probably tired and may have been annoyed with him, but I wasn't angry enough to fight him.")

These types of questions went on for a good while. Lucie would ask me something, Martin would want clarification of what she was asking, even Antonio would bust in with a suggestion or two in English as to how I might word something in order to be clearer. (He wasn't supposed to do that, but I am certain he saw how frightened I was, and was trying to help me the best he could. Thanks, Antonio.) This whole ordeal was beyond draining. I was telling the truth to the best of my knowledge, but I felt like

I was walking through a mined baseball field in the dark, while trying to catch fly balls two cranked-up batters were hammering all over the outfield. I also did not like the way Antonio kept interrupting me mid-answer, apologetically translating, "That is not important" or "She says that is not so important." Uhm . . . YES, IT FUCKING IS. If I was bothering to say it, you can *bet your ass* it was important—I was speaking very, very simply and choosing my words *very, very* carefully. I was also being extremely cautious not to speak too much, as it didn't seem the time to indulge my normally verbose self. As far as I knew, the next ten years of my life depended on how I spoke, how much I spoke, and *exactly* what I said when I spoke. Lucie didn't seem to agree with that, as evidenced by the many times she dismissed me with a "that's not so important" via Antonio. Looking at the translated statement Lucie typed down now, I see where many important aspects of my answers were ignored. She distilled them down to short and rather curtly conclusive sounding statements. I realize today that this was in part probably due to the language barrier, but I definitely got the feeling she was typing down what she wished of my answers, not what I was saying. I can't say for sure (once again, my memory, like every other human, is far from infallible), but I seem to remember questions she asked that I answered that are not on the record at all. I'm sure it was mostly my frayed nerves, but it seemed as if I was being set up for a verdict of guilty. I felt like I was about to hear the judgment at any moment, even though I wouldn't enter a trial courtroom for months.

I asked Lucie if I could see a photo of the young man at some point during the interrogation, and either she replied that the police did not have one (lie) or simply said "no," I cannot remember which. It was very frustrating for me to describe an altercation with someone I only had the haziest of memories of. It upset me quite a bit that she refused to show me a picture. It was like trying to recreate an elaborate painting I had only seen a brief glimpse of in a dream from years ago. I felt certain that if I could see a picture of this young man, it would probably jog my memory, and I could tell them what I knew. I didn't want to hide or deny my actions—I just wanted to know the *truth* of them. Perhaps it was the right thing for her to do as a police officer interrogating a suspect, to not show me possibly deniable aspects of the case. I wanted to know what had happened just as badly, probably worse, as anyone else. I just wanted to see a picture of this young man I had been accused of killing. It didn't seem like too much to ask.

After a long while, Antonio told me that Lucie had no further questions, but wanted to know if I wished to add anything to my statement. I replied simply and truthfully: this was all a terrible surprise to me, and neither my band nor myself were previously aware that anything of this nature had happened. I said that it was awful to hear that someone had been injured and died, that we are dependent on people like this person, the people who support our band. He was a fan, and we would have no reason to want any of our fans to come to harm.

With that, we all stood up and left the office. In the hallway outside as Alex was about to take me away, I told Martin what a horrible job I thought Antonio had done. He just grinned and said, "Yes, he was not the best. But I think this may be to our advantage . . . " then told me someone would come see me tomorrow. Not him, as Martin had a prior engagement to have part of his foot sawed off, but someone would be there. I wished him luck, then Alex took me back to the holding cell from the day before.

I was slightly surprised to be back in the holding cell, as I had expected to return to the hole to await whatever would happen next, and after cadging a smoke from Alex, I asked him what the next item on our schedule was.

"We must go to doctor to find name of your medicine," he said, dragging deeply on his own cigarette. "Now we wait for driver."

Soon the curly haired detective who had driven us from the airport appeared, and after Alex had handcuffed me (once again, not too tightly), it was back through the cop shop and into the basement car park, where we got into the trusty Skoda station wagon (Skoda is the most common brand of car in the Czech Republic) and zipped out onto the streets of Prague. The sun was shining brightly in a beautiful blue sky, and Officer Bart (as I began to think of the driver, since I didn't know his name—plus he just looked like a Bart to me) was a completely different person from the dour-faced, scowling policeman I had seen just the day before. He was acting rather (dare I even say it?) jolly; joking around with Alex in Czech and laughing about whatever it is Czech cops find funny, probably the atrocities that awaited me in prison. Even the music was different; today Bart was feeling good, and seemed to be in a "bad boy" frame of mind, and his choice of tunes for our ride to the doctor reflected it.

Instead of the ghastly, caterwauling, Czech electro-pop from yesterday, he was jamming along to what my friend Bubble calls "roofer rock." Indeed, Bart was *rocking out*, drumming on the steering wheel with his finger tips, nodding his head happily in time to the edgy-but-not-quite-aggressive-enough-to-be-considered-real-punk-or-metal guitar riffs. From time to time he would *really* cut loose, air-guitaring at traffic lights or mouthing a few words of the English lyrics in his heavy accent, and although I'm pretty certain Bart didn't have a clue what any of the songs were about, it didn't really matter. With roofer rock, it's not necessarily about the lyrics, it's about the *feeling*, the feeling of being right on the edge of doing something wild and crazy and totally free (but never having to commit and actually do it). And though I would bet my last dollar that the Czechs have their own roofer rock bands, the very best, most rockin', roofer rock comes from the U.S. of fuckin' A. Luckily for Bart, the radio station DJ seemed to know this, since he was spinning exclusively American tunes, some of which I actually recognized.

After about twenty or twenty-five hard rockin' minutes, we parked on a hill beside a nondescript office building. They let me out of the car and we all walked into the office building, Bart and Alex still merrily chatting away in Czech. Inside a small waiting room Bart and I sat on a bench as Alex talked to a grim-looking nurse in her late fifties. Alex produced my bottle of pills from his pocket and handed it to her. The nurse briefly glanced at the bottle's label and began shaking her head. She said something in Czech to Alex, who seemed slightly put off by her comment as he responded, pointedly gesturing to a computer on the desk of the waiting room office. The woman shook her head again, clucking her tongue as she repeated herself. Alex replied more heatedly, pointing at the computer once again. A sudden fire appeared in the nurse's eyes, and she barked the same brief sentence again, this time in a tone of finality that indicated she wasn't going to put up with any of Alex's nonsense. She reminded me of my Grandmother, a fearless woman who never hesitated to lay down the law as my brothers and I endlessly attempted to drive her to the brink of insanity with our savage, ill-behaved ways.

Enough was enough. The answer was *no*.

Alex literally threw his hands in the air, said something in an apologetic tone to a now very bent-out-of-shape looking Bart, and the three of us walked very rapidly back to the Skoda. In a matter two or three short minutes, the devil-may-care hard rockin' good vibe that had characterized our journey so far had been shattered. We jumped in the station wagon, and Bart proceeded to go completely, utterly, apeshit.

Thus began one of the scariest car rides I have ever take in my entire life. Bart was actually *screaming* in Czech, periodically pounding on the steering wheel with a clenched fist as he burned rubber away from the office, squealing tires and sliding on a patch of gravel into traffic, completely ignoring the stop sign at the intersection at the bottom of the hill. Oncoming cars hit their brakes and blew their horns. Bart flicked them off as he cranked the crappy stock stereo up to speaker-blowing volume and stomped on the gas pedal. Never before or since have the sounds of roofer rock been more terrifying. Bart ignored stop signs. He ignored traffic lights. He ignored the thousands of other cars traveling all around us on Prague's crowded streets. He took corners at speeds that threw me around the back seat of the Skoda, until I managed to fasten my seatbelt with my still-handcuffed wrists. He cursed and screamed the whole time as he sped back to the police station. I couldn't understand a thing he was saying, but I heard one word over and over I had a hunch was the Czech equivalent of "bitch." I wouldn't have to worry about any sort of trial at this rate, for Bart was obviously deep in the grip of a psychotic episode that would surely be the death of us if we didn't get out of that car soon. I began to pray. I really didn't want to die overseas, trapped in a station wagon with two pissed off cops, listening to roofer rock. It wasn't supposed to end this way.

Please God, not yet. Not like this. ANYTHING but this.

The Almighty must have heard my pleas, because pretty soon we were parked back in the basement of the police station and heading back up to the holding cell. The leisurely trip that had taken us nearly half an hour before couldn't have lasted more than ten hair-raising minutes on the way back. I looked at Alex.

"Dude. What *in the fuck* just happened back there? Your driver friend is a *maniac.* I thought we were going to die!" I said.

"Doctor cannot read your medicine. She says we must have translator. I will get translator, then we must go back," he replied with a shrug. Bart had left the cell (probably to go blow off some steam butchering a little old lady or something). I stared back at Alex.

"We have to go *back?*" I asked.

"Yes. I must call for translator now," he said, and left me there, wondering if I could somehow make out a will before stepping into the car again. After an hour or so, Bart and Alex returned to fetch me for our journey back to the doctor's office. As I strapped on my seat belt, Alex said something to Bart, who grunted a short reply and drove us out of the parking garage at a slightly less murderous speed. He was still going fast enough to pull a little drift at the round about in front of the station though, and I heard the tires barking beneath us. Alex craned his head around towards the back seat and looked at me.

"Do not be afraid. Do not worry. My comrade is a very calming driver," he said with a grin.

It wasn't the most relaxing trip, but I was fairly certain we would survive it this time. I was correct, because in short order we were parked back at the office

I saw a female child standing out front, holding a leather-bound folder of the sorts an attorney might carry important legal documents in. As we got closer, I saw that the child was dressed in sensible black pumps, slacks, and a button up shirt; what could be described as business casual attire. *How odd,* I thought, *what a strange way for a child to dress. Maybe kids grow up fast in Prague.*

As we neared the office, Alex called out a question to the child, who replied affirmatively in an adult voice. We reached the office door and she spoke to me in fluent English.

"Hello, my name is Johana. I am here to translate your medicine bottle label."

HOLY CRAP. My translator was a little person! This was *fantastic* news.

I possess a great affinity for little people. I grew up my entire life feeling *different than,* and often was treated as such. My youth was spent catching hell from rednecks and preppy jock types who wanted to kick my ass because I wasn't interested in marching to the banal beat of their drum; in fact I *couldn't* even if I tried—my feet are always out of step. I'm too nerdy, too weird, too much my own quirky self to even attempt to squeeze into what I consider the strangling straight jacket of most societal norms. The few times I have tried, I have failed miserably, as "normal" people can smell something strange on me. While I doubt there are many people who haven't felt ostracized by their peers at some time or the other, and while today I am trying to no longer be shallow enough to judge others just because they seem relatively well suited to fit into society compared to me (you should have seen me at age sixteen though—good Lord, what an asshole), I still feel most comfortable around others who are obviously considered *different than*. I can relate to these folks.

So give me your tired, your poor, your bizarre of appearance and strange of mind. Bring me your freaks and geeks, your weirdos and nerds. Bring me your drunks and junkies, your tweakers and gas huffers. Bring me your dungeon masters and jugglers, your OCD collectable action figure enthusiasts and unicyclists. Bring me your homeless balladeers and bodily fluids performance artists, your jazz fusion flutists and anarchist mimes.

Bring me your little people.

My people. Let's hang.

In short order Johana had taken the bottle, read its label, talked to the nurse for all of sixty seconds, who then signed some sort of paper of approval for Alex. I thanked Johana (whom I would see a lot more of over the next year), Bart threw the nurse a dirty look, and we were off. As we drove back to the station (thankfully at a reasonable, less than terminal, velocity), Alex looked at me incredulously and said, "That woman. She was very small, wasn't she?" as if he had never seen a little person before and Johana had been some creature from Czech folklore who had appeared like magic. I just sighed and nodded. Yes, Alex, she was.

As we neared the round about in front of the station, I told Bart to drift again via sound effects and making steering wheel gestures, and he happily complied. This got a big laugh out of him and Alex; Bart really was an excellent driver (or else he would be dead by now) who should probably quit being a cop to drive stunt cars for a movie production company. He dropped us off in the car park and Alex took me back into the station, this time to the hole. Soon the guard brought me dinner, another tasteless sandwich, and after eating it, I lay there in the gloom thinking about the day's events. There wasn't anything else to do.

At some point in the evening, cell number thirteen's door opened up and a scruffy young man in his twenties was let in, holding the same small bag of toiletries I had been issued the day before. He walked to the bed opposite mine and immediately lay down, staring at the ceiling. I sat up and looked at him.

"What's up, dude?" I asked, hoping he spoke English. He turned his head and gave me a baleful look, then rolled over silently to face the wall, his back to me. *Ooooooh Kay. Not the chatty type, I guess.*

I lay there, trying to fall asleep, but my mind kept racing back to the interrogation room, recalling and examining my statement from earlier that day. I kept asking myself over and over if I was forgetting something, a misplaced piece of the puzzle that was my current dilemma. I couldn't conjure any new memories that would give me any sort of clarification for this problem. I gave up.

Okay, God, I really need you to do me a solid, like right now, dude, I prayed in the dark, *I need you to let me know somehow what happened.*

I need you to tell me if I killed that boy.

No reply.

THE RORSHACH TEST THING (EVERYTHING LOOKED LIKE A BEAR/SKIN RUG OR A BLUE CRAB OR STEAK & EGGS OR A LIZARD OR AN OLD MAN OR FALLEN (SAD), & OF COURSE THE OBVIOUS FREUDIAN VAGINA. THE SUDDEN DOC KEEP ASKING ME WHAT THINGS LOOKED LIKE THIS OR THAT — I HAD TO POINT IT OUT TO HER — BECAUSE, WELL, DUH, THEY LOOK THAT WAY. THE FOOD STUFF MAYBE BECAUSE I WAS HUNGRY. NOTE — I WAS VERY TIRED, RUNNING ON VERY LITTLE SLEEP DUE TO CONSTANT NIGHT NERVES — I'M IN PRISON FOR FUCK'S SAKE! ~~THESE SHE HAD~~ THEN SHE HAD GAVE ME THESE CUBES & WANTED ME TO CONFIGURE THEM TO MATCH PICTURES SHE GAVE ME. THAT WAS KINDA FUN, ESP THE ONE'S INVOLVING NEGATIVE SPACE (CUBES WERE RED & BLACK) — I DID OK ON A NEGATIVE SPACE ONE & ASKED IF PEOPLE NORMALLY HAD TROUBLE — SHE SAID LOTS OF PEOPLE DID. THEN SHE HANDED ME (INDIVIDUALLY) 5? 7? 10? PICTURES THAT LOOKED LIKE CUT OUTS OF 1950'S MAGAZINES, & ONE AMISH SCENE W/ A PREGNANT LADY. MOST OF THE PICTURES LOOKED <u>UNHAPPY</u> — I TRIED TO MAKE A HAPPY STORY OUT OF EACH ONE — I THOUGHT IF I DID A REALISTIC STORY THEY WOULD THINK I WAS A PSYCHOPATH. BUT ALL THE PICTURES WERE DEPRESSING AS FUCK SO I TOLD HER SO. ~~SO~~ I ASKED HER WHY SHE WAS GIVING ME SO MANY SAD PICTURES FOR FUCK'S SAKE & SHE HAD NO REPLY. BUT I LET LOOSE THE CREATIVE BRAIN UNTIL SHE SAID "PLEASE, MAKE THE STORIES SHORTER." I WAS WEARING HER OUT, HA HA! WE HAD TO TYPE AS THE TRANSLATOR SPOKE. I THINK I

chapter eight

In the darkness of the hole, I awoke from a fitful sleep to a guard calling me through the open hatch in my cell door. He handed me a tray with some bread, cheese, and fruit on it. There was also a plastic cup of what I assumed was supposed to loosely represent coffee, a tepid light brown liquid that may or may not have contained any caffeine. I sat with my breakfast in silence, quietly sipping my tasteless brew, eyeing my charming roommate (who wouldn't so much as look at me). Shortly after breakfast the guard reappeared and opened the cell door, calling out to my cellmate. Mr. Personality got up from his bed and walked out without a backwards glance, never to be seen again. Lacking anything else to do, I lay down and went back to sleep.

I woke up sometime later in my ill-lit cubicle of perpetual suckiness and gloom, to the guard opening the door again and calling out "advocate." I was led down the hall into a plain room with a folding table. Inside the room sat Tomas, Martin's bearded young associate. I was very happy to see him, hoping that he would have more news of my case and maybe even a cigarette or two I could bum. While Tomas did have cigarettes, much to my nicotine-fiending bloodstream's dismay, no smoking was allowed in this room. We sat and talked about my case for quite some time, and as I had no writing materials to make notes, all I remember was the priority of making sure the judge granted me bail at tomorrow morning's scheduled hearing. Tomas seemed fairly confident that the judge would set some sort of bail, which raised my spirits a bit. I didn't know if I would have to remain in the Czech Republic if I made bail, and I didn't really care. After forty-eight exhausting hours in the Prague hoosegow, I would have been happy to get out on work-release as a human dartboard in Old Town Square until my trial, if that's what it took. It wasn't that the police or guards had mistreated me; it wasn't even the shit food and "coffee"; it was the endless gloom and the nothingness of the hole that was getting to me. I had no way to stimulate my mind, no books, no writing material, not even a window to look out and briefly feel the sun on my face (hell, I would have even taken a TV at that point). No *nothing* except a head full of confusion, worry, and fear. It was driving me nuts.

I also asked Tomas about how the story of my arrest was being handled in the Czech media; he hesitated: "Not so good, I do not think." I later found out that "not so good" could be roughly translated as "Murderous American singer comes to Prague to destroy the youth of the Czech Republic, hide your children."

After we were done talking, I was taken back to the hole and given a sandwich for lunch. I did some pushups in an effort to exercise my body and tire me enough to go back to sleep. I worked up a nice sweat, but slumber eluded me. After another bit of undeterminable time, the guard opened the door again, this time calling out what sounded to me like "See call old g's." I knew a few OGs I would have loved to have called at that time, but he didn't seemed to offering me a phone. I stared at him questioningly, as I had no idea what he wanted, then he motioned impatiently for me to follow him. We returned to the room I had sat with Tomas in earlier. Inside were seated a mousey thirty-ish looking woman in glasses with a MacBook on the table in front of her, a man in a button up shirt and tie about the same age, and Johana, my diminutive translator from the day before. I said hello to Johana and sat at the table next to the man.

"These people are a psychologist and psychiatrist," she began effortlessly in her slight Czech accent. "They are here to talk to you and perform some tests concerning your mental condition. This is to see if you are mentally stable enough to appear in the court."

Oh boy. The shrinks have arrived, I thought, *This should be interesting. Be careful.*

The duo of dome doctors proceeded to ask me all sorts of questions, what I took to be fairly standard shrink fare. First of all, how was I feeling? (Not so hot, my friends. I was just arrested two days ago by a bunch guys in masks toting enough artillery to wipe out a small country and told I had killed someone. Now I'm in jail in a foreign country. How do you *think* I feel? Got any other head scratchers for me?) Did I know why I was in jail? Was I married? What was my family like? Did I have children? What was my history with alcohol and drugs? Did I want to hurt myself? Did I feel like hurting others? Had I ever been arrested before? Had I ever been institutionalized before? Did I suffer from depression? The woman typed in my answers in her computer, and the man made brief notes on a clipboard. The whole process felt very . . . *dry*; like I was an over-heating toaster oven they were dissembling in order to find out which parts were still in working order.

I answered these questions honestly (and perhaps a bit too cavalierly), except the one about being institutionalized. I did not deem it wise to fill them in on my little weekend jaunt to the psych ward in my twenties. In retrospect, I believe that was the correct choice, for I could see in their eyes and tell by their mannerisms that they were straining to figure out what little boxes to tick on whatever standardized personality type evaluation test form they were filling out. Telling them about that particular bit of stupidity would have in all likelihood led them to immediately brand me as unstable, or at the very least inherently inclined to violence towards myself or others. It seemed as if they wanted to hurry up and compartmentalize my entire psyche so they could wrap me up in a neat little box and present me to the court like a re-gifted damaged birthday present. I was hugely annoyed by this, to be truthful. Humans are complex organisms, complicated in so many ways that we don't understand yet; not one-dimensional characters in an old comic book. I believe the fields of psychiatry and psychology have been of immense benefit to our race (myself included, so no offense to any shrinks reading this—y'all do good work), lending valuable insight to the cognitive process, condition of the human personality, and the often highly convoluted exertions taking place in the murky depths of the subconscious. But it should also always be remembered that any test administered to evaluate this stuff is, at its root, *subjective.* That means any conclusions drawn from these tests are inevitably influenced by the very non-objective mind of the tester. No person is completely objective, not even close. We're *humans*, not Vulcans. All humans, even highly trained shrinks, are prone to errors of judgment, as I would find out soon.

After a while, the psychiatrist spoke to Johana, who told me that he had no further questions. I looked at him.

"So, doctor, do you think I'm crazy?" I asked with a grin.

"No. You are not crazy," he replied flatly, and left. I didn't much care for him anyway. The psychologist woman began asking me question after question about the show, the exact same ones I had answered two or three times already, so asked her if she just wanted me to tell her the whole story. She did, so I told the tale again, exactly as I had the day before, Johanna translating my words almost simultaneously. The psychologist typed out what I said at a decent rate of speed, but I began to wonder why they didn't just tape record the whole thing for accuracy. After I was done telling my story, Johanna told me that the psychologist would now administer some tests, and out came the Rorschach ink blot cards.

I actually got kind of pumped up when I saw the Rorschach test cards in person for the first time, as I had been hoping that it would be one of her methods of evaluating my personality. After hours in my cell, anything would be more interesting to my stimulus-starved brain than staring at a dirty wall in the dark. I shouldn't have been so excited about it, because all the test did was try my patience (or rather, the person administering the test did).

"What does this look like?" she asked.

"A butterfly," I replied.

"Why?" she queried again.

"Uhm, because it *very obviously* resembles a butterfly. Don't you have butterflies here?" I answered.

"Yes, but why does it very obviously resemble a butterfly?" she persisted.

"These look like wings," I sighed, pointing out the wings. She didn't seem too satisfied, but typed a few notes.

"What about this? What do you see here?" She held up a different card.

"A bearskin rug," I said.

"Why?"

Jesus Christ. I pointed out the area that looked like a bearskin rug. She was typing slowly when I said:

"OR . . . it could be a vagina. In fact, any of the Rorschach cards could be a vagina, unless you're about to show me some I've never seen. Is that the sort of Freudian response you're looking for?" I asked.

She typed furiously, but didn't ask me why the card looked like a vagina. The questions continued, my answer always followed with a "why?" from the psychologist. I saw a wizard on one card, an old man falling head first on another (this made me very sad, and I wondered if my subconscious had conjured that image due to the charges against me). For the most part my answers were food related: steak. Eggs. Blue crab. Shrimp. Man, I was starving, and worked that into my replies in the hopes that the psychologist could somehow rustle us up some grub. (Q: "Why does that look like a sunny-side up egg?" A: "Because I'm freaking hungry, that's why. Can we order a pizza or something?") One card looked like a Jackson's chameleon to me (although I found myself wishing it was an iguana, because I hear those can be quite tasty if prepared correctly). This excited Johana to no end, who whipped out her iPhone and showed me pictures of her very own pet Jackson's, fantastic and prehistoric looking reptiles I have always been fascinated by. We began chatting about the chameleons until the psychologist cleared her throat and threw Johana an exasperated look. The final card I saw reminded me of two squatting Shaolin monks giving each other a high-five, and made me think about the Wu-Tang Clan, but I somehow refrained from slipping any mentions of Ol' Dirty Bastard, Ghostface Killah, or the RZA into my answer.

After the Rorschach test was done, the psychologist produced a set of two-tone plastic blocks, each cube diagonally split into equal halves of red and black. She set them on the table in front of me, pulled out a card with a red and black design on it, and asked me to reproduce the design with the blocks, timing how long it took me to replicate the picture. This was a standard IQ test I had seen before, and was actually kind of fun, especially compared to the Rorschach test. My brain was so happy to have a problem that it could feasibly solve, something to concentrate on other than a situation I was currently powerless to change. I found myself quite absorbed in the test, especially the cards she gave me that dealt with negative space. After attempting to reproduce ten or fifteen designs with varying success, she put the blocks away and Johana told me that there was one more test.

The psychologist pulled out a set of ancient looking yellow cards, held one up to me, and asked me to make up a story based on the illustration printed on the card. I looked at the card. It appeared to be originally from a 1940s detective magazine, and was a pen and ink drawing of an old woman collapsed beside a couch, her face buried in her arm, her keys laying on the ground beside her. It was not a happy drawing; obviously something very bad had happened, and in my current state a dead or dying old lady was the last thing I felt like making up a story about. I was tired, hungry, and had had more than my fill of thinking about sad things, so I decided to take control of the situation.

This woman had severely fucked up by giving me this archaic test. She had stepped to me on my home turf: the creative domain inside my head, a limitless place of endless possibilities.

Here I rule with iron-fisted vision; for it is the realm of the story teller, the arena of unfettered imagination, and what I construct there is Holy Writ. I decided that no matter what each picture she presented me with actually reminded me of, I would spin a long, elaborate, and obnoxiously heart-warming tale; concluding each story with a picture-perfect happy ending worthy of the sappiest of romance novels. I was tired of her thinking she could evaluate my personality with some ridiculous inkblots or old magazine illustrations, and I didn't care what she wrote down anymore. I was offended by the simple and highly subjective methodology she was applying to a subject (*me*) who was obviously in no mental shape to be evaluated with any sort of accuracy, and I began to think of her as the enemy. In short, I was depressed, tired, and hungry, but this woman had pissed me off; I wanted to wear her down, to break her. So I did.

The old lady collapsed by the couch was a renowned Finnish molecular biologist who had just won the lottery, who, in a fit of gratitude, had sank to her knees to thank God for unexpectedly delivering her the money she needed to fund the last part of her research, research that delivered an incredibly cheap, globally available, multi-disease cure; eradicating AIDS, cancer, and hemorrhoids on every corner of our planet within a week of its discovery, while leaving her enough cash left over to start an orphanage and still take a nice vacation to Papua New Guinea, where she discovered that her American husband (long presumed dead at sea after his research vessel, the USS *Egghead*, had sank after hitting a reef while attempting to save a pod of baby orcas separated from their mothers by an aggressive oil slick) was in fact living as a full member of an up-until-now undiscovered tribe, the Tooty-Toot-Tootas, a tribe whose spiritual practices had resulted in a perfect society, a place where war and hate did not exist; and after a joyous reunion with her husband, returned to Helsinki, whereupon a lecture by the husband and wife team on the Tooty-Toot-Tootas' way of life was globally broadcast free of charge from Nokia headquarters, and world peace immediately ensued.

Put *that* in your pipe and smoke it, lady.

Depressing image after depressing image was presented. There were lots of lonely people weeping in dim-looking rooms; there were several fearful looking women, crouched and staring pensively at shadowy figures through a half opened door. There were anguished, guilt-riddled looking men and women standing with an arm thrown dramatically across their face, towering over what appeared to be the naked (and possibly dead) body of their latest lover laying in a messy bed, one lifeless arm flopped off the side. These illustrations would have reduced the Dali Lama to a fit of weeping despair, but that's not how this was going to go down. My brain took in each of the obviously despondent people pictured on each card in turn, and then proceeded to twist their appalling dead-end circumstances into exceedingly complex and insanely detailed journeys. These long, meandering narratives all victoriously concluded in saccharine triumphs so sweet that any diabetic within earshot would have immediately gone into a fatal state of high glucose shock. There were only two cards depicting people who didn't appear to be writhing in the throes of the deepest of miseries; one was a farming scene showing what appeared to me to be a few Amish toiling righteously in a field—these folks had all just returned from a magnificent and sexually liberated spring break at Cabo, ending their globe-trotting *Rumspringa* on a very high note (my explanation of the Amish and *Rumspringa* alone took up a good ten minutes).

The other card, the only possibly happy looking one, had a hot rock-a-billy looking chick staring longingly at a ruggedly handsome, Clark Gable-esque, man who appeared to be about to spring into action of some sort. Things obviously not being what they seemed in my world, these two love birds' marriage was currently ending in a hideous divorce, as the action the man (who just happened to be the President of the United States's brother) was about to spring into was gender reassignment surgery in order to work undercover for Al Queda; a medical procedure which would, of course, fail spectacularly due to a relapsing alcoholic plastic surgeon, resulting in a highly publicized murder/suicide that brought disgrace to the entire nation.

Show me sad, I give you happy. Show me happy, I give you the apocalypse. Screw you and your test results, lady. This is my house.

I was having a hard time not laughing as the psychologist dutifully typed out all this nonsense I concocted, because every time I would bring each interminable tale to its seeming conclusion and she would sit back from her laptop with a look of relief, I would add something else. "Oh wait, I almost forgot," I would blurt "this is the best part!" and send my miserable looking character happily tromping off on some bizarre mission to rescue the lone surviving descendent of Gautama Buddha from terminal flatulence, thereby saving the world or some such crap. After about five of these tales, Johana said to me, "She wants to know if you could please make the stories shorter."

"Well, can she show me some pictures that aren't so tragic looking? For fuck's sake, if I wasn't already depressed about being here these pictures would drive me to it, you know? Ask her why she's only showing me sad pictures, would you?" Johana spoke to the psychologist, who didn't deign to reply, but merely held up another dreadfully drawn woeful woman who looked to be on the verge of suicide. *Okay, be that way then,* I thought.

She finally cut me off in the middle of a horrendously cheerful plot twist involving angels, the quest to bake the perfect lasagne, and a genius-level IQ talking pomeranian who was about to reveal the meaning of life live on the BET network. "Okay, okay," she said in a drained voice, and began to put away her cards and shut down her computer. I had won. I got the feeling that I had been like an exotic pet to her; very interesting at first, but not so cute after I refused to be house broken and started crapping all over the living room carpet. She left the room, and it was back to the hole for me. (After I was released I did some research and found out that the test she had given me was the Thematic Apperception Test. The TAT was designed in the 1930s after an undergraduate student told her professor about her homebound ill son making up stories based on pictures he saw in magazines. The stories a subject tells are supposed to reveal sensitive personal information he or she would not otherwise disclose, in fact doesn't even know he or she is revealing since it's contained in a story. My stories should have revealed that I was about to become the Mother Theresa of Metal if the shrink took them seriously at all, which I seriously doubt she did. Just for shits and giggles, Google "1930s/40s Thematic Apperception Test pictures" sometime, and you'll see several of the pictures I did. They haven't changed in three quarters of a century, yet in court this woman would claim that she had given me the latest, most scientifically reliable tests. Ridiculous.)

After eating some "dinner," my cell door opened and in came another young inmate. I said hello to him, but just like my previous cellmate he didn't appear able (or was unwilling to) to speak English. At least he acknowledged my presence with a small wave before crashing out. I was wiped out from my day, and almost immediately fell asleep.

I awoke in the hole, dark as usual, and ate the breakfast the guard brought me. Shortly thereafter a guard took me to the room where my clothes were stored, and I changed out of my jailhouse threads and into my street duds. I was handcuffed and led to a paddy wagon sort of van and placed in a back seat. An iron contraption was lowered over me and firmly locked in place, sort of like the metal safety harnesses on roller coasters, but without the padding. We pulled out of the police station and drove a short while to the courthouse. As we slowed down, through the windshield of the paddy wagon I saw fifteen or so people with cameras and television gear standing outside a locked rolling gate on the side of the building. As soon as they saw the van, they all turned their cameras towards us and began filming and snapping shots. The paparazzi had arrived in full force, and I leaned back away from the windshield to give them as little of a shot as possible. A guard opened the gate, and we drove in and parked. I was let out of the van, and I walked into the building, making sure to hold my head high and keep my back straight, not looking at the paparazzi who were yelling and trying to film through a crack in the gate. I wasn't happy about the cameras, but whenever I couldn't avoid being filmed, these people sure as hell wouldn't see me defeated looking and skulking along like some whipped dog.

I was led upstairs and sat down on a bench outside the courtroom beside Johana, who had told me the day before she would be my translator again. Soon we were joined by Martin (whose foot was now wrapped in a fresh bandage after his surgery), Tomas, and Martin's partner at his law practice, Vladimir Jablonsky. Vladimir was a heavy-set man in his late fifties with a deep, rumbling voice who spoke English in a thick Czech accent. Martin told me that the court was running a little late, as the judge was inside debating on whether or not to allow the paparazzi and press into film the proceedings. Martin also mentioned something about two Americans who were there filming, supposedly making a movie about my band. I wondered if these two were Don Argot and Demian Fenton, documentary makers from Philadelphia we had hired to make a movie about our fans across the globe.

The movie, entitled *As the Palaces Burn*, was conceived by lamb of god's former manager, Larry Mazer. His original idea was to turn the cameras away from the band and towards our fans, particularly fans with interesting stories who lived in economically depressed countries, or in societies where heavy metal was not really accepted, or places that lived under the threat of war. He wanted to show how heavy music helped these fans in their sometimes challenging day to day lives, our band merely being the vehicle to illustrate a more universal point. The movie was never supposed to be about lamb of god in particular, but about the global music community we are part of, and I was pretty pleased the band wouldn't be the focus of yet another usual lamb of god tour dvd (we have several out already). Don and Demian had already traveled extensively with us, filming shows and interviewing fans in Venezuela, Colombia, India, California, and

Israel, and had fit into our crew quite nicely in a short amount of time—these guys could hack it on the road, and we had become pretty close friends. The majority of the filming was supposed to be done, but if Don and Demian were there, it meant the movie was about to go in a radically different direction, one I was none too pleased about—the cameras would be back on me. Regardless, I was disappointed when we were allowed into the courtroom and I did not see them. I would have welcomed most any familiar face, especially that of a friend.

Although Don and Demian weren't there, shortly after being led into the small courtroom and taking a seat on a small bench in front of the judge, about ten other camera men were let into the courtroom and filmed me for two minutes at most. I sat up straight, with my hands clasped in my lap, staring expressionlessly and approximately forty-five degrees downward at a spot in front of me in a modified version of the posture I assume when I meditate. I couldn't exactly crank out a half-lotus in the courtroom without looking like a nut, but I did sit up straight and attempted to clear my mind, striving to appear calm before these jostling camera men. I avoided looking at them purposely, with the exception of one quick glance to see if Don and Demian were present. I didn't want to give them any possible fuel for the over the top tabloid headlines that were being printed daily about me—I could just see tomorrow's papers already: "Blythe stared unrepentantly into the cameras, his ice blue killer's eyes scanning the courtroom as if looking for his next victim." (That sounds ridiculous, I know, but as the reader will later see, it actually isn't at all considering some of the things they printed about me.) The way I was dressed was already bad enough.

What I wore in court was, of course, the clothes I had been arrested in. On my feet were black socks and a pair of size eleven black and red Adidas skate shoes I had bought two weeks earlier in Germany. For pants, I had my favorite threadbare pair of Army surplus store cut-off camo BDU's, held together by road dirt, splotches of white enamel from painting my shed, dental floss, and a few patches, the most visible of which was a row of assault rifle bullets with the words "Made In America" embroidered below them on the leg, and on the other a black square with a chaos arrow and the word "DESTROY" printed on it. The black t-shirt I wore was a gift from my buddy JP of Homage Skate Shop in Brooklyn, NY. It had the words "HB Crew—NO MERCY" printed on the front beside the dancing punk rocker from the Circle Jerks logo. Completing my ensemble was a black hooded sweatshirt with the word "Obituary" printed boldly across the front, the letters filled with the red, white, and blue of the American flag and stylized in the logo of one of my favorite death metal bands of all time. To make matters worse, I hadn't bathed or shaved since the evening of my arrest, and I didn't even have a hair tie to pull back the unruly mass of dreadlocks that covered my head. I had done my best to pull my dreads back and tie them in a knot, but strands of loose hair were sticking crazily out. I resembled a weed-dealing serial killer with a severe lack of regard for personal hygiene. Looking all punk rock in court is not the brightest idea—dress up and look nice when you go to court, no matter what you're charged with. It matters, and it matters *big time*. I know this to be true from experience—one time I caught a whopping *sixty-five* community service hours for pissing in an alley when I showed up to court in Doc Martins, a leather jacket, dirty jeans and bright blue hair. Judge "Rotten Ralph" Robertson had *not* been pleased, and his sentence showed it—the usual punishment was fifty bucks and a scolding.

Sitting in the courtroom in Prague, I realized I was pretty screwed. I really could have only looked worse if I had had on a Charles Manson t-shirt and a swastika carved into my forehead. If good ol' Rotten Ralph back in Richmond had given me sixty-five community service hours for showing up in his courtroom with blue hair on a peeing in public charge, what would this judge possibly do to me for wearing an Obituary hoodie and a NO MERCY shirt to a manslaughter arraignment?

After the cameramen were hustled out of the courtroom, I was told to stand. The judge began by reading a bunch of legal stuff in

Czech, which Johana my translator informed me was the charge against me. Judge Petr Novak was a handsome man in his forties, with a clean shaven head and a not unpleasant manner. He asked me a few general questions about myself and my job, a slight smile on his face as I answered. Then Martin spoke, the judge answered, Vladimir spoke in his gravely basso profondo, the judge replied then made a few statements of his own. This set off a whole new round of statements by all three men, Johana translating simultaneously as best she could. Johana told me that the gist of it was that my lawyers were objecting to my arrest and incarceration on various grounds and that the judge was discussing the eligibility of the charge and the possibility of bail. It was all very fast and very complex, and this would set the basic pattern that all of my future court dates would take for me: swiftly spoken and extremely confusing. At some point the judge asked me how much money could I raise immediately for bail, and after a moment's thought I answered that between my band and me we should be able to get together one hundred thousand dollars without too much of a problem, low-balling him a bit. After more discussion between my lawyers and the judge, finally Judge Novak looked my way and spoke directly to me, staring intently through his wire-rimmed glasses.

"He wants to know why he should grant you bail, and why he should think that you will return to court if he does," Johana translated.

I paused, making sure I was staring the Judge right in the eyes (for I don't trust a man who can't meet my eye, and I wanted him to know I meant business), and spoke slowly and deliberately.

"Because I am a man of my word, my family has been informed of my arrest, and I wish to clear my good name as soon as possible."

The judge stared right back at me for a few minutes, gave me a small smile, then called for a brief recess. I was taken outside by the bailiff and sat back down on the bench next to Martin,

who told me the judge was deciding on whether or not to grant
me bail. Then we sat in silence waiting. I wondered if I had made
a favorable enough impression of being an honest man on the
judge. I hoped so, but I really wasn't too optimistic, considering
my shabby appearance.

Shortly the bailiff opened the court door and we were all led
back inside. I stood before the judge as he read his decision. I
had been granted bail to the amount of two million Czech *koruna*
(crowns), about two hundred thousand American dollars, exactly
double what I had told him I could raise. The judge said that I
would be released when the Czech government had received and
deposited the money, but until then I would be sent to Pankrác
Remand Prison in Prague. The judge also said that he wished the
record to state that he was not so sure that the charge against me
was justified, but that was a matter to be decided at a later time.
Court was then dismissed, and we all filed out into the hallway.
Once there, Martin told me that I might get out of custody as
early as five days from then, providing the prosecuting attorney
(who didn't bother to show up for my bail hearing) didn't raise
any objections.

"But for now, I am going to prison, right?" I asked Martin.

"Yes, you are going to prison."

"Have you ever been to this Pankrác place?"

"Oh yes, many times," Martin said. "Oh, it is a *terrible* place!
Absolutely *horrible*. The worst prison in the Czech Republic." He
visibly shuddered at the memory of being there.

Good grief—it just gets worse, I thought.

"I will see you soon—good luck. Ciao!" Martin said cheerfully
with a little wave as he wobbled off on his bleeding stump. The
bailiff took me to the paddy wagon, and locked me back into my
seat. As we pulled out of the gate and left the courthouse, the paparazzi was snapping pictures the whole time. I sat and stared out
the windshield at the buildings passing by as it started to sink in.

I was going to prison.

part 2

PANKRÁC

—

JULY 2nd, 2012 (MONDAY)
ROOM 808
THE BASEMENT
PRAHA PANKRÁC
THE WORST PRISON IN THE
CZECH REPUBLIC.
MAYBE (?) 8:00 or 8:30 PM

WELL, I HAVE FINALLY DONE IT — LANDED
IN PRISON. I HAD TO COME TO THE CZECH
REPUBLIC TO DO IT, AND IT ONLY TOOK ~~IF~~ TWO
YEARS FOR THE POLICE TO ARREST ME AFTER MY
SUPPOSED "CRIME", BUT HERE I AM.
I WAS ARRESTED WED JULY 2TH 2012 (or
RATHER "DETAINED" NOT QUITE SURE IF IT
WAS ARREST YET) AS I STEPPED OFF A PLANE
LANDING IN PRAGUE — I GOT UP TO THE TOP
OF THE RAMP AND POLICE WERE WAITING
THERE (or A WOMAN WAS COLLECTING
PASSPORTS) THEY TOOK ALL OF OUR PASSPORTS
AND I BELIEVE MINE WAS AMONGST THE LAST.
WE WERE PUT TO THE TOP OF THE RAMP

chapter nine

Ah, Pankrác! Just saying the word (rhymes with "man rats") brings forth a flash flood of highly varied emotions and memories rushing through me—fearful, angry, sad, even bizarrely hilarious and oddly contented thoughts and feelings permeate my being when I remember the reality of my time there. I had no idea what awaited me as the van left the courtroom though. I only knew I was entering an unknown realm, and that I had better do my best to watch my back. I wish I could have kicked off this chapter with a bold, pithy statement about entering the necessary mental and emotional state one needs to survive when going to prison; a strong, masculine, assertive string of rugged, work-boot clad words that would make me look calm, wise, and stalwart in the face of possible long-term incarceration—but I can't. Riding along in the back of the paddy wagon, looking at what little I could see of Prague passing by through the windshield, I wasn't weeping and falling apart at the seams, but I wasn't exactly a model of stoicism either. Mostly I was just confused and very nervous. Just four short days ago I had been sailing on an antique boat through an astonishingly beautiful fjord, heading toward an island where I would rock out in front of a few thousand Nordic fans, not a few of whom were gorgeous, blue-eyed, and extremely well-built women. Now I was riding literally in chains in the back of a beat-up paddy wagon with a blown suspension, heading toward a prison that had been described to me as "the worst" in the country; a prison full of (what I could only assume would be) dour, muscular, and violently-inclined felonious Slavic men. At the very least, I was fairly certain there would be a pretty severe shortage of hot Scandinavian chicks in tight fitting lamb of god t-shirts in Pankrác Remand Prison. I was correct.

Looking back and remembering that ride now, I think I was actually too nervous to be scared, if that makes any sense. Every hair on my body was standing on end, and my adrenaline was flowing. It felt like every single synapse in my body was firing off at once—I was juiced, a ball of jittery energy that had nowhere to roll. I tried to calm myself, but my mind was racing like a tweaker who had won an all-you-can-smoke meth lab shopping spree, sprinting from one extreme to another in milliseconds.

HolycrapholycrapholycrapI'mgoingtoprison!

Calm down, bro, you're gonna be all right.

ManwhatthefuckisgoingonhereIneverkilledanyonehowdidthis happen?

Take it easy, man—you've been through worse. Just be cool, man.

JesushchristI'mgoingtofuckingprisoninaforeigncountrythisissome-craaaaaazyshit.

You've been locked up before and you're still alive. Just keep your wits about you, man.

HolyfuckinghellIdon'twanttogetshankedorrapedI'mgoingtohaveto-fightmyassoffinthere.

Relax dude, you're not going to get stabbed or raped. Just be cool and you'll be all right.

———

I have no idea how long the van ride from court to the prison took, because my psyche was too busy playing a light speed game of emotional ping-pong with itself, but eventually the paddy wagon stopped in front of the solid metal gate of a high razor wire topped concrete wall. The driver beeped his horn and the gate slipped open, a guard holding a black pistol grip 12 gauge Mossberg motioning us in. We pulled forward about fifty feet and stopped. The driver killed the ignition, then turned around, and looked at me through the wire grate that separated us.

"I go inside for a minute. I will be back very soon," he said, his English accented but spoken with ease. He got out of the van and shut his door. There was no air conditioning running, and it was a very warm and sunny day. I began to sweat almost immediately. I sat in the van perspiring for two or three minutes, then he returned and slid open the van door and a delicious breeze blew in.

"I am sorry, but we will have to wait here for a bit. There is some problem going on inside." He reached in and unlocked the metal bar pinning me to my seat.

"Dude, take your time. I'm in no big hurry to go in there," I said.

He gave a little laugh, then asked me, "Would you like something to drink?"

I said I would, and he walked away, leaving the van door open. I guess he knew I wasn't going anywhere—we were behind the prison's tall outer walls now, and I was still in handcuffs. I slid down the seat a little toward the open door, but not too far. I wasn't trying to get blasted by a shotgun toting guard during my first three minutes in prison. I craned my neck to see what I could of my new home. The outside of Pankrác actually looked kind of nice from what I could see—from my restricted vantage point, I saw a fairly neat-looking standard-issue European building. There were even some freshly painted flower boxes lining the short flight of concrete steps leading up to the clean, white building's heavy front door. Maybe this place wouldn't be as awful as Martin said. Soon the driver came back out with two cups in his hand; a coffee for him and water for me. I thanked him and drank my water in two gulps. He took my cup and sipped his coffee.

"I am sorry this is happening for you," he said in a kind voice, "I am a big fan of heavy metal."

I waved my hand-cuffed hands in a *No worries, dude, it's not your fault* gesture and said, "Really? What bands do you like, bro?"

"I listen to Bathory, Finntroll, a little Rammstein," he said. "While we wait, would you like a coffee?"

"That, my friend, would be awesome," I said. He left and walked back into the prison. This was going much better than I had expected. Maybe there would be other early black-metal loving guards and inmates inside. Soon he returned with a mug of coffee with foamed milk on top. I'm a black coffee kind of guy, but I wasn't about to ask this nice metal head guard to go fix me another. I took a sip—it was hot and tasted heavenly.

"Thank you so much—I was dying for a coffee. What would you call this in Czech? Caffe?" I asked, using the fairly universal European term for coffee.

"Cappuccino," he said, with a raised eyebrow and slight grin, his expression saying *Dude, haven't you ever had a cappuccino before?* He pulled a pack of cigarettes out of his jacket, lit one up, then offered, "Smoke?"

"Dear God, yes please!" I said. I hadn't smoked a cigarette in over twenty-four hours, and I was practically drooling over the smell of his smoke in the air. He gave me a square, I put it in my mouth, and he leaned into the van and lit it for me. I took a deep drag, and everything within my entire being instantly changed.

Suddenly, I didn't give two flying shits that I was about to walk into prison for the first time. I didn't care at all that I could possibly remain there for ten years. All the stress left my body and mind, all was right with the world. It was a sunny day in Europe, and I was drinking a cappuccino and having a smoke with my new friend, discussing Scandinavian metal. Life was good; in fact, it couldn't be better.

Whoa! I thought as I quickly came to my senses, *This is* really fucked up. *I'm getting ready to go to freakin' prison and I feel perfectly normal, not a care in the world, just because I'm smoking a stupid cigarette? I must be completely out of my mind! Holy crap, I have to quit smoking these damn things—they are way too powerful.*

———————

I have done just about every drug there is to do—hard, soft, natural, synthetic—you pretty much name it, and more than likely I have drank, snorted, smoked, or gobbled it, sometimes not even knowing what it was (and certainly not caring). I have entered psychedelic states of consciousness so far out there that the entirety of the universe has become my own personal Richard Pryor, every single atom comprising existence itself in a tiny stand up comedian, designed solely to make me laugh. I have flown so high on opiate feathered wings that I told that amateur Icarus to eat my dust and kiss my ass as I blew past him and actually made it to the sun—he obviously didn't know how to party. I have drank so much alcohol that I have woken up in a different state (and I'm not talking about one of mind) with no clue as to how I got there until the sleeping girl beside me, the *crazy stalker girl* whom I had previously been avoiding like a case of the shingles woke up (both of us were fully clothed—thank you, God) and cheerfully informed me that I had called in sick to work last night and that we were on our way to New York City for a romantic weekend getaway, together at long last (*oh God, no—NO!*). I have seen, said, and done many strange things while under the influence of many different substances, but I have never, ever (before or since) done anything that has taken me instantaneously from the worst thing many people can imagine (going to prison) and effortlessly slung me into a ridiculously false five-minute realm of pure bliss like that cigarette did.

Nicotine is some heavy-duty shit. Think about that, kids, before you start smoking. Plus, *it doesn't even get you high*. Why in the hell did I start smoking in the first place? I honestly don't have a clue. But I had a very clear realization in that moment that I absolutely had to quit. Certainly not right then though—that cig-arette was heaven in a cancerous tube, and even though I knew it was telling me a vicious lie, I enjoyed the hell out of that thing. I needed something to calm my nerves, and because I was a nico-tine addict, it did—a nonsmoker would have thrown up all over their cuffs if they had hit that thing as hard as I was. Like everyone else living in a modern society, I was familiar with the terrible cancerous risk to my life smoking incurs (especially being in a touring band, as the health warnings on cigarette packs in many other countries resemble a horror movie), but my nicotine addic-tion made it somehow easy to ignore the truth, just as my addic-tion to alcohol enabled me to drink in the face of overwhelming evidence that I shouldn't. I suppose it's kind of ironic that the best cigarette I have ever smoked was the one that finally made me realize I needed to quit; then again, since that first one sitting outside Pankrác I have developed quite a fondness for cappuc-cino (a coffee drink I had previously always scorned as being for sissies) and have at least one a week. I always think fondly of the guard who drove me to prison as I drink it; so dude, if you ever read this—thank you for treating me like a human being. If we ever meet again, the cappuccino's on me.

After a while a guard called to us. We walked into the building, stopped in front of an office window, where my driver handed the clerk inside a plastic bag containing my belongings. Then we walked a few feet to a large holding pen on the other side of the office, the bars reaching from the floor to the ceiling, where my driver removed my cuffs and ushered me into the cage. He wished me luck and walked away, another guard shutting and locking the door of my cage. I stood there and took a look at my new surroundings.

Inside, Pankrác was not nearly as maintained as its freshly scrubbed outside might lead one to believe—the building was obviously pretty old (at least by American standards). The ceil-ings were quite high, and not much light filtered in through the

few opaque windows set on either side of a large hallway behind another set of bars and leading further into the building.
The black and white checkered floor looked like it hadn't seen a
mop since before the fall of communism, and paint was peeling
on some parts of the walls. Rust splotched the bars of my cage
where God only knows how many layers of enamel had chipped
away to the metal. The area I was in reminded me of an old city
hall whose municipality had fallen on hard times—not only did
they let the janitor go, but were unable to pay their entire electric-
ity bill. It was large, musty, and very dim. I (foolishly) hoped my
cell wouldn't be as dingy as this intake area. I tried to read some
of the graffiti scratched into what paint was left on the bars of my
cage, but it was all in Czech, so I gave up and began doing pull
ups from a section of crossbar.

Almost immediately a window slid open in the wall of the
office that made up part of my cage, and a guard yelled something at me in Czech, shaking his head in disapproval. *Oh, well,* I
thought, *So much for an early prison style-work out.* I got down and
the guard motioned me forward to the window. He handed me
several sheets of paper printed in Czech and a pen, pointing to
lines where I assumed he wanted my signature. I had absolutely
no idea of what I was signing, so I asked him. He replied in Czech
and pointed emphatically at the lines again. It didn't seem like
not throwing down a John Hancock was an option, so I scrawled
a signature nothing like my own (I believe I signed it "Johnny
Rotten"—sorry, Mr. Lydon), then he handed me seventeen sheets
of paper stapled together with the word "instruction" typed in
block letters at the top of the first page. Printed on both sides of
the sheets of paper in well-translated English were the rights of an
accused person who had been taken into custody, and the rules
and regulations governing the prison. The guard shut the window
and I perused the papers. There were rules for the amount of
space each prisoner was allotted within a cell, what a prisoner was
allowed to have in their cell, a seemingly endless list of security

regulations, visitation and telephone policy—seemingly every aspect of prison existence was covered, and it seemed as if this was a very tightly run ship I had boarded, adhering to a precisely formulated and rather draconian plan.

Within a few short days I would discover that this list of rules, regulations, and rights was the single biggest pile of horseshit I had ever read in my life. Pankrác had plenty of rules and regulations all right, but they bore only a passing resemblance to the printed pack of lies in my hands. As for the "rights" of prisoners? Sitting at my desk now and reading paragraph 2 of Section 29, "Satisfaction of Cultural Needs" ("A convict shall be allowed to make a choice of books from the library selection according to his/her interests, spiritual needs and denomination"), I have to smile. Paragraph two of Section 31, "Purchase of Food and Personal Items" ("Prices in the prison shop shall not exceed the price level that is common in a municipality in the area in which the prison is located") actually wrenches a snort of amusement from me. By the time I get to the second paragraph of Section 36, "Convicts' Management Programs and Employment of Convicts" ("Convicts' management programs are divided into the following types: a—work activities, b—training activities, c—special education activities, d-activities of interest, and e—people skills), I'm actually laughing out loud. But my favorite, the one that almost has me rolling on the floor and peeing my boxers with glee, is Section 35, "Protection of Convicts against Illegitimate Violence and against Humiliation of Human Dignity"—oh, this section is the richest!

There are short instructions for prisoners who have been the victim of illegitimate violence or had their human dignity humiliated at the hands of a prison employee (naturally, just report it to a different prison employee and the prison director will take care of it right away, no problem!), but most of it seems directed toward safeguarding prisoners against "illegitimate violence" (man, I just love that terminology) or degradation of their human rights at the hands of other prisoners. During my time in Pankrác, I swiftly came to realize that I didn't really need to watch out for other prisoners hell-bent on humiliating my human dignity. Yes, I was locked up with junkies, rapists, murderers, thieves, con men, and tax evaders; but not a single one of them ever tried to make me feel lesser than myself; in fact many helped me out the best they could, especially when I first got there and didn't know what in the hell was going on. I can't say the same for a few guards. And yes, prison is full of dangerous people, people who can and will hurt you very badly if you act foolishly or get caught up in some shady business. It happens, and it has happened in Pankrác. But I never witnessed so much as a pushing match between inmates in Pankrác, nor saw any prisoners who looked like they had been beat up—by another prisoner. But what do you do when the guards let the police come in from the outside to use helpless prisoners as punching bags for absolutely no reason at all? I did see the end result of that, and it wasn't pretty. I guess police violence isn't considered "illegitimate violence" in Pankrác. I tried to stay aware of every single person around me at all times, but a few of the guards (not all of them) got special attention.

Soon a large guard emerged from the gate leading deeper into the prison, unlocked the door to my cage, and led me out through the gate he had come from. After he had relocked the gate, he motioned for me to keep my hands behind my back as if I were cuffed. I followed him silently down the gloomy hallway until we stopped and went into an equally gloomy nurse's office. There I had my height measured, weighed, and blood pressure checked with one of those old-school manual pump bulb inflated arm cuffs, the ancient and emotionless nurse typing the results at the speed of molasses by single finger pecking into an equally antiquated PC. After what seemed like an eternity, we left the nurse's office, went through yet another gate that had to be unlocked and then relocked, then walked into a bright, naturally lit intersection of hallways. There were a few groups of prisoners passing through the area, escorted by guards and walking with their hands behind their backs like me. Some of them glanced at me briefly without much interest. We were about to turn right and head up a broad set of stairs when a young prisoner with a freshly shaved head noticed me. He stopped dead in his tracks, the inmate behind him bumping into him as his eyes immediately lit up, his face breaking out into a wide, excited, and uncontrollable smile. I know this expression all too well, as I see it with some regularity when I am in public. Sometimes, my wife, friends, or family members will recognize it on people's faces well before I do. It is the look some hard-core fans of my band, even ones in my hometown, will get when they run into me at the grocer's, book store, or coffee shop; the look that precedes them inevitably saying "Randy? Oh my God, it *is* you! I can't believe this! What in the hell are *you* doing *here*?"

Ninety-nine percent of the time, I'm buying groceries or getting gas for my truck or going to see a movie or whatever activity is appropriate for my current surroundings—that is, the same exact thing the fan is doing; especially in Richmond, Va, since I happen to live there. And that's usually my standard reply (although in the grocery store I'm always tempted to say, "Well, you gotta promise me you won't tell *anyone*, but lamb of god is playing a secret show in the produce section. Aisle three, eight o'clock sharp—be there, but keep it to yourself!"), but as the young man resisted the urge to come over to me, threw me the horns, then walked away whispering to the men in his group, I had a feeling he already knew why I was there. Several of the men glanced back at me again, staring openly this time. I supposed the news of my arrival in prison would soon be making its way through the grapevine. This didn't exactly thrill me, as I wanted to maintain as low of a profile as possible, since my arrest was front-page news in the Czech Republic and I didn't know if the inmates believed whatever was being printed about me in the papers. The option of operating completely under the prison population's radar had

just been shot down right in front of me, but instead of getting upset, I quickly (and truthfully) told myself that harboring that hope had been ridiculous and destined for failure from the start. My story was too big, and since every prison is one gigantic rumor factory, I might as well accept my unfortunate notoriety, keep both eyes open for trouble, and wait to see how it would affect my period of incarceration.

The guard motioned for me to precede him up the steps to yet another locked gate. Pankrác Prison is not a group of white painted buildings and a concrete yard surrounded by razor wire-topped walls. It is an endless and bewildering procession of right angle turns, separated every fifteen or twenty meters by heavy grids of floor to ceiling solid steel bars and thick sliding bolts. With every turn of a guard's key, each corridor walked through, every corner turned, a person moves further and further away from the pieces that once defined their life, and deeper and deeper into the ancient belly of their new existence. It is a grim and filthy collage of unhappiness; constructed of iron rodded barriers of finality, and the collective claustrophobic despair of the men and women locked behind them. In the month that I was there, I would fight daily a relentless war to prevent this physical prison from becoming a mental one. If I think about it long and hard enough, the memories begin to overtake me, and I have to fight again to not be overwhelmed by them. The awake, aware human being realizes that this moment is what needs taking care of. Sitting shiva in the dark days of the past is not the act of mourning for lost time or happiness; it is willfully murdering the only chance we ever have to be happy—right now. That is easy to write, but much harder for all of us to actually do. It definitely is for me at times, so now, as I did then, I must just push forward down the next corridor before me and see what comes next.

I walked down a short and low drop-ceilinged hallway (the first I had seen in Pankra), and through a flimsy wood veneer door into a more modern room (and by modern, I mean a circa

1970s orange carpeted, faux-pine paneled, construction company foreman's office, complete with a rickety metal fan and
scratched-up formica-topped desk adorned with a chipped coffee
cup and an overflowing heavy glass ashtray). There were hefty
aluminum rods running the length of each wall, with hundreds
of wire coat hangers hung with burlap sack covered clothes filling their lengths. It looked like the world's biggest and most depressing walk-in closet. A trusty got up from behind the desk and
told me in a halting mixture of Czech and English to take off
all my clothes. I stripped naked in front of the guard and trusty,
who took my clothes except for my baseball hat, socks, boxers
and shoes (he did remove the laces though), draped them on a
hanger, then covered them with a burlap sack and hung them
on one of the rods. He handed me a faded pair of purple sweat
pants about three inches too short for my legs and a threadbare
tan v-necked t-shirt, which I put on. I signed another paper that I
assumed was for my clothes, then the guard and I made our way
back to the staircase we had walked up, and then proceeded to
go down many flights of stairs until they narrowed and ended
in a solid steel door. We had reached the end of the line, and
I correctly assumed that we had to be in the basement of the
prison. The guard unlocked the door, and we faced another gate.
The guard called out, and another scowling prison guard with
a remarkable resemblance to Tom Selleck (if Tom Selleck were
skinnier and had a 1980s-almost-but-not-quite-new-wave spiked-
topped haircut) stepped out of an office door and unlocked the
gate. The guard who had escorted me down handed Tom Selleck,
who gave me a grumpy once-over, some paperwork, then left.
Tom pointed to a bench outside his office where I sat, and called
out down the hall.

A younger guard, standing a good five inches shorter than me
arrived. He had a medium build, dirty blond hair, a fake-looking
tan, and gleaming white teeth that shined as he looked at me
and smiled, listening to Tom Selleck giving him instructions. For

some reason, I immediately distrusted this sporty-looking young guard—he reminded me of the popular rich kids from high school who used to love to publicly humiliate other students whose parents didn't have the kind of money theirs did, as their lack of brand-name clothes made clear to any who saw them.

Bradley. He looked like a Bradley to me (no offense to any Bradleys reading this—I actually have a few friends named Bradley and they are all awesome guys, but this dude was, I'm sorry to say, a serious disgrace to Bradleys everywhere). I decided I would do well to keep my eye on him—there was something about Bradley that led me to believe we wouldn't get along, and he didn't take long to confirm my hunch. Bradley would soon prove to be my least favorite guard in all of Pankrác—I would say that he was the bane of my existence there, but Bradley was too transparent and predictable in his crappiness for me to take his attempts to upset me seriously after a while. He sure as hell tried his best, though.

Bradley and I walked down the hall a few feet and stopped in front of an open cell door. He leaned his head in and hollered in Czech to a shaved bald trusty in his thirties, who quickly took off his headphones and hurried up off his bed a little too quickly (kiss ass), gave me a creepy grin, and went into a closet area beside his cell, emerging with a bundle of items wrapped up in a wool blanket which he handed me. I didn't like the look of the trusty either—he looked like a pedophile to me, a more unsavory version of Uncle Fester from the Addam's Family. I tucked my large bundle under my arm and followed Bradley down the hall. There were solid metal doors on either side of the hallway with numbers painted on them, and we came to a stop in front of 505. Bradley unlocked the door.

"So is this where I'll be staying?" I asked him.

"Yes. For a long time. Maybe a month, maybe longer," he said, smiling at me. Bradley obviously loved this part of his job. He yanked on the door, opening it wide.

"Welcome to your new friend," Bradley said, sweeping his arm upwards and into the room in a grand gesture, as if he were the concierge of a luxury hotel, showing me to the finest suite in the building. "He," he said, pausing for effect, "is a mongoloid," then slammed the door shut behind me as I walked into the cell. I heard keys turning and bolts sliding into their chambers. I was home.

The man before me rubbed his eyes as he got up from his rickety looking metal frame bed. He was a brown skinned fellow with Asiatic features defining his pleasant face, of slightly less than average height, and certainly above average weight for a man of his stature—he had to be well over two hundred pounds, and it wasn't a "firm" two hundred plus he was carrying around. He looked sort of like a Chinese version of the Pillsbury Doughboy, if the doughboy had grown up on a beach in Hawaii working on his tan. We stood there staring at each other. I gave him a smile, and he smiled back. So far, so good. And despite Bradley's dramatic pronouncement, my cellmate didn't appear to be "a mongoloid," as people with Down Syndrome were sometimes referred to during my youth.

"What's up, dude? I'm Randy. How ya doing?" I asked, trying a little conversational English to test the ol' linguistic waters in cell 505. The man just stared at me. I went a little more formal.

"Hello, my good man. This place is really something, eh?" I said. He continued to stare, not with malice, but there was incomprehension written on his brown face.

"*Bonjour, mon ami. Parlez vous francais?*" I asked, hoping that what little I remembered from Madame Degnan's first period high school French class might come in handy. This actually drew a scowl—he obviously wasn't a francophile. I greeted him in Japanese, and I thought I saw a small glimmer of recognition in his dark eyes, but still he remained silent. This was just as well, as my Japanese is horrible at best. Spanish? No reply. I ran through most of the greetings I know from traveling around the world, even throwing in a little Jamaican patois just for the fun of it, but the man didn't utter a word. Maybe he was mute?

Finally, I employed the time-honored technique I have embarrassedly witnessed American tourists use on disgusted locals around the globe: I spoke English as *slowly* and as *loudly* as possible. As all Americans abroad somehow intuitively know, the best course of action when speaking to a confused looking native of the country we are currently gracing with our presence is decreasing the velocity of speech to the speed of wood, while simultaneously increasing its volume to ear-blowing levels. This, of course, automatically grants the listener instant comprehension of our language.

"HELL-O, I AM RANDY," I yelled, pointing to my chest "I AM FROM AMERICA. RAAAAAN-DY. A-MER-I-CAAAA."

My cellmate looked at me as if I were hurting his ears, then smiled and pointed to his own chest.

"Dorj. Mongolia," he said, at a normal speed and reasonable volume level.

He was a Mongol! A real life descendant of the Khans, right here in cell 505 with me! What fantastic luck! Ever since I read *The Adventures of Marco Polo* as a boy, I have been fascinated with Mongolian history, particularly the military tactics and highly structured, horse-riding, arrow-shooting, yurt-dwelling nomadic society Ghengis and Kublai Khan led as they ran through Europe and Asia like a hot knife through butter, looting and pillaging and kicking major ass. The Mongols were so brutal the Chinese had to build the Great Wall to stop them, and that didn't even work. A Mongol! I had so many questions! I wondered if he grilled yak often back home.

"Dorj (rhymes with "gorge"). Mongolia!" I pointed at him, repeating excitedly, "Randy. America!"

"Rurlandy, America," he said, pointing at me and smiling. "Dorj, Mongolia."

It dawned on me that Dorj wouldn't be regaling me with tales of riding the rugged steppes of his homeland anytime soon, as our most successful attempt at conversation so far closely resembled a Tarzan movie filmed in an Eastern Bloc prison. I decided I would have to either attempt to learn Mongolian or teach Dorj some English, because repeating our names and nationalities was already losing its intellectual appeal for me. Thankfully, Dorj motioned for me to put my bundle on the low particle board-topped table in the cell and began showing me the best way to make my bed. The bed was an old metal frame affair, with layers of brown and green paint chipping away to reveal red rust in places, as if a ghetto camouflage job had been done for a hospitalized hunter with no insurance. For a mattress there were what appeared to be three ripped up foam couch cushions laying on top of a metal lattice work with a few springs poking out here and there. Dorj showed me by gesturing that I should put down one of my two wool blankets as extra padding, tucking it around the three cushions, then topping it with the single rough white sheet and other blanket that came with my bundle. There was no pillow. Then Dorj opened the top of two stacked chest-high institutional-green metal lockers, indicating that it was mine to store my belongings. I sat down on my bed and looked at what I had been issued with my sheet and blankets.

Toiletries: One bar of soap. One roll of toilet paper. One toothbrush. One tube of toothpaste. One tube of shaving paste. One shaving brush. One safety razor, single bladed. One purple plastic cup, stained brown interior. One large metal spoon, bent.

Clothing: One hoodless sweat shirt, two sizes too small, same faded purple as sweatpants. One pair very uncomfortable looking (leather?) sandals, dark brown. One pair very thin socks, dark green. One set of pajamas, top and bottom, sinus infection-yellow, mysterious purple stains scattered on fabric. One extra v-necked t-shirt, tan with blown-out collar (a.k.a. "loser neck"), old panty-hose like runs and holes in see-through fabric. One pair "boxers," grey/white, four sizes too big, no elastic in waist, missing one half of sewn-in drawstring necessary to keep on body. One extra large dish towel (for drying body after bathing?), originally white with blue pin stripes, now uniformly blue-gray.

Missing: Books. Paper. Pen. Coffee. Equipment to make coffee. Food. Cigarettes. Lighter. Laptop. iPod. Camera. Skateboard.

Skateboarding area. Surfboard. Ocean. Fishing pole. River. Friends. Family.

Wife.

Freedom.

I sighed and stowed my meager gear neatly in my locker, except for the bar of soap, which I placed on a loosely mounted particle board shelf. The shelf sat above a plain sink that looked as if it was about to fall off the crumbling wall any moment. I turned the single knob on the sink. Ice-cold dirty water rushed out. It never got any warmer, but it did run clear after thirty seconds or so. Great—no hot water for shaving. There was also no mirror in sight, and I hoped I wouldn't make a bloody mess of my face when I attempted to scrape the four-day old beard from my bristling mug. Beside the sink was an old porcelain toilet with a cracked base missing an entire corner. It looked as if someone had begun to bolt it to the floor, but had decided mid-job to go do something more rewarding. The toilet had no handle, but a few lengths of what looked like pajama fabric were tied together as a string, hanging down from a dirty water tank mounted on the wall above the toilet. I gently pulled the string, there was a loud gurgling whoosh, and the toilet flushed with immense power and great speed, water splashing out all over the seat and floor of the cell. Dorj laughed, and I nodded and took a mental note as he indicated that I should lower the toilet lid when flushing. Neither of us wanted a post-poop urine and feces explosion. Beside the toilet hung a moldy shower curtain printed in a rose basket and swallow pattern. It hung from a curtain rod fashioned from a bent piece of pipe that stuck precariously out of the wall, blocking the view of the toilet from the small hatch in our steel cell door, but affording zero privacy for anyone sitting on the toilet from the other inhabitant of the cell.

As I walked around the cell, I noted the ill-fitted and filthy sheet of yellow-green linoleum beneath my feet, unattached to the floor by any sort of adhesive. There were odd pieces of it missing at various places where the linoleum met the wall, and

I guessed that the prison had bought remnants at bargain prices to cover their cell floors. Besides the beds, table, lockers, toilet, and sink, the cell contained two square wooden topped stools, one of which had a chess board scratched in it. There was a crumbling cork board hanging on one wall with a photo ripped from a magazine stuck to it. It appeared to be a picture of some vacantly smiling celebrity I didn't recognize, standing at an awards ceremony with her elderly parents. Someone had taken a pen and blacked out one of her teeth. Beside the cork board, set in a shallow, extremely dusty alcove was a radiator. As I absent-mindedly ran my hand along the top of it, Dorj came over from his bed and withdrew something from the inches pile high of dust beneath the radiator. He smiled, put a finger to his lips indicating silence, then opened his hand. In it was a small bit of blade, stripped from a safety razor. I smiled, and nodded in comprehension as he put his finger to his lips again and replaced the razor, showing me where he kept it hidden.

Seeing the razor instantly improved my morale. It was much too small to be used as any sort of weapon (unless it was somehow affixed to a handle of some sort; a fairly common practice in prison), but I knew it would be a valuable tool. Beside the pragmatic aspects of the razor, its presence in our cell was powerfully symbolic for me. The razor was expressly forbidden, but there it sat nestled in its dusty hiding place; a sharp and physical piece of defiance in this intensely depressing place. It was a tiny metallic refusal to completely accept the current conditions I found myself in, and I was pleased Dorj had already deemed me trustworthy enough to share its existence. I walked over to my bed and sat down, staring at the yellow-gray paint peeling from the high walls of our cell. Dorj dug in his locker and came back with two thin hand-rolled cigarettes, offering me one and twitching his thumb in the universal "do you have a lighter?" motion. I shook my head, and Dorj sighed and put away the cigarettes. At least he smoked, and was willing to share. I looked above me at the single frameless and barred window in the room, perhaps three by two feet in dimension, set in the wall high in between our two beds. The window had two wooden framed panels of glass, one of which was slid open, the only source of ventilation in the cell. I got up from my bed, hopped up on the frame headboard, grabbed two of the six square bars, and pulled myself up for a look. The ground was eye level from my basement perspective, and all I could see through the metal lattice affixed to the outside of the window was a pile of cinderblock and roofing material rubble, sitting in front of a gray wall about ten feet away. The view left a lot to be desired, but at least the window let a small amount of sunshine and fresh air into the cell. The rusty bars began to dig into my palms, and I carefully lowered myself back down onto my bed.

Soon after I got down, I heard the cell door being unlocked behind me. I turned around as the door opened, and there stood Bradley, looking immensely pleased with himself. He crossed his arms and leaned against the frame of the door, smirking at me.

"So, are liking the new home? Your new friend?" he asked with a gleaming smile.

"Yeah. Everything's just great," I replied in a monotone.

"Yes, is very good here," he replied, smiling even wider, then began to walk out the door. The door was almost shut when it stopped, and Bradley popped his head into the room.

"Is there something you are needing? Is there anything else you would like I can get for you?" he asked happily, like a waiter bringing the check to a dinner table.

As a matter of fact, yes, you little motherfucker, there is something else I would like, I thought as I felt the blood starting to rush to my head, *I would like it if just me and you were in a dark alleyway somewhere right about now. I would like that a whole lot.*

I said nothing in reply, staring at him briefly, then turned back around and sat on my bed. He must have seen that he had gotten my goat, because I heard him laugh as he turned the key in the door and walked away. I saw right then that Bradley was definitely going to be a problem, and that I would have to keep a strict watch over my temper around him. Like it or not, he was the one in charge here, and if I let him know he was getting to me in *any* way, I would be giving away what little bit of power I retained in my current situation. Heaven forbid I let him drive me to somehow physically react to anything he did—my situation would immediately go from really, really bad to unthinkable. I'm not some violent thug, but it took me a moment to calm down enough to realize that I couldn't afford the thoughts currently running through my head. In that moment, I wanted nothing more than to smash Bradley a few good ones right in his smug face. I reminded myself that these kind of thoughts get you beaten up, locked up longer, or even worse in prison, and I decided that there was no way I would allow him to make me stay there any longer than I had to.

Dorj could see that Bradley had pissed me off, and waved his hand in dismissal at the door, hissing between his teeth and saying something that sounded like "coondta backhar." I didn't understand what he had said, and didn't even know what language he had said it in, but I definitely picked up on the meaning: "Ah, to hell with that guy. He's just a little jerk." (Soon I would learn that *bachar* was the Czech word for *screw*, the same derogatory term used in America for a prison guard. As for *cunda*, just take a wild guess.) I relaxed and laughed a little, kicking my feet up and lying back on my bed with my hands folded behind my neck. Dorj was doing the same. Might as well chill for a bit.

"Aaaaay, ya ya ya ya ya ya yaaaaa . . . Pankrác," I heard Dorj sigh beside me, marking the first of a million times I would hear him utter this particular mantra over the next thirty-four days. For some reason, I found this hilarious, and began laughing. Dorj began to laugh as well, and before long we were both cracking up and ay-ya-ya-Pankrác-ing away. It was a combination Mongolian/ Czech way of saying *c'est la vie*. What could we do? We were in prison. Prison sucks. Might as well laugh about it. (Even today, when I am vexed by some unavoidable annoyance, I'll catch myself saying it under my breath from time to time. Flat tire on a beach cruiser? Computer hard drive acting up? Flight canceled? Ay ya ya ya ya ya ya ya . . . Pankrác.)

Soon the hatch in our door opened up, and Fester the trusty stuck his head in, yelling something that sounded like "eedlow!" (*jídlo*= food). Lunch had arrived. Dorj went to the hatch and took two plastic trays of food from Fester, who held up a pitcher of light brown liquid, looked at me questioningly, and said "chai?" I brought him our plastic cups, and he poured us each a cup of watery tea before shutting the hatch and rolling the food cart down the cell block hall, hollering *"jídlo!"* and *"chai!"* the whole way in his high-pitched unpleasant voice. Dorj and I sat down at the low table, and he immediately began wolfing down his food with great speed, noise, and ferocity. Dorj ate like he had been waiting his whole life for that particular meal. He sounded like some sort of apocalyptic human vacuum cleaner running on a "complete annihilation" setting, great slurping sounds of sheer mandibular destruction emanating from his rotund brown face. It was impressive, as well as extremely disgusting, to witness. *Well, at least it must be delicious if he's eating it that . . . intensely*, I thought, and took a look at my lunch.

On my tray was a sizable hunk of dark brown bread, a small bowl of clear soup with a few bits of diced carrots floating in it, and a larger bowl of a slightly thicker brownish stew with what looked like an unbaked white sub roll stuck in it. I tore off a piece of the bread and tried it—not bad, not bad at all. (European countries count amongst their citizens superior bakers of bread, apparently even in prison.) The soup was fairly tasteless, made of a very light chicken stock and not much else, so I tried the stew. It had a bit more flavor, and a few tiny bits of what I assumed was some sort of meat in it. Unsurprisingly, the unbaked sub-roll-looking thing in the stew had the same consistency as an unbaked sub roll. I tried a few bites, and while it didn't taste particularly *bad*, it didn't exactly taste *good* either. I felt like I was chewing a mouthful of flour-flavored bubblegum. I gave up on my sub roll after a few hard-earned swallows, finished the stew, then drank the almost flavorless tea and finished up my piece of bread (which was by far the best tasting component of my meal). So far, Czech prison food was ranking pretty high on my list of worst meals ever—it was basically flavorless, and there wasn't much of it. *Oh well*, I thought, *you're not at the Ritz-Carlton. Plus dinner has got to be better. At least there's got to be something solid with the main meal of the day besides bread.*

Oh, how wrong I was. How wrong I was.

Not long after we had finished lunch, Dorj and I were relaxing on our beds when the cell door opened and Bradley stood there, looking slightly irritated, instead of his normal smug self.

"Up! Up! Come, come, both of you. We go," he barked, clearly annoyed at having to take us wherever we were going.

Dorj and I got up from our beds, put on our sandals, and headed toward the door. Bradley held his hand up for us to halt.

"Fix shirt!" he said, motioning for us to tuck our shirts into our sweatpants. We did so, and walked outside the cell, where we were made to turn around, spread our legs, and place our hands on the hallway wall while another guard did a quick pat down. Then we followed Bradley to the end of the hall, where a group of eleven other men were already waiting. Bradley unlocked the gate, and we all walked single file out of the block, hands behind our backs, and up the stairs I had come down earlier. After a good ten minutes of walking up and down stairs and through gates and around corners, we arrived at a low ceilinged holding cell a bit smaller than Dorj's and my room. All thirteen of us crammed in and took seats on the floor and benches bolted to the walls. As soon as the cell door was locked and the guards had walked away, half-smoked cigarettes began appearing from pockets and being lit up, then passed around. I took a look at the men crowded into the cell with me.

Besides Dorj sitting to my left, across from me was a hand-some young blond haired man in his early twenties who looked as if he definitely did not belong in prison. He was well groomed, and except for his prison fatigues, looked as if he had just walked out of the pages of some high-end casual clothing catalog. He kept rapidly glancing around the cell, trying not to look nervous but failing miserably. *Mr. Abercrombie better tighten up or he won't last long here,* I thought. There were three young Asian men squat-ting together in a corner, sharing a cigarette and speaking qui-etly in what I recognized as Vietnamese. A tall, overweight man about the same age as the pretty boy sat on the edge of the bench near the Vietnamese, looking resigned. Beside him was a friendly looking older gentleman who had to be at least in his late sixties, smiling and clutching a soft tan leather attaché in his lap. Next to the older gentleman was a man in his thirties about my height and build who appeared to be sweating out some sort of flu at the moment, as his skin was damp and pale, his eyes glassy. To my right sat what I immediately recognized as a very strung out her-oin junkie of the homeless street punk variety. He was rail thin, filthy, smelled awful, and his thin hair looked as if someone had cut it with a weed whacker. His hair and obvious malnutrition didn't make him look punk rock, it made him look like a chemo patient or concentration camp victim. Finally, sitting and stand-ing near Mr. Abercrombie were three different swarthy skinned men, talking amongst each other. One was thin and quiet look-ing, with sad brown eyes. Another was tall and beefy, and looked almost exactly like my friend Raymond Herrera, a well-known Los Angeles based drummer whom I had toured with before. The last of the dark-skinned trio was very short, had a clean-shaven head, and spoke constantly in a raspy animated voice to the other two. All three were covered in tattoos, and the short one had what I knew to be knife scars on his hands and arms. These three car-ried themselves in a way that immediately let me know that this was not their first day in prison. I guessed that they were *Roma* ("gypsies" being the more vulgar terminology), and I was correct.

The *Roma* were passing a few cigarettes back and forth, and the short one noticed me looking at his. He leaned over and passed it to me, motioning for me to share with the men on my side. I took a few deep drags, and passed it to Dorj first. I wasn't going to make him smoke after the junkie next to me—God only knows what kind of diseases he had—and spoke to the short *Roma*.

"Thank you, bro. I'm Randy. Do you speak English? What's your name?" I asked. The short man sat looking at, then asked Raymond Herrera a quick question, who answered, pointing at me and the short man.

"Englishky? No. Name? Rene," he answered, pointing to himself. Raymond Herrera spoke to him again in Czech or Romani (I couldn't tell the difference), and Rene's eyes got big, then he turned to me with a big smile on his face.

"Aaaah, Americansky," Rene said, pointing at me "rock and rooooool, baby!" and laughed as he began to air guitar. I suppose Raymond had informed him of who I was. I was definitely not going to be the anonymous American on our cell block. Oh well—at least the *Roma* seemed friendly.

"Yes, rock-n-roll," I sighed. "You are *Romani*?" I asked, pointing to him and his two friends.

"Yes, yes. Say Gypsy, Gypsy," Rene replied, then turned back to his friends and resumed their conversation.

"I read about you in the papers," the tall overweight man carefully said, not unkindly.

"Yup, that's me," I admitted. "Do you know why they brought us here?"

"Drug test," he replied, and soon a guard returned with a tray of urine sample cups with printed labels on them, handing one to each of us as he read the name on the label. As the guard left, a collective groan went up from over half the men in the cell. Uh-oh. Although I was almost certain I would pass any standard drug test administered, as I had been clean and sober for close to two years at that point, a part of me harbored a tiny shred of worry. I had just come off a month of festival tour gigs. Backstage at any festival of any sort, anywhere on earth, not just heavy metal—rock, jazz, country, hip-hop, classical, gospel, it does *not* matter—I can assure you that somewhere, someone is smoking copious amounts of marijuana. Even if the musicians themselves aren't smoking it, someone in the crew, either local or band, is getting stoned. That is just a fact of the music business, and I have walked through or sat in countless billowing clouds of ganja smoke in the closed environment of backstage, unavoidably breathing some of it in, much to my annoyance. I don't think there is anything wrong with recreationally smoking a little herb here and there, just as I don't think drinking like a normal person is wrong; although even when I was partying I didn't partake in it much at all—it simply wasn't a drug I enjoyed. And yes, weed has legitimate medical uses, and it *is* ridiculous that it's illegal while cigarettes are not; but just like alcohol, marijuana *is* a drug. It was not something I wanted popping up during a urine screening in prison, especially since I didn't even get to enjoy it when I "did" it. (All you deluded and self-righteous stoners with your hackles lazily raising up right now—calm down, I'm not saying your little magic plant should be illegal; but please, for God's sake stop lying to yourselves—it's a freaking drug. Psychotropic foreign substance + your body = radical change in mental and physical condition. This means you have done a *drug*. Why else would you call it "getting high"? Get over it.)

One by one we got up and went to the toilet in the corner and filled our little cups, carefully placing them on the ground near our feet, except for the junkie beside me. In a moment of opiate-inspired genius, he had placed his on top of the small privacy wall beside the toilet, where it was promptly knocked over by the large overweight man already in the process of filling his own cup. The piss splashed all over the junkie and onto the floor, some hitting my feet. I cursed and jerked my legs back, the junkie cursed and grabbed the cup from the floor, Rene paused mid-story to curse and laugh, and the large man jumped behind the barrier, startled by all the cursing. He emerged sheepishly from the toilet with his cup only half full, apologizing as he wiped his own urine from his hands on his sweatpants. Our little trip upstairs was off to a roaring start.

The junkie was in process of refilling his cup when I heard a man screaming from a cell next to ours, followed by several other voices in the cell yelling in Czech. Immediately four or five large guards came running past our cell, wearing white medical masks, like the ones common during the SARS scare of a few years back, strapped over their noses and mouths. I heard the barred door of the holding cell next to ours being hurriedly unlocked, and the screaming man increased his volume. I heard the unmistakable sound of a scuffle as guards and other inmates in the next holding cell were all yelling over the screaming man. Everyone in my cell had stopped talking and was listening wide-eyed to the ruckus next door, which gave no sign of calming down.

"Dude! What's going on out there?" I asked the urine displacer, as he had spoken in excellent English to me earlier.

"There is a man next door with tuberculosis. He does not want to go to the hospital," he replied, shaking his head. "This is not good."

Tuberculosis? Good God, my Grandma used to talk about how bad tuberculosis was during her childhood! If my Grandma, a woman who grew up during the Great Depression and was one of the toughest people I have ever met, says that something is bad, that means it's *bad*. TB has been pretty much eliminated in America, so I didn't know much about it except that it could kill you—and that it was a highly contagious airborne disease that flourished in crowded places with poor sanitation. Places like Pankrác. I immediately pulled my t-shirt up over my mouth and nose, and most of the other men in the cell did the same. The Vietnamese didn't bother. They just squatted there and lit up another cigarette, probably thinking what a bunch of scaredy-cats we were—Southeast Asia has a ton of weird diseases that aren't common in other parts of the world. The Vietnamese are very tough people, and these guys probably ate tuberculosis with a side of influenza with their morning bowl of *pho* everyday back home.

After another minute of struggling, the guards quickly returned past our cell with the screamer in a brutal-looking restraining hold, yanking him down the hall and out the door as he struggled and yelled in Czech as loud as he could through the beefy arm currently constricting his windpipe. Why on earth he wouldn't want to go to the hospital, I had no idea, but I was glad he was gone. I kept my shirt above my nose just in case any stray tuberculosis particles were still floating about in the air. Soon a guard appeared, unlocked our cell, and called out a Czech name. The piss-soaked junkie stood up and took his second cup of urine with him, holding up his sagging sweatpants around his emaciated waist as he walked out the door. After a few minutes he returned, sans cup, but pressing his thumb into the crook of his elbow, holding a tiny square of gauze in place. He sat down next to me, and within seconds blood had soaked through the gauze and was dripping down his arm and onto the floor. I scooted further towards Dorj. In a matter of minutes there had been piss splashed on me, a hysterical man with a contagious and deadly airborne disease was dragged kicking and screaming past my cell, and now this junkie was bleeding like a stuck pig less than a foot away from me. Things were not going smoothly.

Someone handed the junkie a wad of toilet paper to replace the useless scrap of gauze, but soon it was just as soaked through, and his blood kept dripping down his scrawny arm and onto the cell floor. *I guess that's what happens when you can't find a vein after you've collapsed them all shooting dope,* I thought, thankful that I had somehow never fallen into intravenous drug use. I heard a groan, and looked up to see Abercrombie staring at the blood flowing down the junkie's arm. Abercrombie was very, very pale and appeared as if he was about to either throw up or pass out, maybe both.

"Dude, are you okay?" I asked him.

"Oooh . . . the blood . . . I cannot look at blood . . . it makes me dizzy," he replied in barely accented but very shaky English. Abercrombie looked like he was about to faint, so the quiet gypsy seated beside him got up and let him lay down on the bench. I burst out laughing. I had heard of people who fainted when they saw blood, but I had never seen it happen. I tried briefly to contain myself but it was absurdly hilarious to me that this pretty boy was actually about to pass out at the sight of a little (admittedly probably pretty unhealthy, maybe even deadly) junkie blood—if he couldn't handle this little unpleasantness, how was he going to deal with prison life? It was too funny.

Then I realized what a complete asshole I was being. It wasn't Abercrombie's fault that he was born with genes that gave him a pretty face and a predisposition for falling out when he saw a little of the red stuff. I honestly felt terrible, and no one else was laughing either.

"I'm sorry, man—I'm not trying to make fun of you. You just reminded me of my younger brother, Mark." I lied. "He passes out every time he sees blood, too. He's been that way since we were kids." (Sorry Mark—I had to come up with *something*.) Abercrombie accepted my apology in a weak voice, laying there with an arm thrown across his face, trying to regain his composure. He still looked funny to me, prostrated like a swooning woman on a couch in an old silent movie, but I managed to keep my mirth to myself. One by one, we were all called to a nurse's office where the worst phlebotomist I have ever had the displeasure of being stuck by drained a few vials of blood from each of us none-too-gently. (Dorj and I would later compare the large bruises on our arms.) Abercrombie returned looking even paler than before, the guard basically holding him up. During my turn, I handed a nurse my urine sample, and I watched her do a brief chemical test on it as the needle-wielding sadist drew a few mils of blood. I asked her if I had passed, and she gave me a thumbs-up and told me my urine was clean. *Yay!* I didn't know what the penalty for pissing dirty would have been, maybe nothing, but I knew it wouldn't reflect well on me when it came time for court. I gave Dorj a questioning thumbs-up/thumbs-down gesture when he returned, but he shook his head and gave a rueful hiss between his teeth. I guess Dorj liked to party.

For some reason, it took about two hours for everyone to have their blood taken. Thirteen of us crammed perspiring into that holding cell, the smell of piss and blood and sweat and tuberculosis and God knows what else hanging in the unmoving air. The only upside to this whole ordeal was that the older gentleman began producing full packs of cigarettes from his leather bag, eventually giving them all away. Rene took the cigarettes and distributed them evenly to everyone in the cell who smoked. I felt bad taking so many cigarettes from the old man, so I had Abercrombie ask him in Czech if he was sure about handing them out so freely. He replied that it was no problem, that his lawyer would bring him more. I hope that he didn't have to do a lot of time there, because as I would find out later, getting cigarettes wasn't always as simple as having your lawyer drop off a few packs.

After everyone had fallen victim to the vampire in the nurse's office, Bradley and another guard came back to escort us back to the cellblock. We were walking single file down a long hallway when I heard a strange noise behind me, like air being let out of a car tire. I stopped and turned around and Martin, the man who looked like he had the flu (he had spoken a small amount of English in the holding cell and had introduced himself to me), stood there looking very dizzy. The blood drained from his face, and I saw him actually turn gray right in front of me as he began to fall to his knees. Dorj, myself, and the older gentleman grabbed him before he fell out, and lowered him to the ground. Martin's eyes were rolled back into his head, his mouth had a bit of foam in the corners, and I quickly wondered if he were epileptic and about to go into convulsions. Thankfully he did not, but Bradley and the other guard came back as the whole line stopped, jabbering impatiently in Czech at us, motioning for us to pick Martin up and carry him. They were not in the least bit interested in what was happening with this man, they just wanted him back in his cell. When Martin came to, Dorj and I helped him down the stairs into our cell block, and were walking him to his cell when Bradley stopped us and wouldn't let us help him any further. Martin thanked us and walked slowly and unsteadily down the hall, leaning with one arm against the wall for support.

"That man is sick! He needs help" I said angrily to Bradley, who just shrugged and locked us in our cell. "*Motherfucker!* I hate that asshole *so much*!" I cursed, but made myself calm down quickly, remembering my unfortunate place in this situation. I went to the sink and washed my hands and arms as well as I could with soap and the cold water, and Dorj did as well. We didn't know what kind of sickness Martin had, but neither of us wanted to find out the hard way. I lay down on my bed, wondering what would happen next.

An hour or so later, I heard Fester yelling, "*Jídlo!* Chai!" outside our door. After such a light and terrible lunch, I was looking forward to dinner, which I was sure couldn't be any blander, and had to be more substantial. This time I went to the hatch to get our food, and Dorj grabbed our cups for tea. I took the two trays, each holding a bowl of what looked like the same soup and same piece of bread from lunch and placed them on the table while Dorj got our tea. I turned around to get the rest of our dinner, but Fester had already shut the hatch and moved on his merry way.

A bowl of soup and a piece of bread was dinner? That was it? *You've got to be kidding me*, I thought. But no one was kidding anyone—that was, indeed, it. I would soon learn that lunch was the main meal of the day in this prison (and the Czech Republic in general), and that what we had consumed earlier would pretty much set the standard for *la cuisine de Pankrác*. Dorj had managed to slurp up most of his meal by the time I started on mine, which was just fine by me, since watching him annihilate his meager dinner made me feel a little nauseous. Again though, it was truly riveting (if stomach-churning), to witness him eat—Dorj was a slurper of olympic-level prowess, inhaling everything in front of him in great, sloppy, wet inhalations.

The next several hours were spent sitting in the cell, looking at the walls, hopping up every now and then to take a look out the window, doing a few pushups, and reading over and over the few incomprehensible Czech sentences of graffiti scratched on the walls by former occupants of our cell. Mostly I laid on my bed, thinking about my situation and trying to nap every now and then without much success. Once or twice Fester came by and refilled our cups with luke warm tea. At some point I noticed Dorj fiddling with three small elaborate swans he must have made prior to my arrival in cell #505. They were marvelous constructions, put together from hundreds of tiny pieces of folded up paper. It appeared that Dorj had run out of swan-making materials though, so he amused himself by taking them apart and putting them back together, the entire time whistling the same few bars of what I assumed was some Mongolian folk tune. It was rather soothing sounding, and I imagined him back in Mongolia, riding his horse across the majestic and bleak landscape of his homeland on whatever type of mysterious errand Mongols run when they aren't locked up in Czech prisons.

The sun was still low in the sky when the lights in our cell began to flick on and off, signaling, I supposed, that it was time to go to bed. I had been in bed already for several hours at that point, but I got up and washed my face and brushed my teeth, then said my evening prayers, asking God to give me the strength to get though this ordeal with dignity, whatever its final outcome might be. Dorj watched me hit my knees and pray with a small amount of interest, and when I was done pointed to himself and said "I buddha." Ah, he was saying he was a buddhist (although he actually did resemble very much some of the rounder representations of the Buddha himself I had seen). I gestured that I was a meditator, and indicated interest in if he had the same sort of practice. Dorj gave a short laugh and quickly shook his head no, probably thinking: *Great, another white clown who thinks all Asians like to sit around all day in extremely uncomfortable positions.* Soon the lights went out, and for a short while, what was left of the sun illuminated the cell enough to read a book, not that I had one.

Soon after lights out, the momentary quiet of the day was broken as men began to call out their windows into the prison yard in various different languages, setting off a Tower of Babel–like cacophony of communication, everyone trying to yell over each other to their friends in different parts of the prison. This was not an environment conducive for sleeping, to say the least. I heard a lot of Czech, a bit of German, and some Vietnamese. The Vietnamese were quite loud and seemed to annoy Dorj the most—he imitated them by making quacking noises and moving his hand like a duck's bill (and that is what we referred to them as after I had taught him some English—the ducks). While Dorj was very irate over the Vietnamese (perhaps some sort of inter-Asian rivalry?), I was bothered the most by the loudest of them all—two Ukrainians who screamed mercilessly to each other with great vigor and power, one of them in a cell directly above ours. Even after everyone else had said their goodnights, these two continued to yell at ear-shattering volume to each other for quite some time, the man in the cell above me cursing loudly at the several inmates who yelled what was obviously the equivalent of "Shut the hell up so we can sleep!" in their respective languages. Even after his compatriot across the prison yard fell silent, my upstairs neighbor, Mr. Chatty Cathy of the Ukraine, would repeatedly call out until the other man would wearily answer. I wanted to strangle both of them.

A good hour after lights out, the Ukrainians fell silent, and I lay on my bed in the dark, listening to Dorj snore. Right before

I managed to fall asleep, I got up and grabbed a one-inch piece of red colored pencil lead that Dorj had left on the table, the only writing implement in the cell. I picked a smooth spot on the dirty wall beside my bed. I wrote my name and the day's date in small block letters. Underneath that I made a single vertical mark.

My first day in prison was over.

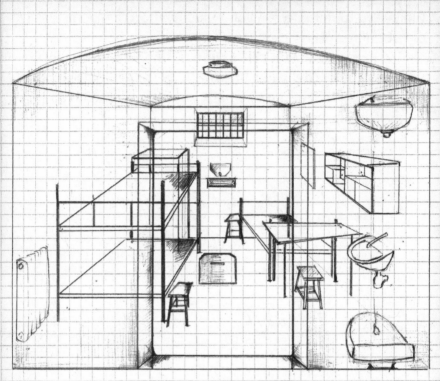

Drawing by GANBOLD
For your book.
05. 08. 2012

BLACK PANKRAC
BLACK DAYS
FINISH!

chapter ten

Pankrác Remand Prison sits south of the center of Prague, built in an area of the city known originally as the Pankrác plain. The word *Pankrác* is Czech for *Pancras*, the name of a citizen of Rome who was decapitated in 303 AD for refusing to make sacrifices to the Roman gods. The Catholic Church eventually canonized him, and Saint Pancras is often evoked, ironically enough in my case, against perjury and false witness, both of which I would fall victim to during my trial. However in the modern day Czech Republic, when most people think of the Pankrác neighborhood of Prague, they don't think about the ancient baroque church for which the area was named. They think about the grim prison I was in, a place where well over a thousand heads have literally rolled and buckets upon buckets of blood have been spilled over the course of its considerable history. The word Pankrác is virtually synonymous with the prison in Prague, for it is the defining landmark of the area, with good reason. At the time of my incarceration, Pankrác was one-hundred-and-twenty-three years old, serving as a prison for that entire time, and the state of the facility showed it.

Construction of Pankrác was started in July of 1885 and completed in August of 1889, the site at that time outside the city limits. In 1926 a large court building was added to the facility, connected to the prison by an underground tunnel still in use today. 1926 was also the year that the prison was approved as an execution ground, at that time conducted by hanging. On December 6, 1930, the first prisoner to be executed in Pankrác did the crazy legs dance at the end of a rope, and between that time and 1938, five more prisoners died by the noose. Everything would change in Pankrác in 1939 though, with the abrupt arrival of the Third Reich in Prague. Pankrác, like virtually every other government-run institution and building in then Czechoslovakia, was seized by the Nazis. The court building housed the Nazi "court," and the Gestapo's Special "Investigation" (i.e., interrogation by torture) Unit did their gruesome work within the prison. The Czech prison guards were quickly replaced by men far more suited to the brutality that was about to ensue, members of the infamous Waffen-SS, Hitler's elite police force that was the military arm of the Nazi party itself. Many members of the SS were later convicted as war criminals at the Nuremberg Trials, and the Waffen-SS itself was classified as a criminal organization due to its intimate ties with (and hideous activities carried out for) the Nazi Party. During the German occupation, thousands of Czechs were imprisoned in Pankrác—normal citizens, Resistance fighters, black marketeers, religious leaders, political figures, intellectuals, writers, artists, and musicians.

From early 1939 until the spring of 1943, inmates were being held in the prison until they were shipped off to either prisons within Germany, various concentration camps, or execution grounds outside of Pankrác itself. However in early April 1943, in a display of the ruthless efficiency typical of the Nazis, executions began to be carried out within the prison's walls. Why bother to send these innocent people all the way to *der Vaterland* when the Czechs could be greased for a lot cheaper in Prague? Pankrác already possessed a functional gallows, which was employed to execute an unknown number of prisoners on site during the German occupation. However, stringing someone up, dropping them, then removing their body and preparing the rope again for the next terrified victim was too time-consuming and just too much work for the Gestapo—more than likely some SS man complained about the backache he had gotten after lifting body after body as his co-worker removed the noose from yet another Czech stiff. Bullets cost way too much money to waste on executing these people, so, for a solution to their conundrum, the Nazis looked to another group of people they were currently kicking the shit out of: the French. Somewhere on the Left Bank of occupied Paris, a Nazi Party official was skimming happily through an illustrated book on the French Revolution, and inspiration struck. He rang up Prague for a chat with his old college drinking buddy from engineering school, and *Voilà! La Guillotine* arrived in Pankrác.

Between April 5, 1943 and April 26, 1945, prisoners were decapitated by the guillotine in one of three cells outfitted for this purpose, primarily in cell #1087, known cheerfully as "the axe room." The guillotine had a basket to catch falling heads; beneath the basket a sheet metal flue ran to a drain in the floor for convenient disposal of all that gushing, messy blood. Near the guillotine was a rack of meat hooks hanging on a track from the ceiling. After a prisoner had been beheaded, their body was simply rolled off the side of the guillotine into a wooden box. Or, I suppose if it was busy day (as I have read in some accounts), the body could be impaled on a hook, then slid a few feet away from the guillotine to make room for the next neck on the chopping block. Imagine that for a second if you will; walking into a room knowing you are about to be decapitated, and the first thing you see is a row of headless bodies hanging on hooks like slabs of beef in a meat locker. Any peace you may have been able to come to with your impending doom would probably be shaken up quite a bit once you entered that real-life chamber of horrors.

Meticulous notes kept by the head executioner, Alois Weiss, show that 1079 prisoners were beheaded in Pankrác, 175 of which were women. There were generally two execution sessions a week, with five to ten prisoners being beheaded in a row, although on August 4, 1944, Alois must have been in a particularly choppy mood, because twenty-nine people paid their first and last visit to the axe room. An execution took, from start to finish, an average of three minutes. The cells of those condemned to die (some for offenses as minor as slaughtering an extra unreported pig in order to feed their families) were within earshot of the axe room, so the sound of the one-hundred-and-thirty-pound sledge and blade repeatedly slamming home as it severed head after head was quite audible to those awaiting execution. Each week, posters would appear all over the city of Prague, listing those scheduled to die in the axe room. If you saw the name of one of your relatives on that list, you could count on receiving a bill in the mail soon from the Nazi party, along with a note explaining that if you didn't have the entire sum immediately, not to worry—you were allowed to pay the cost of your loved one's execution in monthly installments.

At the end of the war, the Nazis dismantled the guillotine and threw it in the Vltava river in an attempt to hide what they had done in Pankrác. But the Czechs had imprisoned the chief of the Gestapo guards, Paul Soppa, who under intense interrogation revealed the whereabouts of its disposal. The Czechs searched the river, found it, and returned it to Pankrác, where it was reassembled (to this day, the guillotine sits in the Pankrác axe room as a memorial to those who died beneath its blade). The postwar executions of Nazis and Nazi collaborators began, and between 1945 and 1948 one hundred and forty-seven of these people were executed in Pankrác, many of them dying in the very prison they had been the overlords of scant months before. The executioner Alois Weiss escaped to his homeland however, where bizarrely enough he would engage in a long and bitter fight with the German government to grant him a pension for his war-time duties as a "public servant." In the 1960s, Weiss even had the cold-blooded balls to write the Czech government requesting a letter confirming his activities in Pankrác, so that he could present it as "proof of employment" to the German government.

I don't know if the Czechs provided him with this, but I do know, in a stunning display of bureaucratic cowardice and capitulation, that the German government eventually granted him his pension, which he lived off of quite comfortably until his death at the age of eighty in Straubing, Germany. Interviews with Weiss in his later years revealed that he felt no guilt whatsoever for executing over a thousand innocent people—hey, he needed a job, right? Ah, those wacky days under the Third Reich . . .

In 1948 the Communist Party of Czechoslovakia seized power, and the new head cheese, a Stalinist president named Klement Gottwald, managed to dial it back a bit in Pankrác. During his five-year run as the most powerful man in Czechoslovakia, a mere 237 people were executed in the prison, 190 of these for political crimes (such as not being a Communist). Admittedly, Gottwald got a bit heavy-handed with the whole "purging" thing during his presidency, being posthumously awarded the title of "Worst Czech" in a 2005 poll, but the killing in Pankrác certainly didn't stop when he left office. From 1953, on through the 1968 Warsaw Pact invasion, and right into the bloody dawn that preceded 1989's peaceful Velvet Revolution (ending the Communist era of Czechoslovakia), an executioner found gainful employment in the prison. The last person to be put to death in Pankrác (and in what is now called the Czech Republic) was a charming man named Vladimír Lulek who had slaughtered his wife and four children. Besides Lulek, there were a few memorable others who died in Pankrác after taking a little dip in Ye Olde Blood Bath: in 1957 they strung up Václav Mrázek, a sexual predator and spa attendant who murdered at least seven women then burgled their homes (in addition to the murders he was convicted of 127 other crimes). Before being hanged in 1961, the lovely Miss Marie Fikákpvá confessed to killing at least 10 newborn babies— she liked to give them a good wallop or two upside their crying little noggins until they shut up. How did she have access to so many of these tiny victims? She was a nurse in the obstetrics department of a hospital, of course.

My favorite though, is Olga Hepnarová, a mentally ill truck driver who became the last woman to be executed in Pankrác in

1975. Olga hated society (especially her family), so after years of deliberating (she started out writing notes at age sixteen that said "I HATE PEOPLE!"), she decided to do something about it. On a sunny July day in 1973 she picked out a tram stop at the bottom of a hill and gunned it, slamming her massive truck into a crowd of about twenty-five people, killing eight and injuring others. To be fair to Olga, she did write a letter detailing her plan which she sent to not one, but *two*, different newspapers several days before she put the pedal to the metal. A portion of the letter read thusly:

I am a loner. A destroyed woman. A woman destroyed by people . . . I have a choice—to kill myself or to kill others. I choose—TO REVENGE MY HATERS. It would be too easy to leave this world as an unknown suicide. The society is too indifferent, rightly so. My verdict is: I, Olga Hepnarová, the victim of your bestiality, sentence you to the death penalty.

Of course the Czech postal system under the oppressive Communist regime wasn't exactly the model of efficiency, so the letter didn't reach the papers until two days after her revenge on her "haters" had already been exacted. Olga was brutal—after wrecking the truck into the people, reportedly she sat calmly in the cab until the cops came, saying, "I did it on purpose!" to any around her who could still listen, and when later asked if she felt remorse for her actions, replied "none." When it came time for her to face the music she did not go quietly into that good ol' truck drivin' night, but fought, vomited, and defecated herself, eventually collapsing and having to be dragged to the Pankrác gallows. Some folks go out kicking and screaming; Olga went out punching, puking, and pooping. You go, girl!

Total known number of executed people in Pankrác in 123 years: 1,580. The actual number is unknown, as only the deaths by guillotine during the Nazi era were recorded, not those who died from hanging, torture, forcible starvation, or just being beaten to death. Then there are all those who died within the prison walls at the hands of other prisoners, untreated diseases, or suicide. Some of this information I learned upon my release, but much of it I found out while still incarcerated. Pankrác is a spooky, spooky place, and at night I would lay in the dark in my cell, listening for the voices of the thousands who died within its walls.

Although in 1989 the death penalty went the way of the Communists in the new Czech Republic, Pankrác stayed open for business—why on earth would anyone want to get rid of a perfectly good one-hundred-year-old prison? The first President of the Czech Republic, Vaclav Havel, did a bit of time in Pankrác for political dissidence during the Communist era. Havel was a brilliant writer, political reformer, and humanitarian—in 2013 it came to light that he selflessly refused the 1991 Nobel Peace Prize nomination, instead suggesting it go to Daw Aung San Suu Kyi, the Myanmar opposition leader in Burma who remained under house arrest for more than two decades. Kyi won the award, and Havel went to his grave having never told anyone about this— what a magnificent human being. So hey, if it was good enough for Havel, then I suppose it was good enough for me, right? Then again, I have notoriously low standards, and several Human Rights organizations don't feel it's "good enough" for *anyone* to live in, especially not the section I was in—the remand section.

About half of the prisoners in Pankrác are serving time, while the other half are waiting to be sentenced (i.e., on remand, like myself). During the time of my detention in Pankrác, I was told there were approximately 1,400 prisoners in house. In 2006, the official capacity for the prison was 858 inmates. Somehow this was mysteriously increased to 1075 inmates by 2012—I say "mysteriously," because from what I could see, there hadn't been anything new added to the prison in decades. In fact, what was there was literally falling to pieces. The years of harsh Czech winters have not been kind to Pankrác, and the place is crumbling like a stale cookie in spots—I saw abandoned sections with broken glass windows that reminded me of downtown Detroit. In startling contrast, if you go to the Pankrác website, everything looks sort of old, but very well kept. There are photos of cells with freshly painted bars in their windows, a patch of green grass running alongside a spanking new razor-wire topped chain link fence, a polished wooden floor gymnasium with inmates playing some sort of indoor hockey, a freakin' *computer lab* with attentive prisoners gathered around brand new flat screen monitors, deeply engrossed in what can only be an educational attempt to better themselves, so that once they waltz out of Pankrác they can all go work for IT companies or whatever—I actually burst out laughing when my wife gave me the link to this site after I was released.

The interior of Pankrác looks absolutely nothing at all like those pictures. Perhaps things are somehow magically nicer and more modern in the area where inmates are serving out their sentences, but it's very doubtful—after all, in 2011, just months before I arrived in Pankrác, prison officials got wind of a five prison coordinated riot in protest of poor living conditions being planned in the Czech Republic. A large cache of hundreds of shanks and homemade slashing weapons was found in Pankrác alone. While I'm certainly glad it didn't kick off while I was incarcerated, I can understand the prisoners' frustration. The place is well over a century old, and its age is very apparent once you're deep behind its walls. In Washington, DC, lobbyists for the thriving prison-industrial complex would have a field day with the unsalvageable conditions of the entire facility; in fact, if Pankrác were in America, they would bulldoze that place quicker than you could say "biohazard lawsuit." All it would take would be one *60 Minutes*–style exposé focused solely on the levels of toxic mold in the cells, and Wal-Mart would be laying the foundation of their newest superstore before the dust from the wrecking ball had a chance to settle, while fifty miles away, BigHouseBuilders, Inc. would be explaining to some small rural community how the construction of a gargantuan new hoosegow, while slightly altering (i.e., *destroying*) the natural beauty of their hick burg, was going to super-charge their economy.

Again, I can't say for certain how the "other half" lives, but I damn sure know how prisoners on remand live. Unless you were lucky enough to have someone living nearby in Prague who would come to Pankrác, pick up your dirty laundry, and drop off clean clothes for you, you were not allowed to keep your own clothing and had to make due with whatever the prison decided to provide you with every two weeks or so. These "clothes" were often little more than rags; literally thread bare t-shirts riddled with rips and holes, and oddly sewn pants that arrived ripped, re-sewn with odd bits of homemade thread, and tied together in places with scraps of bed sheets in order to fit whomever they had been issued to previously (I had to do a ghetto tailoring job on every pair of pants I was issued in order for them to stay around my rapidly shrinking waist line). Gathered together daily in our prison gear in the yard for our one hour of fresh air, the posse on my cell block resembled a small and highly undisciplined army of semi-homeless guys.

Each one of the three different cells I was housed in during my stay was utterly filthy—even if prisoners were given adequate cleaning supplies to scrub and tidy up their cells, which we weren't (we were given a dirty bucket of hot water once a week— that's it. No mop, no bleach, no detergent—we used a scrap of old rag carpet to scrub the floor with), the cell walls were crumbling, the paint was peeling, the plumbing was leaking, the mortar around door frames and cell windows was disintegrating. It was incontestable that nothing had been done to improve the conditions of these cells in years. Dust, dirt, and mildew were more than abundant, as well as various roaches and silverfish, scores of which I would terminate with extreme prejudice. There was also no ventilation in any of the cells, aside from one small window, which provided almost no air flow because our cell doors were kept locked for twenty-three hours a day. As we were only allowed two five-minute showers per week (thank God at least there was hot water in the foul-smelling, grimy shower cell), things in the unventilated cell could get a little . . . *tart*, as one might imagine.

Regular prisoners, according to the Pankrác website, can avail themselves of all sorts of amenities and activities in order to reduce the tension that comes with being incarcerated. I wouldn't know, because I was on remand, along with half the prison. Unless I had a visit from my lawyer or had to see a doctor, I spent twenty-three solid hours a day locked in a dirty cell. The website also states that the average length of a remand prisoner's stay is 100 days, but I met plenty of men who had been waiting to face their charges at trial for much longer than that. The only other native English-speaking prisoner I met, an Irishman I became acquainted with near the end of my stay, told me he had already been in Pankrác on remand for over six months at that point. He hadn't even been *charged* yet. Apparently, the prosecuting attorney couldn't make up his mind on whether to stick my newfound friend from the Emerald Isles with tax evasion or embezzlement. Furthermore, on the website it states that prisoners are separated according to the type of crime they are charged with, violent versus nonviolent offenders. This is also pure hogwash—I was being charged with a violent crime, as were other men I knew who faced even more serious charges, yet I talked to inmates who were charged with possession of drugs, shoplifting, driving while intoxicated, and in the case of my Irish friend, some sort of purely monetary offense. All of us—manslaughterers, drunk drivers, deadly assaulters, rapists, junkies, tax evaders and shoplifters—were in the yard together everyday, one big happy family.

––––––––

*P*rison is not for the weak minded. It is no wonder to me, even after doing such a short amount of time, that so many men and women released from prisons cannot function in normal society anymore and wind up back behind bars again and again. Being locked up causes a profound psychic shift to occur, and the mentality of an incarcerated person is nothing like that of the average person walking free down the street of their hometown. You have to keep your wits about you, you have to watch your back at all times, and everything you do and say is scrutinized, not just by the guards, but by your fellow prisoners as well. Your very life can depend on awareness of these facts. My good friend Cody Lundin, a world famous survival and primitive living skills instructor I train with, says that 90 percent of any survival situation is mental. If you cannot control your head, your body's toast—you have to maintain a positive mental attitude or else you're a goner. I kept his words firmly in the forefront of my consciousness during my time in Pankrác, and I used the only weapon I had available to combat the experience—my mind. I stayed focused, tried to mind my own business, and waited to see what each day would bring. In this process, I tried to learn about myself by looking at my time as a test I was being put to; a test that held dire consequences for failure.

I found out I was strong enough to get by. That was more than enough for me. I don't need to prove to myself or anyone else that I am some sort of Billy Badass, or find out further what prison life is like. Especially not in *Vazební Veznice Pankrác*.

It's a hell hole.

July 4th, 2012
Pankrác Prison
Prague, Czech Republic.

WELL HOLY SHIT IT JUST STRUCK ME ~~TODAY~~ JUST
NOW WHAT TODAY IS — JULY 4th & I AM IN A
CZECH PRISON! OH, THE IRONY OF IT ALL!
I AM CURRENTLY WHISTLING "THE STAR SPANGLED
BANNER" IN HONOR OF MY COUNTRY'S
INDEPENCE — IT JUST GAVE ME GOOSEBUMPS —
OF COURSE THIS ~~OH~~ INSANELY WEIRD PATRIOTIC
MOMENT WAS FOLLOWED BY MONGOLIAN
ROOMMATE, WHO ~~IS~~ NOW ~~WHAT~~ WHISTLING
"WE WISH ~~YOU~~ A MERRY CHRISTMAS!" —
HOLY CRAP THIS IS SURREAL (& TO BE
HONEST, REALLY BIZARRELY HILARIOUS
TO ME). MAN, WHAT I WOULDN'T DO
TO BE AT HOME IN RVA, BARBQUEING
HOT DOGS & BURGERS & STEAKS & DRINKING
A COLD NA BEER, RELAXING WITH
MY BEAUTIFUL WIFE & GOING OUT TO
WATCH SOME FIREWORKS LATER. I WILL

chapter eleven

Spending twenty-three hours a day in the same room, even with the most fascinating of conversationalists, would drive most people completely insane. My cellmate and I didn't share a language, so a good old-fashioned argument about politics or even which Led Zeppelin album was the best (*Houses of the Holy*, of course) wasn't in the cards for cell #505. Even after I began to teach Dorj some rudimentary English, I soon discovered that while he had an amazing talent for learning languages, he would never be mistaken for a member of the intelligentsia focused on expanding his mental horizons. If I were to write a personals ad for Dorj, it would read something like this:

Single/overweight/Mongolian/male seeks like minded/stomached single/Mongolian/female for companionship. Primary interests include: slurping food, drinking vodka, making paper swans, telling racist jokes about Gypsies/other Asian ethic groups/U.S. President Barack Obama, wrecking vehicles, sudoko puzzles, making fun of anyone who does any sort of physical exercise or work, mocking those who use paper for anything other than making swans/wiping butt/rolling cigarettes (esp. reading and/or writing). Must possess firm belief in superiority of Mongol race. Women seeking employed, motivated male need not apply.

While Dorj wasn't the brightest burning candle on the birthday cake, I can have an interesting talk with just about anyone of any background, as I find a large amount of people deeply fascinating. Humans are strange organisms, and I believe there is something to be learned from every single person on earth, even if it's only what *not* to do in life. Or maybe I just enjoy talking to folks different than myself and hearing about their way of living, which is definitely one reason I enjoy traveling so much—there are so many stories out there waiting to be heard, coming from so many different viewpoints and cultural backgrounds. Either way, I was genuinely excited to learn a bit about Mongolia from an actual Mongol, but in the end it wasn't the lack of a conversational cultural exchange in our cell that led me to teaching Dorj English.

It was the whistling.

The nameless Mongolian tune that sounded so soothing chirping softly from Dorj's chubby lips during my first few hours in Pankrác very quickly became a searing white-hot needle of off-key pure Asian pain puncturing my eardrums. It was like the fabled Chinese Water Torture, where endless droplets of water fall individually onto a bound victim's forehead, eventually driving them insane with the constricted and banal repetitious predictability of it all. This was Mongolian Whistling Torture, and hearing the same two-bar chorus during my every waking moment was producing the same result. I had never met a more relentless or uninspired whistler in my life, and it only took a few hours of this to make me edgy. I had noticed that, aside from slurping his food, the only time the man would stop whistling was when I attempted to communicate with him.

I sat on my bed, pondering the immensity of the task before me. *My God, I am totally doomed,* I thought. *How am I going to teach this guy English with no Czech or Mongolian dictionary or basic grammar primer? My grammar* sucks—*what in the hell is a "predicate nominative" again? I should have paid more attention to that sentence diagramming stuff in 6th grade. HOLY COW, I am* most definitely *going to commit a violent crime if he doesn't stop whistling soon . . .* I was beginning to sink into a deep pit of linguistic despair when I realized I had better just suck it up and get started before I choked the whistling, slurping life from him.

"Me teach you Englishky," I Tarzaned to Dorj, who sat up from his bed with a look of surprise on his face, as if he couldn't believe I was going to actually *do something* besides lay on my rack, stare at the ceiling, and listen to him whistle. I grabbed my stack of prison regulations, sat down at our table, found a page with a blank backside, and with our bit of red pencil lead began to write out numbers in a column, from one through twenty, then increasing by tens, hundreds, thousands, etc., on up to one million. Dorj watched me intently as I did this, leaning heavily on my shoulder as he often would later whenever I was writing or reading in an attempt to distract me from my foolish academic pursuits. I lay the piece of paper on the table, took my spoon (which I thought of thereafter as *The Spoon of Teaching*), and pointed with its bent handle end to the first number on the paper.

"One. Englishky, this is *one*," I said firmly.

"One," Dorj said immediately and without difficulty. Hot damn, the kid was a learner.

"Two. Englishky, this is *two*," I said, moving the spoon down to the next number.

"Two," Dorj repeated.

Three and *thirteen* gave him a small amount of trouble, as the "th" sound apparently isn't used in the Mongol tongue, but beyond those two minor hiccups we reached twenty without much incident. Maybe this whole teaching thing wasn't such a bad gig after all; Dorj wasn't whistling, and I was feeling down right professorial as we started at one and began over, counting to twenty three times in a row. As we began counting for the third time, Dorj began to pause and write the Czech word for each number beside its numeric symbol, sounding out the Czech pronunciation for me as we went along. I asked him to write out the Mongol equivalent, and he started to, but I quickly called it off, as I had no hope of remembering the vertical script of Genghis Khan's folk, and attempting to say these words was even harder. Mongolian is a sibilant language with many odd tonal variations, and during my time in Pankrác I was only able to pick up a smattering of it. Czech, although still a very difficult language, was much easier to learn, so Dorj taught me primarily Czech words and phrases as I taught him English. I learned quite a bit of Czech from him, but I almost never heard him use it outside of our cell; it was as if he had been struck mute every time we left #505.

In fact, Dorj was fluent in four different languages (Mongolian, Czech, Russian, and Korean), but acted most of the time as if he only understood Mongolian, which was actually quite a clever maneuver in prison. Guards and other prisoners tended to not pay much attention to him, thinking he was just some lazy Mongol who didn't really understand what was going on around him. Guards wouldn't bother to get upset with him if he didn't immediately do what they asked, as they assumed he had no idea of what they were talking about. Other prisoners didn't ask him for anything for the same reason, and (more importantly) would speak openly in Czech around him about things they might have remained more guarded about had they known he was listening. Once we had cobbled together our primitive mash up of Czech, English, and Mongolian, Dorj was able to fill me in on many of the shadier things going on around us, things I might have not known about had he not been an "unseen" pair of ears.

Unlike myself, no one knew much about Dorj, where he had come from (other than Mongolia), or why he was in prison. He was just another faceless inmate waiting to go either home or to another cell. I envied him his anonymity sometimes, but mostly it came in rather handy in getting the dirt on what was going on in the cellblock. Although eventually he did drive me almost completely insane with his whistling and slurping, for the most part I was grateful to have him as a cellmate. He wasn't a weasel or a mooch (although he displayed zero gratitude for what I did share with him). He wasn't wheeling and dealing from our cell. Beyond his odd racist tendencies (he hated all other Asian ethnic groups, and often referred to President Barack Obama as a "chimpanz") and total disdain for any physical or intellectual activity beyond cleaning our cell or doing sudoko puzzles, he didn't constantly spout off an opinion on much of anything at all. Dorj was just Dorj; a rather simple, yet simultaneously exceedingly clever, chubby Asian whistler. It certainly could have been a lot worse—I could have been stuck with some burly gangster, rapist, or axe murderer who wanted to talk all day long about Czech politics or soccer. As it was, Dorj was just a drunk waiting to be deported for lack of a visa.

Until we began English lessons weightier than counting to twenty, Dorj and I communicated in a confusing (and often hilarious) mixture of pantomime, crude picture drawing, lots of pointing at ourselves and each other, and various sound effects thrown in for good measure. It was like living out a sitcom scripted about two alcoholic Neanderthals busted for some tribal transgression, then locked in a tiny cave together to grunt their way through an endless and extremely convoluted game of criminal charades. Sometimes we would notice how silly we looked mid-way through attempting to act and grunt out some complex concept to each other, and would burst out laughing. The whole thing was completely ridiculous, and I often wished for a camera to film our more ape-like attempts at communication. On either my first or second day in Pankrác, it was during one of these pantomime sessions I learned why Dorj was in prison.

"You," he said pointing at me, followed by "Pankrác," and him pointing to the floor of our cell. Then he turned his palms up, rolled his eyes, and shrugged his shoulders in an exaggerated caricature of a man wondering about something. I realized he was asking me why I was in prison. I also knew that trying to pantomime being a member of a heavy metal band on tour who had just been suddenly arrested on suspicion of killing a fan of my band basically onstage was going to be way beyond my abilities as a mime.

I thought about it for a minute, then said "Policie say," made my hand into a quacking duckbill to indicate talking, then puffed out my chest and frowned like an angry cop. "Policie say. Policie say," I continued, still making the talking hand gesture.

"Ah, policie," Dorj replied, indicating that he understood what I meant.

Then I pointed to myself and said "Me," then mimed a struggle with an invisible opponent, finally pushing them away from me. Then I imitated my opponent falling and hitting his head on the edge of the desk and passing out. Dorj nodded in comprehension. Then he looked at me, suddenly yanked his head to the side and stuck his tongue out in an imitation of a dead man hanging at the end of the noose.

"Kaput?" he asked.

"Yeah. Kaput," I replied, shaking my head.

"Ay, ya ya ya. *Moc Spatny*," he replied, uttering what I would soon learn was the Czech phrase for "very bad." I would hear that phrase many times daily in Pankrác. It was definitely a *moc spatny* kind of place.

"Yeah. It's a pretty screwed up situation, buddy," I said. Dorj looked at me in incomprehension. Time to change the subject.

"You. Pankrác. Why?" I asked, repeating the same series of gestures Dorj had when asking me why I was in prison. Dorj raised his eyebrows and pointed to himself, an innocent expression on his face, as if to say *Who? Moi?*

"Yes. You. Dorj. Pankrác. Why?" I repeated.

Dorj's face took on a positively cherubic expression as he gently placed his open palm against his chest in a gesture conveying delicacy and refinement of nature.

"I . . . ," he said with a dramatic pause, "student. I student. PANKRÁC ACADEME! Bahahahahahaha!" and almost fell off his bed laughing. I started laughing as well, and pointing to myself and saying, "I student, too!" We had a good laugh about our enrollment at Pankrác Academy; then, through a very long and very complex series of gestures and sound effects involving car crashes, heavy drinking, airplanes taking off, horseback riding, and falconry I finally deduced that Dorj: a) loved to drink vodka,

b) loved to drink vodka and drive at the same time, c) had already done a year in a different Czech prison for completely demolishing a truck while drinking said beloved vodka (he pointed out a gnarly scar running down the side of his face obtained during the wreck), and d) was here now because he did not have the proper visa to be in the country. How had he gotten caught without a visa? By drinking vodka and wrecking another truck, of course. Dorj had been in Pankrác for five days before I had arrived, and had been given a hundred-day sentence for his latest exploits, at the completion of which he would promptly be put on a Eastbound plane and deported back to Mongolia. What would he do once he was back home?

"Pure vodka," he replied, tilting an imaginary bottle back and making guzzling noises. Dorj truly loved vodka, and in a minimal manner of speaking, he loved to talk about how much he loved vodka. I heard him wistfully say "pure vodka" (always accompanied by the drinking gesture) several times a day. Thank God we didn't have any vodka, or he would have been shit housed 24/7. I was pretty sure that if he was a disgusting mess when he ate sober, I damn sure didn't want to find out what he would be like drunk at dinner time. Looking on the brighter side of things, since it was pure vodka that had put him in Pankrác, I understood him on a cellular level pretty much immediately—the man was an alcoholic, just like me. I know how alcoholics think, *all* alcoholics; therefore I know how to talk to them, even in caveman-esque sign language. This made teaching him English a lot simpler. After just one week, Dorj had developed an impressive vocabulary, and had an instinctive grasp of pronunciation, even though English is very different than Mongolian. There was no doubt about it, the man had a gift for learning foreign languages, but as previously stated, no one outside our cell knew this. I realized this my second day in Pankrác, when I went out for my first daily "walk."

Prisoners on remand are allowed one hour outside their cell for exercise a day, as my sheet of printed regulations stated, and I was very nervous about going out to "the yard" for the first time.

Visions of getting jumped and/or shanked were running through my head, as I didn't know how the other prisoners were going to react to my (very publicly known) presence. Maybe the young man I was accused of killing had a relative who was locked up in Pankrác, or maybe there would be a prisoner who had a bad experience with Americans and would try to take it out on me. Or maybe someone would want to test the new guy—this is quite common in prison. I had to be ready for anything. I had been on the tier of Richmond City Jail for a bit while waiting for bail, beyond the drunk tank and into the population, and I knew that it was best to mind your own business and steer clear of trouble. I also knew that sometimes trouble comes looking for you, and when it does, you have to maintain face or else be judged a punk. Once you're perceived as a punk in prison, you either have to publicly change that perception, or you have to accept and deal with all the abuse that comes along with it for the rest of your time. I had no intention of causing any problems in Pankrác, but three indisputable facts lay before me: 1) I was in prison, 2) I was not locked up in some special isolation unit for my own protection, like you hear happens to celebrities or politicians when they have to do time, and 3) people who don't even attempt to stick up for themselves don't do well in the general population of prison. That's just the way it is.

I didn't want to become known as a trouble maker or do any extra time for brawling, but I wasn't going to let anyone push me around and not fight back. There was no way I was going to be judged a punk in there—I was way too frightened to allow that to happen. Almost all violence is born of fear, I believe, and I don't mind telling you I was very, very scared of a lot of things at that point in my life. Scared men commit violent acts, and I was prepared to react with extreme force, even cruelty, if I had to. By extreme force and cruelty, I mean stomping on someone's knee-cap with an inside kick until it reversed itself. Ripping their nose completely off their face with my teeth. Permanently crushing their windpipe with a closed fist. Gouging their eye sockets until a bloody eyeball popped out on the end of my thumb. Hurting someone as badly as I could as quickly as I could before they hurt me. These were the type of things that ran through my mind in Pankrác when I thought about fighting, not a gentlemanly boxing match. This was prison, not middle school. That's not tough guy talk, that's the reality of how frightened I was. I'm in no way saying I'm a hard ass, but I've taken a proper beating or two in my life and lived, mostly when I was (surprise, surprise) drunk off my ass. I certainly don't enjoy getting my ass kicked, but I know what it's like, I don't fall to pieces at the thought of it, and if I get in a fight, I know I'll eventually heal . . . if it's not too bad. But I also know that I am a grown man, not an eight-year-old boy, and that a real fight with another grown man could result in severe injuries or even death for one or both of us. I certainly had no wish to maim or kill anyone, but if that's what it took to defend myself, then that is what I would do.

Since I've gotten sober I haven't had to fight; I don't enjoy conflict, and I absolutely despise violence, but if it is going to occur for whatever reason and I'm forced to engage in it, make no mistake about it—I will commit, and I will commit 100 percent. While I am in no way a pacifist, it would take some extreme circumstances to drive me to react with violence to a situation these days—I would have to feel threatened, or feel that my loved ones were in danger. I would rather walk away from a needless confrontation. I have nothing to prove to anyone—I am a grown man, not a high school bully. But prison was one long set of extreme circumstances I couldn't walk away from. I automatically felt threatened just being there, so from the second I walked into Pankrác, I knew I might have to fight, perhaps for my life. This was very scary, but my mentality was such that I would rather take one good beating up front instead of a hundred on the back end. Or, even worse, be beaten up, judged easy pickings, and then raped.

Rape. Now *that's* something that *truly* terrified me about prison. I thought about it quite a bit during my first few days in Pankrác—who wouldn't? I've known both women and men who have been raped, and they have survived, healed, and gone on to live full, productive, happy lives. It is possible to recover from such an unimaginable violation. I knew this. But I'd been through a lot in my life already, and I had no intention of having to experience recovery from being raped if I could help it. If it happened to me, it happened—and it *does* happen in real life prison. I knew this, and I knew I would survive it if it happened to me. But I was determined not to be anyone's bitch, not if I could help it. Once again, this meant constantly keeping my guard up and being prepared for extreme violence, and once again, that's not tough-guy talk, that's pure, naked, shaking-in-your-boots *fear*. When I am really scared, and it's either my ass or yours, I will do my damn best to make sure it's *yours*, every single time without exception.

I. Was. Really. Scared.

———

After lunch my second day in prison, Tom Selleck came banging on our cell door, opened it, and motioned us out. Dorj explained to me that it was time to go out for our walk. According to my prison regulations, I did not have to go outside if I did not wish to; but, despite a healthy amount of fear, I knew it was best to go ahead and just get it over with. I had no intention of hiding in my cell the entire time I was in prison if I didn't have to. It would have driven me nuts; after just twenty-four hours in Pankrác, I was already really sick of looking at the same four walls while Dorj whistled the hours away. We tucked in our shirts, put on our shoes, and walked outside the cell to be searched as we had been yesterday. After we had been frisked, we walked to the other end of the hall where most of the same men we had gotten drug tested with the day before were waiting. We walked single

file up a short flight of stairs, the guard opened a heavy door to
the outside, I took a deep breath, thought, *Well, here goes nothing,*
and out we went.

Outside, instead of the large open area full of prisoners that
I was expecting to see, was a small, empty, enclosed square. On
one side of it was an elevated walkway with two guards patrolling
it on top. Beneath the walkway was a kind of open air concrete
hallway with steel doors set in either side every twenty feet or so.
We walked down the hallway until the guard told us to stop in
front of one of the doors. He opened the door, we went inside,
and he slammed it shut, sliding a heavy bolt home. Apparently
we weren't going to a prison yard today. This was nothing more
than a concrete cage.

The enclosure we were in measured approximately ten by
twelve feet. The plain concrete walls stood about ten feet tall and
were covered in graffiti, either scratched into the surface or written in pen, pencil, or magic marker. The open-air roof of the enclosure was capped with a grid of heavy welded rebar, and the
floor was rough black asphalt. There was nothing else in the pen.
It looked like something cattle would be herded into before being
led off to the slaughter. There were about ten of us in this small
area. This was where we were supposed to "walk"? Like most of
the other men, I picked a spot against a wall with some sunshine
and sat down. The sun felt good on my face, cigarettes immediately began to be passed around, and I began to relax.

Dorj had brought his two rolled up cigarettes out with him,
and he gave me one. I bummed us a light, and we sat smoking as
Rene, the short gypsy I had met the day before, immediately began chattering away in between drags of his own smoke. He talked
and talked, making odd sound effects to punctuate his words. He
seemed to be telling an endless story, and when he would imitate
another person talking, he always changed his tone of voice and
said the same thing: "karfarnukee, karfarnukee, kee kee kee." It
reminded me of the muffled, indistinguishable voices of adults in

the Charlie Brown TV specials. This recurring nonsensical phrase became Rene's nickname—Kee Kee Kee. The other men in the pen listened, laughed at times, and there was general talking amongst everyone except Dorj and me as Rene finished his story. I noticed that all the *Roma* sat together, including a new one who looked like Al Pacino. He even had a nasty scar running down his face, so that is what I called him—Scarface (he was flattered when I mentioned this to him later). There were two other men who had not been with us the day before, a skinny kid with a tight buzz cut who couldn't have been more than twenty-one, and a slightly chubby man in his thirties with a goatee and the sides of his head razored down to the skin. As everyone sat around smoking and talking, the goateed man turned to me and spoke.

"So, you're the famous American that's in all the newspapers, eh? My name is Felix. I heard you teaching your cellmate to count to twenty earlier—my cell is right next to yours. You should get a job teaching in Prague, haha," he said in perfect English.

"*Holy fuck*—you speak English!" I said, stating the obvious.

"Yes. Yes, I do. How do you like our beautiful Czech prison so far?" he replied with a laugh.

Being able to speak to someone actually fluent in my native language was like Christmas in July for me. It was as if Felix (not his real name, for reasons that shall be made apparent later) had suddenly been beamed down from outer space to assist me, the only other human inhabitant on a strange and claustrophobic planet filled with aliens who communicated in a series of karfar-nukee kee kees. I had many questions, and Felix was kind enough to answer them all the best he could. The basement cellblock we were on was the entry point for all prisoners entering Pankrác, and inmates remained there for a month on average before being moved upstairs into general population; sometimes going sooner, sometimes remaining longer. The basement, which I came to think of as "The Dungeon" (since, aside from a brighter paint scheme, that was precisely what it was), was a place where new prisoners were monitored for signs of depression. This made perfect sense—if you want to find out if an inmate is feeling a little down in the dumps, naturally you should stick them in the dankest, darkest, most unhealthy, and *depressing* place in the entire prison and see how they do. Felix had already been in the dungeon for more than a month and a half, his extended stay the result of a fool-hardy bit of truth telling.

"You will be sent to see the prison psychiatrist sometime soon. When she asks you how you like the place, tell her you love it. Tell her you *couldn't be happier* and are making lots of new friends. Whatever you do, do *not* tell her the truth, or you will be stuck down here forever. I was supposed to be moved out of this shit-hole weeks ago," he said.

"Why are you still here then?" I asked, guessing the answer.

"She asked me how I was doing and what did I think of the place so far, so I told her. How did she think I was doing, for God's sake? I had just been arrested and thrown in prison with a bunch of criminals. This place is a rubbish heap. Was I supposed to say that I wanted to live here forever? I guess that answer did not satisfy her very much, so here I am," he said with a shake of his head.

I made a mental note to act happier than a baby in a barrel of boobies when I went to see the prison shrink. I just hoped she wouldn't be asking me why an inkblot looked like a butterfly or showing me anymore depressing pictures. Beyond advice on what to lie to prison staff about, Felix also filled me in on the nuts and bolts of day-to-day life in the Dungeon. The lights came on every morning at 6:00 a.m., except for Saturday and Sunday when we were allowed to sleep in until seven. We had to be up and with our beds made well before 6:30, which was when breakfast came, except on Saturday and Sunday when the first meal of the day arrived at 7:30. Lunch was at 11:30, dinner at four, with lights out every night at nine p.m. sharp. A few times a day, a trusty would come by with tea, or hot water if you had any instant coffee or your own tea bags. You could buy these things and many others (toilet paper, cigarettes, deodorant, snacks etc.) from the prison store by writing down your order on a sheet a guard would bring by your cell Wednesday morning. The guard would return for the sheet that evening during his nightly mail rounds, when he would pick up any correspondence the prisoner wished to have mailed, usually sometime before six p.m. The prisoner's order would be delivered to his cell the next morning. No matter how much money an inmate had in his account, there was a maximum limit on how much he could spend per week at the prison store. I assumed this policy was intended to prevent those inmates lucky enough to have a lot of money on their books from becoming major players in the shadow economy that controls the population of every prison. This economy dictates the interactions of prisoners just as much as its guards (who are often involved in it themselves). Despite what my sheet of regulations said about goods bought from the prison store costing the same as on the outside, prices for things in the prison store were roughly double what they were in a normal store, except cigarettes and rolling tobacco, whose price matching was somehow ensured by the state because of a tax stamp on every packet and bag. I never understood this, as the state was making plenty of money off of everything else in the store, so why not smokes? Maybe the heads of the department of corrections and the Czech version of the ATF didn't get along; I didn't know and I didn't care—the smokes were cheap in there, and I wasn't about to quit while I was locked up.

When I was arrested, I had a single US fifty dollar bill and about 200 Euros in my wallet, which I was told would be converted into Czech crowns and put into my prison account if I so desired. The prison would automatically deduct crowns for the toiletries that had already been issued me, and any money I had left over on my books would be returned to me when I was released from prison and any state mandated legal debts I had were paid. (The Czech government, as of this writing, has made no attempt to return any of the few thousand crowns I had left in my prison account. Hey yo, Mister Prison Accountant—*I want my money.* I know it wasn't that much in the big scheme of things, but it's still *my* money. Pay me, homie.) I didn't know how long it would take to have my money changed into the local currency, but I figured it couldn't be more than two or three days. (I was very wrong about that, in fact I'm not sure my money was ever converted or if it went into some prison clerk's wallet.) As it was Sunday, I would just have to tough it out smoking-wise until Thursday morning, when I would immediately have cigarettes galore delivered to my cell. I began to imagine all the glorious packs of smokes that would be stacked up in my locker like bricks of gold in Fort Knox, and I began to feel magnanimous, asking Felix what brand of cigs the store sold and if they carried his, because come Thursday morning, I was going to hook my perfect-English-speaking, endless-question-answering, main-man-next-door up!

"Thank you, but there is a slight problem. This Thursday is a bank holiday in the Czech Republic, and the prison store will be closed. Orders for this coming week were already taken two days ago, and will be delivered Wednesday instead. You will not be able to have anything delivered until next Thursday, I'm afraid," he said.

A bank holiday? You gotta be kidding me, I thought. We were prisoners, not accountants. Where in the hell would the prison store clerk (whom I assumed was a trusty) go for a bank holiday? To their vacation cell on the other side of the prison? Besides the cigarettes, I had hoped to get some writing paper, a pen or two, and some envelopes and stamps to write my family and band. I had nothing to read and I needed to exercise my mind somehow. Felix told me he had some extra paper he would give me tomorrow during our walk, which I was very grateful for and promised to repay him. What about books, though? I had read something about going to the prison library; did they have a selection of English books I could check out? When would we get to go to the library?

"Oh, we don't go to the library. Once or twice a week the trusty comes by with a cart and gives you two or three books, whatever he feels like. You can ask him if the library person will look for some English books for you though—he might do this for you if he is in a good mood. I think they might have a few. You can have a newspaper delivered to your cell everyday if you like, for a very small fee. You have to submit a request in writing for this during the morning report, though," he said.

Things were looking worse and worse by the second. No cigarettes for at least a week and a half. No trip to the library. A ghoulish trusty who didn't speak English who may or may not try to find me some sort of book I could read. This completely sucked. Well, what was the morning report, and what kind of newspapers did they have to order?

"Every morning you can give the guard who comes by after breakfast a written request for anything you may need—a trip to the doctor, permission to use the telephone, scheduling a family visit. You have to write it out and he will turn it in to the office where someone will review your request. As far as the newspapers, the prison has all the major Czech papers. I think you can order foreign ones, but you must write a request out for this and turn it in during th-"

"Morning report. Right. So, I'm assuming the morning report needs to be written in Czech," I said.

"Of course," Felix replied.

————

Getting anything done in Pankrác, as I would find out, was tedious for even the most experienced of Czech prisoners. Everything seemed to require some written form or the other, none of which I could read, which then took forever to be reviewed. With the exception of *robot*, I couldn't write a single word of Czech. The prison regulations I had been given had not been updated in years, and policies and ways of doing things had changed. Getting things done often depended upon the mood of the particular guard you were dealing with, who may or may not make sure anything you had requested was sent through the appropriate channels in a timely fashion, perhaps even bending a rule or two for you from time to time. Actually, I had no idea of what many of the actual rules really were, as each guard behaved completely differently, some changing in attitude from day to day and situation to situation. The only guard in the Dungeon whose actions and attitude was ever 100 percent consistent with me was also the only guard who spoke more than ten or twenty words of English. This would have been a lucky situation for me, except for the fact that that guard was Bradley. Bradley was consistent all right—he was consistently a dick. While I'm sure every prison has its fair share of bureaucratic hoops through which prisoners attempting to get something done have to jump (as well as jerk-off guards like Bradley), Pankrác seemed particularly inefficient, random, and down right crazy to me. As I have nothing else to compare it to, I could very well be wrong, although any prison that would make Pankrác appear efficient would have to be a complete clusterfuck. The language barrier certainly didn't help me figure out how to accomplish anything.

After we had been in the cage for an hour, the guard returned to bring us back to our cells for the next twenty-three hours. On the short walk through the yard, I noticed many men turning and craning their heads to look at an ancient clock tower that had been obscured from our view in the pen. I turned and looked at it, too—an hour had passed. The tower was the highest point I could see in the interior of the prison, and the clock face on the side visible to me had seen better days—the whole thing looked as if it had just barely survived a bombing raid. The hands of its clock were rusted, its face peeling and missing chunks in several places, entire numbers ripped away to reveal its plywood subsurface. It was a sad looking clock, but I would come to love it more than any other, since for an extended period it was my only way of telling time.

For a few weeks, time as a unit of measure with which to judge my passage through each day simply did not exist for me in Pankrác. The usual concept of time becomes meaningless in prison, especially in a basement cell with one small window facing a concrete wall. Humans both love and despise time. We love it when we have enough of it to finish the things we need to do, or "free time" to do as we wish. We also loathe it when there is an abundance of it, such as the start of our shift at a crappy job, or a particular long and brutal winter. We also detest it when we do not have enough of it, such as when a relative or friend dies "before their time." I have done both, alternately loving and hating time, throughout my life. But love it or hate it, I could always tell my "place" within a twenty-four hour period simply by looking at my watch, and thereby know I was moving forward from minute to minute. The police had taken my watch when I was arrested, and I could not see the passing of the day with the sun's journey across the sky; there were only varying levels of indirect light fading into darkness. Without a watch, time became endless and even more amorphous than it already was. The small marks I made on our cell wall each evening and the moldering clock tower I caught a brief glimpse of once a day became the only way I could tell how long I had been in prison, until my wife brought me a cheap watch during her one visit. I had already been incarcerated for more than two weeks at that point, so my concept of how long I had been away from the outside world was severely askew. I had experienced this feeling before, albeit in a much more pleasant location.

———

A few years ago I spent nine days in the Arizona desert with my friend Cody Lundin on an aboriginal living skills/ survival trip. I was allowed to take no "pre-made" technology except for a bedroll, two wool blankets, a fixed-blade carbon steel knife, a water bottle, and the clothes on my back. After the first six days, everything was taken away except for one blanket and minimal clothing. I spent the majority of that trip, the entire first six days, making everything I would need to survive from natural materials—stone knives, cordage, a bow drill to make fires, a cat tail sleeping mat, hunting weapons and traps, water containers. If I didn't gather it or kill it, I didn't eat. I don't like starving, so I learned to love the taste of pack rat and rattlesnake and cactus fruit. I lived by the fire and became a cave man. It was immensely disconcerting for me at first to not have a watch; then, as I realized that "time" was not important, it became immensely relaxing—I was living by nature's rhythms, by my internal clock. "Time" disappeared. It was wonderful. When we returned to society, everyone seemed so foolish and abrasive to me, hurrying to do this or that. I missed the wilderness; I missed being free of the constraints of *time*. Prison was nothing like this—I was in an unnatural place, and heavily constrained by an unmeasurable sense of time that loomed gargantuan over me like an invisible axe blade.

I really enjoyed seeing that clock tower every day. In a way, the clock tower allowed me to know where I stood in relation to the rest of the world; for although I knew time merely *seemed* to pass at a different pace in prison, it was very hard to keep that in perspective when I had been staring at the same four walls for twenty-three hours a day, punctuated only by crappy meals and whistling. Getting out for an hour to see the clock was an affirmation of the normal passing of time, and of my place within that passage. In a strange sense, it was an affirmation of my continuing existence.

The next day after breakfast, Tom Selleck popped by #505 with a present for me: a paper bag containing most of what had been in my wallet and pockets when I was arrested. This was a wonderful surprise, as I had several things that I would be extremely grateful for in the coming days. There were a few hair ties, business card sized pocket street and subway maps of New York City, a plastic

Fresnel magnifying glass card, various scraps of paper and business cards, a pack of flints for a Zippo lighter, a small book of spiritual readings I carry with me wherever I go, a small change purse I had bought in Christiania (an amazing anarchist city that lies inside Copenhagen, Denmark) that contained a pair of earplugs and six Willie Adler signature lamb of god guitar picks, and a pen and my small Moleskine notebook. I was ecstatic to have my journal and a pen, and after I had put my loot away I tied back my dreads, sat down, and immediately began writing.

———

*R*eading this journal now is a strange experience for me, because it details not just the mundane day-to-day occurrences of prison life, but my mental and emotional state as well. As I read this small book, I can actually feel the sharp fear that pervaded my days. I can also see my attempt to stay positive and grateful in the face of it, and I can step outside those feelings now in a way I couldn't in prison, to analyze them and my actions. I am grateful for this, because I can see that when put to the test, I had come a long way as a human being since my drinking days; I was not completely consumed by anger, hubris, fear, or self-loathing, which were my normal modes of operation. I can forget sometimes what my mental state used to be like when I was in active alcoholism, and be very hard on myself if I feel I am not living up to what I perceive to be acceptable standards. These ludicrous personal standards (ethical, spiritual, professional, artistic) are far beyond attainable for any human being. They are merely a manifestation of my unreasonable pride; kicking my own ass for failing to achieve *perfection* (of all the ridiculous things to expect to attain) is just another ego trip I cannot afford. This self-absorbed and self-pitying self-flagellation gets in the way of me being a productive and useful human being. So it is good for me to look honestly at myself and note my progress from time to time. I'm just a man doing the best that I can—I need to remember that, and without becoming boastful or complacent, give myself a freakin' break every now and then.

I suppose me writing gave Dorj the urge to do something other than whistle, because he fetched our razor blade from beneath the radiator and began cutting the cardboard box his toothpaste had come in into small squares. I noticed him drawing small designs on the squares, and when he was done, he showed me his creation. Dorj had fashioned the thirty-two pieces necessary for us to play chess, drawing the pawns, rooks, kings, etc., on each of the squares. We set the pieces up on the board carved into one of our stools and played a few games. Dorj destroyed me that day, and he destroyed me every day we played afterward. I'm not a good chess player to begin with, and it became pretty demoralizing getting annihilated on the board by an overweight, lackadaisical, compulsively whistling, habitual drunk driver. But it did give me pause from time to time when I became judgmental of Dorj's apparently sloth-like intellect; the man *did* speak four languages to my one, and no moron could play chess as well as he did. As much as Dorj drove me nuts, I was oddly fascinated by him. During my better moments, I thought of him as positively Shakespearean, a modern-day Falstaff sent from Central Asia to test my patience and sometimes provide comic relief during the horrid play I was currently living out. His character was such that he possessed not the tiniest shred of shame or self-consciousness; Dorj was Dorj at all times, and didn't care if you liked it or not. I had to learn a lesson or two from him as a cellmate, because some aspects of the incarcerated life require you to check any self-consciousness you may have at the heavily guarded prison door.

For instance, let's talk about pooping. Everyone poops; we all know this. But if you really want to get down to the nitty-gritty, the very square root of pooping, you need to go to prison for a while. Defecation is usually a very private act for most humans. We lock ourselves up in a bathroom or stall and let 'er rip, striking a match or apologizing for the odor if someone has to use the same toilet after us. Doing a number two is almost always a solo mission; even on camping trips where the only toilet is the great outdoors, we go somewhere away from the campsite and our friends to drop a deuce behind a nice tree. Ask any touring musician what are a few things they miss about home when they are on the road, and almost universally, their own toilet will be among their answers. There's just nothing like taking a crap in your own john. But if you want to know true pooping freedom, spend some time locked up in a small, unventilated cell, subsisting on a primarily liquid diet. Live with an over-weight man who doesn't even chew what little chewable food there is in your diet. Live where you are never, ever, more than a maximum of twelve feet away from the only toilet available, a no-frills, completely exposed, barely-bolted-to-the-floor-at-all affair. You will soon lose any trace of reticence you may have about taking a dump in front of someone else.

After a couple of days in Pankrác with Dorj, my need for poop privacy was utterly and completely extirpated. I take that precious gift with me to this day; I could poop in front of or even with *anyone* now if I needed to without the slightest bit of awkwardness. I could poop next to the President, the Pope, the Prime Minister of any nation on earth. I could take a noisy, smelly crap right beside Mother Theresa, Margaret Thatcher, or Marilyn Monroe. I have never really been a shy or self-conscious person about much, but I do like to have some personal time when nature calls. Pankrác eradicated any poop prudishness I may have had; in some ways, prison will set you free.

———

After we had played a few games of chess, a guard came to my cell and beckoned me out, yelling "Blight! Advocate!" I tucked in my shirt, and took the trip upstairs for my first prison visit with my lawyer. I was frisked once directly outside my cell, then after we walked up a few levels in the prison, I was ushered into a small room and ordered to strip down to my boxers. The guard went through the pockets of my pants and felt my socks to make sure there was nothing in them, then ordered me to take off my boxers and squat. Why in the world anyone would try to smuggle something *out* of prison up their butt was beyond me, but I suppose they had to make sure I wasn't trying to pass my lawyer any contraband, perhaps the secret recipe for the shitty soup they fed us every fucking day. Heaven forbid that ever got out, or gourmands from across the globe would be beating down the prison doors. After the guard was satisfied I didn't have anything I wasn't supposed to, I redressed and he took me into a cell that was divided into two sections by bars; an open area with a desk where Tomas Morycek was sitting and a cage with a stool where I sat. The guard locked me in and left the room, locking the door behind him. Tomas took out some cigarettes, gave me one (for some reason this was against the rules—lawyers were allowed to smoke in these meeting cells, but prisoners weren't—I broke this rule every single time I visited with my attorneys), and began to tell me about the condition of my bail.

My bail had been paid, and I could possibly be released by noon the next day. Supposedly no restrictions had been put on my movements, so I would be free to leave the country; a 2:30 p.m. flight for me to NYC had already been booked by my manager. This seemed a bit optimistic on his part to me, as everything so far in the Czech legal system seemed to take an inordinate amount of time. I was a bit confused by the fact that my bail had been paid and I was still in prison; this was not the way things worked in America. The judge granted you bail, someone posted it, and as soon as they could find you in the jail, off you went on your merry way. I didn't really worry too much about it though; the money was in the government's account. They *had* to let me go soon, right? The Czech legal system couldn't really be all that different, right?

Wrong. *Very wrong.* But I would find that out soon enough.

Tomas and I also talked about my current portrayal in the Czech press. This topic was quite a bit more worrisome for me, because the news was not good. I was told that according to some news outlets, I was being charged with murder. I had savagely beaten a fan on stage. I had killed a woman. I had kicked a kid in the head to death on stage. All sorts of bizarre things had been attributed to me, all 100 percent false. Tomas told me that my lawyers were contacting these newspapers to inform them that if they did not stop printing this nonsense, then we would sue them. Apparently this is standard procedure in the Czech Republic, and happens all the time. The main offender seemed to be a rag named *Blesk*. *Blesk*, as far as I have been able to gather, is a daily tabloid newspaper. It is the Czech equivalent of *The National Inquirer* in America, or Britain's *Daily Star*. It is complete garbage, and almost nobody in the Czech Republic will admit to reading it.

But it is *by far* the number one selling newspaper in that country.

This completely baffles my mind to this day—the Czechs are definitely *not* a dull lot on the whole. Why in the hell so many of them (91 percent as of 2013, according to one statistic I have read) would bother to look at this crap is completely beyond me. I can't read Czech, and even I could tell from looking at copies of *Blesk* in prison that it wasn't fit to wipe my butt with—glaring, bold headlines. Lots of bright colors. Photos of scantily clad women. Lots of exclamation points. *Blesk* is just barely a step up from the rags that print stories about Elvis, Bigfoot, and Hitler cruising around in a spaceship together. But it was the number one selling newspaper in the country, it was printing pictures of me with lurid headlines that said I was a murderer, and according to Tomas, this was a big problem that had to be stopped. It would be even better if we could arrange an exclusive interview with *Blesk* to try to get them on our side a little. It was hard for me to wrap my head around the fact that anyone would care what a trashy daily tabloid had to say about my arrest or case, but apparently *Blesk* held considerable sway, so we had to address the problem. In America, my reaction to any news printed about me by a freakin' tabloid would have been two very short words: *fuck 'em*. Who cares? No one takes that shit seriously where I live. But this was very obviously not America. The court of public opinion can and does affect the court of law at times, and the public opinion was being shaped by the national printed equivalent of the neighborhood fence-leaning scandalmonger. As much as it pained me to admit it, we had to either stop or appease these sons of bitches somehow.

After we were done talking, Tomas pressed a button to summon a guard to collect me. When the same guard who had brought me there arrived, Tomas asked him if he could give me the two packs of cigarettes he had brought for me. The guard curtly shook his head no, Tomas said something else to him, the guard shook his head no again, then finally after a third question from Tomas, held up two fingers. Tomas told me he was sorry, but the guard had told him he could only give me two single cigarettes. It was better than nothing, so I thanked him, and the guard and I returned to the holding cell where I was made to strip again, drop my boxers, and squat. This time, in addition to going through my clothes, the guard made me untie my dreadlocks and he lifted them individually up to check them for hidden materials. Only after he had done everything shy of sticking a flashlight up my butt was I allowed to put my clothes back on and return to my cell.

The refusal of all but two cigarettes and the extensive search of my person was what I came to know to be typical behavior of the guards in Pankrác. By typical behavior, I mean completely random, without pattern or any rhyme or reason. Every time I was allowed out of my cell I never knew what was going to happen. I could be made to strip completely buck naked, I could be told to take off only my shirt, I could be told to keep all my clothes on. Some guards made you strip down to skivvies then drop 'em and squat, some made you strip down to skivvies and would look offended if you started to drop them (I always just assumed that this was going to be the case, and just wanted to get it over with, but more than once I've had guards avert their eyes once the family jewels started to come out). I understand the randomness of the strip searches—it certainly would keep anyone wanting to smuggle stuff around the prison on their toes, but the cigarettes never made any sense to me. Some guards wouldn't let you have a single cigarette, some would let you have just a few, then some let me walk out of a meeting with my attorney with five precious packs in my pockets. I have no idea of what the rules actually were pertaining to cigarettes, or if there even were any. Maybe some guards were just cool by nature, and maybe some were just born dicks. It was always just the luck of the draw when it came to how guards would act around you.

———

The next day came and went without much of any sort of incident (including me being released from the prison). It was dissappointing, but what could I do? Except for our daily walk, Dorj and I never left the cell. We practiced counting to one hundred a few times; that shortly lost its appeal, so in an attempt to keep him occupied and perhaps put a halt to his whistling for a bit, I gave him the Czech version of some of my court papers, which he promptly began turning into a swan. In retrospect, this was a tragic mistake, because a) Dorj could fold and whistle at the same time, and b) he took this as a sign that any paper I had was a swan just waiting to be made. Felix had given me a few sheets of paper to write letters with at walk that day, and Dorj reached over when I wasn't looking and snatched up half of the paper to finish the swan he started with my court papers. I scolded him for this when I noticed the paper was gone, but he just laughed and kept folding and whistling. The whistling was getting to me pretty badly by then, but at least we had a few hand rolled cigarettes and two or three matches. We didn't even have rolling papers, but

Dorj had scrounged around the cell and found a few scraps of an ancient Russian newspaper a previous tenant had stuffed into the crumbling mortar around our window sill, I suppose for insulation during the brutal Czech winter months. Dorj had taken our butts and a few others he had found on the ground during walk and rolled us up a few cigarettes, which we smoked very sparingly. We tried to reserve smoking the roll ups as a sort of ghetto incense for when one of us had to take a poop. We also had four pre-rolled cigarettes ("cadillacs" as I have heard them called in American jails) that I got from creepy Uncle Fester the trusty. He came by with a piece of paper, asking for my autograph, and I told him I would do it for a cigarette. He gave me one, then I showed him one of my lamb of god guitar picks, which he got really excited about and reached out for. I pulled it back, and told him I wanted more cigarettes. We haggled back and forth for a bit, then he went away and came back with a magic marker, a complete prison outfit, and three more smokes for me. I signed the clothes, gave him the pick, and gleefully sat down to smoke. The brief bargaining session had invigorated me; it wasn't so much the actual cigarettes that were awesome, it was the fact that I had gotten something for nothing. I felt like a sleazy stockbroker must when he gets over on a particularly gullible and rich client. The machine of commerce rolled on.

The following day after breakfast, I sat down and began to make a journal entry. A few seconds after I had written the date at the top of the page, it suddenly sunk in what day it was—July Fourth. Holy crap, it was Independence Day and I was in a foreign prison. I am no crazed flag-waving blindly patriotic nationalist, for I believe what Thomas Jefferson famously wrote is entirely true: "What country can preserve its liberties if their rulers are not warned from time to time that their people preserve the spirit of resistance?" Sadly, I have not seen much of that spirit of resistance over the last few decades, a time of government sponsored and sanctioned bloodshed that seems to have gone unquestioned (or at least unchallenged) by the vast majority of the American public. I am a pragmatic man, and as such I acknowledge the need for a strong-armed military in today's world of global violence, as well as governmental agencies that are ever alert to the possibility of terrorist attacks and watchful of the movements of the twisted networks who commit these atrocities. But I find it extremely distasteful when unconstitutional legislation like the Patriot Act is rushed through our senate without even so much as a loud fart of dissent heard (the act passed by a vote of 98 to 1). If you give someone or something with an inherent propensity for abusing power an inch (such as large governmental agencies, as history proves again and again), then they will, without fail, carve themselves a bloody mile. Injustice always prevails when the people blindly accept the dictates of those in power, whether those rulers were elected or seized their positions by the sword. I do not trust the men in power, I do not trust our government, I never have, and I never will. But I love my country, would gladly die safeguarding it if necessary, and consider myself a true patriot. I have been around the world many times, and for all its faults, there is no other country like America. I would not choose to call anywhere else home. For me, my country is its people, not its government, and sitting in that cell on July 4th made me feel a rush of longing to be amongst my people. I wanted to be with my wife and friends, grilling hotdogs and hamburgers, drinking a cold NA beer and watching the kids run around in my buddy Erik's backyard, then going over to Byrd Park in Richmond to sit on a blanket and watch the fireworks. On that particularly American day, as the distance from all that I knew and loved began to drape an extra-heavy blanket of melancholy over me, I decided to combat it by comforting myself with a song I don't normally sing or play. I began to whistle my national anthem, "The Star-Spangled Banner." *O'er the laaaand of the freeeeeeeee*, I sang in my head as I whistled that sturdy old tune aloud, *and the hooooome ooooof the braaaaaaaaaaave* . . .

Goosebumps. Pure goosebumps rising all over my body as the last note faded into the dusty air of my cell. *God bless America*, I thought, *God bless Ameri—*

My weird patriotic reverie was interrupted by the unmistakable sounds of "We Wish You a Merry Christmas" coming from the toilet area behind me, followed by a rapid rendition of "Jingle Bells." Dorj was taking a shit and whistling Christmas carols. *I am going to kill him*, I thought. Then the sheer bizarreness of my current situation suddenly struck me as hilarious, and I began to laugh aloud, Dorj joining me as he farted and whistled "Jingle Bells" again. I turned back to my journal, noted that I would never take the 4th of July for granted again, then crawled back under my sheet to take a nap.

———

I had just started to doze off when the cell door flung open and Tom Selleck began berating me loudly in Czech. I got up from my bed, and he suddenly slammed the door shut again. I had no idea what that was all about, so I just went back to bed—maybe he was in a bad mood that day, but then again he always seemed a little grumpy to me. *Ah, to hell with his Eighties looking ass*, I thought, *might as well go back to sleep*, and so I laid back down and pulled the sheet back over my head to block out what light I could. Almost immediately the door opened again, and Tom Selleck stood there once more, this time screaming even more angrily in Czech. I sighed and sat up, put on a t-shirt and my shoes, then stood up and walked over to the irate guard.

"*What*, dude? What the fuck do you want? Are you taking me somewhere? Let's go then, so I can get back to sleep. Where am I going?" I asked him.

I could almost see the steam rising off of his red face; Tom Selleck was seriously pissed, and I had no idea why. I saw a mighty internal struggle play across his face, the gears turning beneath his jauntily spiked hair as he searched for the words to explain his displeasure. Finally he replied in heavily accented English, the words coming out in an actual growl.

"You . . . are not . . . going," he said, "You . . . cannot sleep . . . under . . . white. Understand?" and made a motion for me to make up my bed.

It was then that I vaguely remembered reading something in my prison regulations about only being allowed to use blankets and sheets to sleep after lights out. The rest of the day, a prisoner's bed was to be neatly made, all corners tucked and the sheet tight around the mattress. The problem with that was that I didn't have a mattress, I had three fucked up couch cushions laying on a metal frame they weren't sized for. The bed also hurt my back like hell to sleep on—the thing was really more like a medieval torture rack with added foam padding from a trailer park yard sale than a bed, so I never really gave a crap how neatly I made it. If they wanted a neatly made bed, they were going to have to give me an actual bed. Until then, I would throw my sheet and blanket over as I saw fit. I walked back to the bed and sloppily drew my sheet back up over the pieces of foam, then flopped back down on it. "There ya go, Tom Selleck. Are you happy now?" I said, not caring if he picked up on his new nickname. Tom just scowled at me, shut the cell door, and I promptly went back to sleep.

A few hours later I woke up to Dorj shaking me and pointing at the cell door. The hatch in the door was open, and I saw a guard's face. He beckoned me with a rapid movement, and I got up, thinking *Christ, what now?* as I walked to the door. As I got nearer to the hatch, I saw the guard had a young face, and he looked rather nervous. His eyes kept darting from side to side, as if he was checking to see if anyone was watching him. When I got to the hatch, I leaned down and he began to speak very rapidly in a heavy Czech accent.

"Randy! I am very sorry for you to be here! I am metalhead and I know you do not belong here! Please do not hate Czech

Republic and Czech people, it is the fucking system! You must go home! You must keep fighting!" he said.

"Bro, it's nice to meet you! I don't hate the Czech Republic or Czech People at all," I replied, because I didn't.

"I am very sorry for not good English, but you must go home! I saw you at Rock-Am Park, watching Alice in Chains with Vinnie Paul," he said, referring to a German Festival I had been at a month earlier, hanging out near the crowd with a good friend watching some bands. "I am drummer, too! Just because some fucking idiot does stage dive does not mean you should be here. I am very sorry! You must go home! We are all metal brothers! You must keep fighting!" he said.

"It's okay, man, it will work out. I'm not sure exactly what happened yet, but I know I never tried to hurt that boy," I said. "Hold on for a minute." I ran over to my locker and got him one of my guitar picks. I gave it to him, and he thanked me profusely, apologizing again for my imprisonment. I told him not to worry about it, it wasn't his fault—the man seemed genuinely upset to see me caged up like that. I asked him if he had a cigarette, and he pulled out a crumpled box with eight or nine different kinds of cigarettes in it. He thrust it into my hands along with a lighter, and glancing anxiously to either side of him, told me he had to go.

"You must keep fighting! Randy, you must go home!" he said, then shut the hatch, and I heard him walking quickly away. I gave Dorj a cigarette, lit one of my own, and sat down to write about my unexpected visitor.

That guard was just the first person since I had been arrested who made me feel like I was still a decent human being. My lawyers were being paid to declare my innocence, but the young man who had just come to my cell was one of *my people*. He had appeared, most definitely against the rules from the extremely nervous look of him, stopping by just to bolster my spirits, perhaps at the risk of his job or worse. He had spoken in a language that let me know he understood me, why I was there, and the difficulties I might face in the future. I'm not talking about his broken English; I'm referring to the silent language that all members of the underground music community I am a part of share. We recognize our own, no matter what color or creed, and this young man had come to me to let me know that my people were thinking about me, that not everyone in that foreign land hated me. I don't think the guard even smoked cigarettes, but had gathered a few for me, bringing me the only gift he could. His visit did me more good than I can explain, and I never even got his name.

So to this young guard, if you ever happen to read this, I would like to thank you—you helped me greatly. I hope we meet again, and if we do, the beers are on me, brother.

———

*L*ater, during our one-hour outdoors, Felix told me that others on the cellblock had known about the guard's visit. Rene began pointing at me, saying "music good for you, rock-n-roll, baby!" I agreed, and when Rene said that it was too bad there was no music in Pankrác, I pointed to my head and told him I had music in my mind.

"Ah, the machine; yes, the machine. In the machine, I free. Searching for free," he said as he pointed to his own shaved and tattooed dome, "but here is home now. Finito," and sadly tapped the ground in front of him.

Rene told me he had not seen his wife for sixty-four months, and had another twenty years' time left to serve in three different prisons. He was scarred and tattooed; an uneducated man with rough manners, and had obviously been involved in some sort of long-term life of crime, but I never saw him behave with anything but kindness to those around him. We never discussed why he was locked up. I had no problem asking anyone what their charges were in Pankrác, because everyone I talked to knew why I was there and would speak openly to me about it, but for some reason I never asked Rene. We would talk about family and tattoos and music and art (Rene was an accomplished artist with pen and paper who made me several sketches as gifts or trades), but not about his crimes. Maybe I never asked him because I didn't want to know what he had done—this was a man with the numeral thirteen tattooed on the back of his head because M is the thirteenth letter in the alphabet, and his daughter's name was Maria. He spoke of her as fondly as any father I had ever talked to had about his own daughter. Whatever he had done, it didn't matter now. He was one of my homies on the block, he showed me respect, repaid me when I loaned him smokes or coffee, and even helped me out when he could. The outside world, and what he had done in it, was something that had no bearing on our relationship inside. In prison, unless you are a sexual offender, child abuser, or psycho killer, not many inmates will stand in judgment of your actions. No one goes to prison on a winning streak, so there's really no room or patience for holier-than-thou attitudes. I certainly tried not to judge anyone, because at the root, we were all the same—in the machine, searching for free.

———

Men in prison also share what they have when they can. If you are greedy, you will be treated as such. After I finally got some money on my books, I had more to share than most men in Pankrác. I was always as generous as I could be with the inmates I knew, but I was careful who I shared with, as I didn't want to become known as a rich push-over in the general population—carelessly displaying wealth is not a good maneuver in prison (or anywhere, for that matter—besides the fact that you look like an asshole, you are just painting a target on yourself). One person I always shared with was Rene's friend, the Quiet Gypsy. He never spoke much at all (and that's why I just called him the Quiet Gypsy, or T.Q.G. for short—the dude was totally silent most of the time), had no money on his books that I could tell, but had a generous heart. He displayed this quality during walk that day when he reached into the waistband of his pants and pulled out a fat plastic baggie of the good stuff.

Coffee.

Holy crap, the dude had *coffee.* He began portioning it out into scraps of paper, standing in the corner of our concrete cage while the rest of us watched for guards on the walkway above. It looked totally sketchy, exactly resembling the countless drug transactions I had witnessed or been a part of, except the gear was just good old java. We were not supposed to carry anything except cigarettes out of our cells during walk, so the coffee was against the rules. If the guards found any contraband on you when they searched you before heading out to walk, you could kiss it goodbye—this could and did happen from time to time. T.Q.G. had risked having his coffee taken, just so he could share it with us, and I immediately took a liking to him. I didn't have any paper to take coffee in, so Rene tore off a corner of the baggie, poured me a share, and carefully sealed it with a lighter; once again in the exact same precise manner as drugs are dealt sometimes. I thanked T.Q.G. with great earnestness, and he waved me away in an almost embarrassed manner.

You can bet your sweet ass that when my wife brought me some expensive packs of instant coffee from America a few days later, the Quiet Gypsy immediately got a healthy portion. I remember those who look out for me.

I was also happy to see Martin, the man who had passed out in the hallway after our doctor's visit the first day. He looked a lot healthier, and I asked him what had happened that day. He told me that he had been dope sick, withdrawing from heroin since he had first been locked up nine days ago, and had not been able to sleep. This surprised me, because I have seen many dope sick junkies kicking before, but didn't see it in him that day. Martin had been in the hospital ward for the last few days, being given nutrients and ten milligrams of diazepam (a.k.a. Valium) to help him sleep as he kicked the dope; if an inmate was judged as having sufficiently bad drug withdrawals the prison doctor would sometimes do that to help wean them off. That was it though—the whole time I was in Pankrác, I never once heard mention of any sort of alcohol or drug rehabilitation programs or educational classes, and I met plenty of guys who were in there because they were drug addicts. Martin had been arrested for shoplifting a lighter from a convenience store—he needed it to smoke the heroin he had just bought and stashed in an alley. He told me that once he left prison, he was done with drugs. It was ruining his health and his life, he couldn't believe he was doing time in prison for stealing a plastic lighter. He told me he wanted to stay clean, to not live that terrible way anymore. I told him that I was an alcoholic, not a drug addict, but that I knew many, many drug addicts. It had been my experience that almost none of them were able to get and stay clean without some sort of help, so I wrote down the name of an international organization that has helped many of my addict friends and strongly encouraged him to look them up the same day he left prison, as they would surely have an office in Prague. He thanked me, and told me he would. Martin wasn't a bad man, he was a man with a drug problem. I realize that this is very hard for some people to grasp, but it is true—not all drug addicts are horrible human beings. Most of them just need help breaking the chains of their addiction, not a prison sentence. Of course for some alcoholics and addicts, a prison sentence is the only way they will begin to grasp the ramifications of their actions and get clean. Then there are those unrepentant criminals who most definitely need to be locked up for the good of society. But most drug addicts I have known started off as decent, normal citizens, only becoming involved in a life of crime after their addiction led them down that dark path. Before it kills the addict, in order to feed itself, addiction will almost always eventually lead an otherwise sensible person into committing actions that would horrify them if they were not caught in its vicious grip. Alcoholism and drug addiction have existed for as long as alcohol and drugs have existed. That is longer than humanity's written record, and that is not conjecture, that is scientific fact. It has not changed in thousands and thousands of years. Unfortunately, our way of dealing with this problem hasn't changed that much either. I hoped that Martin would learn from his mistake and be one of the lucky ones who managed to break the cycle, or he would wind up dead, insane, or back in prison.

I cannot express how grateful I am to be sober today. It is everything to me.

––––––––

That evening when Uncle Fester made his normal rounds yelling "Chai!" I asked for hot water instead. I dumped a huge lump of the instant coffee into my mug, stirred it up, and immediately took a huge gulp. As I almost choked on the gritty mouthful, I quickly realized that the coffee was not the pre-brewed and freeze-dried instant variety I had expected, but was instead finely ground roasted beans. Dorj had been watching me, and laughing at my ignorance and haste as I spit out the bitter brew, signaled for me to wait five minutes. I did, the grounds settled, and it turned out to be a halfway decent cup of coffee. At the very least, its robustness was miles above and beyond the barely flavored hot water the prison doled out each morning as an excuse for coffee. I get my taste in coffee from my mother's father, Papa, who drank it strong enough to put hair on your chest, because he was a man, by God. He would yell at his wife, my Nana, if she made a pot that most humans could consume without their hearts exploding, "Sarah! You know I can't drink this stump-water!" Whoever Pankrác's barista was, they were definitely a stump-water kind of guy, and I cursed him most mornings until I got some instant coffee to stiffen up his disgracefully diluted drink.

Uncle Fester also came around that evening with a cart full of books from the prison library. As he poked his head into the cell door hatch, he held up a few paperbacks and asked me, "Book?" I practically ran to the door and snatched the books out of his hands, but upon opening them saw that they were printed in Czech. I sighed, handed them back, and asked him if he had any English books instead.

"Englishky for book? No. Next tomorrows maybe. I ask for you," he said with his signature creepy grin, and slammed the hatch shut. I heard Dorj laughing again, and I wheeled around to face him, irritated by his mirth.

"You no want book?" I said, lapsing into the broken English that seemed to be the most effective way of communicating with my slothful cellmate, "Why you no want book? You can read Czechsky, you fat motherfucker. Why you no want book?"

Dorj waved his hand in dismissal. "Bah. I no read book. Book *spatny*," he said "I pure vodka. Pure vodka *doubry* (good)."

"Maybe you should have read a few books on how to get a visa instead of drinking so much goddamned pure vodka, then your fat ass wouldn't be stuck in this shit hole with me," I barked, but Dorj just laughed, said, "Pure vodka" once more for emphasis, whistled a bar or two of "Jingle Bells," then rolled over and went to sleep. He was grinding on my nerves more and more each day.

The next day, Tom Selleck opened our cell door and yelled "doctor!" Dorj and I got dressed and followed a dense-looking pimply-faced guard upstairs to see whatever passed for a member of the medical profession in Pankrác. First we were taken to a large and dusty room with two walls of floor to ceiling dirty glazed windows. The room was completely empty except for a steel table and a rickety looking x-ray machine. The thing looked ancient, and as I held a slate over my chest so they could x-ray my lungs, I wondered if this contraption had been calibrated since it had arrived at Pankrác, or if I was being blasted with a lethal dose of Cold War–era radiation.

After we had both been sufficiently zapped with the Commie beam of deat—I mean *x-rayed*, Dorj and I were taken to the holding cell we had first been in when we had our blood taken. The guard took Dorj, who was gone for at least forty-five minutes. I sat in the cell alone, staring at the walls and wondering what in the hell they were doing with him that took that long. Finally, Dorj returned looking really pissed off. As I walked with the guard out of the cell, Dorj looked at me at and said, "Doctor very stupid man!" *Great.* The guard led me into an office, pointed at a chair in front of a large desk, sat down in another chair a few feet from mine, and promptly started to nod out. I looked across the desk at the white-haired man seated behind it.

The doctor appeared to be somewhere between two and three hundred years old; three hundred and fifty at maximum. A long, lit cigarette dangled between his lips, perched there like a failed surgeon general's warning, perhaps as a smoldering act of defiance against what he felt were unnecessarily hasty, perchance even *risky*, pronouncements by modern medical science on the hazards of tobacco use. His bulbous crimson nose had an amazing web of exploded capillaries spreading across it, resembling a miniature subway map of Tokyo wheat-pasted onto a misshapen red golf ball. White hair sprouted crazily from his head and ears. Around his neck, wrists, and on his wrinkled nicotine-stained fingers were heavy gold necklaces, thick linked gold bracelets, an expensive gold Rolex, and several hefty jewel-encrusted gold rings. In front of the doctor was what appeared to be the first ever production model PC, which his rheumy eyes stared at from beneath droopy lids. The doctor looked very confused by the computer, maybe even afraid of it. Every minute or so he would extend a single bony finger out and peck a seemingly random key, then quickly withdraw it, like he was testing the machine, poking it to see if it would suddenly spring to life and attack him, or perhaps explain the mystery of fire. I fully expected him to emit chimpanzee-like "ooh-ooh-ooh" grunts at any second. A large ashtray, over flowing with butts, sat on the desk beside the computer's keyboard. With his cigarettes and gaudy jewelry and obvious incompetence with even severely outdated modern technology, he looked like an ancient bookie trying to figure out the spread on some futuristic calculator. He seemed to be completely unaware of me, even though I was seated no more than three feet away from him.

I turned to look at the acne-faced guard who had brought me there, wondering if he would alert the doctor to our presence, but he was fast asleep. As I sat there staring at the drool running down the side of his face, he began snoring loudly. He wasn't doing much of a job guarding his charge, and me a supposedly violent criminal! Not for the last time during my stay in Pankrác, I was struck by how easy it would be for me to just smash the life from someone who was supposedly there to keep me under control. There were even a few times during my incarceration where I was escorted through the prison by a lone female guard who was significantly smaller than me. This petite woman turned her back quite carelessly on me as we walked alone up and down some staircase. I never saw that even in the drunk tank back home—the guards there were all beefy dudes who looked like they were used to rough customers. If I were a female prison guard, I wouldn't turn my back on me for a second, no chance, no way. All around me in the doctor's office were heavy or sharp objects that would have made perfectly fabulous killing weapons. I could have reached any of them with just a few quick steps. The guard was asleep, and the doctor was way too old and oblivious to stop me. I could have ended both of them right there, very quickly.

I'm not saying that I wanted to hurt anyone, or had any urge to, just that while I was in Pankrác I often noticed how so very easily I could. I don't normally think these sorts of thoughts, but prison seemed to bring them out of me. Maybe it was some sort of ancient survival instinct, trying to assert itself in this strange place. Or maybe I am just a man with an inherently violent, criminal, bestial nature; but I don't really think so. It was being in prison that brought these darker aspects of myself to the fore so regularly—it's not like I go to the coffee shop and randomly start fantasizing about strangling the barista to death, even if he screws up my drink.

The guard must have sensed these twisted thoughts, because he woke up with a start, throwing me a suspicious glare from one piggish eye before immediately dozing off again. The doctor continued poking at his computer keyboard every minute or two, still showing no signs of realizing that I sat directly in front of him. The office was dead quiet except for the snores of the guard and the occasional clack of the computer's keyboard as the doctor depressed a solitary key. After about five or six minutes of this weird silence, I couldn't take it anymore.

"Hello, Doctor," I said loudly, "what seems to be the problem today? How may I help you?"

This cheery announcement had an immediate effect on the doctor, who bolted upright (in reality it was more of a creaking semi-vertical lurch, his actual bolting days being long over), dropping his cigarette into his lap and retrieving it with a muttered curse. He looked at me, completely surprised by the sudden appearance of this knotty-haired tattooed stranger. His previous unacknowledging manner had been so complete, I wondered if he was thinking that perhaps one of his pokes at the computer had summoned me from the ether, causing me to appear like magic, even though I had been right in front him for several silent minutes. The doctor brushed some ashes from his clothes, took a long, pensive drag on what was left of his smoke, exhaled noisily, then spoke to me in a deep voice made raspy by years of chain smoking.

"You . . . are . . . Czech?" he slowly asked me, suspicion riding the tobacco-roughened edges of his rumbling voice.

"No, American," I replied, wondering how my initial use of English hadn't alerted him to my status as a foreigner.

"Ah, Americansky. Goot, goot," he replied, as if my nationality had cheered him up. Perhaps he had been having a Communist-era flashback, and my unexpected appearance had made him afraid that I was a member of the secret police come to question him. He was more than old enough to have lived through the darkest of those times, when such concerns were a very valid part of life in the country. The doctor then pulled out a clipboard with a chart on it and proceeded to very, very slowly ask me a long line of questions about my general health, of which I understood about half, and those with great difficulty.

"You . . . haf . . . dee-yah-bate-ees?" No, no diabetes.

"You . . . haf . . . arch . . . problem?" No, my heart seems to be fine.

"You . . . haf . . . some . . . tromer?" Well, I suppose we've all suffered some trauma throughout our lives, but there's none I'd care to discuss at the moment, so no, no trauma, so to speak of.

Then the doctor's eyes narrowed, and I could see suspicion returning to his gaze as he asked me, "You . . . haf . . . some . . . invariable . . . disease?"

"I'm sorry, I don't understand you," I replied, hoping that there was no disease in Pankrác so ruthless that I would absolutely contract it, no matter how strong my immune system was.

"You . . . haf . . . some . . . wind . . . marriable . . . .disease?" he said, a hint of malice creeping into his voice.

"I'm very sorry, but I still don't understand what you are saying," I said, thinking that a) I was already married, and b) even if I was single, I would never wed something as fickle as a weather pattern.

The doctor began to stand, then, quickly thinking better of it, leaned some of his considerable bulk over the table and pointed his cigarette accusingly at my crotch. "You . . . haf . . . some . . . wenairial . . . disease!" he practically shouted, ash flying from his smoke onto the desktop. This time it was a statement of fact, as if he had just caught me red-handed, shagging his favorite teenaged granddaughter in the barn out back.

"No! No! Absolutely not! No venereal diseases!" I stuttered, glad that the family jewels were in fact healthy, and wondering what this angry doctor would have done to me if they were not.

"Ahhhh, goot, goot," the doctor said, "this is gool for you," and he seemed to relax. *Whew,* I thought, *that was a close one,* as if I had actually done something to escape his ire other than have a healthy penis.

As the doctor extinguished his cigarette and lit up a fresh one, a pleasant-faced brunette nurse in her late forties entered the room and broke out in a huge and beautiful smile when she saw me. "Ah, you are music man! I like Beach Boys!" she said in a very sweet tone of voice.

"Really! I *love* the Beach Boys," I said (because I do, and am slightly obsessed with them and their story), immediately breaking into "Barbara Anne." The nurse was simply thrilled by this, and let out a loud shriek of glee as the doctor and now awake guard stared at me in amazement, as if they had never heard anyone sing before. After I ran through a quick verse and chorus of "Barbara Anne," the nurse gave me a quick round of delighted applause, then turned to the doctor and abruptly began screaming at him.

Her transformation from squealing school-girl music fan to screeching, malicious-hearted harpy was so abrupt and unexpected I actually jumped in my seat. I had noticed before that the key components of the Czech language as it is spoken in prison (which is very different than the Czech you hear strolling through the streets of Prague) are: 1) blistering speed, 2) ear-splitting volume, and 3) an overall verbal tenor that suggests deeply, deeply seated unhappiness and anger at everything and everyone around the speaker, especially the person being spoken to. But this woman had been so childishly pleasant to me at first, so pleased with my singing, that I had forgotten for a second that, just like the Beach Boys and their music, there was a very dark core hiding beneath that sugar-coated shell—how could there not be? She worked in a prison. The nurse let the doctor have it for a minute or so, then he, too, underwent a transformation, shedding a century or two and giving it back to her just as loudly. Where before the doctor had been speaking slowly in a deep and unintelligible, yet mostly pleasant, approximation of the English language, he was now bellowing fiercely in Czech. After about two minutes of seemingly mutual hate-filled invective, Adolph Hitler–like in intensity, the nurse stomped out of the room and the doctor picked up the phone beside him and slowly, slowly pecked out a number.

As he brought the receiver to his furry ear, a female voice blasted out of it in a deafening greeting of "ahoy!" which the doctor promptly answered with his own scream of "ahoy!" before beginning to berate the woman on the other end (this is one of many linguistic quirks of the Czechs I never figured out—another being that every single Czech woman's last name seems to end in *ova*—despite the fact that the Czechs are quite clearly landlocked, they all turn into Popeye when they say hello). After the doctor was done bawling her out, the woman responded with twice the energy and fury, her voice somehow seemingly louder in my ears than the doctor's, even though it emanated solely from the tiny speaker of the phone's headset. The doctor and the woman on the phone went back and forth like this for approximately five minutes, the doctor scribbling a note or two on a yellow pad in between verbal barrages. The two finally reached a satisfactorily aggressive enough conclusion, and the doctor slowly hung up the phone. He then screamed something ending in *ova*, which I could only guess was the nurse's name, as she reappeared and immediately began screaming at him again. The doctor and the nurse yelled back and forth for a few minutes until she left; then he picked up the phone, slowly dialed a number, and the whole procedure, ahoys and all, began anew.

This process was repeated without variation, and I exagger-
ate not one bit, for at least forty-five minutes. The nurse running
in and out of the room, the screaming, the infuriated sounding
phone calls, the ahoys—it was nerve shattering, and I was beginning to become a bit unwound. Throughout all this ruckus, the
guard fell back asleep, not stirring or moving an inch, a large wet
spot growing on his crotch where the drool dripped from his chin
onto his lap. I was amazed that anyone could have slept through
the commotion, which had sounded to me like three Slavic pi-
rates exchanging screamed insults with bullhorns before sailing
their ships into battle with each other on some strange Eastern
European inland sea. I was starting to actually consider using
some of the weapons I saw around the office to shut these people
up when things mercifully began to draw to a close. Finally, after
all feathers had been sufficiently ruffled and nasty enough parting shots fired, quiet descended over the office again. The doctor seemed to have forgotten me, and returned to poking at his
computer again, until I cleared my throat to get his attention. He
looked up from the computer screen and noticed me as if for the
first time; then a hint of recognition crept into his eyes. He smiled
warmly at me, like I was an old friend who he hadn't seen in
years who had decided to pop by for a surprise visit while I was
in town.

"Soooo . . . " he said, lighting his fiftieth cigarette since I had
been there, "You . . . haf . . . some . . . problems?"

*Yes. Yes, I do have some problems. I am in an ancient Czech prison,
stuck in a filthy cell with a Mongolian Slim Whitman who is surely going to put me in the looney bin, one whistle at a time. I don't speak the
language you were just screaming in, and I will not suddenly become fluent in it, no matter how loud anyone yells it at me. I resent the fact that
you people serve me "food" that I wouldn't slop the hogs with back home
in old Virginny, that I am wearing rags, and that I sleep on a metal torture device that would cripple Charles Atlas for life after just one hour on
it. I am confused and I am scared, I am thousands of miles away from*

my wife, my family, and my friends, locked in a basement cage; and I have absolutely no idea of when or even if I will be let out. You bet your cob-web covered ass I've got some problems, doc.

"No. No problems at all," I said.

"That is goot for you," he replied, blowing smoke in my face, "gootbye."

It had been the strangest visit to a doctor in my entire life, and I was not sorry it was over. Almost as soon as Dorj and I were back in our cell though, Tom Selleck opened the door again, pointed at me, yelled "advocate!" and off I went back upstairs. Martin was in the attorney/client cell waiting for me, bringing good and bad news. The bad news was that the prosecuting attorney was determined to keep me in prison, and for the moment it seemed he was able to; he had made it known he would raise an objection to me being granted bail. This confused me at first; in America, to the best of my knowledge, if a judge decided to grant you bail, once it was paid you were free to go. In the Czech Republic, things worked a little differently. A prosecuting attorney could object to you being granted bail, or the conditions of your bail, and then the matter would have to be considered by another court. In the meantime, you remained in custody, whether or not the bail had been paid. My bail had been paid in full by my band, who had borrowed the rather large sum of money from our record label. Close to a quarter million dollars sat in some government account somewhere in Prague, and I sat in prison. Not only that, but Martin told me that even if the court reviewed the conditions of my bail, found them satisfactory, and decided to let me go, the prosecuting attorney could raise yet another objection, which would have to be seen by *another* court, who would decide whether or not to let me go. Things did not look good for my immediate release, and apparently the prosecuting attorney was a real jerk to deal with for my lawyers. In America there is generally a sense of professional courtesy amongst lawyers, even if they are taking the opposing sides of a case. Things are often worked out, hopefully fairly and in the best interest of all parties involved, with a level of civility. This was not the case with the prosecuting attorney, a Mr. Vladimir Muzik. Martin told me that when he had called Muzik to discuss the case, Muzik was rude to a level of belligerence, yelling at him that he was a busy man and didn't have to talk to Martin. Martin seemed to think that Muzik would wait until the last moment possible to raise his objection, thereby dragging out the process as long as possible. Martin told me I could feasibly be released within a few days, but not to get my hopes up. He didn't want me to develop unrealistic expectations about my situation, explaining that if the prosecutor played the system correctly, more than likely I would be spending at least a few months in Pankrác.

I appreciated his candor. I am a man with a severe distaste for sugar-coating. I prefer to know the reality of any situation I may be in, good or bad. That way I can make an educated decision concerning my next course of action. I like to hear the truth, and if I speak, I like to speak the truth, even if it makes others uncomfortable. I have managed to offend a few folks over the years by speaking my mind—to some I am too blunt. And during my drinking days, that was definitely true on occasion. Today, I temper my honesty with as much tact as I can muster. I think I do a pretty good job, but I still manage to piss people off from time to time. I'm a nice guy with great manners; honestly, I am. But if I say something, I mean it; so if we ever meet, don't ask me a question if you aren't prepared for the answer. I'm going to do my best to not be a dick, but I'm not going feed you a line of bullshit or say something because I think it's what you want to hear.

In prison, the more I knew about the reality of my situation, the better off I was. Martin gave me a little more reality during our visit, showing me a photo from *Blesk* with the headline "THE DEATH GRIP!" or something to that effect printed boldly above it in Czech. The photo was of me onstage, kneeling on top a young blond man, my hand wrapped up in the collar area of his shirt, still singing into the microphone. The young man is beneath me, throwing up the horns. Apparently some video and photos of the wrestling incident I had related to the police during my interrogation had surfaced, this being one. I looked at the young man in the photo, and his appearance matched my hazy memory of him from that night, including his complete disregard for the fact that I didn't want him onstage. Any moron looking at the photo could tell that the young man wasn't being choked; people don't "rock out" when being choked, they instinctively try to break free so they can breathe. But in typical tabloid fashion, *Blesk* had printed this photo of what was assumed as definitely being the dead young man in question (the paper identified the man in the photo as Daniel) with a glaring lurid headline in order to sell more copies of their useless rag by demonizing me. This sort of journalism disgusts me, and it always has; it's irresponsible and can have very real repercussions on innocent people's lives. But once again, Martin was giving me what I wanted and needed—the truth about my situation, which at that moment was being affected by a very public falsehood. He reiterated the importance of us arranging an interview with *Blesk* to try to get the paper on our side, which still stuck in my craw, but I knew I would have to play ball if we wanted them to stop portraying me as a murderous maleficent monster. Suing them would be both costly and time consuming, and by the time any sort of libel suit went to court, my manslaughter trial might be over. The damage would be done. So I swallowed my pride and disgust and told him to set it up.

Martin also had a couple of photos of Daniel taken from one of his social media accounts. He handed them to me, and I took a long, hard look at them. In one, Daniel sat cross legged on a dirty carpet in front of a half stack and Randall amp head, holding a black guitar upright on his lap. There was spray painted carpet tacked onto the walls of the room, and a few beer bottles in a corner. I instantly knew where he was, as I had spent a large portion of my life in rooms that looked exactly like it. Daniel was in his practice space. He was one of us, a musician.

Looking carefully at these photos, Daniel looked just like countless lamb of god fans I had met over the years; hell, he looked like he could have been *in* lamb of god. Long blondish brown hair, a black t-shirt and jeans, facial hair, happily sitting in a dirty practice space holding his guitar in front of his rig—I had seen both Mark Morton and Willie Adler, our two guitarists, in that exact same position many, many times, even dressed precisely the same. But I didn't recognize his face. These photos didn't exactly look like photos of the person I had wrestled with; his hair was a bit darker and looked to be thicker and wavier than the stringy blond I dimly saw in my mind's eye. I also did not remember the young man having any facial hair, but as someone who has grown and shaved off many different styles of beards since I started growing one, I knew that didn't really mean anything. The different shade of his hair didn't amount to much either; over the years, my own hair has been more colors than a warehouse full of house paint. Remembering my own youth, I took into account that young people's appearances often change, and I tried to write off the differences in the photos as negligible, but for some reason I couldn't. The young man onstage with me looked vaguely familiar, but the person in the practice space was a total stranger. I searched my mind, trying my best to match the picture of this young guitarist with something in my memory, but I could not.

I am sorry you are dead, I thought as I stared at the photos, *but I don't recognize you, bro. I don't know who you are. I wish I did, but I don't. I guess I will find out sooner or later.*

Martin wasn't all doom and gloom though; he informed me that lamb of god's lawyer, Jeff Cohen, would be in Prague in five days; with him would be my wife, Cindy. Martin had worked it out with the Czech authorities so that Jeff would be able to visit me as some sort of legal consultant. Jeff wouldn't be allowed to represent me in court, but he would be allowed to help my Czech lawyers with the case, as he was familiar with both myself and my rather specialized area of employment. It would be nice to see Jeff, but of course I was more excited about the arrival of my wife. I was allowed one ninety minute visit from a friend or family member every two weeks, and the visit had to be arranged far in advance. My family couldn't just pop by the prison and ask to see me, neither could my friends in touring bands (although some tried, and were turned away—shout out to my hometown homies, Tony and Municipal Waste, for representing the RVA at Pankrác!); I had to write a request for them to be let into the prison, this had to be cleared, etc. etc. It was nothing like the movies; no guard was going to unexpectedly sling open a cell door and yell "Blythe! You have a visitor." I was also allowed one large package a month, either delivered by a visitor or by post. I told Martin I would put together a list of things I needed which he could email to Cindy: cigarettes. Coffee. Candy. Writing utensils. Paper. Books. Sweet lord have mercy, *books*. I couldn't wait to read something other than the insurance card in my wallet. It was killing me.

Besides news, Martin had brought me three packs of Marlboro Reds, which the guard let me keep this time—totally random, that place. When I returned to my cell, I heard Felix's voice float through my cell window from next door.

"How was your visit with your lawyer? Good news, I hope," he said.

"Some good, some bad; but I guess that's life, right? He did bring me some cigarettes. Would you like a couple?" I asked.

"Of course! That would be brilliant. Hmm . . . how to get them over here, though," he said.

I couldn't just cruise over to Felix's cell and start passing out squares, and I didn't have the necessary equipment to "play horse." Playing horse was strictly forbidden; Felix had explained the activity to me during walk. It required a fair amount of string of some sort, as well as something that could be used as a weight. You tied the weight to the end of the string, stuck it out your window, and swung it side to side until the person in the cell next door could grab the weight. They then tied their own piece of string to your string, you tied whatever you wanted them to have to the end you still had, then they simply pulled it over to their cell. Drugs and other contraband were often passed from cell to cell this way, so if you got caught there would be repercussions— we weren't even supposed to talk to each other through our windows, a rule everyone broke anyway depending who was on guard duty. So far Tom Selleck hadn't yelled at me for talking through my window (unlike Bradley, the jerk), so I asked Felix if he thought maybe the guard would pass him some cigarettes from me if I asked.

"Maybe. It will depend on his mood," he said doubtfully.

As I began to knock on our cell door, calling out I was almost immediately halted by a grumpy sounding Tom Selleck right out-side my door. "Fuck off!" he yelled, without bothering to open the hatch in the door to let me ask him my question. I wondered if he had heard us talking about the cigarettes, and this was his way of saying no, or if he just didn't give a crap about what was going on in our cell. *Well, at least I'm not asking for a roll of toilet paper or medical attention,* I thought. We had already been out for walk that day, so I apologized to Felix and told him I would sort him out some cigarettes the next day.

After breakfast, I sat at our table thinking about the son of a bitch prosecutor and his likely plan to keep me in Pankrác for at least the rest of my favorite time of year, the summer. Right at that moment, that hot, humid, most magical of seasons in the American South was slowly passing me by thousands of miles away, and I wanted to be at home in Richmond, riding mopeds with my wife, skateboarding with my buddy Josh, and fishing in the James river with whoever wanted to go. I wanted to be at one of the beaches I loved so much down in Cape Fear, North Caro-lina, going surfing or fishing with my brother Scott, or just swim-ming in the ocean and looking at the pretty girls with my brother Mark. I wanted to take a trip up to the Blue Ridge mountains with

Cindy, driving along Skyline Drive, then snuggling up in front of a campfire after the sun went down and the mountain air cooled. I wanted to go to my hilarious mother-in-law's house in Northern Virginia and eat a bunch of homemade Chinese food and listen to her tell stories about growing up in China. I wanted to kiss my Grandma on the cheek and hold my cat Henry and go out to eat some fresh local caught shrimp with my Mom and wrestle with my nephew Lucas. I wanted to hang out at my Dad's house and look at his latest woodworking project, and talk about books with my step-Mom Cheryl and joke around with my brother Andrew after everyone else had gone to bed. I wanted a lot of things, and as I caught myself getting madder and madder I reminded myself that people in hell want ice water. I needed to get my wanter fixed. Getting angry wasn't going to do me a lick of good, in fact it would only hurt me. I have come to realize that useless, directionless anger is one of my greatest character defects, and when I indulge myself in it, I am remaining in a problem, not its solution. Anger is a natural human emotion, and it has its place and uses, but when I get mad, *really mad*, it can be frightening to others and myself. Winding myself up like the iron core of an electrical transformer always leads to an explosion, and I can't afford explosions in my everyday life. I certainly couldn't afford one in prison, so I decided to do something that always helps balance me when I am distraught or angry. I wrote a gratitude list.

———

A gratitude list is simply a written collection of ten or so things you are grateful for in your life. I had been introduced to the practice by my friend Bill Griggs years before when I was doing a terrible amount of whining. Anyone can benefit from writing a gratitude list, and I try to do at least two or three a week to this day. When you *consistently* and *honestly* take a look at the things you actually have to be grateful for, your perspective changes, and you begin to realize what is really important. Go ahead, try it. If you're reading this and thinking that your life is so bad that you don't have a single thing to be grateful for, I don't mind telling you here and now that your priorities are all fucked up. Consider this a friendly kick in the ass from good ol' Uncle Randy. You need get off the pity pot, put on your big boy or big girl pants, revaluate your situation, and give it a try. I'll even give you the first two items: *1) I am grateful to be breathing (because if you're reading this, I'm assuming you're alive—that's something), and 2) I'm grateful that that jackass Randy wrote about gratitude lists in that crappy, long-winded book of his, because I don't want to remain miserable forever and this could conceivably one day help me pull my own head out of my ass. At least I got something out of all his rantings.*

I was definitely full of anger as I squatted on the pity pot that day, so I took out my journal and pen. This is what I wrote:

Gratitude List, July 6th, 2012

1. I am grateful that I am sober.

2. I am grateful that I have a beautiful wife who loves me and is coming to see me in a few days. She is interested in my welfare and has been helping with my case.

3. I am grateful that I have a loving family who must be very worried about me. I know they love me, even when they don't understand me.

4. I am grateful that the US and UK press seem to be on my side to my knowledge.

5. I am grateful that I have a cool cellmate, Dorj, who has a good sense of humor and makes me laugh.

6. I am grateful that Felix next door is cool and speaks English—thank God he is next door to help me out. I must return the favor.

7. I am grateful that I do not lack money—even though this place is frustrating, I am not poor like some people in here. I will eventually get to order stuff.

8. I am grateful that I am of good health physically and mentally. I must exercise both body and mind daily.

9. I am grateful that my mind is spinning still in creative directions—I must focus it on these things and learn and profit from this experience.

10. I am grateful for zazen (meditation). I must practice it more diligently.

11. I am grateful that my fellow prisoners have been kind, friendly, and sharing to me, even though they do not have much. I must repay their kindness and good deeds in turn.

12. I am grateful for the relative quiet of this prison so far. No drunks, no blasting music 24/7, no goddamned television driving me nuts. In some ways it is better than tour. I must take advantage of this.

13. I am grateful that I have pen and paper and time to write. I must sharpen my skills.

14. I am grateful I have a few cigarettes left. I should either quit or enact stricter rationing discipline. Probably quit, but even if I run out, I will make it no problem.

15. I am grateful I get three square meals a day. Although not exactly the finest of cuisine, I definitely will not starve in here, even though portions are plain and small. That is a lot more than many people have in the world. I must remember this, and be grateful for food, clothes, and shelter—all of which I have.

———

As soon as I started the list, I began to feel better. When I was done, I sat and re-read it a few times. One word in number fourteen's entry kept on jumping out at me: *discipline*. If I was going to maintain a positive mental attitude, then I needed to enact some discipline. As I pondered the word, I began to hear a song from Black Flag's classic 1985 live album, *Whose Got the 10 1/2?* At the end of the album's twelfth track, "My War," singer

Henry Rollins screams, "Yes! Annihilate! Destroy! The discipline! *I am the discipline!*" He does this with vicious, bloodcurdling, utterly committed conviction in his sandblasted voice. "My War" has always been one of my favorite songs, and hearing it in my mind made me feel even better. I grabbed the paper wrapper I had saved from our roll of toilet paper and at the top of it I wrote *THE DISCIPLINE* in large block letters, underlining it. Then I began to write out a precisely ordered daily schedule of exercise, meditation, and writing. I decided I would regiment myself, do my best to adhere to my self-imposed schedule, and maintain the discipline. I posted this schedule on the tattered cork board in our cell using four dabs of toothpaste, stared at it a bit, then began doing pushups.

The discipline would be continually refined and added to throughout my stay in prison. There were many days when lights out arrived before I had time to complete everything I had scheduled for myself for that twenty-four hour period. There were also days I slacked off, but I always picked it up again the next sunrise. The discipline kept me busy; it kept my body active, my mind sharp, and my morale up. I did not aimlessly drift through my time in prison, trapped in endless speculation about my fate. If I had, then I would have been a cloudy-minded emotional wreck. Discipline will save you when the chips are down. Discipline will temper you and turn you into steel when your ass is burning alive in the flames of life's hard times-furnace. My discipline enabled me to keep a relatively clear head on my shoulders, and I am grateful for it to this day. My gratitude list had brought me my discipline; for me the two are inseparable. When I am being an ungrateful S.O.B., my discipline gets tossed out the window.

After lunch, Bradley came to the door, scowled, and sternly said, "If you want shower, you must come now"—somehow that little jerk even made getting clean sound like a threat. Dorj and I gathered our tiny towels, soap, razors, and shaving cream, stripped down to our boxers, and followed Bradley two or three doors down the hallway to the shower. I could hear running water and laughter inside, and although I was a bit nervous about taking a shower in prison with a bunch of naked inmates (I am not shy at all about nudity, but we all know what happens in the showers in prison movies), I was really looking forward to getting clean. Bradley opened the door, steam billowed out, and Raymond Herrera and Scarface waved us a naked and cheerful hello. Dorj and I walked in, hung our towels and underwear on a hook, and began showering in the large, dim, and dingy shower room. As there were only two shower heads, the four of us had to alternate between scrubbing and rinsing, but everyone was very polite about it. No one hogged the water. It felt indescribably good to wash the dust and sweat from my body. I was just about as happy as one can be in a prison, laughing and scrubbing away, when I almost gave myself a heart attack.

What is the one thing you know most definitely *not* to do if you go to prison? The one bit of knowledge you have gained from watching prison movies, the piece of advice that is drilled into every young man's head as soon as he is old enough to really understand what long-term incarceration can entail? That one, singular, most important thing you are told not to do *under any circumstances* in a prison shower, as it will surely lead to the most horrific, painful, and humiliating consequences imaginable if you are an idiot and actually do it?

You all know what I'm talking about. And yes, I did it.

I dropped the soap.

Twice.

The first time I dropped the soap, I was standing beneath the shower head, blissfully rinsing away a thick mixture of dirt and lather when Scarface made some joke about Bradley, cursing in Czech about the stupid *bachar* and imitating his Napoleonic manner. I began to laugh, accidentally squeezing the white bar of soap in my right hand. The slippery bar shot upwards and outwards towards Scarface, and I stood transfixed, frozen with horror as I watched it fly from my grip. Time seemed to slow to a snail's pace, and like a slow-motion dream sequence in some terrifying movie, the bar of soap hung glistening in the air for a long moment before landing on the shower floor.

Noooooooooooooooooooooooooooooooooo . . . I actually heard my voice echo in my head, sounding like a 78 rpm record playing on 33. I do not believe my back has ever been straighter in my entire life as I lowered my naked body to the ground using only my legs, keeping the appropriate orifice aimed due south at all times in a defensive maneuver designed to retain my honor. No one seemed to notice that I had committed this terrible *faux pas*, and I relaxed a bit. Mere seconds later it flew out of my nervous hands again, and I stiffly lowered myself down to pick it up once more. *My God*, I thought, *they're going to think I'm flirting with them.* But once again, no one seemed to notice (or maybe they did, and I'm just not as cute as I was in my twenties), and I finished showering without any further incidents. After I was done, I grabbed my towel and dried off the best I could, which was not very well given the smallness and pitiful condition of the rough rectangle of cloth. There was no mirror in the bathroom, so I shaved blind, Dorj helping me by getting the spots I had missed. I decided to grow a goatee, as that meant less wear and tear on the single blade safety razor, which was basically useless after two or three shaves.

Later at walk we had a new inmate join us, a stocky, muscular Russian named Pavel. Pavel had a huge sack of tobacco, plenty of rolling papers, and was quite generous with both. Pavel asked me in halting English about my charge, as apparently he was getting hit with a variation of the same thing. I explained my charge and its penalty, five to ten years with no time off for good behavior. I referred to it by its paragraph number in the Czech legal code, 146, which was how prisoners seemed to discuss their charges amongst each other. Rene and everyone else (everyone is a lawyer in prison, by the way) seemed to think I would have it dropped to a lesser variety of manslaughter, which carried a penalty of two to eight years, some of which could be knocked off for good behavior. I asked Pavel about how he had landed in Pankrác, and he ruefully shook his head, saying he had been out on the town with his girlfriend when a group of guys started hitting on her. He told them to knock it off, a fight erupted, and he punched one of the men in the face. The man fell down, hit his head on the cobblestone street, and went *kaput* right there—end of story. He was also charged with manslaughter, but his paragraph was 145, which carried a sentence of ten to twenty years with no time off for good behavior. Like most Russians I have met, Pavel looked like he could more than handle himself in a fight, but he had a very gentle manner about him that made me believe his story—he just didn't give off the vibe of a troublemaker. I felt sorry for him.

———

Sitting in my cell as the sun went down, I began to think about my possible sentence. I could do a year or two no problem, and do it with a smile. Ten years though? I decided I could do that as well, but that I could not ask my wife to wait for me that long. I would not *want* her to, although I believed she would, because she is a good woman who has already been through a lot with me. Cindy was still in her thirties, she could go and find someone else, start anew. I loved her too much for her to be alone for that long. I would want her to go and build a new life, to pursue happiness. She deserved that. The thought of separating from my wife was sad for me, but I grew even sadder thinking about her heading into her fifties, alone with no husband to speak of except a box of letters sent from thousands of miles away. I felt that would be wrong of me to put her through that, and whether or not I was an innocent man didn't matter much if I went away for a decade.

Hopefully things wouldn't come to that though, and I banished the thoughts from my mind. The whole time I was in

Pankrác, I tried my best not to think about my wife too much. Not because I didn't love her; indeed it was quite the opposite—I loved her so much it hurt far too badly to ponder a life without her. Things would happen the way they were going to happen, and if I was found innocent, then there wouldn't be any problem. If I was found guilty and had to do a year or two, I would have plenty of time to miss her then. If I got ten years, then I would go about coming to peace with being alone. But not until then. At present, what I needed most was a clear head. I had to stay in the moment, and not mope over my woman.

Lights out came, and I lay there on my lumpy cot, listening to the nightly Tower of Babel as the prisoners called across the courtyard to each other. The goddamned Ukrainian above me was the loudest as usual, and kept on screaming to his comrade even after all the other men, including his friend, had stopped talking. I knew that yelling at him would do absolutely no good, in fact it would probably just piss him off and make him scream louder and longer, but he was driving me insane. I hopped up from my bed, grabbed the bars of the cell window, and got ready to curse him out. Suddenly, I was struck by how much I must resemble a monkey in a cage at the zoo, swinging from the bars, furious at my captivity. I began to laugh and get down, when an idea struck me.

I carefully let go of the window's bars, balancing on the iron railing of my bed, and cupped my hands on either side of my mouth, forming a bullhorn. Then I let rip with a Tarzan yell, just like Johnny Weissmuller did in those old black and white movies from the 1940s.

"Ooooooo-aaooo-aaoooooooooooooooooooooo-aaoo aaaaaaaaaaaaaa . . . " My jungle call echoed off the gray walls of my concrete home.

And the prison exploded into animal noises.

Monkeys, goats, cows, chickens, dogs, elephants, pigs, cats— you name it, I heard it coming screaming out of cell windows. It was completely *awesome*, it went on for a good while, and it drowned out the Ukrainian (who I'm sure was losing his mind over being out-yelled). I lay back down on my bed and smiled, listening to the menagerie that had erupted all around cell #505. I thought back to what Rene had called out to me as we all returned to our cells at the end of walk.

"Randy, go home! Go home, Randy."

I was trying my best to do just that, which didn't amount to much. But I had just spent my first week in prison, I was still alive, in good physical and mental shape, and I had a smile on my face. Fuck the prosecuting attorney, fuck the judges, fuck the cops, and fuck the assholes that ran this prison.

Fuck 'em all.

BEING COOL + BUYING ME SMOKES + COFFEE. HE GETS SOME
SWAG FOR SURE IF I GET HIS EMAIL + ADDI AFTER ALL THIS
IS DONE. ANYWAY, THEY WOULDN'T LET ME KEEP MY SMOKES
ONCE I WAS BACK IN PANKRÁC (WHICH BY THE WAY, IS A
WHOLE AREA/NEIGHBORHOOD, NOT JUST THE NAME OF THIS
PRISON), FUCKERS! PRISON RULES - ALSO - THE YOUNG FUCK
FACE GUARD WHO 1ˢᵗ PUT ME IN HERE TOLD ME THE OTHER DAY -
"FOR YOUR FUTURE, YOU MUST STAND UP WHEN WE OPEN THE DOOR" -
FAT CHANCE FUCKFACE, UNLESS ITS FOR ME TO GET UP
+ SIEG HEIL HIM JUST TO LET HIM KNOW I THINK HE'S
A FUCKIN' NAZI. THAT DUDE (WHO I WILL CALL
BRADLY, BECAUSE HE LOOKS LIKE A BRADLY) IS A FUCKING
DICK - I WOULD EAT HIM ALIVE. THE SAME DAY HE CAME BY, POPPED
THE HATCH AND SAID "GOOD NEWS FOR YOU!" + I SAID "OH YEAH?"
+ HE SAID "YES, LUNCH IS HERE" + SAID IT WAS GOOD NEWS
SINCE I WAS HUNGRY + HE SAID "OH YES, + THE POLICE ARE
COMING" - YEE FUCKIN' HAW ASSHOLE, I ALREADY KNEW THAT, +
IT TURNED OUT GREAT, SO SUCK IT. THE OFFICE TO CHANGE BACK INTO
MY PRISON CLOTHES CLOSED @ 3 SO I AM STILL IN MY STREET DUDS.
WE ANYWAY, WE ATE DINNER, SMOKED UP OUR LAST STUDENTS, +
CRASHED. / TODAY WE AWOKE WITH NO SMOKES - DRAT!
(I NEED TO USE DRAT MORE OFTEN), HAD BREAKFAST, CRASHED
SOME MORE, THEN IT WAS OFF TO THE PSYCHIATRIST
TO MAKE SURE MY LEXAPRO DOESN'T RUN OUT (FUNNY,

chapter twelve

My second week in prison began with me sitting down to do something I absolutely loathe—writing a letter to the press. In my life as a musician, I prefer to let my work and my actions speak for themselves. I don't like explaining myself, my band's music, or our show, especially to the press. In fact, I hate doing interviews when we put out a new record or go on tour, because I honestly really have nothing to say. I'm not the band guy who says, "This is our greatest record ever! We are so proud of it!" in the press. I view that kind of crap as the hot air that it is. I mean, who is going to tell an interviewer, "You know, this record is pretty good, but I like the one we did two records before it waaaaay better," even if it's the truth? "Just listen to the damn record and come to the show, and if you like it, cool. If not, I'm sure you'll let us know"—that's my ideal answer to all questions concerning any upcoming releases or tours by lamb of god, or any other music I may put out in the future. Unfortunately, that doesn't help sell many records or concert tickets, so I talk to the press and answer the same questions over and over. Then, once the reviews come out, good or bad, I try not to look at them. What other people think and say about my music has absolutely no bearing whatsoever on what I do and how I do it. Besides, brutal criticism from total strangers, sometimes directed at you *personally*, is the price you pay for daring to stand in the ring and fight instead of sitting on your fat ass in the bleachers, heckling and drinking over-priced shitty beer. I'll take the ring any day—I'm not really a sidelines kind of guy.

But I wasn't putting out a new record or going on tour, I was facing a manslaughter charge, and I was being demonized by the national media of the country I was incarcerated in. I couldn't just ignore that kind of press, like I could a crappy record review. I still wasn't exactly sure what had happened that night in 2010, but I honestly believed I never purposely attempted to harm anyone (which was the nature of the charge against me), and I wanted to state that as loudly and as clearly as I could for the record.

"Greetings from Pankrác Prison in Prague. I, D. Randall Blythe, am writing this to inform anyone who may care of my status and position concerning my current incarceration in the Czech Republic . . . " The statement went on to elaborate on five main points: 1) a profession of my innocence, 2) my complete surprise and displeasure over not only being arrested but not being previously informed in any way of the charges against me by either the Czech or American governments, 3) a statement that I had suffered no abuse at the hands of either inmates or prison employees, 4) a few words of reassurance for my countrymen and women back home that I was both physically and mentally fit, and could not complain of my circumstances as our men and women of the armed services live through far worse in the course of their duties, and do so without whining, and 5) an expression of my sorrow over Daniel's death, regardless of my guilt or innocence.

I worked on the statement until we were called to go outside for a walk, which, as it was a Saturday, occurred at 8 am. As we were being led back to our cells after the hour outside was up, Felix turned to me and said, "And now, we will be locked in our cells for twenty-seven and a half hours." Agh! No! Don't say that! He reminded me of some of my band and crew members who like to start counting the days left on a tour way too early into a run. "Hey! Only forty-seven more shows to do until we get

letters, two English books, and two printed out emails. One was from my drummer, Chris. He wrote me to say that the band was working as hard as they could to get me out of there, and that the support for me from the music community was overwhelming. Several very well-known musicians, people from groups far bigger than ours, were speaking up publicly about my situation. The fans were sticking with me, a White House petition had been started and was rapidly gathering signatures, and people were sporting "Free Randy" shirts already. It was good to know that I hadn't been forgotten by the music family I had been a member of for my entire adult life.

The other email was from my wife Cindy, and I must have read it fifteen or twenty times that day alone. "Honey, I don't even have the words for how sorry I am about what you're going through. Even just saying that falls terribly short. I know you're staying calm and strong—you continue to amaze me with what you're capable of doing, of handling . . . "—the beginning of that letter was all I needed to feel better. I just needed to know that my wife knew I was okay, that I was maintaining a stoic attitude, that I was still the man she knew I was and would continue to be. She had given me that in a few short sentences, which was a precious gift to me. I didn't worry about myself that much when I was in prison—there were scary moments, but I had handled them so far without freaking out and I knew I would continue to do so. But make no mistake about it, I am a worrier by nature—about other people. If someone I care about is going through a particularly rough spot, I will worry about them until I am almost paralyzed with anxiety. This is counter-productive of course, and I try not to worry so much, but I can't help it a lot of the time. And I had been very worried about my wife, because I knew that me being locked up would pain her. After I read her letter, I wasn't so worried, because I knew that she could sense I was okay. The letter went on to let me know that she had seen pictures of me in court, and could tell by my face that I was remaining calm. She also knew that I was okay because she had heard I was learning some Mongolian from my cellmate (in later letters from other friends, they said similar things—they knew I was doing okay because I was still trying to absorb some culture, even in prison). Reading Cindy's letter had made even more determined to not let the weight of my uncertain future crush me under its fearsome heel. I would soldier on, and do what I could to run a tight mental and physical ship. Energized, I made a small sign for our cork board on a square of paper. It read in bold letters: *Maintain Discipline.* I stuck it up, then plopped down on my bed to look at the two books Martin had brought me.

Ah, books. *Books I could read.* By this time, I hadn't cracked open a book in almost two weeks, the longest period I had gone without reading since I had first learned how, and I was starting to get a little nutty from the lack of mental exercise. The first one I picked up was *The Quest,* by Wilbur Smith. From what I could gather after a brief perusal, it was a historical novel set in ancient Egypt, and seemed to center mainly around the activities of a slave who had been castrated. Well, at least there wouldn't be any dirty parts to get me all worked up and missing the wife. *Hmmm, could be interesting, but I'm really not a huge fan of the whole slavery and penis removal thing,* I thought, and picked up the other book. This one also involved a bit of forced physical mutilation, but seemed to have a slightly more hopeful bent to it. *Unbound: A True Story of War, Love, and Survival,* by Dean King, was about thirty women who had survived the Long March, a massive and brutal 4,000 mile retreat across China on foot by Mao Zedong's Red Army from the soldiers of Chiang Kai-shek's Chinese Nationalist Army. The book's title was taken from the ancient Chinese practice of binding girls' feet at a young age (thereby permanently deforming them) in order to make them develop the "lotus gait," a mincing way of walking primarily on the heels that was deemed erotic by Chinese men at the time. The women of *Unbound* had rejected this barbaric process, and saw

Mao Zedong's Communist Party (which opposed foot binding) as progressive and feminist, so they endured the Long March, even though several of them were later persecuted by the Communists during Chairman Mao's Cultural Revolution in the '60s and '70s. My wife's mother is from China, I have family there, and I find the history of the land fascinating (especially the complete and abrupt overhaul of national identity that came with Mao's rise to power), so despite the lengthy list of character names in the front of the book (all those Wangs and Yangs and Tangs looked pretty confusing), I decided I would probably give *Unbound* a go before *The Quest*. Plus, although the subject matter looked pretty grim, at least the Chinese women had rejected foot binding and had decided to walk on their own two normal feet; once somebody cuts off your pecker in ancient Egypt, you just have to deal with it and come to some sort of acceptance, I guess. My decision was made final the second I read the author's brief bio on the back dust jacket: *Dean King lives in Richmond, VA.* My homeboy! I settled down with the book, and made a mental note to contact King one day and tell him how reading a hometown author's book in prison had cheered me up. (So thanks, Dean—it really did!)

The next morning after breakfast Bradley came by #505 and opened the door. Dorj and I were both laying on our beds, me swiftly decimating *Unbound* (it was a good book) and Dorj whistling. Bradley didn't appear to really want anything. I think he was just bored and wanted to see if he could piss me off.

"When I open door, you must stand up!" he ordered.

"Yeah, dude, whatever." I said, returning to my book. Neither Dorj nor myself moved an inch.

"You must stand up when I open door!" he repeated, agitated by our insolent non-compliance.

"I heard you the first time. Are you done here now? I'm trying to read," I said, peeking over the top of my book. Dorj rolled over on his side and closed his eyes.

"For future, you must stand when I open!" he almost shouted. Bradley was getting worked up. This gave me *immense* satisfaction.

"I wouldn't hold my breath waiting for that to happen if I were you. Don't let the door hit you in the ass on the way out," I said, then returned to my book.

Bradley looked confused by my colloquial English. He cursed in Czech, then turned swiftly, stomped out of our room, and slammed the cell door shut. Dorj and I immediately burst out laughing. I knew Bradley could hear us, as he was still locking the door and we were howling quite loudly. There was no way I was going to get out of bed and stand up for that jerk. Actually, I had briefly considered hopping up, snapping to attention, screaming *Seig Heil!* and throwing him the ol' Hitler salute while laughing in his face just to let him know what a joke of a tiny little wanna-be fascist I thought he was, but quickly thought better of it. I didn't know if he would try and spread rumors that I was some sort of neo-Nazi (after all, the Czechs had had a pretty rough time of it with the Third Reich in the very prison I sat in); plus, just laying there seemed pretty darn effective at getting under his skin. As long as I didn't physically attack him, I figured he couldn't do too much to me or really make my life much worse. What was he going to do? Throw me in prison? Screw him.

I spent the rest of the day reading *Unbound* and working on a second draft of my letter to the press. Every now and then, as he was prone to do, Dorj would snort his derision at my foolish bourgeois pursuits as I read or wrote. I asked him why he didn't get a book to read—surely our ghoulish trusty could find him one in Czech, and by then I knew he could read Czech perfectly well. Or he could borrow one from another prisoner; I had seen several inmates exchanging books during walk.

"Bah—book *spatny* (no good). Pure vodka *mots doubri* (awesome as hell)!" he said, then took a long, deep, satisfying imaginary slug of Poland's best.

I honestly could not grasp this mentality—even during my drinking days I read constantly, and as we had no pure vodka (or anything else, for that matter) to keep us amused, reading a book seemed to be the logical answer to the pressing problem of what to do with our abundant spare time. But Dorj never once touched a book the entire time I was in Pankrác, and to this day I honestly doubt he has ever read one, period. Dorj not only refused to do anything that might be good for him, he scoffed at me whenever I engaged in any activity designed to keep myself mentally and physically fit. I would do pushups, and no matter how many I would crank out, he would laugh at me when I was done and say, "You like girl! No strong, hahaha!" It was like having the world's worst personal trainer in the cell—a fat, lazy, fiending alcoholic coach who offered no advice, no support, and no encouragement; only a terrible and monotonous whistling work out soundtrack and a harsh broken English critique of my performance once I was done. Dorj would crush me at a game of chess if I happened to feel like being further demoralized that day, or do the Sudoko puzzles sandwiched in between photos of topless women and the horoscope in *Blesk*; but that's about as far as he would go when it came to mental exertion. Whistling, eating, making paper swans, and calling President Barack Obama a "chimpanz" was about the maximum distance he was willing to walk down his short and narrow intellectual alleyway.

Dorj really had a hard-on for Obama for some reason—on the rare occasion we were given a banana with our breakfast, he would laugh, and hold out the banana to me, saying, "For Obama! Ah-murica president black chimpanz!!!! Ah hahaha! You President Obama chimpanz! Hahaha!" Then he would peel the banana and eat it while making monkey noises, saying, "I Obama! I Obama, hahaha!" On this particular day, after he had already been laughing at me for reading, Dorj started in with the whole Obama bit. I had had about enough of his racist crap, and so I yelled back at him in broken English/Czech: "Mongolian president chimpanz! You *manelka* (wife) chimpanz! You mother chimpanz! Dorj is chimpanz! All spatny Mongols, chimpanz, goddamn it!" Dorj just stared at me like I was an idiot.

"No! No chimpanz Mongolia—Mongolia, *zima* (cold)! Chimpanz, no *zima*. Ahmurica, *teplo* (warm). *Teplo*, yes chimpanz. Ahmurica, *teplo*. Ahmurica many chimpanz, okay?" he said, scowling at me. Clearly, I was a moron with no knowledge of global climates or simian temperature preferences. For all I knew, Dorj might actually have thought we had wild chimpanzees running around in America, so I just shook my head and gave up. I couldn't believe I was in a European prison, having to defend my President's honor from racist remarks, and reduced to counter-attacking by calling my Asian cellmate's mother a chimpanzee. It was too ridiculous to actually get riled up over, so I did what I always did whenever the absurdity of my situation struck me—I laughed. Even if Dorj and I had spoken each other's languages perfectly, he seemed pretty set in his ways. I didn't harbor any delusions about him suddenly embracing a broader, more enlightened way of thinking just because I yelled at him that my President was not an ape, which was about the extent of my linguistic rebuttal powers in our shared crude English/Czech/Mongolian patois. I couldn't even get him to accept that reading a freaking book was a worthwhile activity for *me*, much less convince him to open his mind a bit on the topic of race relations. Plus, Dorj's skin was a few shades darker than Barack Obama's, so it was especially funny when he would yell about my "black" President. I had no choice but to laugh at his ridiculous gibes.

Dorj did perform one valuable service for me later that day, bestowing an honor usually reserved for academics who have to spend phenomenal amounts of time and money to achieve what I did in just two short weeks as a jail bird: he gave me my doctorate. As I sat writing, Dorj came over and leaned on my shoulder, peered at my writing, then picked up *Unbound*, thumbed through it, slammed it back down on the table, then started pointed at me and laughing. Christ, that guy was getting on my nerves.

"*What?*" I asked, "What's so damn funny, lard-ass? Is it the reading? The writing? My black President again? What?"

"Ahahahah! You doctor now! You doctor!" he said, imitating me reading and writing.

"No Dorj, I'm not a goddamed doctor. I'm a singer and a jail bird, just like you," I said.

"No, you doctor now! You read book, you write, you in Pankrác! Amurica, Hahvad University. Czechy, Pankrác Academe! You doctor, Pankrác Academe! You . . . Doctor Pankrác! Ahahahahahaha!" he hooted, and fell back on his bed, convulsing with laughter and blurting out "Doctor Pankrác!" every now and then.

And that is how I became a doctor, and Doctor Pankrác was how Dorj referred to me from there on out, until after a particularly bad case of gas, when I earned my second doctorate, and he began calling me Doctor Bomba. After I asked him what the Mongolian word for swan was, he became Doctor Khun (pronounced *hoon*), since he made swans just about as much as I read and wrote. Every morning immediately after waking up, he greeted me as I had taught him to: "Good morning, Doctor Pankrác, how are you today?" "I'm fine, thank you for asking, Doctor Khun. Would you care for some moldy *hleb* (bread)?" I would reply. As a doctor, I figured it was my duty to teach my fellow doctor some etiquette so that he could behave in a dignified manner suited to a man of such high scholarly distinction, but Dorj never got past saying good morning. You can only polish a turd so much.

The next day a few hours before lunch, I heard Felix calling to me through his cell window. I climbed up to my own window so we could chat, and he told me that he had just heard the guards talking about me. They were saying that the police were coming for me later in the day. I asked him what for, and he told me he didn't really know for sure, but thought that maybe they would be taking me somewhere for further interrogation. This immediately sent the wheels in my head to spinning—I didn't know what they wanted, but I was damn sure not going to say a thing until Martin Radvan was in the room with me. The presence of my attorney during any questioning was my legal right under Czech law, and I began to imagine myself arguing with whoever would be interrogating me this time, insisting that they summon Radvan or I wouldn't say a thing. Despite their threats, I would stonewall them, I would be as stoic as Marcus Aurelius, I would remain calm like the eye of the storm—the hatch in our cell door opened and Bradley peeked his head in, just as I was telling my imaginary interrogator that I would have his head on a spike in front of Prague Castle if he didn't summon my lawyer immediately.

"Good news for you!" Bradley said through that crappy bleached smile of his.

"Oh yeah? You tested positive for syphilis?" I asked.

"Lunch is here!" He laughed.

"That's *great* news, because I'm starving. I can't wait to see what delights the cooks came up with today," I said, smiling right back at him.

"Oh yes," he paused. "*And* the police are coming," he added, obviously excited at the thought of me being questioned more.

"I already knew that. I asked them to pop by and bring me a hooker," I said.

Bradley smirked at me, then slammed the hatch shut. Man, that guy sucked, but he had actually done me a service by interrupting my ridiculous interrogation fantasies. Smart-assing off to him had made me stop predicting worst-case scenarios, one of my most unfortunate mental traits that I couldn't afford to let run rampant in prison. Being prepared for hard times is one thing; actively sketching out insanely detailed blue prints for structurally unsound buildings and erecting them on mental fault lines is another. Most bad things I imagine simply do not happen—if they did, life as we know it would have been wiped from the face of the earth decades ago. I did not have to wait long to find out what the police wanted anyway, as they came for me shortly after lunch. A guard took me upstairs to the laundry room where I had handed over my street clothes, and a trusty gave them back to me. The trusty and the guard led me into the office area of the laundry section, and told me to change out of my prison duds. As I changed in front of both men, I began laughing. Everywhere I looked, I saw a familiar face.

The walls of the office were covered with pictures of my friends.

Apparently the guys who ran the prison laundry were metal heads. Above the desk were posters of Machine Head, Killswitch Engage, Shadows Fall, and Metallica, all bands I had toured with several times and dear friends. Over in a corner beside an industrial sized tub of detergent I saw Zakk Wylde, Ozzy Osbourne's old guitarist and frontman of Black Label Society—I'd known him since 2004. I'd put down some road miles with Dimmu Borgir, and there they were, sneering above a pile of dirty towels, adding a comforting bit of homey Nordic evil to the dark faux-pine paneled walls. And on the wall right beside me was a large poster of Slash from Guns-n-Roses, ripping away on his guitar—I had been stage right shooting pictures of him playing with his current project and rapping with him afterwards backstage just a few weeks ago in Belgium. It felt like I was back on tour, backstage with the bros at a festival for a moment.

"Dudes!!! What's up?!" I said to all my guys on the walls. The guard looked at me like I was crazy, but the trusty I handed my prison clothes to shot me a smile. He understood why I was happy—he was obviously one of my people. Just seeing all these faces I knew personally in such a depressing and unexpected place did me a world of good. On the way out I passed Lemmy from Motörhead, standing on stage with one arm raised. I smacked my hand against the wall and gave him a high-five—I didn't know Lemmy, but I figured he wouldn't mind.

Downstairs at the prison entrance where I was first admitted to Pankrác were three plain-clothes detectives—one was the speed demon who had taken me on such a terrifying ride through Prague to identify my medicine. I hoped he wouldn't be driving us wherever we were going (he did, of course). Another was a gigantic grim-looking ball of muscle whose name I never got—I

don't know if he could speak. The third detective, a fit and pleasant looking man with short dirty blond hair walked up to me, introduced himself as Charlie in excellent English, and told me they
were going to carry me to an eye doctor, as there was something
wrong with my eyes.

"I don't have any eye problems," I said "I just wear glasses."

"Yes, but the police want you to go get your eyes checked. We
have to go to a doctor about 100 kilometers away—this is the only
doctor in the Czech Republic authorized to do such examinations
for the police," he said.

"100 kilometers away! I'm going to miss my one hour of going outside—it starts soon," I said.

"Yes, but I think it is better than being in prison, don't you? It
is a nice drive," he said

I couldn't argue with him there, so off we went, me and the
hulking silent detective in the back seat. After being locked up
in prison for a couple of weeks, it was quite strange to see people walking the streets in regular clothes, headed wherever they
wanted to go, not herded down dingy hallways in ill-fitting prison
pajamas like a bunch of miserable cows. We sped through the
outskirts of Prague and into the sunny Czech countryside, which
was quite beautiful at that time of the year. Mile after mile of rolling fields full of corn, wheat, and other crops passed; I saw thousands of sun flowers taller than my head planted in orderly rows.
I rested my head against the window, looking out at the fields
and forests passing by—the landscape reminded me very much of
Southampton County, Virginia, an area I had spent much of my
childhood in, roaming the woods and peanut fields of my Grandmother's farm land. For a few moments I tried to forget about the
handcuffs around my wrists and just enjoy the ride. Not too long
after we had been in the countryside, Charlie asked me if I would
like something to eat, perhaps some cigarettes and a coffee? I told
him I had no money, and he said not to worry—these things were
not very expensive, they would buy them for me. We would stop

at a gas station soon for smokes, with an adjacent McDonald's for food and coffee.

McDonald's—*yuck*. "The American Embassy" as I like to call it (you will see those familiar Golden Arches rising like two high-cholesterol boils from the city streets of just about every country on the planet) had *terrible* coffee, and I'm not too fond of their food either—it's garbage designed to make people as fat as possible while providing minimal nutritional value. But as the old saying goes, beggars can't be choosers, so I graciously accepted his offer, all the while mentally cursing that clown Ronald for conquering Europe far more effectively than any imperialistic despot ever had. Soon we were parked at the gas station next to McDonald's, and Charlie and the driver left the car to go get us food and smokes. I looked over at the huge man crammed into the back of the Skoda next to me and gave him a smile. He gave me his version of a smile back, which resembled his cheeks dead lifting about five hundred pounds—even his face looked like it worked out. He didn't seem *mean*, just . . . big. I guess Charlie and the driver felt better protected against the might of my 165 pounds of fury with an elephant in the back.

Soon they returned with coffee, a water, a pack of smokes, and a brand-new lighter for me, and burgers for themselves. Despite the awfulness of Pankrác's cuisine, I politely declined their offers of food—I couldn't bring myself to eat Mickey D's that day, but in retrospect that was highly foolish of me—I just hadn't been in prison long enough. Had it been a week later I would have gorged myself until I had a Big Mac heart attack. As Charlie gave me my coffee, he told me he was going to remove my handcuffs and open the car door so I could smoke while they ate, but that I shouldn't go anywhere. I told Charlie not to worry, I wasn't going anywhere, and thanked him for the coffee and the smokes. I lit up a cigarette, careful to blow the smoke away from the eating detectives (manners are manners, y'all), and took a tentative sip of the dreaded McDonald's coffee.

I nearly went into shock after just one taste—it was absolutely *fantastic*. Strong, dark, aromatic, and full of flavor, but not burnt or bitter. I took the lid off the coffee and looked—yes, the brew even had a slight crema resting beautifully on its black surface. I stopped for a moment and reminded myself that I hadn't had a decent coffee for a while, just in case I was overreacting, then took another sip. Nope, it really was that good. If McDonald's had coffee that delicious in the States, I would go there everyday, and Ronald's unholy plan for obesity-based global domination be damned. I finished my cigarette and drank my coffee as slowly as I could while the men ate, then we hit the road. Charlie did not re-cuff me. I thanked him for that, and again for the cigarettes and coffee.

"It is no problem. And it is not like I enjoy having to handcuff you," he said with a kind smile. "My policy is that if you are reasonable, then I will be reasonable."

Charlie really did seem like a reasonable man, a guy just doing his job. As sad as it is, the world does in fact need homicide detectives—I know that if a friend or relative of mine was murdered, I would want someone trained in police work to help me find out who had done it. I have had many, many run-ins with cops over the years, and a lot of them have been unpleasant. I have known racist cops, sadistic cops, power-tripping cops, and straight-up criminal cops who got a piece of the action wherever and whenever they could. But I have also known some very, very cool cops who honestly just want to help keep people safe.

Don't get me wrong—I still avoid the police whenever possible. Cops make me nervous, because I know what they can do. I've felt the end of a nightstick in my ribs more than once. But only a complete idiot would hold on to the knee-jerk idea that all cops are bad people—I know, because I was that complete idiot for a long time. As I've gotten older, I've had to learn not to throw a rock at every bird I see just because a seagull pooped on my head once at the beach. And since Charlie was treating me like a human being, just taking me to get my eyes checked as he had been told to do by his boss for whatever reason, I did my best to act reasonable. We actually had quite a good talk on the way to the optometrist, discussing how he came to be a detective (all detectives in the Czech Republic have to be regular beat cops for several years before they can move on to their area of law enforcement), and how I had come to be a professional heavy metal musician. Charlie's favorite band was Metallica—he had seen them at least fifteen times, he said, so I told him a few funny tour stories about those guys, and we even argued a little bit about which record of theirs was the best (my overall favorite is *Ride the Lightning*). As we were riding and talking, I began to notice how badly I smelled in comparison to the three men in the car with me. Normally, when I am stuck with a bunch of dudes (i.e., on tour with a bunch of other unwashed heathens), I only notice how clean and different women smell (I would describe it as "delicious"). But I was so ripe I could really notice the smell of freshly washed clothes, clean skin, and shampooed hair of the men surrounding me. That I stank made me feel self-conscious, so I apologized to Charlie.

"Dude, I'm really sorry about the way I smell right now. I don't have any clean clothes and they only let us shower twice a week in that shitty prison. Normally, I'm a pretty clean person, but being in Pankrác isn't exactly like going to a Swiss spa," I said.

"Do not worry—you don't smell that bad," he said kindly. "We have to deal with much, much worse; mentally ill homeless people and drug addicts who *really* stink. You are fine."

After about an hour of driving, we reached the city where my appointment had been scheduled (I believe it was a town named Pardubice, but I cannot be certain), and soon we were pulling into the parking lot of a nondescript office complex. Next to the offices was a funereal home, which shared the parking lot. Someone popular must have been getting planted that day, as a very large number of mourners were exiting the building right as we pulled up. They were dressed mostly in the traditional black, and weeping women dabbed their eyes with tissues as they passed slowly by mere feet outside my window. I was relieved when we continued past the funeral home and around the corner of the office complex, out of the mourners' view—I didn't know if they would be putting me in cuffs again to see the doctor, and I didn't want to frighten or upset these obviously saddened people any further. It was a strange thing to be out in public yet still a prisoner, escorted by three burly and openly armed policemen. I felt as if everyone who saw me might recognize me as the evil American, as my face had certainly been on the front page of the news, and videos of me in court had been shown on Czech national television. I was grateful when we got out of the car to go into the office, Charlie made no motion to cuff me again, because it was evident that this was just a regular doctor's office, and I could spot a few patients waiting to be seen in the small waiting room up front. It would have made me feel pretty awkward to sit next to the mother waiting there with her pre-teen daughter had I been in cuffs. As it was, I was self-conscious enough already; I was in dirty clothes, I was unshaven, and I stunk pretty badly. None of the people in the waiting room seemed to notice though as Charlie talked to the receptionist, who shortly opened a door and ushered us down a back hallway and into a large examination room to meet the doctor.

The doctor introduced himself with a smile; he spoke perfect colloquial English and didn't seem disconcerted at all by the fact that I was in his office with three cops, a man under armed guard and charged with killing another human being. The doctor and one of his nurses administered the same basic battery of tests I have been taking off and on since I was in the second grade, when I first got glasses. The doctor was quite friendly as well, and we chatted about various things while I took the tests; it was very nice for me to speak in my native tongue with a person who had not a trace of awkwardness in their speech. Except for the police presence, I could have been in any optometrist's office back at home, getting a regular old eye exam. The doctor even scolded me for smoking, asking how many packs a day I smoked; when I told him one, he laughed and said, "So that means two. You should really quit, you know." I realized that the day's trip—the coffee, the conversation, seeing a bit of nature, even the vision tests—had made me feel more like a regular human being than I had in quite sometime.

After the tests were done, the doctor wished me good luck, and we got back into the car for the ride back to Pankrác. Charlie let me smoke before we left the parking lot, and again during a brief roadside stop for the driver to take a leak in one of the sunflower fields. He told me he would try to convince the people at the prison to let me keep the pack of cigarettes he had bought me, but it was unlikely that they would (and once we were back in Pankrác, he did try—no dice). As we neared Pankrác, the song "One" by the heavy metal band Metallica came on the radio, and I asked the driver to turn it up, which he did. "One" was the first song by Metallica to crack the Top 40 charts and garner them a bit of mainstream acclaim, winning the first Grammy ever given for best metal performance. It is a fantastic song, but much like "Stairway to Heaven" or "Free Bird," it had been played to death by commercial radio for over twenty years by that point, and just like those songs when I listen to Zeppelin or Skynyrd, I normally skip the track when I crank some Metallica. But on this day, I had never been happier to hear the opening samples of machine guitar and mortar fire, Kirk Hammett's crystal clear guitar intro, and James Hetfield's rich voice singing the opening lines:

"I can't remember anything, can't tell if this is true or dream . . . "

Hearing music made by friends of mine was like getting a call from home, and that song did me more good at that moment than they could ever know (thanks, dudes), and we pulled into Pankrác with it blasting—Charlie even let me stay in the car until the song was over. The irony of rocking out to some of the lyrics behind the gates of a prison did not escape me ("darkness/imprisoning me/all that I see/absolute horror/I cannot live/I cannot die/trapped in myself/body my holding cell"), but as their grim musical tale of a severely wounded war veteran trapped in his own body ended, I walked through the front door of Pankrác with a little more pep in my step. I said goodbye to Charlie, and he wished me luck. The laundry office was closed for the day, so I was led back to my cellblock wearing my street clothes. Bradley was waiting, that stupid grin of his plastered on his face.

"So, you have nice day with police?" he smirked as he opened my cell door.

"You're goddamned right I did. It was *fucking great*," I said. "The police were super nice to me, and we went for a nice long drive through the country. We stopped for McDonald's, and they bought me cigarettes and coffee. Then I sat around in an air-conditioned office talking to a guy who spoke perfect English, and we listened to heavy metal on the way home. I even heard some of my friends' music; plus it was *beautiful* outside, too. Did you have a nice day in this shitty basement?"

"Why are you wearing these clothes? You must change into prison clothes," he said, obviously disappointed by my cheery report and trying to regain the emotional upper hand.

"No can do, chief—laundry is closed. It sure is nice to not wear those crappy pajamas though," I said, and flopped down on my bed with a smile. *Suck it, Bradley.*

———

The next day after breakfast, a guard who spoke excellent English took me for a visit to the psychiatrist. I had written a note earlier in the week, which Felix translated into Czech for me, requesting an appointment to ensure that my rapidly disappearing prescription of Lexapro was refilled. While I hoped to eventually get off the drug (and eventually did, during the writing of this book), I did not want to stop taking an antidepressant cold turkey in prison. I was scared of what would happen to my mind, as my brain chemistry might still be all screwed up—I had put in twenty-two years of hard drinking and drugging, so I had without question, done my best to make it so.

The shrink was a sour-faced woman who, with the guard acting as a translator, asked me the standard prison shrink stuff: How are you doing? What is your mental state like? Have you been depressed at all? What do you think of the prison so far? Are you having any problems getting along with the other inmates? I had been warned by Felix about this woman, so I knew just what to say.

I told her the truth.

"Well, I must tell you the truth and say I'm doing just fine, m'am," I chirped, sounding happier than an injury claims lawyer at a thirty-car pile up. "I have all the things I need to survive. I have food, clothes, and shelter. I am grateful for these things—many people in the world are not so lucky. They don't get three meals a day. They are forced to wear whatever rags they can scrounge up. They don't have a bed to sleep in. And many of my countrymen and women are at war, stuck fighting in the desert somewhere, with people who hate them and are trying to kill them. They have it much worse off than me. So no, things really aren't so bad here when I think about it that way." The shrink looked up at me from her notepad, her face brightening like an elementary school teacher who had just discovered a star pupil in a class full of juvenile delinquents.

"Well! I certainly wish *all* the prisoners here had such a good attitude," she said, making a note for the prison pharmacist to send me 10 milligrams of Lexapro daily, and I was off and back in cell #505 in a short amount of time. In-and-out in about ten minutes. Easy-peasy-Japanesey.

What I had told her *was* 100 percent true; I *was* grateful I wasn't starving, I *was* grateful for clothes and shelter, and the men and women of my country's armed forces *did* have it a lot worse than me, and no one had tried to kill me in Pankrác . . . *yet*. And really, I honestly did think about all of these things on a daily basis. That's the truth, and my gratitude list reflected it. But our interview would have gone very, very differently had I not been carefully choosing my tone of voice and words to convey an almost moronic sense of contentment with my lot. Had I not been afraid of being locked in the basement longer, or pissing off the psychiatrist so much she refused to authorize my drugs, I would have said something like *this:*

"How am I doing? *HOW AM I DOING?!?!?!?* How in the fuck do you *think* I'm doing, you sloth-witted bitch? *I'm in prison. In a foreign country. I'm doing terrible.* Who gave you this job, Bozo the Clown? What do I think of the place? Am I depressed? Have you bothered to look around? Have you ever seen the basement of this dump? For Pete's sake, have you ever even tried *the soup*? My God, do you even know where you are right now, you mutton-headed shrew? *Of course* I'm depressed, *of course* my mental state is a little bit on the grim side right now. What do you expect out of me, cartwheels and a thank-you note? Jesus H. Christ, if all I have to do to get a gig as a psychiatrist in this country is ask unbelievably stupid questions with excruciatingly obvious answers, then as soon as I get out of this hideous den of sorrow and woe, I'm going to take your fucking job and figure out a way to stick *you* in the basement with Cuckoo Khan the whistling wonder. I'll let *you* rot down there for a couple of weeks, then ask *you* the same asinine questions you just shot at me out of that clueless gob of yours. Then we'll see whose mental state needs evaluating."

But I had been forewarned by Felix, so I played the game and acted like a grateful little criminal. If I was going to be stuck in Pankrác until my trial (and as each day passed, this seemed more and more likely), I wanted to be moved out of that dark basement, upstairs into population, and properly medicated so I didn't flip my wig. I wasn't happy about having to play suck up, but sometimes discretion truly is the better part of valor.

After I got back from the shrink, Bradley popped by to tell me that I had to change out of my street clothes immediately. He seemed really bummed that I was just kicking it in my normal duds. When I laughed in his face and told him that these were the only clothes I had to wear, unless of course he wanted to lend me his, he stomped off in a huff to find someone to take me to the laundry. He came back shortly wearing a triumphant grin and said that a guard would take me upstairs soon to change. No one ever showed up to collect me, and Bradley looked extra pissy at lights out when he saw me lounging in my camo shorts and skate shop shirt. *Read it and weep*, I thought as I pointed out the printing on the shirt with a smile as he peeked through the cell door hatch. *No Mercy, Bradley, you insufferable douchebag.*

The next day the guard came and yelled "Advocate!" and up I went to see my lawyer, or in this case, lawyers. Seated with Tomas Morycek was Jeff Cohen, and I had never been happier to see his face. Besides the fact that I loved Jeff as a person, besides the fact that he was there to help my Czech lawyers out, besides the fact that he would be able to explain to me in plain English from an educated point of view what in the hell was going on with my case so far, besides the simple fact that his was a comforting familiar face—Jeff was an *American. He belonged to my team.* He was my countryman, and I had not seen one of those in a few weeks.

Jeff had also brought me four packs of cigarettes (the guard only let me keep one) and a book. Jeff has a highly developed sense of irony, and as he handed me the book he said, "You know, I was talking to some people about what to bring you to read, and some of them suggested giving you really long stuff, like *War and Peace*, to eat up some time. But I said, 'Fuck that!—there is only *one* book Randy needs to be reading right now,' and this is it, baby."

I looked at the book in my hand. *The Trial*, by Franz Kafka. Jeff had brought me *The* fucking *Trial; the singular* weirdest, most depressing, surreal fictional account of an arrest and prosecution by a court of law ever written. To make things even worse, it was written by Franz Kafka. In Prague. Two or three miles away from where I sat at that very second. I hadn't cracked open any Kafka since high school, and I had never bothered to read *The Trial*, but I was vaguely familiar with the book's plot—Josef K. wakes up one day and is arrested out of the blue for an unspecified crime by two agents working for an unknown agency. The rest of the book just gets stranger and stranger as Josef K. struggles to understand the nature of the nameless charge against him and the bizarre and convoluted "court" that automatically assumes his guilt. In the end, he is executed with a butcher's knife, his last words being "Like a dog!" Josef K. dies a bloody death, never even knowing what he has supposedly done wrong. It is, like virtually all of Kafka's work, a very, very dark book. Any hopes I might have had for a little light reading, something to take my mind off my bizarre situation, perhaps a nice mindless fantasy novel, were dashed immediately.

In press coverage of my legal ordeal, the term *Kafka-esque* would be repeatedly used to describe the predicament I had found myself in. The journalists who bandied that term about were not so much hitting the nail on the head as dropping an atom bomb on the freaking thing—the parallels hit a little too close to home for comfort. I had been suddenly arrested one day while going about my normal business, and told to my disbelief that I had committed a serious crime. Although, unlike Josef K., after a short while I was made aware of the charge against me, I still had no memory of committing any such action, and all the same began to be plagued by self-doubt and consumed by worry for my future. There was a strange (and to my American eyes) inscrutable legal system arrayed against me, one I labored mightily to understand, and which seemed to employ a strange set of arbitrary rules that simply did not make sense to me. These occurrences and emotional downward spirals were what filled the pages of *The Trial*, just as they filled my current life. Even the setting of some of the scenes in *The Trial* perfectly mirrored my surroundings—dark,

dim, crumbling buildings with dirty rooms full of unhappy people. Surely Kafka had at the very least glimpsed Pankrác at some
point in his travels through his hometown, if he did not know
someone languishing behind its walls. The whole thing was just
too eerie for my tastes, but I tried to smile as I thanked Jeff for the
gift. After all, reading material was scarce, and while I decided I
would eventually read *The Trial*, I hoped it would be somewhere
far, far away from Prague and a few years into a (hopefully) free
future. (But Jeff Cohen is a very smart man, much smarter than
me; he knew me and he knew what he was bringing me. His
choice was perfect—I did wind up reading *The Trial* during my incarceration, and after my initial misgivings, found the similarities
both fascinating and helpful when thinking about my situation.)

After saying hello, Jeff and Tomas and I discussed the status of
my case, focusing mostly on how to make my already paid bail
effective—getting me released. The prosecuting attorney had made
good on his plan to raise an objection to my bail, claiming I was
a flight risk, and now an appellate court would review my case
again to determine whether or not I would be released. It seemed
asinine to me that almost a quarter million dollars had been paid
and I still wasn't out of prison, but my team (suddenly I had "a
team" of lawyers, something I had never wished for before in
my life) were doing everything they could to secure my release—
talking to the police and judges, trying (unsuccessfully) to parlay
with the prosecuting attorney, carefully reviewing any available
evidence arrayed against me with a fine tooth comb, looking up
legal precedents, filing complaints and objections, and possibly
hiring a private detective to try to dig up new evidence and get
me out of the country once I was released. I began to feel better
now that Jeff was there, a man I had known and trusted for many
years, and he seemed to be fired up and ready to kick ass and take
names. The long and short of it wasn't very surprising to me—the
prosecuting attorney was being a complete dick to my attorneys
and was doing his best to keep the wheels of the system spinning

in order to keep me incarcerated. But I was extremely grateful that someone was there to ask the hard questions about the Czech legal system for me. I needed answers, because rotting in prison after paying bail was still not processing too well in the old ramen noodle helmet.

My favorite part was the private detective, though.

"You're gonna fucking love this guy, Randy! He's *brutal*—he's all ripped, ex-KGB, a *Krav Maga* expert, and he's got a fast sports car with black tinted windows he's going to pick you up in, to get you over the border and the fuck outta Dodge as soon as you are released," Jeff said.

Now we're talking, I thought, my Cold War secret intelligence fantasies returning full force. A grim and burly Muscovite skilled in the deadly arts would come in secret to get me out of the country under the cover of night in a low, fast car. There might even be the possibility of gunfire, or at the very least a bribe paid at the border (definitely handed over in a leather attaché case—I made a mental note to ask Jeff to make sure he had one of those). The prospect of adventure never fails to excite me, and a furtive high-speed midnight escape across the Czech border sounded like just the thing to get the old adrenaline flowing again and banish the Pankrác blues. I hoped I would get a forged passport or a disguise to wear, perhaps a fake mustache. At the very least, I needed a fedora.

During our visit, I was also able to slip Jeff a note for Cindy (a list of supplies I hoped she would be able to bring me the next day) and a letter to my friend Jamey Jasta asking him if he would print and distribute a fanzine I had already begun mentally outlining about my life in prison. Giving Jeff the note and letter was strictly against prison regulations, and I was searched before our meeting, but I simply stuck them amongst the legal papers and notes I had made concerning my case—I was allowed to carry those kind of documents to any meeting with my attorneys. Any correspondence of a personal nature was supposed to be reviewed by the prison censor before leaving Pankrác, but Cindy would be there tomorrow, and I was pretty sure the prison officials wouldn't be too jazzed about me publishing an underground paper from behind the walls of Pankrác. But I am a writer, a punk rocker, and a dissident involved in the self-published underground literature scene since my early twenties, and I will not let my creative voice be silenced or censored. Plus the Czech Republic had a long tradition of *samizdat*—Václav Havel himself, possibly the most revered man in modern Czech history, had been imprisoned after writing and distributing his long political essay, *The Power of the Powerless*, a brilliantly executed expose on repression and the dissent it fostered that severely rankled the fur of those in power within the totalitarian system of Communist Czechoslovakia. If Havel could do it, then I damn sure could and would.

Jeff also asked me on behalf of my manager Larry if I would be willing to tour shortly after my release—we had an upcoming run of the States already booked. This request initially irritated me greatly, as the very last thing I wanted to think about at that moment was traveling and playing music with my band. Traveling and playing music with my band was what had landed me in prison in the first place, and the last thing I cared about at that moment was hopping up onstage and *entertaining* people, for fuck's sake. I wanted to do a lot of things, and running around and screaming like a lunatic for our fans' amusement was not one of them. But a lot of money had already been spent on pre-production for the tour, lawyers don't come cheap, and cash was flowing away from my band's bank accounts quicker than a fish off the hook at low tide. My band is my business, and my business was hurting pretty badly at that moment; so I held my tongue, sighed and thought, *Well, what did you expect? The show must go on*, then told Jeff to let Larry know I would tour as long as I had a week or two to see my family first. As our meeting drew to a close, I told Jeff to let Cindy and my family know I was doing just fine. I did not want them to worry any more than they already had, and I knew a quick update from someone who had seen me in person would do them some good. Jeff told me Cindy was doing well—tired and slightly overwhelmed, but well. On the way back to my cell, we stopped by the prison laundry where I turned in my street clothes and got back into my prison uniform. One of the metal head trusties who worked in the laundry room slipped me a few loose cigarettes with my clothes, and I signed an autograph on a scrap of paper for him. It was also nice to see the posters of all my friends again.

I woke up the next morning and shaved with cold water from our sink, then did my best to scrub my body and make myself as presentable as possible, even applying a little mint toothpaste to my arm pits for deodorant as Dorj had taught me. I was extremely excited to see my wife, and didn't want to look anymore disheveled than I had to. Cindy and I are used to being apart for long periods of time—it's been that way since the very beginning of our relationship—and she knows that the road isn't exactly conducive to maintaining good hygiene. All the same, whenever I return home from tour, I do my best to wash the road dirt from my body, shave my face, and put on some semi-clean clothes before we are reunited. I try to leave as much of the road on the road as possible, to become a semi-normal human being while I am home. My wife didn't start dating a rockstar, she started dating a dishwasher who was in a band that made no money. Having a beautiful, intelligent woman who loves me for myself, not my job, is one of my greatest blessings. And although she loves me, stinky or not, I try not to take that for granted, and make an effort to clean up a little for her after I've just spent a few months sweating amongst the savages singing for my supper. I didn't have a shower available that day, or clean clothes, or even deodorant, but I made an effort. Shortly after lunch a guard came for me, and I went upstairs to see my wife.

I was searched thoroughly, then seated in one of a long row of two-sided open-air cubicles. There was no glass partition or phone to speak into, and I was told that I may kiss my wife one or two times, but that guards would be watching at all times. Any other physical contact was to be kept to a minimum. I sat there for two or three minutes with butterflies in my stomach, then a group of visitors was led into the large waiting room, my wife amongst them. Those that had brought packages for inmates placed their bags and boxes of stuff on a long table and a guard carefully inspected each item, then they were allowed to sit down across from their incarcerated loved one and the ninety minute visit began. I saw my wife walking towards me, and a smile broke out on my face.

Cindy was dressed conservatively in a modest dark dress, and appeared quite calm, if a little tired, after her long journey. She in no way gave off the appearance of a frightened woman. I was immensely proud of her for this, as I guessed there would probably be paparazzi stalking the prison gates, waiting for her arrival (I was correct). There had been no public announcement made of her trip to the Czech Republic, but the press had informers amongst the prison staff, and I knew her scheduled visit would not go unnoticed—my case was too big for a visit from my wife to slip through the cracks. Since I knew the reporters would be there to hound her, I wanted her to show no fear or weakness in public, and she didn't. It does not suit my nature to have a panicky, crying wife, a frail woman who would shield her teary face and run away from those kind of needling bastards. I did not marry a weak woman, and she walked tall that day, just as I knew she would. She did not burst into hysterics at the sight of me, she did not weep later when confronted by reporters after our visit, and if she cried at all during my time in prison (for I have never asked her if she did, and it does not matter to me), I know that it was behind closed doors, with family and close friends. I am a fighter, and like both the men and women of Ancient Sparta, a true fighter must have a fighting spouse as well. Half of Cindy's family is from China. In China, you maintain face. She maintained face, and did both me and her people proud that day.

To be honest, much of what was said during our visit is but a vague blur in my mind. I was just glad to see those beautiful (and thankfully dry) eyes, to kiss her sweet lips once or twice, to hear her speak as she let me know that both she and my family were holding up well. Until after my trial was over, the only time I almost broke down and cried was when we spoke of my family. In a few short words, she let me know that my family loved me and was standing behind me 100 percent during my current ordeal. While I already knew I really had nothing to worry about in that department, it still did me a lot of good to hear the words said, and my eyes did mist up a tiny bit.

I believe I tried to keep our conversation light for the most part, telling Cindy a few general and humorous things about my life in Pankrác, mostly funny stories about how Dorj was driving me nuts with his incessant whistling, and making fun of the sad state of my prison issue clothes—one pants leg was hemmed two or three inches higher than the other. But I do specifically remember one quiet thing I said to her, something I had to get off my chest to the woman I loved so. I needed her to hear this, to know the reality of my situation, to be aware of the source of the growing darkness her husband was carrying around inside his gut like an iron fist slowly squeezing his entrails tighter and tighter. I looked around to make sure a guard wasn't too close to us, and leaned in close to her face.

"Honey, I think I killed that boy," I whispered.

"What?" she whispered back.

"I said, I think I killed that boy. I'm not 100 percent sure, but from what I'm hearing it seems like it to me. I never set out to hurt anyone, and it wasn't my fault—there were people all over the stage at that show, no security that I could see, it was a total nightmare gig, and I don't remember even seeing this kid at all. But from what the police and papers report the witnesses are saying, I do believe it was my hands that killed him," I said.

"Oh honey, you don't know that!" she immediately replied, "We don't have any idea if what those people are saying is true or not. And from the video I've seen, there seems to be all sorts of different ways that kid could have gotten hurt."

Cindy was referring to low quality cellphone camera footage the police had obtained of part of our concert. During this video, the young blond man that everyone assumed was the dead person in question left the stage several different times, including a particularly nasty bouncer-enforced tumble. I had only heard of the video, but parts of it had begun circulating the Internet, the footage shown in slow motion on many sites. After watching this video, some armchair detectives were claiming that a segment of it showed me brutally shoving the man off the stage, resulting in a mortal injury. I would watch this video countless times later, carefully analyzing the contact I had with the young man. Only a complete idiot who, for their entire life, had somehow existed outside the physical realm with no knowledge whatsoever of the capabilities of the human body nor possessed the innate basic grasp of the laws of inertia and gravity that allows us as humans to move through our existence without constantly traumatizing our bodies would have come to that conclusion. A person would have to be colossally, incomprehensibly *stupid* to think that I could have flung the man from the stage with such force that he flew through the air the way he did in the footage. My left arm is quite clearly behind my body as the man begins to come forward from behind me, my hand looks to be on the scuff of his neck, then follows along with the man as he leaves the stage. I remain singing into the microphone in my other hand the entire time. Anyone who watched this and thought I was able to reach around behind me and toss one-handed another adult human being from the stage like a rag doll, must have been raised entirely by a video game console and thus been under the delusion that I was some sort of superhumanly strong multi-tasker. They would also have to be partially blind to not see the beefy security guard who came rushing out of nowhere and shoved the man from behind with great force with both hands from the stage. But I had not seen this footage yet, and only had a vague idea of what it contained. The only information I had came from hazy memories and reports by the papers and police saying that I was a savage, aggressive man who had purposefully injured another. Again and again they said that I was a killer. I knew I hadn't purposely tried to harm anyone, but I was beginning to feel that there had to be some kernel of truth in the disheartening information I had available to me at the time. My psyche was slowly being worn down by prison and bad press. I was grateful to my wife for bringing up an obvious point—everything against me at this point was hearsay, not documented fact. The fist in my gut didn't disappear, but it relaxed a tiny bit.

Cindy also let me know that the English-speaking press that bothered to report my situation seemed to be doing so fairly, and that more and more people from our music community had been speaking up on my behalf, showing support, and wanting an answer to the question of why I remained incarcerated after my bail had been paid. Two such people were Sharon and Ozzy Osbourne—I had toured with Ozzy a few times, and although we were not close, I was loosely acquainted with both the legendary singer and his equally legendary no-nonsense manager wife. It touched me deeply that these two people, both figureheads of the business I was in, were speaking on my behalf. Ozzy Osbourne was in *Black freakin' Sabbath*, for Pete's sake. I wouldn't have a job without him—he and his band *created* heavy metal. I was even further humbled later when I found out that Ozzy and Sharon had done more than merely speak up in the press for me. During my incarceration, my publicist and dear friend Maria Ferrero had begun reaching out to people in the industry I knew in order to obtain letters of character reference—these things can make a big difference during a trial. After I was released from Pankrác prison, Maria forwarded me a copy of a signed letter the Osbournes had written to Judge Petr Fassati (the official who was in charge of my bail), speaking positively of my character. Not only that, to my complete shock, they ended the letter by pledging to put on an OZZfest concert in Prague, the proceeds of which would be donated to a charity of Judge Fassati's choosing, if my bail would be honored and I were to be released from prison. While the Osbournes are very successful people, and I'm sure their bank accounts reflect that success (Ozzy is revered by all who listen to heavy metal, and Sharon is one of the shrewdest businesswomen on the planet), the cost and organizational effort involved with putting on an OZZfest concert is immense—I know, for I have toured with the traveling heavy metal summer camp in both 2004 and 2007. Those tours did wonderful things for my band's career (as well as giving me many life-long friends), and even though I got "called to the principal's office" a few times for various drunken lunatic offenses (you know you're screwing up when you get blessed out for acting too wild on a heavy metal tour—sorry, Sharon), these two kind souls were making a concrete effort to help me in the best way they knew how. To this day, I am awestruck by their selfless gesture on my behalf, acting solely out of concern for one of their extended musical family. Furthermore, their kindness is yet another example of people judging a heavy metal book by its cover—Ozzy himself is definitely no stranger to controversy (or court cases, for that matter) and has been reviled throughout his career by fundamentalist religious groups as a negative influence on the youth, hell-bent on spreading Satanism and death. But I know "The Prince of Darkness" to be a kind and gentle man, and I remain indebted to him and his wife for all they have done for me and my band.

The visit from Cindy came to an end all too swiftly—I honestly can't remember how our conversation ended, or even kissing her goodbye. Perhaps my psyche has blocked this from my memory, for it would have been an undeniably painful thing to watch my wife walk away, knowing that the grim, helpless feeling of leaving her husband behind bars that only a prisoner's wife knows had to have been hanging over her. I never wanted her to have to see me like that, a caged man in ill-fitting rags. The man she married on the sandy shore of a North Carolina sea island was fiercely independent and ill-suited to confinement of any sort. It must have hurt her greatly to see me deprived of my freedom, a thing she knew I valued so highly. If I know myself at all, and I do, my worrying soul would have been in overdrive at causing her concern. The next day, an inmate would give me a copy of *Blesk* with my wife's picture in it—the paparazzi had indeed cornered her as she left the prison grounds. Cindy did not run, hide or weep at the appearance of these people—she spoke briefly of her sadness at the death of the young man, and of her belief in my innocence, then went on her way, head held high. While I was happy to have a photo of my wife, and would look at it from time to time, I did not display it openly in our cell, or look at it too often. Even today, my heart grows heavy if I look at, for it is a picture of a beautiful woman in pain—I can see it in the eyes I love so much and know so well.

Once I was back in my cell, I sat down on my bed to look through my package of loot. Cindy had brought me several things I had requested via Martin, and some stuff she had just known I would want—she is my wife, after all. There were two pairs of high quality flip-flops—a pair for me and a pair for Dorj, as I wouldn't have felt right about rocking new kicks while he was stuck with Pankrác bo-bos. There were two cartons of Marlboro Reds, straight out of Richmond, VA, as well as several individually packaged portions of Starbuck's Italian roast instant coffee to go with the cigs—my mornings were about to get a lot more civilized. There were several bags of my favorite varieties of fruit-flavored candy—I go through phases of eating a lot of candy (terrible for the teeth, but in that moment I did not care one bit). There was a huge volume of Sudoko puzzles I had requested in an attempt to keep Dorj occupied. There were letters from my family, pens and paper with which to write my own letters, and there were books. *War and Peace. The Hobbit. The Complete Short Stories of Ernest Hemingway.*

Books. The mere presence in our cell of those most holy of civilization's achievements instantaneously gave me a surge of relief and hope. I had requested the Tolkien for escape, the Tolstoy for sheer girth, and the Hemingway for both pleasure and study. Amongst the letters from my family, my father had also included some books, one being *Letters and Papers from Prison*, by Dietrich Bonhoeffer. I read the back cover of the book with a skeptical eye—first it was Jeff with the nightmarish Kafka, now my own father had turned against me—what were these two men doing, collaborating on how best to make me even more depressed about my current location? But just like Jeff Cohen, my father is a very, very smart man, much smarter than I, and he had picked a volume that would provide me great comfort, not mere escapism, in the weeks to come.

As the title suggests, *Letters and Papers from Prison* is a collection of personal correspondence and essays written in prison by a German Lutheran minister named Dietrich Bonhoeffer. The book was first published posthumously, as Bonhoeffer was arrested by the Nazi Party in 1943 on suspicion of involvement in a plot to assassinate Adolf Hitler (which he was), and subsequently executed by hanging in 1945. Bonhoeffer was a man with a steel backbone and superb moral character; an outspoken critic of Hitler and his persecution of the Jews, he died naked at the end of a rope after climbing the steps to the gallows proudly, silently, and completely composed. Although little known during his life, Bonhoeffer's works became hugely influential in later years, the story of both his dissidence and eventual martyrdom in the heart of Nazi Germany a great source of inspiration for those who struggled through the Civil Rights era in the United States, anti-Communist factions in Eastern Europe fighting to throw off the oppressive weight of the Iron Curtain, and those on the front lines of the anti-Apartheid movement during their brutal struggle for freedom in South Africa. My father would have known that a work by a man such as Bonhoeffer would greatly help me, and it did—I plowed through it rapidly in prison, completely entranced after reading the first passage I randomly thumbed to.

In a letter to his parents dated May 15, 1943, Bonhoeffer writes: "Of course, people outside find it difficult to imagine what prison life is like. The situation in itself—that is each single moment—is perhaps not so very different here from anywhere else; I read, meditate, write, pace up and down my cell—without rubbing myself sore against the walls like a polar bear. The great thing is to stick to what one still has and can do—there is still plenty left—and not to be dominated by the thought of what one cannot do, and by feelings of resentment and discontent . . . "

If there has ever been a more magnificent and useful piece of advice written on how to maintain one's emotional sovereignty and a positive mental attitude in prison, I have not read it. In fact, I would whole heartedly recommend the entirety of *Letters and Papers From Prison* to anyone who is incarcerated, or suffering under any form of real oppression. Bonhoeffer was a product of his time, and as such his views on some subjects (such as the role of women in marriage) are a bit dated (to put it mildly), and some readers may not enjoy the theological slant of the book, but it is an undeniably remarkable work produced by a human will working at its best and highest level; a well-written record of immense internal fortitude in the face of a world gone mad with unthinkable atrocity. To read of Bonhoeffer's stoic life as a prisoner of the Reich made my current woes seem trivial at best, and I would often turn to his dying work for inspiration and solace in times of despair. This is what a good book can do for you that no insipid television show or inane Internet video will ever come close to achieving; it can reach down through the ages, hurtling past the clutches of death itself, to prop you up when you are alone and at your lowest. If you don't believe me, try watching re-runs of whatever your favorite television series was ten years ago the next time you are faced with a potentially life-altering dilemma and see how much wisdom you can glean from that drivel. I'll take

Ernest Hemingway, Rick Bragg, Helen Keller, Pat Conroy, Vacláv Havel, Malcolm X, and Mark Twain. I'll take Dietrich Bonhoeffer, thank you very much.

I spent the rest of the evening smoking as many cigarettes as I wanted, drinking instant coffee, reading books and letters from my loved ones, and trying not to eat all of my candy at once. To have at my ready disposal these normal, everyday things that I usually took for granted gave me great pleasure, and I fell to sleep more content than I had in quite some time.

———

The next morning, I awoke from a wonderful dream about hanging out with my brother and a still-alive Bob Marley. Oddly enough, almost all my dreams in prison were really good ones; I believe that it was my subconscious's way of protecting my psychic health. To pass the sleeping hours in Pankrác suffering through nightmares would have undoubtedly made it harder to remain positive while awake. The whole thing already felt like a bad dream at times anyway, so getting a sound night's sleep without doing battle with the strange demons that lurk in the human subconscious was a blessing. Often I would be with my wife, family, or friends in my dreams, doing things I enjoyed, almost always outside in nature. (Not to mention the occasional random crew of topless hot chicks who would sometimes inexplicably suddenly appear and briefly go jogging by—why can't this happen to me in real life? It seemed a perfectly reasonable occurrence and not out of place or odd at all in my dreams.)

After I cleared the cobwebs from my head, I sat down and finished the final draft of my statement to the press, then ate breakfast in our hot cell. Along with our usual hunk of bread, Dorj and I had received a couple of oranges in perfect condition. The oranges were a rarity in and of themselves (most of the time we got mealy apples if we got fruit at all), but to get fruit that was unbruised, not overripe, and without critters of any sort crawling inside was truly an uncommon treat. After we had enjoyed the oranges, I took the peels, scraped what stringy rind was left on them off, then set about very finely julienning the peels with our razor blade before finishing them with that most precise of cuts I had learned during my kitchen slave years, the brunoise. I took the diced peels, put them on a scrap of newspaper, and sat them out to dry in our dusty window sill. After they had dried, I placed them in an empty yogurt container and sat them between Dorj's bed and mine as a ghetto air freshener. Aside from our toothpaste and lone bar of soap, the orange peels were the only thing in our stifling cell that smelled good—the rest stank of sweat, mold, and dusty decay. And while they did not provide a very powerful aroma, the act of creating something, *anything*, that improved my circumstances in the slightest bit cheered me and gave a sense of purpose to a listless, hot morning. Anything I could do rather than sit and worry over my future (something I currently had absolutely no control over) improved my morale.

Another thing that always cheered me up was the simple act of laughter. I made sure I found something funny in my grim surroundings every single day without fail. This was perhaps easier for me than it would have been for many, as I had spent much of my adult life living in filthy punk houses with alcoholic and drug-addled roommates. These were men and women who had mastered the fine art of finding humor in living in squalor. Once you have paid rent to rest your head in a hovel known affectionately as "Dirtbag Manor" (a truly disgusting place), the blow of living in a crumbling century-old prison doesn't land as harshly as it probably would for a child of privilege who had never had to hand-wash piles of mouse turds off his plate before using it every single time. My old roommates at Dirtbag Manor, Steve and Matt, would burst into uproarious laughter any time one of us would look at our filthy house and say, "Can you believe we are stupid enough to actually give a landlord rent to stay in this shit hole? My God, we are paying good money to wallow in freakish misery! Fuck it, hand me another beer, bwuahahahahaha . . . " It was absolutely *hilarious* to us that we were living out our lives in a place that would give anyone with an ounce of sense the creepy-crawly heebie-jeebies just walking through the living room—of course the massive amounts of shitty beer and high quality drugs we were ingesting probably did their bit in lowering our standards to the point that life in Dirtbag Manor seemed not only not completely insane, but acceptable, and yes: very funny.

Even now that I'm sober, have money to pay my bills, and no longer live in a house that resembles a cockroach's wet dream, I often laugh when I find myself in a really depressing situation. I'm not talking about bitter gallows humor, or chest-beating chuckles of bravado; I actually find acute misery *hysterical* at times—as long as it is my own. I can't laugh at other people's pain (as long as they aren't complete assholes); I find people who do so distasteful and *weak*. Very, *very* weak. But I have a finely tuned sense of self-deprecation, and I enjoy laughing at myself—when things in my life go awry, I think my automatic defense mechanism is laughter. Laughing in the face of a bad situation tends to do me a whole lot more good than getting angry or crying. Pankrác, with the exception of one other truly horrific occurrence, was the worst situation I had ever been in. So I laughed—a lot.

My wife and family know that I love to have a good laugh, and I am constantly joking around with them when we are together. But since I had been arrested, I worried incessantly about them worrying about me. Sitting at the table in our cell after breakfast, I had a sudden flash of inspiration—I would write them a very humorous letter. If they knew that I was still laughing, that I still had a joke on my lips, then they would truly know that I was doing okay in there. I grabbed a pen and a sheet of paper and began the letter, deciding I would take all the bizarre happenings and weird stuff I found funny about Pankrác and cram it all into one twenty-four hour period, a sort of gonzo version of Solzhenitsyn's

One Day in the Life of Ivan Denisovich. I wrote about two pages of stuff that made me laugh out loud when I re-read it (if I am laughing at what I write, then it's generally a safe bet that others will, too), then stopped because my hand began to cramp (I was writing in very small block letters in order to conserve paper). As I was putting away my writing materials, Tom Selleck opened the cell door, yelled, "You clean cell now!" in his usual cheery voice, and a trusty pushed in a small throw carpet made of rags just like the one underneath our sink, emptied our galvanized steel bucket that functioned as our trash can, and filled it with hot water. Dorj and I put our stools on top of our table, then I used our small hand broom and dustpan to sweep the dirt from our floor the best I could. Dorj motioned for me to sit on my bed, then he took our old throw carpet, dunked it in our already filthy bucket of water, and began furiously scrubbing our floor with more vigor and speed than I had previously seen him display during any other activity besides eating. After he had worked up a good sweat, I took a scrap torn from one of our foam couch cushion "mattresses" and scrubbed the table, then the sink, and finally our toilet the best I could. When the trusty came and took away our old throw carpet, Tom Selleck poked his head in the door, briefly looked around, and said, "good," before slamming the door shut.

I was glad we had passed muster, but in reality all we had really done was move around the dirt in our cell. This frustrated me to no end—you can't clean something when you don't have clean things to clean it with—but the place did look a tiny bit more tidy. Dorj had really busted his ass scrubbing the floor, and I was grateful to have a cellmate who at least valued cleanliness, no matter that we had absolutely zero way of attaining it. If cleanliness is next to godliness, then Pankrác must be Satan's Siamese twin—the only way that place will ever be truly clean again is if they drop an atom bomb on it.

The next day I read quite a bit and worked some more on the first draft of my letter to my family. Before lights out, I sat re-reading what I had written, making a few small notes in the margins, and laughing hard out loud at times at the high weirdness I was trying to relate to my people. My second week in prison was coming to a close—I didn't know when or if I would be let out, my band was in debt for paying an expensive bail that seemed to be worthless, the prosecuting attorney was a rampaging asshole determined to play the system and keep me in prison. I was stuck in a tiny filthy cell with a fat whistling Asian from hell, and I hadn't had a solid meal in quite some time. But I was laughing my ass off on my shitty bed, and I knew I would laugh tomorrow, too.

But the guards would be having a laugh as well the next day.

TUES. JULY 17th, 2012

IT HAS BEEN AWHILE, 6 DAYS TO BE PRECISE, SINCE I
HAVE WRITTEN IN HERE. MANY THINGS HAVE CHANGED, YET
AT THE SAME TIME VIRTUALLY NOTHING OF ANY IMPORT.
I AM NOW IN A BIGGER CELL, WITH 2 ROOMMATES, AND
ASTONISHINGLY YET ANOTHER MONGOL HAS BEEN ADDED TO
MY POSSE, A COOL BUSINESSMAN ONE YEAR MY SENIOR NAMED
NBOLD, WHO APPARENTLY IS WANTED BACK IN MONGOLIA
FOR SOMETHING GONE SOUR. IT IS GOOD HE IS HERE NOW —
THE ROOM FEELS BIGGER, & DORJ HAS SOMEONE TO OCCUPY HIM
NOW. THE WHISTLING HAS BEEN FOR THE MOST PART REPLACED
BY INCESSANT JABBERING IN MONGOLIAN, 90% OF IT DORJ'S,
WHO OFTEN LAPSES INTO AN INCREDIBLY ANNOYING WHISPER
BY THE END OF THE DAY, EXHAUSTED BY HIS CONSTANT TALKING.
STILL, IT'S BETTER THAN BEFORE. I HAVE BEEN IN PANKRAC
MOST OF 18 DAYS NOW, IT'S BEEN 21 SINCE MY ARREST OR
CUSTODY OR WHATEVER IT WAS CALLED. THE LAST WEEK HAS
BEEN A LOT OF LETTER WRITING, INCLUDING THE LONG COMEDIC
ONE TO MY FAMILY, WHICH I HAVE CUT BACK TO ONE PAGE A DAY
NOW FOR THE FIRST DRAFT — IT IS EXHAUSTING TRYING TO BE
FUNNY FOR SO LONG — IT DOES MAKE ME SMILE AS I WRITE IT,
BUT I AM WRITING A BIT MORE CAREFULLY NOW, PAYING
A LOT MORE ATTENTION TO MY WORD CHOICES & SEARCHING FOR

chapter thirteen

Although my wife was still in Prague for a few days after our visit, she was not allowed to visit me again, nor was anyone else, besides my lawyers. Luckily my lawyers still included Jeff Cohen, who came to see me on an almost daily basis while he was in the Czech Republic. There was no real news about my case other than what we already knew—my bail money was sitting in some government bank account, I was sitting in jail, and the prosecuting attorney wanted to keep me there. But it was still nice to see someone from home, and it did my heart good to know that Jeff was in constant contact with my wife and family during this time, giving them updates on my unchanging status—at least they knew I wasn't being tortured or hadn't been killed by another inmate.

On the first day of my third week in Pankrác, Tom Selleck was returning me to my cell after a visit with Jeff when I noticed that he seemed to be in an unusually good mood. Normally Señor Selleck had a sour-puss grimace seemingly permanently grafted to his face, as if he were constantly just catching a whiff of a really smelly fart, but today there was what could only be described as a twinkle in his eye. I even saw him throwing me a sly sideways grin from time to time as we walked towards my cell. He looked like a man trying to hold in the punch line to a really funny joke. I began feeling slightly nervous, as I had an uneasy feeling that whatever was giving old grumpy pants Selleck a case of the yucks probably wouldn't be quite so amusing to me. As we stopped in front of cell #505, Bradley walked over, stepped in front of me, and casually leaned against the door. He looked like he had been granted an extra portion of shit to stuff into his usual shit-eating grin. Uh-oh.

"Ah, Blight," he said. "It is very happy day for you! It is moving day!"

Tom Selleck actually gave out a chuckle as Bradley moved to the side so he could open the cell door. It was the first time I had ever heard him laugh, and I did not care for it one bit. Stepping into the arid air of #505, I saw a sweaty Dorj bent over his stripped bed, stuffing his belongings into a make-shift pack he had fashioned from his wool blanket. He had already stripped my bed, and had put my sheets into my own folded up blanket. Most of my belongings had already been placed neatly beside my bedding.

"We come back in ten minutes. You will be ready for moving then," Bradley smirked as Tom Selleck shut and locked the cell door.

"Dorj, what the fuck?" I asked. "Where are we going, Doctor Khun? Upstairs?"

Dorj shrugged his shoulders, cursed in Mongolian, and kept on packing. I got the distinct feeling that we would not be moving upstairs, as Bradley had seemed entirely too chipper about us leaving #505. Upstairs we would have been out of his jurisdiction, beyond his range of operations, and safe from his infantile attempts at making our lives miserable. No, there had to be something else going on, some sort of hideous surprise Bradley could barely wait to spring on us. I sighed, and carefully packed my books and other things into my make-shift knapsack. *Well, at least they can't move us down another floor*, I thought.

Over an hour later, Bradley and Tom Selleck reappeared, both looking as if they were about to burst. Dorj and I gathered up our pathetic bundles and walked out of the cell, following

Bradley and Tom Selleck as they turned left and headed down the basement hallway. We had passed a mere six doors when they stopped in front of cell #512. Tom Selleck unlocked the door with a huge grin, and Bradley made the same grand sweeping gesture he had when first putting me into #505. "Your new home!" he said, choking back a laugh. Tom Selleck stood beside him, his hand held over his mouth to cover his own mirth. I looked into the cell.

The cell looked to be slightly larger by a few square feet than our last one, and was furnished exactly the same, except for the addition of a two-level bunk bed on one side of the cell across from a normal single level cot. On the top bunk sat a stocky Asian man of a lighter skin tone than Dorj, his chiseled facial features sharper than Dorj's dough-boy mug. He hopped nimbly down from the bunk and said something in Czech. Dorj immediately burst into a rapid fire barrage of Mongolian, to which our new cell cellmate replied in kind. I heard the cell door slam shut behind us, then Bradley and Tom Selleck exploded into laughter outside in the hallway. In between guffaws I heard the words "Americansky," "Mongolsky," and "dva," the Czech word for two.

In 2012, the number of people living in the Czech Republic was approximately 10.5 million total. Of that number, around 6,000 were Mongolian, Mongolians comprising .057143 percent of the Czech Republic's population. That means that for every 1,750 persons in the Czech Republic, one would be a Mongol. One in 1,750—supposedly there weren't even 1,750 inmates in Pankrác, so the chance of getting a Mongolian cellmate was pretty slim to begin with. The odds of winding up in a cell with *two* Mongolians? Astronomical.

I had two Mongolians.

I put my stuff on the single bed (Dorj had immediately tossed his on the bunk below his countryman) and sat down, listening to the two Mongolians talk. Actually, I listened to Dorj jabber at the other Mongol, who tried to reply every now and then, only to be cut off by our chubby cellmate, who had been transported to a state of ecstatic verbal bliss now that he had someone he could blabber to in his native tongue. Dorj spoke Mongolian in a high-pitched voice I hadn't heard him use before, starting each sentence in an excited girlish tone and finishing in a sibilant hissing whisper. Every three or four sentences he would burst into a fit of high-pitched giggling before continuing on. His new manner of speaking immediately began to grate on my nerves very badly. I looked at the other Mongol, whose eyes were starting to glaze over under the force of Dorj's vocal barrage, and decided to come to the rescue and introduce myself. I hoped he wasn't a whistler.

"Dorj! Give it a rest. You're burning the dude's ears up," I said, interrupting him mid-giggle. Dorj glared at me, but shut up for the time being.

"Hey bro, my name is Randy," I said, extending my hand for a shake "You speak any English?" I asked our new cellmate.

"I am Ganbold. Yes, I learn some English from my son. I not very good at English, but some little learnings," he replied, shaking my hand.

"Your English is way better than my Mongolian," I laughed, and we began to rap.

Ganbold was a businessman one year my senior who had been living in Prague for well over a decade. He had been arrested the day before by the Czech police at the request of the Mongolian government, and was being held in Pankrác until the Czech government decided whether or not they would deport him back to Mongolia. According to Ganbold, he had been running an employment agency for Mongolian people in Prague, finding job placements for them as work was scarce in his home country. Apparently he had a business partner back in the Mongolian capital, Ulan Bator, but something had gone sour. Suddenly he had received several massive bills for back taxes from the Mongolian government, taxes he claimed to have already paid through his business partner, who had (conveniently enough) recently seemed to have disappeared. He had been writing the Mongolian government, emailing scanned receipts for the taxes his business partner had provided him when the Czech police showed up at his office, arrested him, and whisked him away to Pankrác. Now he was frantically trying to figure out a way to avoid being deported, as according to him, a Mongolian prison was an excellent place to get one's throat slit while sleeping. This was confirmed by a few emphatic and theatrical hand-to-neck motions from Dorj. The government of Mongolia was rife with corruption, and Ganbold had a suspicion that the tax dollars he had sent to his business partner had made their way into not only his partner's pockets, but into some crooked government official's as well. He had a bad feeling that if he went back to Mongolia, he might just disappear while in prison—apparently not an uncommon occurrence in a country that still had a significantly high percentage of nomadic people in its population, and a shaky national head count as such.

"I think this man will make it very bad for me to return to Mongolia. Very bad," Ganbold said, referring to his absentee business partner. He didn't appear particularly terrified, but it was pretty clear from the way he spoke (and Dorj's throat slitting motions) that Mongolia probably wasn't the best destination for him at the moment.

I immediately took a liking to Ganbold; out of all the men I knew in Pankrác (myself included), he seemed to be the least "criminal." There was absolutely nothing shifty about him—he came across as a straight shooter, someone who had gotten a raw deal at the hands of a less than scrupulous business associate. Although a great number of men in prison will tell you they are innocent, going on to explain in great, convoluted length how *they* are really the victim in their situation, I actually believed Ganbold's tale of woe. There was just something about him that made me feel he didn't belong in there with the rest of us, an open way he had about him that belied no hidden acts or dark designs. As we talked, I learned that he had gotten divorced ten years ago from his wife, and had just started dating again for the first time in a decade at the insistence of his seventeen year old son.

"My son say to me, 'Dad, you must have woman. Is no good for man to be alone for so long'. I finally say okay after many alone years. Two month ago, I meet very nice Mongolian woman—so beautiful. Now I am in Pankrác. This prison no good for my new love romancing," Ganbold said, shaking his head sadly.

"Man, that blows," I said, "Hell of a way to start off a relationship."

"I must write her letter! But I have no paper or pen for writings," he said.

"No worries, man. I'll loan you some paper and a pen," I said, and fetched writing materials from the pile of stuff on my bed. I handed him a few precious sheets of paper and a good pen, and Ganbold sat down at our table to write while Dorj and I set up camp in our new cell. From time to time, Ganbold would stop writing, look up at the ceiling, and sigh as he searched for the right words to try to convince his new lady friend he wasn't a criminal. He looked liked a love sick teenage boy writing to his girlfriend, desperately trying to squash an ugly high school hallway rumor that he had made out with another girl. Dorj stared at him as he wrote, then turned to me with a scowl.

"Ay ya ya ya ya, Doctor Pankrác. Look—he write. He like you. He doctor, too. Probably even like read book. Ay ya ya ya ya—two doctor," he said, his disapproval very evident at having another cellmate with a propensity for chirography.

"Yes, he is doctor, thank fuck. But you doctor, too. You Doctor Khun, hahaha!" I laughed.

"You two are . . . *doctors?*" Ganbold asked incredulously.

And so began Ganbold's pursuit of his doctorate. For the next week, we called him "Student Ganbold," and required him to address us by our titles, Doctor Khun and Doctor Pankrác, at all times—the man couldn't very well just walk into a cell with two doctors and immediately expect to claim his place amongst that most elite of Euro correctional fraternities, the Doctorhood of Pankrác Remand Prison. There had to be a trial period to see if the new man would crack under the pressure of incarcerated life, to ascertain if he had the guts to live day in and day out crammed in a grimy airless cell with two other men, eating garbage and sleeping on a torture device, and still have the spirit to laugh heartily in the face of *bachars* like Bradley whenever they came around to be a dick. In prison, doctors of our sort didn't whine and complain—little bitches did. Ganbold displayed exemplary behavior during his first week—no whining, complaining, bitching, snitching, or mooching (although we freely shared what we had with him). Right from the beginning of a very scary and stressful time in his life, Ganbold carried himself in a manner befitting a doctor; so at the end of his seventh day in prison I took pen to paper and drew up a fairly elaborate diploma with his full name, leaving a blank line for his doctor title. Dorj and I each signed it, thereby conferring upon him all the rights and privileges one could expect as a doctor. But exactly what kind of doctor was he? After a brief hushed conference on the bottom bunk with Dorj, we agreed that Ganbold was a doctor of an amorous sort, as he was constantly mooning over his girlfriend. He did this silently, without complaint, writing her long letters daily and sighing periodically to the ceiling, but we knew what was going on. It was obvious that the thought of losing her was just as disturbing to him (if not more so) than the prospect of a Mongolian prison; in fact his possibly doomed romantic affair had been one of the defining features of his character during his week as a student. Taking this into account, I quickly penned in his doctor name, handed him the diploma, Dorj and I shook his hand, and he became a KISS song.

Ganbold was now Doctor Love.

But on that first day, he was just Student Ganbold, and although not quite a doctor yet, I was still glad to have him join us. For some reason, despite the fact that our new cell was only slightly larger than our last one, the addition of another person did not make me feel more cramped or crowded. On the contrary, my days seemed to be roomier and more full of possibility and humor now that Ganbold had arrived—he was a good man, with an even keeled temperament, and was quicker to smile than frown. Of course, I do believe that Dorj and I got very lucky—we could have been crammed in with some terrible ill-tempered brute, or a child molester, or a mooch. But Ganbold was none of these things, and it was really nice to have someone who spoke a modicum of English in my cell, a man who neither whistled nor ever once uttered the phrase "pure vodka" in my presence. When Tom Selleck and Bradley popped by to check on us an hour after our move, they actually looked dismayed to find the three of us sitting in our cell, chatting affably over Marlboro Reds. I was surprised they didn't immediately move us again—obviously they had been hoping I would be upset by the addition of yet another Mongolian into my already cramped habitat.

Ganbold's arrival did change Dorj's primary means of amusing himself, though. While the whistling nearly totally and instantaneously disappeared, it was replaced by a never-ending stream of Mongolian delivered in that hideous girlish whispering giggle Dorj had first used when speaking to our new companion. Until the day I left Pankrác, I listened to this entirely one-sided conversation go on from sunup to well past sundown, Ganbold quickly abandoning the idea of contributing anything to the dialogue other than a noncommittal grunt periodically. This did not seem to bother Dorj one iota—he would carry on speaking Mongolian even when Ganbold's loud snores from the bunk above him filled the cell air, competing nicely for sonic dominance of cell #512. Neither Ganbold nor myself were paying the slightest attention to his blabbering; Dorj might as well have been speaking to a plate of braised turnips (although they would have been slurped up within seconds of being placed in front of him, and he would have just had to carry on speaking to an empty plate). Ganbold seemed only slightly irritated by Dorj's incessant self-amused spiel, merely raising his eyebrows at me once or twice a day in a "I wish this dude would shut up" expression from his top bunk. I, however, wasn't handling Dorj's new-found loquacious-ness so well—his constant torrent of effeminate-sounding prattle had started to activate my throttling instinct. I seriously wanted to choke the shit out of him, and began noticing my hands clench-ing and unclenching of their own accord from time to time. Once again, English lessons saved the day—right from the beginning of his stay with Dorj and me, I began to polish up Ganbold's rough grasp of my language. Dorj actually had the decency to shut up while we were doing lessons, aside from correcting Ganbold's pronunciation from time to time, or explaining in Mongolian what a word meant. For all his faults, Dorj's talent for languages was phenomenal, and he could be quite helpful at times as I taught Ganbold English.

––––––

The next day when we went outside for walk, Bradley and an unfamiliar guard came to escort us. Unbelievably, just like Bradley's usual comrade in arms, the new guard looked exactly like the actor Tom Selleck. But whereas Tom Selleck #1 was stuck in the glory days of the 1980s with his spiky hairdo and large, lux-urious mustache, Tom Selleck #2 was a Tom Selleck for the new millennium—his mustache was trimmed much more sensibly, and his hair was cut quite a bit tighter to his head. Tom Selleck #2 also seemed to be a more jovial breed of man; Tom Selleck #1 was always scowling whenever he came by, but Tom Selleck #2 greeted us with a smile as he opened the door and said something in Czech in a pleasant tone; something that obviously meant "It is time for your walk, if you so desire to participate, my friends." His Czech was very strange, a deep, back-of-the-throat version of the language I had not heard before—perhaps he was from some far-flung border province of the Republic. Not that I understood much Czech at all, but Tom Selleck #2's Czech was truly bizarre— it sounded as if it consisted of varying tonal inflections of just one word, something that sounded like *yarl*.

"Yarl, yarl, yarl," he said with a smile before he closed the door to our outside cage, pointing to his watch and holding up a single finger, indicating that he would be back in an hour to collect us, "Yarl? Yarl!" Tom Selleck #2's intense love of this word, to the exclusion of all others, was not noticed by myself alone.

"'Yarl'? What is this 'yarl'? Is this this man's name?" Ganbold asked me. I had no idea what a "yarl" was, but it became Tom Selleck #2's other nickname immediately. How could it not? It's all the man ever said.

I introduced Ganbold to all the guys at walk, and soon he was laughing and speaking in Czech with everyone. While we were outside, I noticed that Felix wasn't present—this was the second or third day in a row I hadn't seen him. I asked his young, shaven headed cellmate, George, where he was, but George didn't speak much English, shaking his head and rubbing his stomach like he had a tummy ache. I gave George a couple of cigarettes to take back to his cellmate, making a writing motion while telling George I would send a note for Felix with him soon. George squirreled away the cigarettes and nodded that he understood me.

I was pretty bummed about not having Felix next door any-more, as he spoke excellent English and had been a great assis-tance to me in communicating with the guards. Plus, he was just a nice guy, and it was pleasant to chat with him through our cell windows. His cellmate, George, always seemed a little odd to me though. He smiled incessantly whenever I would speak to him, but made no efforts at communicating with anyone else when we met up for our daily walk. None of the other men seemed in-terested in talking to him either, and he always seemed to be the last to be given a drag off a cigarette when the smokes were being passed around. Of course, George was always trying to mooch cigarettes off me; maybe he had been hitting the other men up too much before I arrived. For whatever reason, George seemed strangely distanced from the rest of us when we were outside for walk—something about him seemed not quite not right.

At walk, I always enjoyed "reading" the graffiti on the wall of whichever concrete cage they had put us in that day—I use the term "reading" very loosely, because it was written in many, many different languages, most of which I had no comprehension. I did find tags from a few Americans, including Honolulu Joe, and Rex from Arkansas. Seeing their scribblings brought me great joy, especially Honolulu Joe's, as he drew palm trees and a nice beach scene beside his name. I also saw the logos of a few punk rock and metal bands, obviously drawn by fans, and decided to throw my own into the mix—"D. Randall Blythe/lamb of god, Euro Prison Tour, Pankrác, Summer 2012" went up on quite a few walls in Pankrác, and while I certainly had no wish for any of our fans to wind up in prison, I thought it might be cool for a lamb of god fan to see that if they ever were unlucky enough to wind up in that dreadful shit hole. I had just finished tagging the wall with a rapidly drying Sharpie on that particular day when I saw some English graffiti I hadn't noticed before near the top of the wall. In block letters, someone had written "Oh God, Oh my Lord, why me?" A few feet down the wall, in the same handwriting, was "I am too good for prison!" Not far from that, the same person had scrawled, "Prison is the worst place one could be in life." Reading this stuff highly annoyed me—why did this guy have to be such a little punk bitch in *my* language? I really hoped he wasn't an American—I hadn't met any other Americans in Pankrác, and I didn't need guys like this running around giving us a bad name. Obviously he wasn't too good for prison, otherwise he wouldn't have wound up in there. And I could think of quite a few places that were far worse to be stuck in than prison. Compared to, say, a combat zone in Somalia, Pankrác was Disney World. I re-read the part about being too good for prison, and wished that the whining, embarrassing, scribe was in the cage with me right then, so I could slap the shit out of him.

The next day Jeff Cohen flew back to America, and I spent most of my waking hours working on the comedic letter to my family. I was about to start writing again after breaking for yet another tasteless dinner when I heard a noise that made me drop my pen and run to our cell window. I hopped up on Ganbold's bunk, and right outside our cell was a ratty looking black cat. I called out to the cat, wishing I had some sort of solid food to offer it, but the cat just sat on the pile of rubble outside our cell and stared at me in the imperious manner of cats all over the world, meowing from time to time. I was glad to see an animal other than a rat or cockroach, but the sound of its meow that had drawn me to the window brought on a sudden wave of worry and homesick sadness. I missed my elderly cat Henry, and I began to wonder how he was recovering from a recent brutal shaving fiasco. Henry was over seventeen years old, and that evening as I lay on my cot, I thought about how I may never get to see him again. I did not sleep well that night.

When everything that you know and love is taken from you, the smallest, most mundane things, stuff that you normally pay no attention to, like a random alley cat passing by your window, can have a very large emotional impact.

———

The next day I got a visit from Tomas, who not only brought me some cigarettes and a couple of books (one being an English/Czech dictionary I had requested; the other a slim, informative, and highly amusing book called *Xenophobe's Guide to the Czechs*), but good news about my bail as well . . . sort of. There had been a hearing the day before concerning the prosecuting attorney's objection to my bail, and the appeals court had rejected his attempt to have my bail reversed. I was free to leave the country and go home—as long as I was able to pay double the amount of my original bail. Eight million Czech crowns, about 400,000 U.S. dollars. My bail was approaching the half-a-million-dollar mark, but Tomas informed me that my band had agreed to pay it and would be sending the money soon—he assured me that I would definitely be released, it was just a matter of when.

Another $200,000? Where in the hell would we get that kind of cheddar? My band couldn't just call up a Czech bail bondsman and give them 10 percent down, like they could have in America (I didn't even know if they had bail bondsmen there, period). Lamb of god had already borrowed a large chunk of cash from our record label, and I had serious doubts that they would fork over double that amount for a band that hadn't brought them a single gold record after eight years. But Tomas reassured me they had agreed to pay it, and the check would be in the mail very soon. (I would later find out that some rather well off friends had gotten together and agreed to loan my band the money. While it would be incredibly tacky to print their names here, I cannot thank these people enough. So if y'all ever read this—you know who you are—thanks. I owe you big time.) He also told me that upon receipt of the money by the Czech government, the prosecuting attorney had a three-day period in which to file yet another objection to the conditions of my new bail, which would then have to be reviewed by another appeals court. Tomas didn't seem to think that the prosecutor would have any reason to file another complaint, but I did—he wanted me to remain in prison.

Emotionally, the lowest hour I spent during my entire time in Pankrác was when I was informed that my bail had been challenged the first time. I had been told that I would be walking out of the prison gates soon. I was happily convinced that I would be free at some point in the very near future, I had believed that I would be on a plane back to America, I had begun dreaming of seeing my wife, family, and friends, I had started to think about eating something other than soup. In short, I had begun to count my chickens before they had hatched, and when all the eggs were smashed to bits by the strange legal procedures of the country I was locked up in, I had learned a very harsh lesson. After laying on my cell bed and feeling extremely sorry for myself for about an hour, I gave myself a swift kick in the ass for being a fool and made a vow to never count on anything before it happened ever again, especially not in prison. Until I left Pankrác a free man, I would consider the prison my home. I would not give up hope of being released, but I would do my best to not think about what I would do once I was on the outside. For my own emotional health, I would try to cultivate the attitude and habits of a monk cloistered in a very strict monastery, expanding my mental and spiritual life while doing what I could to maintain my physical well-being. I was no longer willing to climb on board Ye Olde Emotional Roller Coaster and suffer the brutal whiplash that occurred every time I raised my head to look towards the end of the ride and freedom, only to have my neck almost broken when it took yet another steep plummet downwards around the next corner. The prosecutor was delaying every chance he could, dragging out the process as long as possible and playing systematic legal games with my freedom. I had learned over many years of alcoholism and a bit of bad luck here and there how to endure pain, but I had not always done so in the smartest manner. Like the old saying goes, pain is inevitable, but suffering is optional. I do not enjoy suffering, so I decided I would keep my head down, dig in hard, and focus only on the present as much as possible.

————

The next day when we went for walk, I smuggled out a letter for Felix in my underwear to give to George, in case my English-speaking friend still wasn't feeling well and decided not to come outside. George had a letter from Felix he had snuck out as well, and we exchanged notes after the door to our cage was locked. I sat down, leaning against the warm, rough concrete wall in a spot where there was a beam of sunlight, lit a cigarette, and read Felix's letter. *Hello, you criminal,* Felix wrote, *Randy, could we borrow your lighter for today? I will have one tomorrow with shopping. I am not going for walk because of them silly people. I heard they were calling me names and talking rubbish about me, saying stuff like I am racist, etc. Don't need to listen to this shite mate, you know? Thanks for the lighter and ciggies—Felix*

I was a bit surprised to read that the other men considered Felix a racist, as he had never displayed any sort of prejudice in my presence, and was in fact a very well mannered man. I did get the feeling though that, much like myself, prison was very intellectually boring for him, at times excruciatingly tedious—Felix was a well spoken, obviously educated man. Sometimes at walk, I would ask him what the other men were talking about if their conversation grew particularly heated, and he would dryly reply, "The usual criminal prison bullshit. I try not to pay attention to what they are talking about—it's always the same old crap." I had heard the gypsies talk about creepy Uncle Fester the trusty being prejudiced, saying that he was always making racist jokes when he brought them dinner, and that I definitely believed—something about him rubbed me really wrong. But Felix? I just didn't see it. At walk, we spoke colloquial English, rapidly enough that the few prisoners around us with minimal fluency in my language would not have been able to follow our conversation at all. If he had wanted to make racist remarks he certainly could have, and it has been my experience that real-deal virulent racists cannot restrain themselves from mouthing off about their wacko beliefs whenever they can without fear of reprisal. But perhaps I had missed something along the way, some subtle cultural indicator that my American eyes were untrained to spot—the Czechs were comparatively reserved people after all. I didn't think much more about it until we returned to our cell after walk.

"Randy, those men no like you giving letter to George. They see you give letter and wonder what it say," Ganbold said as soon as we were back.

"What? Really? Why do they care? It's just a letter for Felix, asking him why he's not at walk," I said.

"These men say Felix no good person in here. These men say he is *informanté*. They say he watch and tell *policie* things," he said.

Holy crap, I thought, *Felix is a squealer?*

"That reason why he no come out for walk. These men say they will . . ." and Ganbold made punching and stabbing motions.

"Look, tell them I was just asking where he was, because he's the only other guy in here who speaks English well. I don't know anything about any *informanté*—I don't even understand what everyone is saying anyway, because I don't speak Czech. I couldn't tell him anything even if I wanted to," I said.

"I already say this to these men. They know—they no angry with you, they angry with Felix. You are okay. But no more letter, okay? Is not good for you—these men no like it," Ganbold said.

"No worries about that—no more letters to Felix for sure. Just tell them to be cool, okay?" I said.

In prison, there are countless sets of eyes on you at all times. You have to watch every little thing you do, every move you make, no matter how innocent, in front of both the guards and your fellow inmates. I have talked to friends who have done time in America, and heard stories of men getting beaten up or worse over a stupid misunderstanding. You have to watch your ass at all times, and a highly paranoid attitude is a perfectly reasonable, even logical, state of mind to maintain in prison. Even in city lockup, I had always tried my best to keep to myself for the most part and mind my own business, because the less involved you are with anyone the less trouble they might bring you. But I was in a place where I did not understand the vast majority of what was being said around me, and had no way of hearing the dark whispers about Felix that were currently circulating through the cell block. And maybe he *was* talking to the cops—why did he say in his note that the other men were calling him a racist, not an informer? Probably because he knew that it would make me begin to question whether or not he was spying for the cops, exactly as I was doing at that very moment. As I sat thinking about it, I honestly didn't believe that Felix was a stool pigeon. I didn't then, and I don't today (hence his pseudonym)—I knew he had been arrested during a domestic disturbance, and was in prison on what I understood to be a simple minor assault charge incurred after a mutual drunken fight with his girlfriend. He was not proud of this, but his sentence was not that heavy at all, just a few months. Perhaps I was being naïve, but it just didn't make sense—I didn't see what he possibly had to gain by being an informer for the police, or really what information he could give them—he had been stuck in the basement longer than normal, not in general population upstairs where there was more interaction between prisoners and where one might actually overhear something worth the police's time. Like everyone else on our block, he barely saw anyone other than his cellmate. I had a feeling that because Felix didn't really participate much in the bull sessions that happened everyday at walk, that because he was an educated man, that perhaps someone thought he was a snob, maybe even a racist, and had decided to start a rumor that he was a squealer. Regardless of my personal belief, I wouldn't be writing him anymore letters. Being seen passing a smuggled note to a rumored squealer's cellmate (whether or not he was actually a squealer didn't matter) was not a good look—it's a good way to catch a shank in the side. Rumors can get you killed in prison. This is the reality of life behind bars.

But Felix being a squealer was not the only thing the men had told Ganbold about my former neighbor; apparently his cellmate, George, was in there on a rape charge. I asked Dorj if he had heard this as well, and nodded and made a humping motion, then imitated a screaming woman in distress. *Jesus H. Christ,* I thought, *No wonder no one talks to that guy.* I had asked George what he was in for and he had told me something about getting in some knock-down bar fight and beating three guys up, but I hadn't given his story any credence, as he had also told me and the other men at various times that he was a) a professional body guard, b) a professional soccer player, and c) independently wealthy. Obviously none of these things were true because a) he wasn't muscular or tough at all (I had seen him struggling to do just a few push-ups), b) he was clumsy as hell, and he always looked like he was about to trip over his own big klutzy feet, and c) he never had money on his books for cigarettes and was always trying to bum smokes from me or scrounge up butts. I had noticed that he was a pretty weird dude, but I figured he was just some goofy social outcast kid who had gotten busted for something stupid like weed, and was merely trying (and failing) to impress the real criminals while he did his little bid. If what Ganbold had told me was true, then the men were ignoring George for a very different reason than his annoying tall tales.

It has always been my understanding that sex offenders, especially pedophiles, occupy the lowest rungs on the prison ladder and are treated so badly that they often have to be placed in special cell blocks with their own kind for their own protection. These men, the child molesters and rapists, are often beaten severely (sometimes to death), and raped themselves if the nature of their crimes become public knowledge within the prison walls. I had not seen anyone act aggressive towards George at walk, but I now understood the aloof attitude the other men displayed towards him. And while I didn't really believe that Felix was a stoolie (and had no real way of finding out), the more I thought about George, his tall tales, and his almost desperately happy manner whenever I talked to him, the more I believed his dishonesty and weirdness and shunning by the other men could be explained by him being in there on a sex offender charge—he was trying to cover something up. In a concrete cage of men who are all very used to deception, it's hard to hide anything, and I had never felt entirely comfortable around him for some reason. I just had a strange feeling about the kid, and now it was starting to make sense.

That day's hour outside had not been my finest—through no fault of my own, I had been seen openly passing a note intended for a squealer to a goddamned rapist. This is the kind of shit that can happen when you land in prison in a foreign country and aren't careful enough, and I would be even more cautious who I talked to or associated with for the rest of my stay there. As I was so well known as a foreign rockstar who was arrested completely by surprise, I didn't really fear repercussions for what was obviously an ignorant mistake on my part, but when you can't speak the language of the facility you are in, the standard prevailing prison paranoia becomes even more heightened. Anything can happen at anytime, and Czech-illiterate foreigner or not, I had to watch my ass.

Later that afternoon, I was cheered up by an unexpected person: Tom Selleck #1, who popped by the cell to drop off the order form for tomorrow's shopping—Martin had deposited some Czech currency in my prison account, and I was supposed to write out what I wanted from the store, then turn in my order when the guard made his evening rounds. The goods would be delivered the next day. Felix had shown me an order sheet before. The only problem was that the list was written in Czech, and I hadn't the foggiest of what it contained. Not only that, Felix had also told me not to pay attention to the list, as it was very old, the prices were incorrect, and it hadn't been updated in years—the store apparently had much more available than what was on the list, and he told me he would help me order what I needed when I had some money on my books. But now, due to the nasty rumor surrounding Felix, I couldn't afford to talk to him anymore. I looked at the list and shook my head sadly—finally I had the money to buy some basic things I needed, but the situation was still utterly hopeless. He looked at me and said "Problem?" When I said that

I couldn't read Czech and had no idea of what I was doing, to my immense surprise he smiled broadly, took the list from my hand, and said, "I help you now!" in a very kind tone of voice.

Tom Selleck #1, the grumpiest screw I had met so far in the whole joint, was actually going to *help* me? Until that moment, I had never once seen an expression on his face that could be called anything other than a scowl or frown; Selleck #1 was a man you would look at if you ran into him on the street and immediately think *Good grief, I wonder who peed in his cereal this morning?* It came as a complete shock when he smiled at me—I would have thought cracking a grin would have broken his face. It seemed almost *unnatural*, and his sudden warm-hearted and helpful manner made me suspicious; I expected Bradley to pop out from around the corner at any second with another Mongol to stuff into our cell. But T.S. Numero Uno seemed genuinely happy to help me as I pantomimed things I wanted, like cigarettes, deodorant, shampoo, and razors. Ganbold came to the door to help out, as he spoke Czech, and Dorj remained mute as always whenever there was anyone else around. Tom told Ganbold some of the food items the store had available, and between the two of them I soon had a full order sheet ready to go. I thanked Tom Selleck #1, and stood there in our cell shaking my head once he had gone— what had happened? Maybe he had just been having a bad few weeks? Or maybe Mrs. Selleck had broken him off a piece and he had gotten laid the night before. Who knew? Nothing about the guards in that place was ever predictable.

After dinner, Tom Selleck #2 came by for the evening mail call, and the random temperament of Pankrác's guards raised its weird head again. Tom Selleck #2 opened our cell door, smiled, and asked if we had anything to give him. I handed him my grocery order and a visitation request form I had filled out—my parents were making the long trip to Prague to see me if I was still locked up in two weeks, the next scheduled visitation period. On the form I had written my parents' full names, addresses, and passport numbers, exactly as I had been instructed by Tomas earlier; I even had showed it to Ganbold to make sure I had done it correctly. Tom Selleck #2 took the forms, briefly looked over my grocery list, nodding in approval as he pointed at my order for a spicy dry salami, then began reading the visitation request form. His normally cheerful expression suddenly grew dark as he read the form, then he pointed to where I had neatly printed my stepmother's first name, and began barking at me.

"Yarl! Yarl yarl yarl, yarl? Yaaaaaarl?!?" he said, shaking his head in disbelief.

"Uhm . . . it says 'Cheryl'? That's my stepmom," I said, as he continued to stab at her name with his finger.

"Grrrr . . . YARL. Yarl yarl yarl yarl, yarl yarl! Yarl! Yarl?" he said, as he ran his finger over the plainly printed word *Cheryl*, then thrust the form back into my hands with a look of complete disgust. He shook his finger at me, then locked the cell door. A few seconds later he returned with a brand-new blank form, thrust it through the cubby hole in our cell door, gave me a few exasperated *yarls* for good measure, then slammed the hatch shut. I could hear him stomping away down the hall and yarling away; clearly something had just gone terribly awry, but what? He had obviously been quite agitated by my stepmother's name—was *Cheryl* an obscene word in Czech? Did he have an ex-girlfriend named Cheryl who had done him wrong? I knew Cheryl had traveled in Europe years ago right after she had graduated college; was it possible that *she* had broken his heart during a brief but torrid Euro summer romance years ago? Or had somehow offended him so badly that he had never forgiven her? Cheryl is a wonderful lady with excellent manners, so I didn't think so. I studied the paper, then looked up at Ganbold in confusion.

"This man says he cannot read name on paper. You must write again" he said.

I looked at the paper. I had been very careful to print as neatly as possible, and Cheryl's name didn't look any different than the

other words I had written down in precise block letters. I handed
the form to Ganbold and asked him to see if he could read her
name.

"Shar-lurl?" he said.

Close enough. What in the hell was going on with the Sellecks
today? First Mr. Miserable himself, Tom Selleck #1, had suddenly
turned into a ray of sunshine and was acting all buddy-buddy;
then Tom Selleck #2, who up until just a few moments ago had
been the nicest guard I had interacted with in Pankrác, had gotten all pissy over my stepmother's name—he wasn't even the one
who approved visitation requests, he was just a screw on my cell
block. Was it possible that they were trying to mess with my head
for some reason? I had heard of good cop/bad cop, but good
Tom Selleck/bad Tom Selleck? There was no rhyme or reason
to this terrible place at all. I sighed and sat down to fill out the
new form, printing the word *Cheryl* slightly larger than the rest. I
hoped it wouldn't offend anyone else who read it.

As the days went by, Dorj had continued to blabber on in his
swishing Mongolian, and my nerves became more and more on
edge. I was not getting enough sleep, as his new found loquacious-
ness often went on for at least two hours after lights out. While I
lay on my rack gritting my teeth, Ganbold (who seemed immune
to the constant assault in his native language) would be snoring
quite loudly on the top bunk, and below him Dorj would go on
and on, his words eventually slowing until he literally fell asleep
mid-whispered sentence. Telling Dorj to shut up did absolutely
no good, as he would only be silent long enough for me to start
to fall asleep, then, without fail, just as I began to drift off into
slumber he would giggle and start yapping again. During the day
it was even worse, so in the morning after my shopping had arrived, I put everything away, gave Ganbold and Dorj a pack of
cigarettes and a fresh razor each, and announced that it was time
for English lessons. If I had to listen to Dorj talk anymore, at
least it would be in my language, which he did not speak in a

hideous whisper. We started with counting, as we always did, and everything was going great until we hit the mutual bane of our numeric existence, the number thirty.

As I had noticed the first day I began teaching Dorj English, the *th* sound presented a bit of difficulty for those who grew up speaking Mongolian—I cannot say for sure, but based on my limited experience, it doesn't seem to exist in their language. For almost three weeks now, I had been trying pretty much daily to get Dorj to say *thirty* correctly, but all I ever got out of him was "lurty." Today was no different; for some reason, although he would fudge the *th* for *three* and *thirteen* (it came our sounding almost like *tree* and *tert-teen*), he absolutely refused to make even the smallest *th* concession for *thirty*, and all I ever heard was "lurty." Ganbold would at least *try* to make the *th* sound (*thirty* came out as *shirty*), but Dorj wouldn't budge an inch. I could tell he was doing it on purpose, more than likely just to spite me. The numeral thirty had never pissed me off so badly before.

"Thirty," I said.

"Lurty," Dorj repeated, a smug, implacable look plastered across his round, brown face.

"Let's try that again. Thir-ty," I said, leaning forward.

"Okay . . . lur-ty," he replied, leaning forward himself, mimicking my movements and intonation perfectly while neatly neglecting to match my pronunciation.

"No! *Thuh thuh thuh! Th!* Thhhhirrrr-ty!" I said, getting irritated.

"Yes, lurty. Luh luh luh Luuuuurrrr-ty!" Dorj replied with a grin. I felt like strangling him.

"No! Not *lurty*, you fat motherfucker—*thirty*! *Thuh-thuh-thuh!* We've been on this for three weeks now—SAY IT, GODDAMMIT, I KNOW YOU CAN DO IT! *THHHHHHHHHHHHIRTY!*" I practically screamed, exaggerating the *th* sound to the point of ridiculousness, spit flying from my mouth.

"No! No *thuh-thuh-thuh!* No thurty! Lurty! Lurty, lurty, LUUUUUUUUUUURTY!" he yelled back, sticking out his tongue like a snake and hissing as he finally made the *th* sound. "No *thh-hhh! Thuh! Thuh!* Bah! I no cobra! Englishky stupid!"

I knew it! I knew he could make the *th* sound! For some reason he had just found it distasteful to do so; but from there on out, anytime during English lessons that I had to correct Dorj's or Ganbold's pronunciation of a word containing *th*, I simply said, "cobra!" and they would laugh and try their best to say it correctly.

The rest of the day passed without incident; when Tom Selleck #2 came to collect my newly filled out visitation form, he gave it a brief once over, pointed to my stepmother's name, said "Um-hmmm . . . yarl" in an approving tone, and that was that.

The next day, as my third week in Pankrác drew to a close, I caught myself day-dreaming about getting out soon. As much as I fought against it, I felt myself developing a short timer's mentality—this would not do. My release had not yet occurred, and if my experience thus far had taught me anything, it was that there were no guarantees that things would unfold according to any sort of plan. I had been working on the comedic letter to my family, and I began imagining myself happily in America with all the people I loved, thinking that it wouldn't be too much longer before I was home. I noticed this, and quickly reigned myself in. I put down the letter to my family, took a fresh sheet of paper, and wrote a letter to myself. I put it in an envelope, addressed it to myself care of my wife, and stuck a stamp on it. I gave the letter to the guard at the next evening's mail call, wondering when I would next read it.

I've never received that letter. Perhaps it was against prison regulations to write to one's self, and they just never sent it. Or maybe they thought I had gone crazy in there, talking to myself, and the prison censor just threw it away. Maybe it got "lost" along with several other letters I mailed from Pankrác and have been told never arrived by the intended recipients. I don't know, and I don't know what the letter said—my journal merely mentions that I had written and mailed one. I hope it said that I was doing the best I could to make the most of my time in a really bad situation, and that I should remember that when I got out, and make the most of the opportunities presented me.

It's what I'm trying to do right now.

TRIAL & HAVE TO APPEAL, I WILL BE ALLOWED TO STAY OUT ON BOND, SAME ONE, UNTIL THE APPEAL TRIAL AS LONG AS I SHOW UP FOR COUNT ON TIME & CONDUCT MYSELF WELL, WHICH I ABSOLUTELY WILL - I WILL BE HERE 3 FREAKIN' DAYS EARLY. I HOPE I DON'T MISS CHRISTMAS - PROBABLY WON'T, BUT WHO KNOWS? TODAY DID HAVE ONE PARTICULARLY NOTEWORTHY ASPECT: BREAKFAST. THE FOOD HERE HAS BEEN LESS THAN STELLAR TO SAY THE LEAST, BUT TODAY'S BREAKFAST OFFERING WAS NOT ONLY INSULTING, IT WAS INHUMAN & SHOULD BE CRIMINAL. MY NORMALLY HAPPY NURSE LADY DIDN'T LIKE MY SONG "DOUBRY RANO, MÉLATCHKO"(GOOD MORNING MY SWEETHEART) THEN THEY GAVE US THE NORMAL ROLL THING, AN APPLE, AND WHAT LOOKED LIKE A WHOLE STICK OF MARGERINE OR BUTTER - IN FACT, THAT'S WHAT I THOUGHT IT WAS AT FIRST. I ASKED GANZBOLD & HE SAID IT WAS A SPECIAL MORAVIAN SYR (CHEESE) AND WAS A SPECIAL TREAT TO CZECHS. HE UNWRAPPED MES & IT LOOKED ALL WET & SLIMEY. THEN THE ODOUR HIT ME. I HAVE NEVER, EVER, SMELLED ANY FOOD THAT SMELLED THAT BAD - IT SMELLED LIKE THE BOTTOM OF A WET DUMPSTER ON AN AUGUST DAY IN NEW ORLEANS. IT WAS ACTUALLY NAUSEATING. GANZBOLD TRIED A BITE & ALMOST THREW UP. HE SAYS NORMALLY IT IS STINKY & STRONG, BUT TASTES GOOD, BUT THIS CHEESE HAD TO BE OUT OF DATE (LIKE ALL OF OUR FOOD) AND WAS SPOILED & AWFUL. I HAVE NEVER SMELLED ANYTHING THAT

chapter fourteen

*L*ooking through the journal of my time in Pankrác, I can see the rapid, steady, reactionary progression of paranoia, cunning, and self-preserving deceit in my psyche. Unless you are placed in solitary for the entire duration of your incarceration, to exist in prison is to master the arts of misdirection and obfuscation, and a person resolutely determined to remain completely open and honest would not fare well behind bars. Prison is not the place to wear your heart on your sleeve, nor the locale to practice absolute truthfulness—you will only be taken advantage of by your fellow prisoners, and in many instances, by less than scrupulous guards. Make no mistake about it, regardless of your guilt or innocence, prison teaches you how think like a criminal. It does this by almost automatically developing a persecuted, criminal train of thought in inmates, even in those trying their best to do their time quietly and just get by until their release. I think this is one of the biggest reasons why so many ex-cons have such a hard time re-entering normal society; when your every action and word is shaped by a siege mentality for an extended time, when the motivation for virtually every act committed by those around you must by necessity be questioned, then it's hard to have trust in any of the human components of the system that keeps modern society functioning with at least a modicum of civility. Prison is a system as well, but to move safely and efficiently within it, one must develop character traits that would be seen as evidence of extreme neurosis or sociopathic tendencies on the outside. My writing from that time is full of sentences that only I understand the true meaning of, coded phrases detailing the constant stream of little white lies, forbidden actions, and plans to work outside the parameters of the prison rules in order to remain sane and comfortable inside while awaiting my release.

For instance, I know that anytime I wrote about admiring Dietrich Bonhoeffer's witty written manner when penning correspondence, I was referring to smuggling a letter to someone on the outside without going through the prison censor (living as an inmate charged with plotting to kill Hitler in a Nazi prison, Bonhoeffer had to do quite a bit of this). Whenever I wrote down any thoughts I was having concerning details of my case, I did so in general terms; obtuse sentences full of tiny in-jokes with grim punchlines that brought no laughter to my lips. And on the first day of my fourth week in prison, I wrote about shaving with a new safety razor I had gotten from the store, and what a shame it was the prison didn't seem to have a recycling program, as all the old plastic razors and toothbrushes just went into the trash, destined for the landfill. That meant that I had taken my old plastic safety razor, broken it apart, pulled the blade from it, and was considering affixing it to a toothbrush handle (I never wound up doing that, as it would have been pretty hard to hide, but I did keep the razor, as our old cutting tool was left behind when we switched cells—it seemed too risky to carry it with us). I wrote about the reality of my day-to-day life in such a cloaked manner because I never knew when the guards would do a cell inspection.

Cell inspections occurred at random intervals, sometimes once a week, and sometimes for four or five consecutive days. Prisoners had to leave their cells while the guards had a look around, banging on our lockers and bed frames with a long flexible stick, poking through our meager belongings for stashed contraband. I had no idea of exactly how hard they searched through our belongings, but it varied from day to day and guard to guard. Sometimes we would return to our cell after an inspection and the whole place would be a mess, clothes rearranged, beds in disarray, the contents of our lockers strewn about. Other times it looked as if nothing had been touched at all. I knew for certain that my journal had been looked through before, as my bookmark was in a different place, or it had been moved from my locker to my bed while my other reading and writing materials remained in their normal place. I had no idea if any of the guards could read English, or if they were legally allowed to seize my journal and take it in for inspection by someone who could. It was better to be safe than sorry, so I wrote about anything the authorities may not like in deceptively plain, obvious terms, the subtext of which was only apparent to me.

I had just finished stashing our new razor underneath a bit of torn linoleum and hiding the broken remains inside various bits of trash in our rubbish bucket (if the guards saw a disassembled handle, they would certainly wonder where the blade had gone) when we heard the familiar yell of "Kontrol!" and were herded out of our cell so the screws could do their thing. Luckily they didn't find our newest bit of contraband, but I remember sweating as I leaned against the wall outside our cell, wondering if they would put me in the hole if they discovered the razor—it had been my doing, so I would have to take responsibility. I also remember the sound of the search; each guard seemed to have their own rhythm with which they searched a cell, but they all sounded the same to a certain degree. First there was the yell of "Kontrol," followed by a deep bass thumping as they slapped our mostly empty metal lockers, then a staccato clinking sound as they drug their stick across the radiator in each room, and finally a higher pitched clicking sequence as they did the same to the bars of our bed frames. I heard this sonic pattern echoing throughout various parts of Pankrác every single day. It was part of the rhythm of the prison itself, and my mind filed the grim beat away for use at a later time. There are several such sound patterns from prison stored in my mental hard drives, and I can hear them as clearly as if I were still in that cell—once you've spent enough time as a musician, the part of you that is always looking for the next song can never be turned off, no matter your surroundings.

Shortly after our cell inspection, we lined up to go for our walk. I noticed that several of the men on our cellblock were not present; Martin the junkie was gone, and two of the *Roma*, Scarface and Raymond Herrera, were absent as well. Once we were outside, I asked Rene where they had gone, and he told me they had been moved upstairs. Raymond had been Rene's cellmate, and he had been given a most unpleasant replacement.

Rene's new cellmate was the ugliest man I had ever seen in my life, bar none. A scrawny youth of average height, he looked like an anthropomorphized cross between a weasel and a chimpanzee. His long, pointy, ferret-like nose protruded in front of two, black beady eyes ringed with dark circles and sunk into a craggy simian brow. His pointy, yellow teeth were freaking enormous, sitting crookedly in his maw like an oversized orthodontist's nightmare. His ears were large and floppy, his skin filthy and marked up with terrible, randomly placed jailhouse tattoos. He had a strange, crusty fungus coating his long, pointy fingernails, which hung at the end of arms that draped ape-like almost to his knees. His hair was lank, greasy, and had been hacked into a crooked, bizarrely asymmetrical version of a mohawk. The man looked to be in his mid-twenties, and obviously had not bathed in quite sometime. And lo, the stink of the speed freak (that most annoying of all drug addicts) was upon him, and wrought in me great trembling and despair. It wasn't his homeliness that instilled immediate revulsion in me—despite his wretched hygiene, his unfortunate visage was no fault of his own. What turned my stomach and filled me with dread was that horrible tweaker gleam in his eye; the crazed twinkle I recognized the second I saw him watching me light up a cigarette. He immediately broke into a slanted yellow grin, and began slinking towards me. *Fuck, the tweaker is gonna hassle me for smokes*, I thought. I knew this would not be a quick process—nothing ever is with them.

Alcoholics, coke heads, burn-out stoners, heroin junkies—none of these people are a bundle of joy to be around. But a speed freak? A goddamned tweaker?

You are *doomed*.

The hideous power of the tweaker to destroy your sanity lies in the unholy potency of his drug of choice, methamphetamine. Meth allots the tweaker plenty of time to ponder deeply the nature of his own personal reality, and after staying awake for days on end (sometimes up to a week or more), the psychosis that shrink-wraps itself around his head like some sort of malnourished epileptic octopus must be *expressed* somehow. Twitching, humming, and obsessively repeating non-sensical phrases, the tweaker begins to turn his awful and inhuman speed-fueled powers of concentration towards "projects"—these can assume the form of completely dismantling your brand-new computer to see what makes it tick, endlessly organizing and rearranging the beer bottles in your recycling bin, or, worst of all, explaining to you in great jittery detail the secrets of the universe (the understanding of which has been bestowed upon them by their newly developed "psychic powers"—a common tweaker delusion, I shit you not). The tweaker never rests or slumbers, merely twitches slightly slower from time to time, for those who soar aloft on wings of meth are above petty mortal concerns such as sleep. The tweaker's ultimate goal is to pull down all those around him into his delusional, self-aggrandizing, hideously spinning world of shrieking bat-shit bonkers insanity, and woe be unto the person who gets caught in the crooked crosshairs of his bloodshot, dilated-pupiled eyes.

Chimpo Weaselman (as I came to call him) was fresh to prison (this time, at least), and was obviously still coming down from a binge—the signs were unmistakable. He tweaked his way over to me, then standing entirely too close for my comfort, held out his hand in a begging gesture and said quietly, "You give me cigarette?"

"No. I do not give you cigarette," I said.

"Yes. Cigarette for me. Thank you," he said, stepping in closer in an attempt to narrow the distance between us and execute some sort of tweaker mind control trick. I do not like close-talkers to begin with, and in prison every time someone had tried to close-talk me, they had been quietly attempting to beg something from me. I placed my foot directly in Chimpo's path, halting his advance.

"No. *Fuck no.* No cigarettes for you. Beat it," I said, standing my ground.

Chimpo Weaselman changed directions smoothly, slithering sideways to initiate a flanking maneuver; but I merely pivoted on my heel and slid my blocking foot around with him, effectively maintaining my defensive perimeter. He was beginning to piss me off. He looked at my foot and sadly frowned, as if to say, *Oh come now, there's really no reason for all that.*

"Cigarette . . . for me!" he said one last time, as if a bright and novel idea had just popped into his head.

"I said 'no!' No fucking cigarette for you. You need to fuck right off and step away from me," I said, raising my voice and visibly clenching my fists—I don't trust tweakers, and they can become violent if the mood strikes them. Rene noticed that I was getting agitated, and said something to his new cellmate in Czech, who gave me an oily smile and slunk away to bum a smoke from someone else.

Another new inmate to the block was Ollie, a French-speaking Czech who spoke a bit of English. Ollie had been living abroad, primarily in Monte Carlo, for the last decade, having only recently returned to the Czech Republic in the last month and somehow winding up nearly immediately in Pankrác. I never bothered to ask Ollie what he was in for, but I don't think it was a violent crime; he was a very smart, well-traveled educated guy who knew a lot about international politics, as well as being well-versed in the currency exchange and tax rates of many different countries (which made sense, Monte Carlo being a huge international destination for gamblers). I got the feeling that his criminal activities probably revolved around obtaining money by fraudulent means, which in all likelihood was why he had to leave Monaco in the first place. Regardless of whatever his crime was, Ollie was a very pleasant man to talk to, and between his remedial English and my remedial French we were able to enjoy a nice conversation about the various countries we had visited in our travels.

Near the end of walk, Chimpo Weaselman approached me again as I was speaking with Ollie, and he attempted to bum a cigarette again. After I brusquely informed him I would never give him a cigarette as long as I still drew breath, he then asked me to buy him some coffee and sugar from the prison store with my next shopping order. For a second I was so astounded by his request that I just stared at him—did he think that I was merely averse to parting with cigarettes, but would have no problem with buying him whatever else he wanted? Then I remembered that he was a tweaker, and tweakers are not known for their unshakeable grasp on logic; plus, he was probably just trying to get his filthy paws on any sort of stimulant he could. I told him I wouldn't be buying him coffee, sugar, cigarettes, or anything else for that matter, that he was wasting both his and my goddamned time, and that I didn't appreciate that one bit. I don't believe he understood most of what I said other than "no," but he seemed to get the point.

———

After breakfast the next day, both Dorj and Ganbold went back to sleep, and I decided to take advantage of the silence in the cell and get some work done. As I sat enjoying the quiet, writing letters and outlining an idea I had for a novel, I noticed how oddly comfortable I had become in prison. I had a daily schedule, I followed it fairly religiously, and I was getting a lot of writing done. I had (admittedly crappy) food, clothes and shelter; I had more than enough cigarettes, some half-decent instant coffee, and a few snacks. I had plenty of books and time to read them. The basic building blocks I needed for a happy life (sans wife, family, friends, and freedom, of course) were in place—I can get by with very little and remain quite content. Within just four short weeks of my arrest I had settled pretty easily into my new life as an inmate, and while I wasn't overjoyed to be there, most of the time I was not freaked out in the least bit that I was in prison. This worried me—while I value my ability to acclimate to difficult situations as one of my best character traits, I was concerned my adaptability to my latest hardship would eventually morph into apathetic acceptance of my lot. I wasn't quite ready to throw in the towel and reconcile myself to my fate as a jailbird yet, and I definitely didn't like how relaxed I was feeling at the moment. I pondered this oddly nonplussed state of mind for a bit, then suddenly realized that after years of constant touring, I was simply enjoying the quiet and relatively small amount of interaction with the rest of the human race I had at that time.

I was forty-one years old, and had been on the road or in a studio pretty much constantly for over a decade. I was almost two years sober, and since I didn't party anymore, I could no longer cope with being constantly surrounded by loud, obnoxiously wasted people by doing the logical thing and getting loud and obnoxiously wasted myself. I did not enjoy being around all those fucked up people anymore—in fact, most of the time I didn't enjoy being around most people *period*, drunk or sober. Touring is nothing if not an ever-changing, highly concentrated revolving group of people centered around your current location, most of whom want to talk to you, and on the road there is no peace, no quiet, no solitude, and no escape from all the attention that comes with being a public person. For some band guys that's perfectly fine; the constant attention they get from fans and the press is a balm for their troubled, insecure souls. All of those people wanting to meet them, constantly complimenting them, telling them that they *love them* validates their inflated self-image, even their very existence. Everyone wants to be loved, but there is a huge difference between the true, lasting, unconditional love of good friends and family, and the temporary adoration of people who only love their *idea* of what you are, not the actuality of you as a person. While I was grateful that people appreciated my artistic output, enabling me to travel the world and pay my bills by doing what I love, I neither wanted nor needed that kind of external validation. What I wanted and needed was some freaking peace and quiet. I wanted to sit still for a moment, to escape my job as a traveling, screaming, black-t-shirt salesman and just read and write for a bit. For quite some time, I had been longing to erect a barrier between myself and that noisy, hectic life; just long enough to catch my breath and relax without being "Randy from lamb of god." I never imagined that that barrier would unexpectedly arrive in the shape of prison walls. I relaxed a bit, stopped freaking out about not freaking out, and reminded myself that I might as well take advantage of my removal from society while it lasted.

I needn't have been worried about becoming too comfortable in my surroundings, as Dorj soon woke up, and with a giggle, immediately began talking in Mongolian. Ganbold continued sleeping peacefully, emitting a snore every now and then, and I put down my pen and stared at him with irritated envy. But in that moment, I was grateful to be stuck with Dorj, for he truly was slowly driving me insane with all his whistling and whispering. As long as I had him as a cellmate, I knew I would possess a fierce urge to get as far away from Pankrác as possible as quickly as possible. I was greatly relieved when a guard came to the cell and announced that my lawyer was there to see me. Tomas had come bearing good news—two new witnesses had come forward of their own accord and had given testimony to the police. The witnesses, a couple who had been at the 2010 show, told a much different version of what had happened that night at Club Abaton from the three young men (all friends of the deceased) who had been interrogated so far. Their description, not quite as muddled and conflicting as the three testimonies already given, worked more in my favor. In addition to this surprising but welcome new development, Tomas also informed me that I would be released within a week, as my bail had made it into the Czech government's bank account. I didn't bother to ask why I was not being immediately released, as I had given up any hope of trying to understand the strange Czech legal system and the sluggish pace at which it seemed to resolve issues of bail and recognizance. I thanked him for bringing me the news, but took it with a grain of salt—I would believe I was to be free only when my feet no longer paced the filthy linoleum floor of my cell.

That evening though, I began to think about what my release and return to America would entail, and felt a rising tide of anxiety. Aside from the small handful of fans I had briefly met in the highly restrictive environment of Pankrác, and a single written interview that Martin had finally arranged with *Blesk*, I had left my life as a public person outside the prison walls. I now know that during my incarceration, a very large number of people whom I had never met were very concerned for my well being, and that my imprisonment was a daily topic of discussion for many. But in prison, I had no way of knowing these things (aside from the odd letter from my wife or bandmates)—I was a number, just another prisoner in ill-fitted rags, albeit one whose highly publicized criminal charge every other inmate was aware of. The press surrounding my case came to me only in small bits and pieces, and for the most part I was completely unaware of the outside world's perception of my dilemma—hell, my own perception of my dilemma wasn't exactly crystal clear. If I ever was finally released and got to go home, I knew that my relative separation from the world would very swiftly change. My family and friends would all want to see me. I would have to go on tour and make some money, and many, many people would want to talk to me about prison and my case. The music press would be ringing my manager's phone off the hook with interview requests. Just the thought of trying to explain to all of these concerned people what prison was like, my vague understanding of my legal situation, and what I guessed the future might hold for me made me feel panicky. I became acutely nervous at the thought of walking out of the prison doors, but not for the usual reasons some inmates get apprehensive about their release; if I were released soon, I wouldn't have been incarcerated anywhere near long enough to forget what regular society was like, and my job would still be there when I got out. But my release carried its own unique set of problems. Most regular everyday criminals don't walk out of prison as a top news story in their profession's personality driven media, and I decided right then to deny all requests for interviews until this thing was resolved. I had no desire to endlessly repeat the same depressing answers to the inevitable question of "What was prison like?" (And I don't today, hence the book in your hands at this second.) I did not want to have to say "I'm sorry, I can't discuss that at the moment" over and over when the press asked me about the incident that had landed me in jail—I had very little information, and I honestly didn't know exactly what had happened. Plus, it's not exactly the swiftest game plan in the old playbook to start running your mouth to media outlets before the very serious criminal charges you are facing have been resolved. Loose lips sink ships, and except for my lone *Blesk* interview done at the advice of my attorney, I had remained silent, and went to sleep that evening firmly resolved to continue doing so. (I had written my page and a half statement to the press, and had given it to my Czech lawyer, but Martin said it was too long and that *Blesk* wouldn't print it—this irritated me greatly, as I had chosen my words very carefully, deemed each one necessary, and hadn't written it for *Blesk* in the first place. The statement had been tightly structured, said all that I wished to say at the time. I had penned it primarily for the English-speaking press to begin with, and I considered the fact that my voice was only allowed to be heard through a goddamned *tabloid*, that daily printed T&A photos, as a profound insult to my intellect.)

The next day, despite my anxiety from the night before, I awoke with a song on my lips, and I couldn't wait to sing it to my Czech bride. My *Pankrác manželka* ("Pankrác wife," as Dorj and Ganbold referred to her) was the Beach Boys–loving nurse from my long, arduous visit to the ancient prison doctor. Each morning she rapped on the cell door briefly, opened the hatch, and chirped

"Oh, Blight! The music man! Goot morning!" as she handed me my antidepressant pill. She seemed extraordinarily happy to see me every single time she came by, and her kind smile was truly a bright spot in my day. Dorj and Ganbold would immediately begin snickering the second she was gone, then start ribbing me, laughing and saying that once I was released, this woman would surely follow me to America to break up my marriage.

"Bahahaha, Doctor Pankrác! You go to America, Pankrác manželka come, too—find your home! Knock on door in morning! 'Ahhh, Blight, my music man! I love you!' Bahahaha! American manželka soooooo angry! Big fighting! Bahahahahahaha, Pankrác manželka in love with you, hahahahaha! Big troubles for you—*two* manželka now, bahahahahaha! Doctor Pankrác, you fucked!!!"

It *was* pretty darn funny in that grim place to have this cheery woman so happy to see me (and a nice feeling to boot), so in honor of my Pankrác manželka, I had begun composing a brief song to serenade her with. I had arranged the lyrics to the tune of Elvis Presley's "Are You Lonesome Tonight?", practiced it a few times for Dorj and Ganbold to check my Czech pronunciation, who were certain she would immediately kick down the cell door and attempt to rape me as soon as I let my serviceable baritone loose. I hadn't performed for an audience in a while, and was actually looking forward to singing for this woman. The Mongols sat on their bunks expectantly, waiting for the show to begin, and shortly before breakfast came the familiar rap on our cell door. The nurse greeted me in her usual cheery manner, and as she handed me my 10 mg Lexapro tablet, I began to sing.

"*Dobré ráno / miláček* (trans: "good morning, sweetheart") / good morning / my looove / how are youuuu? / It's so goooood, to see you agaaaaain / I must thank you, my loooov-" WHAM! I was heading into the second half of the first verse when the nurse's face abruptly twisted into a dark frown and she unceremoniously slammed the cell door hatch shut right in my grill. Well, *damn.* Maybe she hated Elvis? I should have recycled a Beach Boys tune, maybe "Surfer Girl." Behind me I heard the Mongols explode into laughter.

"BAHAHAHAHAHA!!! Doctor Pankrác, she no like your song! Pankrác manželka, *hate* your song! Pankrác manželka, shut door in face, wham, fuck you! You need new job! You *terrible* singer, Doctor Pankrác, bahahahahahaha!!!"

The Mongols continued to make fun of my morning's melodic malfunction up until Bradley came to take us out for walk, and after the relentless joking, I desired some peace and quiet. So for the first and only occasion during my time in prison, I decided to stay inside and not go out for walk. Besides not having to hear about what an awful singer I was for an hour, I would possibly be able to get some writing done in peace.

The hour alone went by all too swiftly, but Ganbold returned bearing good news about my case. Apparently the news of my imminent release was in the Czech papers, and the men were all talking about it at walk. From what Ganbold had gathered, the prison was required to release me within forty-eight hours of a judge signing some sort of paper, which he was supposedly going to do any day now.

"These men were upset you not come out for walk today; they say that you go to America soon. These men say you must come tomorrow, so they can say goodbye. And they all talking about this man, Ozzy Osbourne. They have picture of him in paper with your name under. Do you know this Ozzy Osbourne man? He is very famous, and says good things for you in paper! You go home soon!"

Wow. Although I tried not to let myself get excited or develop any expectations with the arrival of this seemingly definitive good news, it was difficult not to smile. I wished I had been at walk, to try and get Ollie to explain exactly what the paper said—surely we could have piecemealed it together between a bit of French, a dash of English, and the tiny smattering of Czech I had learned. I also wondered what Ozzy had had to say—what guy in a metal band wouldn't? The communication barrier that was currently one of the most maddening aspects of my life was firmly in place though; and as Ganbold's English (although far superior to my Czech) wasn't the greatest, I could glean no more than a few sketchy details from his account. I hoped one of the men would bring the newspaper article to walk tomorrow so that I could try and make some sense of it.

The next morning, my nurse returned and was as pleasant as ever—of course, I wasn't singing any Elvis to her either. This morning she didn't even say hello, just handed me my pill, winked at me, and said "Aaaaaaah yo!" in a disturbingly erotic high-pitched purr. My Mongols burst into laughter as usual as soon as she was gone.

"Okay, dudes, what the fuck does 'Aaaaaaah yo' mean?" I asked.

"It mean 'Ooooooooh yes!', bahahahaha! You Pankrác man-želka, is sexy babika (grandmother)! Bahahahahaha! 'Aaaaaaaah yo, I love you Doctor Pankrác, I am sexy babička for youuuuu, aaaaaaah yooo!' Bahahahaha!!!" Dorj said, wiping tears of laughter from his eyes. The jokes never seemed to stop in those days.

Ganbold had told me that at walk the day before, the men had been talking about a rumor of a "special breakfast" we were to be served the next day, some sort of uniquely Czech delicacy that some of the men were excited about. By the time Uncle Fester came around with the breakfast cart on this particular morning, I was quite curious as to what that "special breakfast" would be. I would have loved some waffles, but as we weren't in Belgium I didn't bother to get my hopes up. Ganbold and Dorj were discussing how nice it would be to have some horse milk, according to them a common breakfast item in Mongolia. Horse milk didn't sound too appetizing to me, but I would rather drink a five-gallon bucket of it straight from the mare than take one bite of what arrived on our food trays on that morning. As we took out trays and sat down at the table to eat, I saw an apple, the white bread roll we were given, and what looked like an entire stick of butter in a foil wrapper. A quarter pound of butter was the Czech idea of a good breakfast?

"What is it? A stick of butter? That sucks," I said.

"No, no—it is special *syr* (cheese) from Moravia in Eastern Czech. It is good!" Ganbold said, and began to peel the foil away from his cheese stick. The cheese was a pale yellow, and seemed to be . . . slimy. Slimy cheese? It didn't look too appetizing to me, and I began to have my doubts about this "special syr." I noticed that even Dorj (who normally finished his breakfast in two or three slurps while I was just starting in on my morning coffee) looked a little apprehensive and hadn't touched the foil on his cheese stick. Ganbold held the cheese up to his nose, took a whiff, winced, then shrugged and took a healthy bite off the end of the stick. Right at the very second his lips closed around the slimy yellow bar, the odor hit me, and instantaneously, with great heaving violence, I began to gag.

Olomoucké tvarůžky, as the cheese is known to the Czechs, is produced in the small town of Lotice in the Moravia region of the Czech Republic. Renowned for being a particularly pungent product, the cheese is always accompanied by breath mints when served in restaurants. The malodorous nature of the cheese is perhaps not surprising, as according to some accounts, it is fermented under hunks of rotting meat (I can't say for sure if this is true, but I wouldn't doubt it). In the humble opinion of this writer, it is the worst smelling food on the face of the planet (far worse than the fabled durian fruit); in fact, it is one of the worst smelling things on this planet *period*. I have eaten some downright weird shit in my day, and I like to think of myself as a man of adventure when it comes to traveling and food (although lamb of god's guitarist Mark refers to my dietary habits abroad slightly less nobly as "sport eating"). I am lucky enough to traverse the globe singing for my supper, and I feel that it is my duty as a privileged citizen of the world to sample the local cuisine wherever I go, to eat what the locals eat, with the locals, in the local spot where the locals eat it. To know a country's food is to know what fuels its people's very lives, and I have witnessed my open-minded attitude towards eating abroad grant me an immediate measure of both trust and respect from previously suspicious locals. It has also granted me several miserable hours immobilized on the local toilet, but that's beside the point. In my travels, I have consumed with great gusto a huge and varied number of very strange looking, smelling, and tasting things (often cooked on a dirty street corner in a makeshift mobile kitchen that would cause an American health inspector to instantly drop dead from shock right on the spot)—I come, I eat, I conquer the brutish and xenophobic stereotype of the ugly American abroad. Furthermore, I have enjoyed many, many amazing meals this way. If you work for a promoter or venue and I am coming to your town, take me to the dirtiest, least glamorous, hole-in-the-wall restaurant where men with mud still caked on their boots from work wolf down hot plates of whatever the local specialty is. Order me some of that, the good stuff you grew up eating. Feed me *your food*, and I will *love you* for it.

Unless you happen to be a local cheese lover from Lotice, Moravia, in the Czech Republic—in that case, I will never, ever, ever join you on a culinary adventure in your town, and I will not care one bit if you think I am a close-minded American cheese-bigoted pig. The smell of the *olomoucké tvarůžky* was so mind-and-nostril-blowingly repugnant that just the thought of being anywhere near the Lotice factory where it is produced in large quantities sends a shiver down my spine. I am surprised that anyone can actually breathe the air of Lotice for longer than five minutes and survive (for surely it must carry the lethal, fetid aroma of the *tvarůžky* upon its winds), much less actually reside there. *Olomoucké tvarůžky* smells like a place where sewers go to die; it is a crime against God, nature, and the human race, and as the product of Ganbold's moment of temporary olfactory insanity hit his tastebuds, he turned green (yes, Mongols can turn green), bolted from his chair, and began loudly trying to puke up the cheese into the toilet.

After he was done, Ganbold staggered back over to the table, saying, "I think this *syr* is maybe badly old. It is not tasting like that when I eat before."

"Does it always smell that bad?" I asked, holding my t-shirt up over my nose for lack of a gas mask, still gagging.

"Oh yes. Very strong," he said, picking up the cheese and moving to throw it into our trash bucket. I stopped him, grabbed an empty plastic grocery bag my groceries had come in, and tied all three sticks of the *olomoucké tvarůžky* up in it, triple knotting the bag to make sure it was completely airtight. I was putting the bag into the garbage when Dorj told me to save it.

"Why, for fuck's sake?" I asked, pausing above the bucket. "What will we use it for? A biological weapon?"

"No. You give to begging Chimpo man. He no ask you for nothing after he eating *syr*, hahaha," Dorj said with a giggle.

After lunch Bradley came to get us for walk, and I smuggled the bag of evil out in the waistband of my pants. The men were all happy to see me, and although no one had brought the previous day's article about my release with them, Rene seemed particularly impressed by it, clapping me on my shoulder several times and saying, "Ozzy Osbourne says good things for you. Yeeeeah, rock-n-roll baby! Randy, go home!" I pulled out a cigarette and lit it, and sure enough, Chimpo Weaselman began making his unctuous way towards me, his dirty hands already clasped together in supplication.

"Cigarette for me?" he whined.

"No, still no cigarette for you," I said, grinning as I pulled the bag of cheese out of my pants, "but I brought you this. Special *syr.*"

His eyes lit up and he snatched the bag from my hands, scurried over to a corner, and began untying the knots that held the terrible smell of the cheese inside. Then Dorj, Ganbold, and myself stood transfixed, staring with appalled fascination as Chimpo proceeded to unwrap then cram all three bars of *olomoucké tvarůžky* into his hideous mouth, chewing the unholy cheese with a look of pure bliss on his face. He swallowed the gooey putrid mess, belched loudly with great satisfaction, then began licking the foil wrappers.

God in heaven, I thought, *he's not even human*. George came over to ask me if I had anymore *syr*, but Ollie barked at him in Czech to go away. "Do not talk to him," he said, throwing George a hard look, "He is a bad person in here. He is a *délinquant sexuel*."

Fuck, only the two creepiest guys in here like that god-awful cheese— maybe Chimpo's a sex offender, too? I thought, *No woman in her right mind would sleep with that ugly motherfucker; especially not with a load of tvarůžky on his breath. Maybe the stuff is rapist fuel—is there such a thing as immoral cheese?*

The next morning a guard came by with the day's mail, handing me a post card and a letter, both from lamb of god fans. A few letters from friends and family back home had made it to me thus far, but these were the first two pieces of correspondence I had received from strangers. One was a post card with the face of the Joker from Batman printed on it, his nefarious grin surrounded by blood-red letters reading, "The only sensible way to live in this world is without rules!" On the back of the post card was a short message wishing me well, telling me to hang in there, and letting me know that my community was thinking of me. "This is going to make one hell of a story for ya when you get exonerated," the neatly printed message read in closing. There was no return address, and it was signed simply "Metal Dave from Seattle, WA." I read the postcard a few times, then stuck it to our cork board so that I could see the Joker's face. The post card added a bit of color to our drab cell, and in that dark place with so many confusing rules, its bloody message brought a defiant smile to my face more than once. The prophetic post card sits in front of me on my writing desk as I write this, so thanks Metal Dave—I hope to see you down the road sometime.

The other piece of mail was a lengthy letter from a man named Gavin Piercey in Canada discussing what was going on with the public reaction to my trial, wishing me well, and also just telling me about he and his wife Donna's life. Gavin had even included a photo of himself and his wife, and it was immensely pleasurable for me to read about normal, everyday things. By the end of the letter I felt as if I had actually come to know the man a bit. Both the postcard and Gavin's letter had cheered me up quite a bit, and I immediately began writing Gavin a reply. I did not take the kindness of these two strangers for granted, and the time they took to send me a bit of encouragement was not spent in vain, for their messages did me more good than they will ever know.

That day at walk there was yet another addition to our regular group, an ancient and filthy *Roma* who had obviously been living on the streets before landing in Pankrác. As the man scoured the ground for cigarette butts, I was appalled by his pitiful physical appearance. He had dirt caked under his long finger and toenails, his skin was weathered and scarred, and his tell-tale shaking hands betrayed the discomfort of an alcoholic in the grips of withdrawal. The old man looked to be in his eighties (although hard living had probably added a few years to his appearance), and I wondered what he possibly could have done to have wound up in Pankrác, for he was very frail and looked utterly lost—he belonged in a hospital, not prison. Rene spoke to him quietly in the Gypsy tongue, but the man made no reply and continued looking for cigarette butts until someone gave him a half-smoked cigarette. He inhaled it in what seemed like one mighty drag; then someone else gave him another half cigarette, which he also made astonishingly short work of. Noticing me smoking, he teetered over to me and began begging me for a Marlboro. Although I felt sorry for him, I had no intention of giving this power smoker any of my precious few pre-rolled cigarettes. The old man was relentless though, so finally I emptied my Marlboro box of cigarettes and put them in my pocket, took some of the rolling tobacco I always carried outside to share and half-filled the box with it, threw in a few rolling papers, and handed it to him. He put the box in his pocket and, without saying thanks or batting an eye, began asking me for the cigarette I was smoking. This rudeness annoyed me to no end, so I firmly told him to kick rocks, which he eventually did, but not before asking me for my cigarette a few more times. After more fruitless attempts to weasel the smoke out of my lips he gave up, and soon realized I wasn't going to budge. Then he changed tactics and began incessantly asking me for my lighter, and when the guard came to take us back inside, I gave it to him just to shut him up, as well as in the hopes that he would leave me alone the next day (he didn't). At first I had felt sorry for the old man, for when I looked at him I saw what awaited me if I ever started drinking again: homelessness, delirium tremors, prison or the insane asylum, and finally, a painful, lonely, pathetic death. But his lack of gratitude and unremitting mooching had aroused my ire, and I was glad when he was gone a few days later. I am a patient man with those who suffer from alcoholism, even the ones in the midst of a good bender, for I have been there myself many times. But a blatant lack of manners from someone who isn't currently plastered out of their mind, ancient alcoholic or not, offends me to the point of instilling coldness in my normally compassionate heart.

The next day brought a disheartening visit from Martin, who informed me that the merry-go-round with the prosecutor was continuing. Martin's partner Vladimir had been at the police station earlier that day on business concerning a different case, and had been talking to Lucie (the detective who had arrested me) in her office when the prosecuting attorney happened to call. Vladimir overheard him asking Lucie when the police would need me again for interrogation, and she told him that they didn't. Then he asked her what kind of a person I was, to which she said, "He's a normal guy." Apparently he wasn't too happy to hear that I was no longer needed for questioning, or that I wasn't some frothing-at-the-mouth psycho-killer. From listening to Martin, I had a hunch that to Musik, the prosecutor, I was not a human being. I was a notch he could put in his belt; a high profile case he wanted to win in order to advance his career, not a man looking at five to ten years of his life vanishing behind a prison wall. Musik would prove my theory correct again and again throughout my incarceration and trial, playing the system the best he could to keep me behind bars and even showing a callous disregard for the opinion of the officer who investigated my alleged crime. (I was later made aware that upon reviewing the available evidence and testimony, the investigating detective recommended in their report to Musik that I be charged with a lesser crime than manslaughter. The prosecutor ignored the report, refused the recommendation, and told them to charge me with manslaughter.)

Martin also informed me that the prosecutor had until midnight the next day (which was a Friday) to appeal my new (and now paid-in-full) bail, and that he would most likely wait until the very last minute to do so. Then I would be stuck in Pankrác through the weekend until Monday or Tuesday, when a second appeal court *might* convene in order to review Musik's complaint and *maybe* make a decision on whether or not the eight million Czech crowns my band had paid were a sufficient enough reason to release me. And even then, Martin told me, the prosecuting attorney could write a brand-new arrest warrant for me in order to keep me in prison, saying that the police needed me for further questioning. I could appeal that, then he could appeal my appeal, and so on and so forth.

"But the police told Musik I wasn't needed for questioning anymore!" I said to Martin, trying to keep my temper.

"I do not think he will tell the court that," Martin said.

As hard as I was trying to keep my chin up, I was slowly being ground down by this constant stream of conflicting good and bad news. It seemed like every time it started to look like my situation had taken a turn for the better, things suddenly got worse. The silver lining peeking out from behind a lifting dark cloud always turned out to be a patch of acid rain, and despite my best efforts to not develop any expectations, I was becoming demoralized. I began to wonder if it wasn't best for me to simply not know anything that was going on with my case at all—every time I tried to make sense of it, it just got more confusing.

Finally, to make things even weirder, Martin told me that another young man had come forward and had been interrogated by the police as a witness, but not in regards to seeing me allegedly pushing the deceased fan off the stage. This young man was claiming that *he* was the one I was seen wrestling with onstage in the photos that all the Czech papers had printed, *he* was the one who was in the video that was circulating on the internet. I didn't know what to make of this strange new development—was this guy just some attention-seeking crazed fan? Or was it possible that he really *was* the guy I remembered tussling with onstage? I hadn't seen the video yet, but I remembered the disconnect I had felt when I had tried to match the photo of Daniel in his practice space Martin had shown me with the hazy memories of what occurred that night. Something had been off, something hadn't quite lined up correctly. Martin didn't have a photo of the new witness yet, but when I would see it later I would understand why I couldn't connect the dots when I had first seen Daniel's picture.

I went to bed that evening with a head full of confusion, anger, fear, and sadness. I lay there in my bunk, trying not to be overwhelmed by what was happening to me, but it was very hard. I asked God to give me the strength to get through whatever was coming my way with some dignity, and if he was feeling extra-generous at the moment, to grant me a little understanding of what in the hell was going on. I wanted an answer. I wanted to know what had happened so badly I could taste it. It is a very odd feeling to go to sleep wondering if you killed a man or not. I would get my answer eventually, but that night God was silent, as he had been every night since I had been arrested.

DUDE! Come on! Kick down a little insight, would ya? I'm not asking you to get me off the hook here, I just want to know what I'm dealing with, okay? I could handle this a whole lot better if you would just somehow let me know what happened that night. Is that too damn much to ask? Help a brother out, okay? I prayed. I don't have to use flowery language for my God to get my drift, and I'm sure he understood me that evening.

He just wasn't talking.

From my first day in Pankrác, I had done my best to remain fully grounded in the reality of my situation. Following the advice of Zen Buddhist monks and recovering alcoholics everywhere, I tried to "stay in the moment." This very second is all that truly exists, and I have heard it said that if you have one foot in the past, and one foot in the future, you are pissing on the present, so I clung fast to each moment as it occurred. I had bolstered this effort with a bit of philosophy stemming from my punk rock roots, fiercely embracing the concept of P.M.A. (positive mental attitude), a gift given to me by the seminal Washington, DC hardcore band, Bad Brains, in their song, "Attitude": "Don't care what they may say, we got that attitude! Don't care what they may do, we got that attitude! Yeeeeeeeah, we got that P.M.A." I would screech through the small square hatch in our cell door, drawing confused looks from Uncle Fester as he shoved cracked plastic trays bearing approximations of food into our home.

"Stay in the moment, maintain a positive mental attitude, and you will get through this. Stay in the moment, maintain P.M.A., maintain P.M.A., maintain P.M.A. . . . " I told myself over and over. Be present. Observe strict mental discipline. Do not lose hope.

But unless you are a one-hundred-year-old Zen master and have spent your entire life in a cave meditating in a heightened state of mental, physical, and spiritual awareness, this is the hat trick that is almost impossible to pull off, especially in prison. How do you maintain a hyper-vigilant awareness of each second, trying to squeeze the most out of it, while still retaining P.M.A. manifesting as hope for a better tomorrow, the whole time trying not to think about the future too much? Especially when a lot of the "moments" you are attempting to stay in just flat-out *suck*?

I thought I had learned my lesson after my bail was appealed the first time. *Don't start thinking about home. This is your home now. Make the most of it, because it hurts too much to build expectations up, only to have them crushed beneath the heel of a bureaucracy you cannot hope to understand. You had better square yourself away and PDQ, soldier, because this is reality, and bellyaching about it is about as useful as a screen door on a submarine.*

But in prison, as the minutes, hours, and days stretch on, you can easily start to lose track of time and any sort of rational perspective. If you don't watch it, you can easily venture into the forbidden realm of the overly cerebral. This is a dangerous place to go, at least for a man like me, someone who, as I've said, can envision the complete annihilation of the entire human race at the tiny microbial hands of some catastrophic nonexistent virus given thirty seconds and sufficient negative stimuli, say blowing a flat tire on my bicycle on the way to the coffee shop.

A wise man once told me "Son, don't go up in your head without adult supervision," advice I had stupidly ignored the night before, after Martin's visit, much to my detriment. It was a terrible idea, but I began to *think*. The new witness who was completely disrupting any of the accepted ideas about my alleged actions. The prosecuting attorney's endless manipulations of the strange Czech judicial system that continued keeping me in Pankrác day after interminable day, one last minute protocol filing after the other. I had finally begun to let this (by now) entirely predictable course of events get to me, and became angry and resentful over the games being played with my freedom. My inner self-pitying squalling brat surfaced, and I let him run free through the chambers of my mind. Mommy's little monster cursed his fate, despaired his present living conditions, and pined for his wife and home. I decided to throw a very quiet, completely internalized, utterly berserk mental hissy fit. This was a deadly mistake, and I paid for it by falling into a deep funk on my cot, staring at the crumbling ceiling until lights out. I had prayed to God for some guidance, had received none, and promptly blew a mental gasket. Laying there full of bitterness over an answer I was not hearing, I tossed and turned and cursed the screaming Ukrainians on the floor above me until I passed out.

That same wise man who had let me know my mental playground required a responsible chaperone had also told me, "You can start your day over anytime you want to," so I woke up the next morning and swiftly jumped off the pity pot, determined to start again.

Screw Musik, and screw this shit hole of a prison. This place cannot break me, this place cannot break me, this place cannot break me . . .

Over my first cup of instant black coffee, I remembered that it was shower day. This thought completely banished my dark mood of the night before, since my twice weekly shower had become one of the highlights of my existence in prison. Not that I was in a hurry to get into a steamy room with a bunch of naked men, but I was always pretty ripe after a few days in that ancient dump with no shower. Since the Playmate of the Year hadn't shown up to scrub my back yet, and since Bradley and the Sellecks simply refused to have the jacuzzi installed that I had repeatedly requested since my arrival in Pankrác, I was more than grateful for the opportunity to scrub my body, with or without nude convicts. When you live in a 123-year-old, moldy basement that has zero means of air circulation in July for days on end, even in the relatively cool Czech Republic, things can get . . . tart. We all just wanted to get clean.

Disease and infection flourish in dirty, unsanitary places, and make no mistake about it, Pankrác was (and I'm sure still is) a filthy, filthy place. Whenever there is a natural disaster with long-term effects, public utilities are cut off. People always die during the aftermath of these emergencies due to lack of proper sanitation. Pankrác was an unnatural disaster, and it was hazardous to let us shower as little as we were allowed. I had gone for up to two weeks without a shower back in my freight hopping days, but that was only because one was not available. The prison shower wasn't as good as most dressing room showers in the crappiest of rock clubs (and I have washed the show grime off of my body in some *sketchy* backstage showers), but it meant hot water. Hot water meant I could shave, and there would be a few minutes of feeling like a human being again before the sweat and dust covered my increasingly skinny form.

When Bradley or the Sellecks had a day off, there were a few fill-in guards who only seemed to be on the cell block for a single day at a time. One of these was a short fat man I called Archie Bunker due to his age, rotundness, and temperament. On this morning, Archie Bunker showed up shortly after breakfast, yanking open our door and yelling "Sprcha!" (shower) in his normal charming fashion. I didn't much care for Archie; so far he had been nothing but grumpy around me, throwing me a wrinkled stink eye whenever he had to let me out of my cell for walk or a visit from my lawyer—as if it was *my* fault that he was at work in this depressing relic instead of reclining in his la-z-boy, shoving *knedliky* (Czech dumplings) into his pie hole and tipping back a few pilsners. My personal opinion of Archie wasn't on my mind, though, as I grabbed the three gallon ziplock bag my wife had so smartly packed my Marlboros in (it served as a great shower bag) and held it behind my back with both hands, per prison regulations. I followed his lumpy squat form the short distance to the shower cell, and I could hear voices echoing from inside the cell as Archie unlocked the heavy steel door.

You never knew who or how many men you would be showering with—the number varied at the seemingly random whim of whichever guard was running the block that day. Sometimes it would be just you and your cellies, a rare, luxurious, occasion where you could take your time and really scrub yourself clean. Most of the time there was a lot more man ass to deal with, though. On one particularly bad day there were nine of us in that two shower head cell, everyone taking turns getting wet, jumping from underneath the shower heads, soaping up, lathering, and jumping back under to rinse off. On this day, it didn't sound too loud from behind the closed shower door though. *Good—we can actually shower in relative peace today*, I thought.

The first thing I noticed when the door opened was an amazingly foul smell carried out on the blast of steam that always billowed forth into the cooler hallway air when we went to shower. I cannot really do the malodorousness of this scent justice by analogy, as I have nothing else sufficiently mephitic to compare it to. Incredibly, even the dreaded *olomoucké tvarůžky* paled in comparison; I suppose my best attempt at a description would have to include bacon wrapped scallops gone rotten in a New Orleans alleyway dumpster in August, a urine soaked mattress in a skid row flophouse, the feces-filled oldest toilet in the world (it's a squat-style hole in the floor of the public bathroom at the Great Wall of China, and I remain scarred by that experience to this day), and the unwashed feet of an extremely lazy fry cook in a greasy spoon truck stop diner in southeastern Georgia. It was overwhelming and immediately made me gag.

Through watering eyes, the next thing I noticed were the two men already in the cell. Chimpo Weaselman was standing beneath one shower head and scrubbing away on his spindly form. *Great.* He flashed his freakishly gigantic simian grin at me from underneath his minuscule brow and mangy crooked mohawk. *Ah, it's the famous American rockstar,* his eyes said, *Welcome to the shower—do you have any cigarettes/coffee/sugar/happiness I can leech from you?* Chimpo was even uglier naked; I couldn't stand the sight of his pleading apish visage atop his badly tattooed scrawny body, so I looked to the other man preparing to occupy the remaining shower head.

Apparently Chimpo was no longer Rene's cellmate, and had been placed with a slow-moving, quiet Roma with a pleasant face and disheveled Buddy Holly hairdo. He had landed on the block the day before, and at walk had seemed to be a nice enough, if very shy, fellow. Chimpo's new celly stood beside the steel table we put our clothes on with his back turned to me, unwrapping what looked to be approximately fifteen feet of ace bandage from around his midsection. *Jesus, he must be recovering from being stabbed at least twenty times with that much bandage,* I thought. The wrap itself was filthy, with yellow-brownish splotches of what I took to be dried pus all over it. I noticed that his skin was scaly and an angry-looking dark purple beneath the bandage as it left his narrow back. His epidermis looked like it had been trapped beneath the mottled cloth for months, perhaps years. What had happened to this man? As the last of the bandage fell away from him onto the floor, I saw him fiddling with what appeared to be plastic aquarium tubing. Where did that come from? Was it some sort of drug smuggling apparatus? And what in God's name was *that smell?* What in the hell was going on here?

Then I saw it.

The colostomy bag.

Up to this point, I had only had one other close encounter of the colostomy kind, but it had definitely been memorable, and being in my band had brought that experience about as well. Lamb of god was playing down South somewhere, when I looked to my left across the dimly lit stage and saw what looked like a fan attacking my guitarist Mark. This person was jumping around with his arms around Mark's neck in a sort of headlock, as Mark inexplicably continued to play guitar. Mark does not particularly like to be touched by strangers, especially when he is playing guitar. Baffled, I took off full tilt across the stage to deal with this lunatic before Mark brained him with his guitar, fully intending on tackling and subduing him until security could remove him from our stage and hopefully the venue. (We may argue constantly amongst each other, and there has been a blow or two thrown in our less than finest moments, but if you are not one of us, you do *not* touch my band mates.) I had reached terminal velocity about three feet away from this latest fiasco, and was preparing for impact (and whatever happened to come after), when our lighting guy suddenly threw on some par cans that brightly illuminated the whole stage. As my eyes adjusted, I quickly noticed two things. The first was that the man had one leg. The second was a colostomy bag, full of waste and still attached to the man's innards by plastic tubing, flopping around the stage like a muddy channel cat on a dry riverbank. The fan had his arm around Mark's neck, a huge grin plastered across his face as he hopped up and down on his one leg. The look on Mark's normally composed face can only be described as priceless. It was beyond hilarious.

But I had no time for belly laughs, as I was hauling ass and about to send this man flying off his single leg with the might of all 165 pounds of my lanky frame. I tried to put on the brakes, but my inertia was too great, so I performed an extremely awkward leap up and to the side of them, narrowly missing wrecking into the pair. It wasn't so much of a leap as it was a flying vertical stumble, but I managed not to smash into Mark and his new monopodular friend. As I began my short descent, I saw the colostomy bag laying directly beneath me and getting closer very rapidly.

It's strange how time always slows down for me in extremely stressful situations, and I remember like yesterday my feeling of helpless horror as I saw my right foot bearing down on a direct collision course with the bag of waste; a size 11 Vans covered comet about to make its disgusting impact on the surface of planet poop. The bag glistened darkly, lurking on the stage below me, far worse than any cow pie I had ever squished between my toes as a boy running barefoot through the fields of Southampton County, VA. My mind raced as I braced myself for the worst—would it explode underfoot, a truly terrifying weapon of ass destruction? Would the tube disconnect and blast our unsuspecting audience with a foul spray of pee-pee ca-ca, the way that bastard Governor George Wallace had his police thugs fire hose Civil Rights protestors in 1960s Birmingham? Would the tube remain connected, shooting the waste back up into this fan, poisoning his insides and eventually killing him? *Why does this kind of stuff always have to happen to me, not normal people? Oh God, I'm going too fast, going way too fast, can't move in time, oh no here it comes . . .*

And my foot slammed into solid wood, missing the bag by a centimeter. Someone hustled the fan off, and that was the end of it. I've often wondered how a one-legged man with such an obvious disregard for the safety of his colostomy bag (it's not like he was inconspicuous) managed to get past security and onto the stage in the first place, and when asked about our strangest fan interactions, Mark or I would invariably bring up that night.

"My God," I would laugh, "Can you imagine how bad it would have looked if I had smashed that guy? I can see the headlines now: 'D. Randall Blythe, singer of metal act lamb of god, tackles crippled fan, exploding colostomy bag in process. Dismayed audience members sprayed with infectious human waste. Lamb of god forced to cancel current tour as former fans nationwide boycott band, calling Blythe "a heartless monster," a risk to the public health, and demand his arrest.'" It was all very funny in retrospect.

The current matter at hand was not amusing at all. Very real headlines had made me out to be a monster, I was in prison and charged with killing a fan of my band, and amazingly, yet another colostomy bag had appeared in my life, this time in the worst possible place—a disgusting shower cell that was my only meager hope for getting my already disgusting body somewhat clean. I watched in horrified fascination as the Roma unhooked the tubing from his stomach, carried the bag with him under the running shower head, and dropped it carelessly on the floor. As the water ran over his head, instantly tamping down his curly pompadour, the man turned around to face us, smiling. There was an open vertical incision on his belly, perhaps two inches wide by four inches tall. Something pinkish and grey protruded from the hole in his gut. It looked like someone had unzipped him and part of his intestines were bulging out. Directly below the incision was a rather sizable uncircumcised penis. It was covered with large, very noticeable warts. I felt my testicles trying to crawl up inside of me to safety. I stood frozen by the changing table, petrified and slack jawed as my brain tried to process this awful visual collage.

The man squirted green prison canteen shower gel into his hand and began to carefully clean his abdomen, then lathered up the rest of his body. He saw me looking at him, smiled, and held up the bottle of shower gel, offering it to me in a friendly way. This kindly gesture unfroze me, and I shook my head no with a weak smile, holding up my ziplock containing my own shower gel. I turned around and saw Dorj and Ganbold standing behind me, staring at the man in mute horror. We milled about in the entry way to the shower, repulsed and unsure of what to do. Finally Dorj sighed and resolutely strode into the shower. It was the singular bravest act I ever saw him commit in the thirty-four days we spent together.

Ganbold and I looked at each other, gulped, and after a few seconds of hesitation followed Dorj into the shower. The next five minutes were a grim, nervous, all-male nude dance of avoidance. Chimpo Weaselman would stand under one shower head, lathering and rinsing, laughing and oblivious to the exposed innards of his warty new companion standing a mere four feet away. Dorj, Ganbold, or myself would be underneath the other head, soaping, scrubbing furiously, and rinsing as fast as we could. Then the quiet Roma would take Chimpo's place, and who ever was under our shower head would leap out from beneath it, joining the other two in hugging the shower wall, as far away as possible from the water bouncing off his terrible smelling wound and knobby unit. There was no joking, no laughing, no talking at all from the men of cell #512. No lollygagging or relaxing for that precious extra minute beneath the only hot water we would see for the next three or four days. I don't believe the three of us even washed our hair. We did not want to be in that shower with that man, and I could see by the crestfallen look on his normally cheerful face that he knew it. The room smelled absolutely atrocious, a sauna reeking of excrement, disease, and the sweat of panicked, repulsed men. Dorj, Ganbold, and I washed as quickly as we could, stepped over to the steel changing table bolted into the dirty tile wall, dried ourselves hastily with our threadbare towels, and put our clothes back on. Ganbold began slamming his fist into the steel door, yelling in Czech for the guard to let us out.

I looked back and saw the Roma staring at us with sad, dark eyes as the water fell on his head. I was immediately filled with shame at reacting to his presence the way I had. I had made him feel bad. The colostomy bag was not his fault, the fact that I was in this prison shower with him was not his fault, and his sexual health was none of my concern. My shame was shortly replaced with a rising fury directed at whoever had decided to put us all in the shower together. This was a man with a specialized medical condition that needed a sanitary environment. *My God, I could see his insides.* He had a severe case of genital warts and his bodily fluids were splashing about as he cleaned himself. I didn't know how contagious any other diseases he may have had could be in that steamy environment, and I grew more indignant towards the apathetic wardens of this crumbling edifice with each passing second I spent locked in that mildew stained cell with the quiet man.

And truth be told, I hated him for a few seconds. Hated him for his venereal disease, hated him for his open wound and exposed intestines, hated him for his smell, hated him for arousing the sense of panicked disgust that more and more threatened to consume me the longer I remained in his immediate vicinity. Most of all I hated him for his eyes; his dark, mournful, eyes that made me hate myself. I knew he knew I was revolted and angered by his presence, and in that moment, to my shame, most of me simply did not care.

This is what prison does to you—it dehumanizes you, and quickly strips away the polite pretense of societal norms and niceties. It forces open your eyes with a cruel and brutal speculum of despair and self-preservation, showing you the ugliness in others, and the ugliness in yourself. It will swiftly turn you into an animal if you let it.

After what seemed like hours Archie Bunker reappeared to let me and the Mongols out of the shower room. We poured out too quickly for his liking, and he looked frightened at first, then annoyed, fingering his nightstick and barking at us in Czech to slow down. Tom Selleck #1 must have just arrived for his shift, as he poked his head out of the office to see what the commotion was all about as all three of us began jabbering simultaneously at Archie in Czech, Mongolian, and English. I have no idea of what exactly Dorj and Gambold said, but I'm sure it was along the same line as my epithet filled tirade.

"WHAT. THE. FUCK. WAS. THAT? Archie Bunker, have you lost your *fucking mind?* There's a dude in there with his goddamned *guts* poking out of him! My God, man, that is SO GROSS. He's got warts all over his johnson and it smells like hot death in there! Warts, Archie, BIG ASS WARTS ON HIS DICK and a hole in his gut—the motherfucker looks like a human piñata about to pop. We could be catching all sorts of weird shit in there! You cannot put us in there with that guy again, no way, there is no way, NO FUCKING WAY, ARCHIE that we are ever doing that again! Negative, you bald dumb-ass! You have to fix this situation, like NOW."

Since we weren't speaking Czech, Archie ignored me and Dorj's hysterics and barked replies at Ganbold, interrupting him curtly all the way during the fifty-foot journey from the shower back to #512. Archie was beginning to look really peeved with Ganbold, and every time my Mongol cellmate would start to say something else Archie would snap "Neh," then something else in Czech, over and over. We reached our cell, he opened the door, impatiently motioned us inside, and slammed it shut with a scowl. We all looked at each other.

"Ganbold, what did the *bachar* say? We cannot shower with that guy—it's not safe for us! Did he say it won't happen again?" I asked.

"No. This man, all he says many times is 'No! No, this is normal.' This other man has disease. This is NOT a normal! This is a *mots patny*!" Ganbold said.

"Normal? *Normal?* Fuck him! We are not showering with that guy again, no way! Maybe it's normal where he comes from to shower in a disease factory, but it's not normal for me. I'll stay dirty before I ever get in that shower with that dude again. I need to talk to the health department in here or whoever, but we are not doing that again!"

So far my only experience with the Pankrác "health department" had included tuberculosis, bleeding junkies, and an ancient chain-smoking doctor. As I thought about this, I began to envision days without showering. We sat down on our cots, silently shaking our heads. Dorj wasn't even whispering or whistling.

This was bad. This was unacceptable. I had to think of something.

The solution to our dilemma came shortly, but from an entirely unexpected source: the British. A half hour ŏr so after our very distressing shower, I was sitting in my boxers, stewing and already sweaty again when Tom Selleck #1 came and flung open the door. As he told me to get dressed quickly, he looked completely out of sorts, almost frantic. I threw on some pants and a t-shirt, and he made motions for me to tuck it into my waist band. Then he noticed and pointed at the large holes in my shirt, shook his head, and told me to change it. Much to my initial dismay, so far no one in Pankrác had paid the slightest bit of attention to the terrible condition of the clothes inmates were issued. *All* of my t-shirts had had holes or been threadbare, and I had not been given a single pair of pants that fit. *What in the hell is going on here?* I wondered, *Did he schedule me for a photo shoot? Are we going to church or something?*

Right as I finished tucking in my other t-shirt, a group of about seven or eight well dressed men and women, accompanied by Archie Bunker and another very large and muscular guard, appeared outside our cell door. All the men had on nice suits, and the women wore sharp business attire as well. They looked completely incongruous in the basement cell block, and for a second I just stared at them; their sudden and well groomed appearance seemed so out of place to my eyes that they might as well have been space aliens popping down to earth for a surprise visit.

"Hello, are you David Blythe?" a tall, gray haired man asked in a crisp British accent.

"Uhm, yes. Yes, I am," I stammered, flabbergasted at hearing my last name pronounced correctly for the first time in almost a month.

"We are representatives of an organization that is working to improve conditions for British prisoners incarcerated abroad. Do you mind if we ask you a few questions?" he asked with great politeness.

"Uhm, sure. I mean, no; no, I don't mind at all. You *do* realize I'm an American, right?" I said.

"Yes, we are familiar with your case. But there are hardly any British prisoners in here, and you speak English, so we decided to come talk to you."

The tall man, who seemed to be the leader of the group, asked me a few brief questions about the conditions of the prison and my treatment by the Czech authorities. I told him the truth; that I had not been mistreated by the Czech police or abused by any guards or inmates, but that I found the prison to be old. *Too* old. The entire time I talked with him, the big guard that was with them stood right beside me. He kept fidgeting and glancing at me with a strange look on his face every time I spoke—I did not like this one bit. He was making me nervous, standing so close with his hulking presence. I couldn't tell if he was trying to intimidate me or was nervous himself. I didn't know if he didn't understand what I was saying, or did and was throwing me warning glances, letting me know there would be repercussions if I began bad mouthing the prison or its staff. Archie Bunker looked pretty nervous, too, but his face was pissing me off, as I now understood why I had been made to change my shirt so quickly. *Oh no, we can't have the visitors knowing what it's really like in here, now can we, Archie? Inmates walking around in threadbare rags full of holes doesn't look so hot to people from the outside world, does it? Why didn't you bring them around for a little colostomy bag shower show time, you little bald cock sucker?*

The situation had come about without warning and was so foreign to me that I found my normally loquacious self slightly tongue-tied. In retrospect, I can think of a very long laundry list of things very wrong with the prison that I could and should have told them about (including our laundry). If I had known they were coming in advance I could have just written out that list, then invited them to stay for lunch so they could literally get a taste of what life in Pankrác was really like (of course the kitchen probably would have rustled up some steaks from somewhere), but as it was I just sort of stood there nervously mumbling and

staring at their clean clothes. Since the man had said he was familiar with my case, I did mention the fact that I was extremely
frustrated over my bail situation, and that I thought the Czech legal system an archaic hold over from the Communist era badly in
need of an overhaul. A man of Middle Eastern descent in the back
of the group, apparently the group's official tour guide, grinned
ruefully and spoke to me in a Czech accent.

"Well, we are still learning . . . " he said sheepishly, as if the
Czech Republic had just declared independence a month ago.

"Still learning? You guys haven't been a Communist country
since 1989. Almost a quarter of a century isn't long enough to
figure out if the four hundred thousand dollars of bail in your
government's bank account, the bail I've had to pay *twice* now,
is good enough to let me go until trial? I'd say you guys need to
learn a little faster," I barked, surprised at the sudden vehemence
in my voice. The guard beside me jumped, the tour guide looked
uncomfortable, and I saw one of the women with the group jot-
ting something down on a clipboard. My voice had come back,
and I had just begun to tell the man about the concrete cage we
were crammed into for our one hour a day walk when he turned
to the Middle Eastern Czech and asked if they could see it, then I
was put back in my cell and they were gone.

About fifteen minutes later, a Czech woman I didn't recognize
appeared at my cell with Archie Bunker. Via Ganbold's rough
translation skills, she told me that she was Pankrác's social worker
(I never would have believed they had such a thing if she hadn't
been blatantly hustled down there immediately after the Brits had
left), and wanted to know if I was having any problems in the
prison. Telling Ganbold to make sure that he was being absolutely
clear, I told her in an angry voice about our shower earlier that day,
about the man and his colostomy bag. I repeatedly used the word
disease, explained that the Roma needed to shower in a sanitary environment by himself, and said that under no circumstances would
my cellmates and myself ever be showering with that man again;
furthermore, I would be contacting my embassy immediately if

someone tried to make us. Archie Bunker stood beside her nodding his head, saying several times that it wouldn't happen again. The woman took some notes on a clipboard and then left.

We never had to shower with the man again, but I will never forget the sad way he had looked at me, nor my anger and shame over my repulsed behavior.

Cindy would tell me later that virtually all the useful information she had discovered about the rules and regulations concerning my incarceration in Pankrác came from websites run by the British government. The British government at the very least gave the appearance of caring a whole lot more about the welfare of its citizens imprisoned overseas than my own government, which was basically useless as a source of information. That didn't surprise me one bit, as the American government couldn't even be bothered to let me know I was wanted for manslaughter in a foreign country. Their silence was one of the reasons I was behind bars in the first place, and I have to fight hard not to become very angry when I think about it. I've never received any sort of explanation from my government that made any sense, and I don't expect to. But to the Brits, I would like to extend a hearty thanks for making useful information available for relatives of its citizens, as my American wife availed herself of it (and for coming to check up on me as well). Cheers mates!

That evening I went to bed feeling almost victorious, having watched Archie Bunker standing there shaking his head like a buffoon and having to eat crow over the whole shower incident. I felt slightly vindicated, as the last day of my fourth week in prison had been pretty rough on me, and the previous one had been no picnic either. But the next day at walk, I would find out that I wasn't the one who had had the worst day on the cellblock, even with the awful shower.

Not by a long shot.

I GOTTA QUIT SMOKING!

(CONTINUED FROM FRIDAY, JULY 27th, 2012)

WORKER WOMAN (HUSTLED DOWN HERE NO DOUBT AFTER THE BRITS LEFT FOR DA MALE CONTROL) ASKED ME IF I WAS HAVING PROBLEMS IN HERE - I TOLD HER "NO, NOT FOR THE MOST PART" (CUZ IT'S TRUE - I GUESS MY STANDARDS ARE LOW, HAHAHA) EXCEPT I STARTED EXPLAINING THE SMOKEING INCIDENT & GANBOLD TRANSLATED - I WAS VERY EMPHATIC THAT I WOULD NOT DO THAT AGAIN - THE SAME OLD-ASS GUARD EXPLAINED THAT "IT WOULDN'T HAPPEN AGAIN" - YEH FUCKIN' A RIGHT IT WON'T. THEN TODAY AT WALK, THE QUIET GYPSIE (ONLY ONE LEFT OF THE O.G. GROUP - RENÉ WENT UPSTAIRS YESTERDAY) TOLD US THAT TWO POLICE WALKED INTO HIS ROOM TODAY RIGHT AFTER SHOWER, PUNCHED HIM IN THE FACE & KNOCKED HIM DOWN - THEN THEY SAID "COME ON, GET UP, YOU'RE A MAN, RIGHT?" HE GOT UP & SAID "OK, WE'RE FRIENDS NOW" & SLAPPED HIM ON THE SHOULDER & LEFT. THESE WERE FUCKING COPS, NOT GUARDS - RACIST ASS PIGS - BUT THE GUARDS HAD TO LET THEM IN TO DO THIS TO THIS MAN - THIS PLACE IS MORE & MORE FUCKED UP THE MORE I KNOW ABOUT IT. YESTERDAY WAS BAD EMOTIONALLY - BETTER TODAY, AS I SAID, BUT TODAY IS WAS MORE ILL PRANKAC-REALITY STYLE. I WROTE A LETTER TO CINDY & DECIDED THAT IT WAS OF A NATURE THAT SHOULD REACH HER AT A DIFFERENT TIME OR VIA BONHOEFFER METHODS - I AM LEARNING

chapter fifteen

Violence is a reality in prison; for some inmates it is merely the continuation of a life lived violently on the outside. For some prisoners with particularly vicious temperaments, they have to be isolated in special heavily guarded sections for the protection of others. Violence can erupt instantly in any section of a correctional facility though, and a wise inmate is alert at all times to its possibility. Every prison, no matter how well run, is a powder keg—Pankrác was an ancient one that had developed many holes in its seals. By this time, it was clear to me that it was a decaying relic completely unfit for human habitation, hence the foiled riot planned the year before. I was entering my fifth week in Pankrác, and I had not witnessed any beatings or stabbings yet, but I was watching my back and waiting. I knew that if I stayed there long enough, I would inevitably see some violence, or at least its after effects. All I could do was remain vigilant and hope that it wouldn't involve me.

As crappy and rundown as the place was, in Pankrác I contemplated my possible sentence and decided that if I wound up doing serious time, I would rather do it there than in an American prison. My reasoning for this stemmed from a lucky accident of birth—the color of my skin. The inmate population of Pankrác was for the most part homogenous—white Europeans—and I did not see evidence of the widespread racial tension that exists in American correctional facilities. There were a few different ethnic groups represented in the prison population, mostly Vietnamese and Romani peoples from what I saw, but I did not see or hear of any signs of racial based gang activities. I asked a few inmates about this, and they informed me that gangs formulated around an ethnic identity didn't really exist in Pankrác, and that they had only seen such things on American television shows. Other than learning that a few of the Vietnamese who were always huddled together at walk (they seemed to stick to their own kind tighter than any other ethnic group I saw) were the ones to go to if I wanted some drugs, I just didn't see much evidence of inmates congregating based solely on race alone. Surely there were gangs of some sort inside the prison, but I didn't consider five or six quiet Southeast Asians hustling pain pills, coke, and a little weed a gang. This is not the case in American prisons, where white, black, and Hispanic gangs have a very significant presence. These gangs periodically engage in bloody warfare behind prison walls, and it is best to not become involved with them or their activities, but that is no guarantee you won't get caught in a melee and beaten up or stabbed simply because of the color of your skin. Racial tension is very real in American prisons, and I had felt that tension even in the Richmond City Jail on my very first trip downtown.

Taking a lazy stand against a blatantly unjust system, I had refused to do any of the sixty-five community service hours that the infamous Judge Robertson had given me for peeing in an alley. I had a warrant out for my arrest for failure to appear, and a cop had recognized me out and about on my bicycle one fine Friday afternoon, so into the paddy wagon and off to the pokey for the weekend I went. I was sitting beside a huge, muscular black man, both of us in cuffs, waiting to make the one phone call you're allotted when arrested, and thinking that I didn't want to spend the money that I would have to pay back to someone after they came and bailed me out. Court would be in session Monday morning, and this was such a trivial matter that (provided I didn't get Judge

Robertson again) the judge would probably just roll his eyes, tack on a few more hours, and tell me to get the hell out of his sight and go do my community service. I decided to spend the weekend in jail rather than spend perfectly good drinking money on this matter, but figured I'd better at least call my roomate Clay to let someone know I was in jail. The inmate ahead of me finished up with his call, and the phone was handed to me. I dialed up Clay, and luckily he answered.

"Clay, look dude, I'm downtown in jail. They picked me up on Grace Street for failure to appear. Court isn't until Monday, so I'll see ya then," I said.

"What?!? Shit. Well, do you want me to come bail you out?" he asked.

"Nah, I don't think so. Fuck it—waste of money. I'll just wait it out," I said.

At this point, the very large and very black man seated on the bench inches away from me (who, of course, could hear my entire conversation) leaned over with a big grin on his face and said almost directly into my ear

"You better tell your boy to come get you out before some big nigger *fucks* you."

"What? What was that?" Clay asked.

"Clay, never mind. I changed my mind. Come get me outta here, bro," I said.

While I'm pretty sure my ebony friend was merely trying to scare my twenty-something year old skinny white ass for kicks, he definitely succeeded. And having been to jail for the night on other occasions (thankfully without having any sort of sexual experience, interracial or otherwise), I have felt the tension more than once, seen the way the different colors seemed to stick together, and noticed the ways eyes follow across a tier when a group gets up and moves as one to a different location. An American prison is not a place where the politically correct get together to put aside their petty differences, hold hands, sing *Kumbaya*, and "celebrate diversity." In Pankrác, since the majority of the inmates were white, and (luckily for me) so was I, the racial tension just wasn't there for me. In fact, the most racist person I met in Pankrác was my cellmate Dorj, but he just seemed to hate *everyone* that wasn't Mongolian, and did nothing about it but talk shit. So while I expected to eventually see some violence amongst the inmates, maybe a personal beef settled in the yard one day, I didn't expect it to be of a racial nature, or to come from any sort of organized group like a gang. The place was a shit hole, but I was used to shit holes, and I would rather deal with settling a beef with someone over a personal matter in a dump than have to fight for my life in a clean prison over something as inane as race.

But some inmates in Pankrác weren't born into the prevalent ethnicity, and despite the fact that most everyone I knew seemed to get along regardless of race, sometimes racially motivated violence arrives from members of an organized group who aren't inmates at all.

As we lined up to go out for walk that day, I noticed Rene talking in hushed tones to his friend the Quiet Gypsy, the one who had so kindly shared his coffee with me during my first few days in Pankrác. I noticed that T.Q.G. was walking rather slowly on the way out to our cage, and had his hand pressed to one side of his face. Once we were outside and locked in, he sat down slowly, as if he was sore, slumping against the wall, still holding his face. Rene began asking him questions, to which the Quiet Gypsy simply shrugged and periodically spoke a few words of Czech. Rene appeared angry, and I noticed all the other men were silent and paying careful attention to the conversation going on. I heard Rene curse, then sit down beside T.Q.G., gently placing his hand on his shoulder and shaking his head in disgust.

"Rene, what's going on? What's wrong? Did something happen to him?" I asked, pointing at T.Q.G., who sat silently rubbing his jaw.

"*Policie, policie,*" Rene said bitterly, then spat to the side.

"Police? What the fuck?" I said. Ollie walked over, and in a mixture of French, English, and Czech, explained what had happened.

The Quiet Gypsy had just gotten out of the shower yesterday, and after being returned to his solitary cell (he didn't have a cellmate at that time), he was beginning to get dressed when a guard opened his cell door. Two large policemen in uniform immediately walked in, the door was shut behind them, and without warning, one punched him in the face hard enough to knock him to the floor. He lay there stunned for a second, then the police began to taunt him, saying "Come on, get up, you're a man, right?" The Quiet Gypsy began to get up when the other policeman punched him in the face, knocking him down again. The policemen continued berating him until he stood up, but this time they smiled, clapped him on the shoulders, and said, "Okay, okay; you *are* a man after all. We're friends now, right?" Then they laughed and left.

I asked the Quiet Gypsy to show me his face; there was a large bruise on the left side of his jaw where the policemen had struck him, and a couple of teeth were loose in his head. I asked him why this had happened, and he just shrugged his shoulders.

"He is a Gypsy. The police do these things if they wish," Ollie said matter-of-factly by way of explanation.

This immediately enraged me to the point that I began shaking. The Quiet Gypsy was the most mild-mannered man I had met in Pankrác, a slender, reserved fellow of very few words who had never asked me for a thing but had always been willing to share what little he had. I stood there cursing at the rough concrete walls around me, impotently clenching my fists and trying not to tear up, consumed by a deep hatred. I was so angry for T.Q.G.—there was nothing he could do about the abuse, no one he could complain to about his mistreatment. Who was he supposed to tell, the police? A guard? The cops were the ones who had administered the beating, and a guard had let them in to do it, remaining quiet while it occurred. Complaining would probably only result in another (probably worse) beating. T.Q.G. was just another Gypsy in a Czech prison, and as Romani people are the victims of widespread discrimination in the Czech Republic (and across Europe), he could be mistreated without anyone giving a fuck. (We found out later that day the reason for the beating: Someone T.Q.G. knew on the outside, another Roma, had resisted arrest earlier that day. The two arresting officers, after kicking the shit out of the resisting Roma, decided to come to Pankrác and use T.Q.G. as a punching bag just to get that last bit of aggression out of their systems.) So while I was lucky to be a white man in a white prison in a white country, my quiet and generous friend was not.

In the United States, there are approximately one million Romani people, aka Gypsies. Unlike Europe, the Romani population largely assimilated into American society quite some time ago, and the term "Gypsy" is not used as a racial slur the way it often is in Europe. Most modern day Americans aren't really aware of the Romani population in their midst; in fact, the majority of Americans don't know what a "Gypsy" really is. When they think of one it's generally some woman with big earrings and a colorful scarf tied around her head who reads palms and tarot cards for a living, or a Walt Disney-esque group of exotic dark skinned nomads who travel in a covered wagon across the land as tinkers, sharpening knives and repairing kitchenware for money, playing lively music around a campfire in between polishing their crystal balls. As a child in the American South, I heard more than one parent tell their misbehaving child to straighten up or they would "sell them to the Gypsies," but they might as well have been talking about the boogie man as no one I knew had ever seen hide nor hair of a Gypsy (this saying comes from the old superstition that Gypsies are predisposed to kidnapping *gadje* children for some odd reason).

In America, the term Gypsy is also often broadly used to describe anyone who wanders, rather than a specific ethnicity. And although the term *gypped* (to have been cheated by someone out of something) originally comes from the term Gypsy (as they were stereotyped as con artists and thieves in America in the past), and as such is definitely offensive, the majority of modern day Americans don't associate it with Romani people, or know its etymology. Most Americans generally don't associate Gypsies with Romani people period, because they don't know that Romani people even exist.

This is not the case in Europe, where members of the Romani diaspora are far more widespread, are not as assimilated into the different countries they inhabit, and are subject to all sorts of hideous discrimination. The term Gypsy in various European languages is very often used with derision (even though some Romani organizations include the word in their name). I myself would not have used the term, except that all the Roma I met in Pankrác referred to themselves as Gypsies and told me to do the same—I think this is probably because I spoke English, and Gypsy is an English word, the Czech being *Cikán*. Before I went to prison, I was aware that the Romani people suffered quite a bit, even in modern day Europe, sometimes even legally under populist laws (there is a long history of this throughout Europe dating back to before the Middle Ages, and the first anti-Romani laws went on the books in 1583 in what is now the Eastern Czech Republic). I had seen a few impoverished looking Roma on the streets of various European cities, but it wasn't until I came to Pankrác that I actually met anyone of Romani descent, and began to learn first-hand of the discrimination they faced there. In 2007 the Czech Republic and neighboring Slovakia were reprimanded by E.U. officials for antiziganism (discrimination against Romani people) after it was discovered that they were forcibly segregating Roma children from normal schools. Romani children were (and in some places still are) removed from public schools, placed in substandard educational facilities, or even in classes for the mentally handicapped. Violent attacks on Romani people (both as communities and as individuals on the street) are common in Europe, and the language used to describe them by some government officials is alarmingly similar to that used by Hitler's thugs prior to the mass Romani slaughter of the 1930s and '40s— unclean. Dangerous to society. Parasites.

I despise all forms of racism. I am lucky I have wonderful parents of above-average intelligence who taught me to think this way from birth. However, while I understand how racism works and the way its moronic cycle is perpetuated, I still have very little tolerance for it from anyone with any sort of link to the modern world (an ancient computer with a dial-up Internet connection will suffice), regardless of race, color, or creed. It is unacceptable to me not merely because I was raised to view it as immoral, but primarily because *as a rational adult human being with a brain in my head*, I can very clearly see its *base stupidity*. Stupidity offends me. Throughout recent history, during times of extreme unrest, people of all colors have experienced moments of clarity from whence they suddenly began the process of rejecting the dunderheaded racially biased beliefs pervasive amongst their peers. From Oskar Schindler witnessing the brutal liquidation of the Krakow Jewish ghetto at the hands of the Nazis during World War II, to Malcolm X's trip to Mecca where he worshipped with fair-haired blue-eyed Muslims in Islam's most sacred site during the Civil Rights struggle of the 1960s, individuals have had their preconceptions shaken and begun to *use their brains*. Growing up in the American South as a boy, I personally witnessed people of an advanced age make a conscious decision to question what they had been taught to believe their entire lives when they began to realize that their parents were *wrong*. It is not an overnight process to unlearn a lifetime of what basically amounts to primitive superstition, but in this day and age, where an unfathomable amount of information is instantly and freely available to anyone with a smart phone, there is no excuse to not at least make a start. I don't want everyone on the planet to get together, hold hands, and sing *We*

Are the World or some hideous feel-good shit like that, I just want people to act like they use their brain for something other than switching TV channels. We do not live in the 1800s anymore, and there is absolutely no excuse for this sort of ignorance.

After walk I went back to my cell and finished my letter to Gavin, the lamb of god fan from Canada. The letter wound up being quite long, nine pages, and included a history of the prison, an outline of my daily schedule, and a crude drawing of the layout of my cell. Near the end of the letter, I asked him to scan it and post it on the internet if he would, as I wished fans of my band to know that I was alive and well, if pretty unhappy about my current situation. After seeing T.Q.G. holding his face, I was thoroughly sick of being muzzled. I was sick of the climate of fear I was living in, sick of the constant circus that was my bail situation, sick of it all. I just wanted to go home, and if I couldn't do that, I wanted to be heard. (I was free by the time Gavin received the letter, so he never posted it. He had scanned it though, and I have a copy of it still.)

I spent most of the next morning working on a letter to my family to prepare them for their upcoming visit. In the letter, I very strictly emphasized that they were not to get emotional in front of the paparazzi, who would undoubtedly be waiting to hound them outside the prison gates. Like my wife, I would not have my mother and stepmother be seen crying on Czech TV or in a newspaper. I wasn't really worried about the old man; while I knew he wouldn't be overjoyed to see me behind bars, I also knew he would keep a stiff upper lip in public. But I was slightly concerned about the ladies; I wanted them to be completely dry-eyed and walk with their heads held high when the press jackals came sniffing around, and I informed them in no uncertain terms that it should be so. While I was working on the letter, a guard came by with something absolutely wonderful for me: a battery powered FM radio. I had asked Martin to purchase me one and drop it by the prison, and although it took the prison over a week to inspect the radio to make sure there was no contraband inside, it had finally arrived. I placed the radio on the table, turned it on, and after scanning through several nauseating pop music channels and a bewildering bit of Czech talk radio, I found what I was looking for: the local classical music channel (98.7 on the FM dial, if you're ever in Prague). I am not an aficionado of classical music, I cannot recognize but a handful of pieces by name, I cannot tell you much about any of the great composers, but I do enjoy listening to it. It's relaxing, cerebral music, and it's great to write to. It had been quite some time since I had my own source of music available, and although I would have rather have had my fully loaded iPod, I was very grateful to have found some classical. (I figured Prague had to have a classical channel; after all Mozart did work there.) I returned to my letter, feeling some tension leaving my body as the orchestra began to work on my subconscious. I wrote smoothly and without as much angst, for music had entered my life again, and suddenly everything was beginning to look up.

Until five minutes later, when Dorj started complaining.

"Bah. Music *spatny*. Screech, screech, screech. No good. Turn off," he said, imitating a violin player hacking away with a bow.

Enough was enough, and I had had more than enough of my obnoxious cellmate.

"Dorj, *shut the fuck up*. For five weeks now I have had to listen to you whistle and whisper and slurp your goddamned food like a pig. I do not give one single solitary fuck whether or not you like classical music. I do not care if it pile drives you through the gates of insanity. I do not care if it makes you bury your head in the toilet and drown yourself to death, *kaput*! I am going to listen to some music, and there is not a goddamned thing you can do about it, so once again, *shut the fuck up*."

"Fuck you!" Dorj said, scowling like a four year old on the edge of a tantrum.

"Fuck me? No, *fuck you*, you fat motherfucker. Whistle over this," I said, and turned the radio up as loud as it would go.

Dorj crossed his arms and huffed and puffed on his bunk, but didn't make a move to touch the radio. I was glad he didn't, because I was pretty pissed off, and may very well have hit him if he had gotten up from his bed and in my face. He had finally driven me to the very edge of mental instability, and his whistling chickens were about to come home to roost if he tried to deprive me of one of my only joys in that sordid place. The music sounded absolutely atrocious coming out of the crappy boom-box speakers at top volume, but it did the trick. I couldn't hear Dorj *at all.* After an ear-deafening two or three minutes, I turned the music down to a tolerable level, and looked at Dorj.

"Now, if you will stop bitching like a little girl and play nice, I'll keep this at a reasonable level," I said.

"Bah. Music *spatny,*" Dorj said. But he just rolled over on his side to sulk, eventually falling asleep. Ganbold sat on his top bunk, shaking with silent laughter. After a while, he hopped down from his bunk, grabbed our Czech/English dictionary, looked up a word, and said quietly as to not awaken Dorj, "He is a pleasant."

"A pleasant? No, Dorj is definitely *not* a 'pleasant'. What do you mean?" I said.

"Yes, yes; he is a pleasant. From village," Ganbold said, pointing to a Czech word in the dictionary. I looked at the English definition.

"Oh, *peasant.* No *L* sound; pleasant means something entirely different. Yes, Dorj is most definitely a peasant," I laughed. I had never had the occasion where I felt the need to use the word *peasant* to describe another human being, as it seems a bit archaic, not to mention insulting to farmers and rural people (from which I am descended), but it worked perfectly in this situation. Dorj *was* an unpleasant peasant, and whatever village he came from, I'm pretty sure he was known as its idiot.

Later that evening Martin came by with some entirely expected bad news: predictably, the prosecuting attorney had raised an objection to my newly doubled and paid in full bail, and had (just as predictably) waited until the very last moment to do so. His

reasoning for the objection was so feeble as to be laughable—
Musik tried to justify it by saying that the Czech court would not
be able to get mail to me in the U.S. to inform me of my new
court date, and that furthermore, even if the court somehow was
able to miraculously put enough postage on a letter to get it to
America, I was never home long enough because of my touring
schedule to check my mail anyway. I laughed out loud when I
heard this, as I was starting to realize that my antagonist didn't
possess the most brilliant of legal minds. Where did he come up
with this crap? Maybe he was drunk when he wrote his objection.

"Really? That's the best reason for keeping me in this dump he
could cook up?" I asked Martin.

"Yes, I know, it is ridiculous. Your manager has already written
a letter to the court saying that he will inform you of any developments with your case no matter where you are, which we will
try to get to the appeal court before they review your case again,"
he said.

"They gotta throw this out. That's the lamest thing I've ever
heard out of a lawyer—it sounds like Musik is running out of gas,"
I said.

"Yes, but still, I do not want you to get your hopes up too
much. The court will hopefully decide to reject his complaint
sometime this week. Then they have five days to write up and
send their opinion down to the lower court, which will order your
release. But do not forget, within the first forty-eight hours of the
lower court receiving the appeal court's opinion, Musik can write
a new request to place you in custody again. Then you will be
stuck here until we can appeal to the Czech Constitutional Court,
which will take at least two weeks. I am sorry, Randy, but I do not
want to promise you something that may not happen," he said.

I thanked Martin for his candor and went back to my cell. Martin had always been a straight shooter with me, and I had grown
quite fond of him, even though lately when he popped by it was to
deliver consistently bad news. I had taken this latest development

pretty well, as it was pretty much a given that Musik would object to my new bail. And while I had basically given up on the bail situation and was almost entirely convinced by this point that I would remain in Pankrác until my trial, I felt slightly better about my chances in court. I was no lawyer, but considering the facts that both the U.S.A. and the Czech Republic no longer generally delivered mail by horseback and airplanes existed, even I could have come up with something better than the cockamamie excuse that getting a letter to me was simply too difficult for our countries to achieve. I began to wonder about Musik's courtroom capability, but I would find out all about his obstinate nature later.

The next morning Ganbold had to go see the prison doctor for some reason, and when he returned I saw him speaking outside our cell in a very excitable manner to two guards I didn't recognize. It appeared as if they were briefly arguing over something, then they must have acquiesced to Ganbold's wishes, as I heard him enthusiastically thank them several times in Czech. The cell door was locked, and Dorj immediately began to pepper Ganbold with questions in rapid-fire Mongolian. They talked briefly, then turned to me with doleful expressions on their faces. Something was up, and from the looks of my cellmates, it wasn't good.

"What now?" I asked Ganbold.

"Doctor Pankrác, this very bad news for you. Me, Dorj moving upstairs today. *Bachar* say you must stay here. They give you two new men for this room," he replied solemnly.

"WHAT?" I exploded. "I've been here just three days less than Dorj and I *still* don't get to go upstairs?"

"No. *Bachar* say they bring Chimpo Weaselman and other man to room after we go. I sorry, Doctor Pankrác," he said. This immediately sent me over the edge.

"No! *No fucking way*. I am *not* living with Chimpo. I refuse! No way! I am calling the *bachar* back right now! I must talk to them," I said, getting up from my bed to go and bang on the cell door. Ganbold got up and stopped me.

"No, Doctor Pankrác, no. I ask these men for you to go up-stairs, but it is *mots spatny*. These *bachar* no like you. Say you must stay with Chimpo. I sorry, Doctor Pankrác. Very sorry," he said quietly.

I sat down at our table and buried my head in my hands. This was unbelievable. The absolute worst. I was living in a nightmare. Dorj may have driven me completely nuts, but he was a far cry from Chimpo Weaselman. The thought of being locked in a cell with Chimpo twenty-three hours a day, constantly doing battle over cigarettes, coffee, and whatever else I possessed made me be-gin to start contemplating my options for suicide. *Oh sweet Jesus, what if he got his hands on some speed somehow?* What then? I began to see extra time being piled onto my sentence as I envisioned myself snapping and knocking his gigantic teeth out. I would never ever leave this terrib-

"BAHAHAHAHA! Doctor Pankrác looking so sad! Big joke onto you! We all go upstairs now, bahahahaha!" Dorj said, wip-ing tears of laughter from his eyes. I looked up at Ganbold, who quickly (and somewhat ashamedly) told me that the guards he had been arguing with were originally only going to take Dorj and myself upstairs, but he had somehow convinced them that as a Mongol he needed to remain with his chubby countryman. He had told Dorj this, who then persuaded him to play the joke on me.

If I hadn't been so relieved that I wasn't bunking with Chimpo, I would have assaulted them both.

———

A half-hour later we were packed and ready to go. Bradley came and opened the cell, and the three of us walked to the end of the hall, where Felix sat with his belongings on a bench outside the cellblock office. We took a seat, and soon two guards came to escort us upstairs. I picked up my bundle, and ignoring Bradley's smarmy hoot of *bon voyage*, walked out of that basement forever. Goodbye Bradley, and go fuck yourself. Goodbye Archie Bunker, I hope you choke on a *knedliky*. Goodbye Tom Selleck #1, you turned out to be pretty cool, may your '80s hairline never recede. Goodbye Tom Selleck #2, you weird bipolar motherfucker, I hope you learn a different word than *yarl* one day. Goodbye *Pankrác Manzelka*, our love was never meant to last so please don't show up in Richmond, my sexy babika. Goodbye moldy basement. Thirty-one days in you was thirty-one too many.

The long hall that housed our new cellblock was much airier, with a large set of open floor to ceiling barred windows at the end. Bright, blessed sunlight streamed in through the windows, and a slight breeze blew down the hall. Things were looking better already. The guards walked us almost all the way to the end of the hall, stopping in front of cell #176, our new home. A trusty came to the room as the guard was unlocking our cell, and in perfect English told me that the tier would be leaving for walk in twenty minutes, so we should just arrange our stuff later if we wanted to go outside that day. I thanked him and took a look around our cell. It was laid out basically the same as our previous one, but smaller, with lower ceilings. It also looked to be even older and more dilapidated; paint was coming off the wall in great swaths, the toilet was in worse shape than the wreck we had had downstairs, and the dirt coating the cell somehow looked more ingrained. The cell was also hotter, as we had moved up several floors.

Overall, the move had been a huge downgrade, which is really saying quite a bit, as our other digs hadn't exactly been palatial. But as they say, location is everything, and we were more than happy to trade a little space and cool air for a room with a view. I looked out the barred window and saw the low skyline of the Pankrác suburb for which the prison was named, stretching in all directions above the endless garlands of razor wire that topped the prison walls like cruel dull-gray strands of deadly DNA. I could see the outside world, and after a month of staring at a pile of rubble and concrete from the ground level windows of the subterranean mold terrarium I had been living in, my imagination was fired. I saw a woman hanging laundry from her balcony on the upper level of an apartment building across the street, and I wondered about the life she lived a stone's throw from the prison. Did she ever wonder about the men and women inside? Did she know anyone in Pankrác, inmate or employee? Did her eyes even register the crumbling bulwark outside her front window anymore, or did her brain block it out, a regrettable and aesthetically unpleasant bit of scenery piggybacked atop her cheap rent? I would never know a thing about the woman, but I would often look for her out of that window, and my ruminations on her life were a source of pleasure for me, cerebral calisthenics that stretched the myopic boundaries that prison life imposes on an inmate's mentality.

I turned from the window as a guard unlocked our cell to collect us for walk, and quickly grounded myself in the reality of my situation and surroundings. Now I would walk the yard in general population for the first time, and I knew it would be critical to remain alert and show no fear, as there would be many sets of eyes on me, watching and judging the way I carried myself, looking for weakness. As Gandbold, Dorj, and I were escorted to the end of the long line that stopped at the main gate of our tier, I heard the whispers begin as I passed one by one by the hundred or so men already in place to walk outside. I neither stared at nor averted my eyes from the men, strolling casually with my head held high and my shoulders squared. When we reached the end of the line, I saw many heads turned towards me as the men pointed and talked in low voices amongst themselves. In the past, after my brain had been marinating a few hours in a sizable amount of high-quality lysergic acid diethylamide, sometimes I had been possessed by the irrational fear that everyone surrounding me was looking at me, whispering amongst themselves, discussing the particulars of my warped state of mind. Of course that had been groundless psychedelic induced paranoia, but the looks and whispers in that prison hallway were very much real. All the inmates knew exactly who I was, why I was there, and they were, in fact, talking about me. Like the first day I had gone out for walk in the basement, I mentally prepared myself for the possibility of sudden violence being directed my way. A tattooed bald man in his late forties with a gaudy silver medallion around his neck seemed particularly intent on staring at me, but I couldn't tell if his look was hostile or merely curious, and I made a mental note to keep my eye on him. I had the strong feeling that if something was going to go down, it would happen outside and it would happen today. I prepared myself to move swiftly and without mercy, as my actions would have to make a strong impression, whatever their consequences may be. As we waited to walk outside, I talked and joked casually with Ganbold, trying my best to appear disinterested in my surroundings, the whole time my heart hammering in my chest. It is a frightening thing to be the focus of one hundred strange prisoners' blatant attention, and it was an experience I will never forget.

The guards unlocked the gate and we all filed out, walking down the flights of stairs with our hands clasped behind our backs, my cellmates and I near the front of the line. I could feel the eyes on the back of my head, and as soon as we were outside I took a seat on a bench bolted to the ground sitting flush with a tall chain link fence so that my back would be protected. I lit a cigarette and waited as the men filed past me into the yard.

The yard was a long concrete rectangular courtyard, slightly larger than a standard sized tennis court. Three of its high walls were walls of the prison buildings themselves, the fourth being a twenty-foot high concrete barrier separating our yard from another, and I could hear prisoners from another cellblock talking and laughing on the other side of the dissecting wall. Inside our courtyard was a cage within a cage; another four walls of heavy-duty chain link fence, the tops bent inward and topped with several rows of razor wire. There were three concrete Ping-Pong tables bare of nets, but no one seemed to have paddles or balls anyway. The middle of the yard had a rope strung across it from two poles, and twenty or so of the men split into teams and began playing volleyball with a frayed ball that lay by the make shift net. Other men produced chess sets and began setting them up on benches, or just sat down to chat. The rest of the men began lei-surely walking in a circle around the perimeter of the courtyard, stretching their legs after twenty-three hours in their cramped cells. I noticed that several men had on their own clothes; clean t-shirts without holes and non-prison issue sweats or track pants, but most wore the same uniform as me. I began to see men I knew; Rene, Scarface, Raymond Herrera, Martin, and the scrawny junky who had bled all over the place in the holding cell while we were waiting to be drug tested were all on my new tier. The junky looked remarkably healthier; his strange haircut had been tightened up, and there was a bit of pink in his previously sallow complexion. I got up from the bench and said hello to the men I knew with high-fives and fist bumps all around, joking about our new and improved surroundings. I saw many of the inmates continue to glance at me from time to time—it was good for them to see that I already had friends in the place. After a bit, Ganbold and I began to walk around the yard. As we slowly circled the volleyball court, the inmates began to lose interest in my passing and I started to relax a bit. I was a passing curiosity they seemed to have noted and forgotten—except for the bald man, who by this time I was convinced was definitely giving me the stink eye. Although bigger than me, his bulk was of the flabby sort, and I was certain I could take him as long as I moved quickly and he didn't have a knife. The search we had undergone outside our cell before walk had been perfunctory at best, and anyone wanting to could have easily smuggled out a small shiv. As we circled the yard, I kept my distance from the man, as well as my eye on him. He never made a move towards me for the rest of my time in Pankrác, but he would throw me strange looks everyday at walk, and I was always ready for him.

As I walked with Ganbold, I saw two odd-looking men, seated apart from everyone else, their appearance so out of place that it gave me sudden pause. They were large, muscular, and as we passed them by I heard them quietly speaking English in an accent I couldn't quite place. They were so foreign looking that it took me a second to realize the reason their appearance startled me—these were the only two black guys I had seen in well over a month. As I passed them by several times, I strained to hear what they said, but I couldn't make out enough to put my finger on their accent. They were definitely speaking English, but so softly I couldn't tell if they were Jamaican or from some other island in the Caribbean, some African nation, or even from somewhere in America. Aside from my two Mongols, they were the smallest ethnic minority I had seen in Pankrác, and I made up my mind to speak to them the next day and find out where they were from. I hoped they were American, or at least Jamaican, so that I could talk to them about familiar places on my side of the world.

A few rounds into our walk a Czech man about my age came up, introduced himself in English as Jacob (not his real name), and began to walk with us. Jacob had heard all about my case, and although not a fan of heavy metal, he did listen to underground music of the industrial variety. We walked a bit, discussing various groups like Skinny Puppy, Front 242, and Einstürzende Neubauten, and it was extraordinarily pleasant for me to discuss music with someone knowledgeable about bands the general populace is not usually aware of. All of us who reside in the broader music underground, no matter what specific genre, carry a passion for our bands and their efforts; groups consciously attempting to do something divergent from the mindless, plastic, cookie-cutter tripe that pollutes the airwaves. And we like to discuss the finer points of these bands, to intensely debate the merits of their various records in a way the average pop fan never bothers to. To us, music isn't something you listen to for a few months then throw away, it's something you *live*. I can still remember very well the first time I heard the Sex Pistols—the music was *real*, it had *substance*, and *it changed my life*. Jacob was the first inmate I had met who understood the power of this kind of music, and it was a relief to discuss something other than court cases and cell block rumors for a change. But as we walked, I did wind up asking him why he was in prison. He told me he was there because of drugs, heroin specifically.

"Ha ha, I know a little something about that kind of thing," I laughed. "But I had to quit all that crap. It was killing me. I haven't had a drink or a drug in almost two years now."

"Really?" he asked, "I have tried to quit several times, but the drugs are too powerful. I always go back to them after a few days."

"Bro, it can be done. After twenty-two years of partying, I quit at the beginning of a heavy metal tour, on the road, where people actually want to *give you* free drugs and booze. I had been trying to quit for four years before I finally had enough. If I can do it, you can do it, man!" I said.

"Then I must try again," he said, "because I am going to die if I don't stop. Heroin has already put me in this place. It will kill me if I go back to it."

"Yes, it will. But you don't have to die, man," I said, and began telling him about my life as an alcoholic. I told him about many things from my past over the next few days as we walked and talked in that yard together, things that were not wise for someone in my position to tell anyone in a prison, but I was not afraid. I made a judgment call and went with my gut, and I decided to help this man who came from a different branch of my tribe. I could see that Jacob was hurting badly inside; he had assaulted his own father in order to get money for heroin, and was full of shame and self-loathing over what he had become because of his drug addiction. His two cellmates were drug dealers who constantly discussed how they would restart their business the day they were let out. Jacob was frustrated, confused, and scared. I am not an expert on alcohol or drug addiction, nor am I a substance abuse counselor. I do not have a vast amount of scientific knowledge concerning the particulars of any sort of addiction, or the low down on the latest developments in addiction treatment. What I am is a common, run-of-the-mill *drunk* who did a lot of pretty messed up things while I was messed up. And as such, I can talk to someone who honestly wants to stop living in their problem from a place of experience, and I can relate my struggles in a language they can understand. I can stand before them as a sober man and let them know that if they truly want to, they *can quit*. People just like myself told me that very same thing, drunks and drug addicts who had put down the bottle or the bag of drugs (or both) before it had killed them. They told me I didn't have to live that way anymore. I finally listened, and those people saved my life. The least I could do to repay them was try and help this poor man.

As the walk came to an end, Jacob filled me in on a few helpful details about life in population. The next day was shopping, and we would actually go to the prison canteen to pick out what we wanted. ("It's like going to heaven," he said.) If you had someone in Prague willing to pick up and do your laundry once every two weeks, you could wear your own clothes. I didn't have any clothes other than the ones I had been arrested in, so that was out, but Jacob told me he would loan me a real towel, a pair of track pants, and a few t-shirts. He told me the hours for our daily walk, and which days we showered. Finally, he said that once a week we were allowed to watch an hour of TV in the hallway, which was almost always a soccer game (we were in Europe, after all). This hour of TV also always turned into one big nerve wracking screaming match between all the inmates gathered to watch. I asked him if there were any drug counseling sessions or trips to the library available that we could go to instead—nope.

This astounded me. Even in population, there was absolutely no attempt made to provide inmates with any sort of manner to better themselves. Incarcerated people don't need a fucking soccer match, they need something that will help them gain knowledge and change their ways, at least if there is to be any hope of rehabilitating them so that one day they can rejoin society as useful members. I looked in my stack of prison regulations later, and found a brief mention of drug counseling services being available to juvenile inmates, but that was it. I guess in Pankrác if you're an adult drug addict they just give you a few tranquilizers to help you kick, like they did for Martin, then either you stay clean or wait until you're in population to buy drugs from the inmates who sling them. (Synthetic morphine was the currently available flavor on our tier, and if it had been a mere two years earlier, I would have been as high as gas.)

We got back to our cell and put our belongings away, then to my astonishment Ganbold produced a plastic mirror he had borrowed from the guards downstairs earlier that day. Ganbold began shaving in the sink using the mirror, and I asked Dorj why he hadn't gotten us one before.

"Bah. No need mirror. For woman put make up on face," he scoffed.

Dorj's Asian beard wasn't what you would call full so *he* may not have needed a mirror, but my scruff comes in thick and heavy, so I was grateful to have one to shave with instead of blindly hacking away at my face. After Ganbold was done, I grabbed my shaving brush, paste, and razor, went to the sink, and got a good look at myself for the first time in a month. I had grown a goatee in order to save wear and tear on the cheap single blade disposable razors I used, and as I lathered my face, I saw the age that had come with my short time in prison.

My skin was pale, much too pale for the time of the year, and I was thin from lack of decent food. I noticed the worry lines emanating from the corners of my eyes, which were ringed underneath

by dark circles from constant tension and lack of sleep. And for the first time in my life, my beard was streaked with gray.

I have never been a beauty queen, but I looked like shit.

Oh well. You're forty-one, not seventeen anymore. The way you've lived, it's about damn time the old dog started getting a gray muzzle. And this is prison, not a beauty parlor, buddy, I thought, and shaved my face, thankful for the mirror despite the rough picture it presented.

The next day after breakfast, those of us with money on our books lined up outside the prison canteen. Jacob was there, and as we sat waiting our turn in the store, we talked some more about drinking and drugs. I had spent the previous evening writing a five-page letter that described the last few days of my drinking, and I gave it to him, hoping he could find something of use in my story.

I had been on the very last leg of a tour cycle that ended in one of my favorite places on earth, Australia. Lamb of god had a day off in Brisbane, and I have friends there, so that evening I met up with them at an Irish pub named Gilhooley's on Albert Street, just a few blocks from my hotel. We were knocking back a few pints when a fan of my band walked over to our table, bringing his drink, and uninvited, without a word sat down and began staring at me. *Great.*

"Um, hello? Can I help you?" I asked the young man.

"You're Randy. You're the singer of lamb of god," he said, as if somehow I had missed that fact.

"Yes, that's right. It's me, in all my ridiculous glory. We'll be playing tomorrow night. Tonight though, I'm just hanging out with my friends. I don't get to see them very often, so we'll see you at the show, dude," I said, hoping that he would get the point and leave me alone. The fan just stared at me. It was uncomfortable, and weird.

"Yes, but you're here now. You're Randy," he said, reemphasizing his startlingly obvious point. He continued staring at me. *Oh boy.*

"Look dude, I gotta take a piss. I'll catch you later. Like to-morrow night, understand? Nice to meet you. Goodbye," I said, and throwing a look at my friends that said *Help me out here*, I got up and went to take a leak. When I returned, the fan was still sitting at our table. I glared at my friends Leila and Jeffo. *What the fuck, guys? You were supposed to get rid of this dude.* They both just shrugged helplessly at me. Obviously, I would have to handle this matter myself. I was a few drinks deep by this point, so getting mean wasn't a problem.

"Well, dude, if you're going to sit here like a bump on a log and just fucking stare at me like a monkey in a zoo, you had better make yourself useful. I'll take a pint of Cooper's pale and a shot of Bushmill's. So will my friends," I said.

"What?" he said, confused by the drink order. This guy was thick.

"Three pints of Cooper's pale ale, and three shots of Bush-mill's Irish whiskey. You're buying. Chop chop. My friends and I are getting thirsty here," I said.

"Uhm, okay . . . " he said, then slowly turned from me and went to the bar, glancing worriedly over his shoulder as if I might suddenly disappear, a figment of his imagination.

"Jesus Christ, why didn't you guys get that freak to fuck off?" I asked Leila and Jeffo.

"We tried. We told him to go hang out with his own friends over there at the bar. We asked him to leave you alone. We told him that you were trying to enjoy your night off in peace, but he just kept saying 'Nope, I'm drinking with Randy. That's all that matters,' over and over. He's an odd one," Leila said.

"Yeah, he's a total punisher. Not too bright, either. But I bet he'll leave after we order enough drinks on his tab," I laughed.

I was wrong. Leila and Jeffo and I went from bar to bar, and the fan followed us everywhere we went, buying drinks when I ordered him to as I tried my best to burn up every last Australian dollar in his wallet. But for some reason I couldn't get drunk, despite the prodigious amount of shots and pints I poured down my gullet. The fan, however, was getting completely wasted. His eyes were crossing and he was having a difficult time staring at me anymore, although he did his best. The night ended on a beautiful rooftop bar, with Leila, Jeffo, and I making a sport of confusing and abusing the young man. We acted as if I was really in Australia to help produce Jeffo's imaginary new reality TV show (named, cleverly enough, *The Jeffo Show*), taking imaginary phone calls, screaming at imaginary producers, talking about imaginary publishing rights we had to attain in order to use Led Zeppelin's music as an imaginary soundtrack for the imaginary show, and asking the fan his opinion on all sorts of imaginary technical matters, then berating him when he confessed to not having any idea of what we were talking about. All of it was very quick, very witty and very off the cuff, and all of it was very, very cruel. While it had been indescribably rude of the young man to attach himself to me and my friends in the first place, in all fairness to him, he was a complete idiot, and currently a very drunken one at that. After last call had come and gone, we finished our drinks and walked out onto the street. I said goodbye to my friends, then telling the young man to leave me alone and go home, I walked back to my hotel, leaving him wobbling unsteadily on a street corner, more fucked up than a football bat. I drank a few more beers on my hotel balcony, then went to sleep.

The next morning I woke up with a crippling hangover. Despite the hideous way I felt, the night before I hadn't been able to reach that comfortable place alcohol had taken me to so many times before; a numb, murky, zone of white noise where all the things about my life and myself that bothered me were shut out for a few hours. I had drank my face off for free, but the booze had finally stopped working. I made a pot of coffee, walked out onto my balcony, sat down, and lit a cigarette. Against the wall in front of me were empty bottles of beer, standing in a neat row, the well-ordered evidence of what my life had become. It was a

beautiful day, and as I sat there looking at the beer bottles, I realized I didn't feel like doing *anything*.

The Brisbane Botanical Gardens were right down the street,
a mere two blocks' walk from my hotel, and I didn't want to go
and look at any of the beautifully foreign plants I find so fascinating Down Under. Directly across the street was one of my
favorite bookstores in the world, Folio Books, but I had no desire
to browse through their compact but magnificent selection. All
around me were great restaurants, yet despite an empty stomach
I didn't feel like eating a bite. Most tellingly, in my refrigerator
were several cold beers—the only thing I felt like doing was drinking them. But when I thought about it, I didn't even feel like
doing that. I was dead inside. I couldn't think of a single thing
I wanted to do. I had become nothingness, trapped in a human
body. What an awful, soul-crushing feeling that is.

Staring at the row of empty beer bottles, I saw that they were
a metaphor for my life. On the outside, if you didn't look too
closely, everything was in order. I had a dream job, and somehow
still maintained a regimented enough life to function on tour. I
had money in the bank, and I had a home. My wife had somehow not yet left me, and I still had friends and family who loved
me. But like the row of beer bottles in front of me, I had become a mere receptacle for alcohol, a garbage can to throw booze
and drugs into. Now I was empty, just like those bottles; and just
like those bottles, all it would take to bring me crashing down
was one slight nudge. I thought of the fan from the night before,
about what he had told my friends.

I'm drinking with Randy. That's all that matters.

I myself had been drinking with Randy for twenty-two years,
and it *had* become all that mattered. I was desperately unhappy. It
was time to try something else, or I would die.

That night I walked onstage with a pounding head and did
my job, trying really hard not to fall completely to pieces in front
of over fifteen thousand people. I had to keep my head down at

times during our set so that no one would see the tears streaming down my face. I was terrified, empty, and heartbroken; but I dug in and did my job.

That was my first day sober. I haven't had a drink since.

I wrote this story out and gave it to Jacob because I had a feeling he was teetering right on that very same emotional razor's edge, that point where a person takes a leap of faith to one side and gets sober, or slides down off the other and eventually dies of their problem. For people like us, a life spent dancing in the middle is impossible—the razor eventually slices us in half if we try. On a scale of one to ten, there are no numbers in-between. It's one or ten. All or nothing. Do or die. I hoped that sharing my story with Jacob would help him see that he could start doing and stop dying. He thanked me for the letter, then it was my turn to enter the canteen.

Normally only one prisoner was allowed in the canteen at a time, but Jacob spoke in Czech to the guard and the clerk, who let him enter with me and act as a translator. The canteen looked like the inside of a tiny convenience store in a bad part of Detroit, just without the beer and wine selection—everything was behind what looked to be bullet proof glass. At first I was confused by this—I realized that I was locked up with a bunch of criminals, some of whom had presumably knocked over a liquor store or two in their day. But really, what could possibly happen inside the prison to warrant bullet-proof glass for the store? Were there inmates possessed by uncontrollable urges to rob store clerks, pathological stick-up men who would escape their cells only to make their way to the canteen to try and empty the non-existent cash register? What would they load up on? Cookies and cigarettes? Then what? There would be no get away car waiting as they left the canteen on foot, running wild-eyed into the prison hall, arms laden with toiletries, instant coffee, and rolling tobacco. Then I thought about it and realized that the clerk wasn't an inmate—the glass was for her protection, in case a riot broke out. I have always thought that working in a convenience store would require a special kind of mental fortitude (an almost super-human, herculean ability to deal with the general public that I am fully aware I do not possess); and although there was no graveyard shift or drunken maniacs wandering the aisles of the prison canteen and shoplifting, the thought of being stuck in the only area of a rioting prison with large quantities of cigarettes sent a shudder down my spine. You have to have balls of steel to be a check out clerk in a prison canteen, and the lady behind the counter, although very patient with me as Jacob helped me suss out my order, looked tough as nails. I finished my shopping, went back to my cell, handed Ganbold and Dorj a few packs of smokes, then it was time for walk.

I passed the two black men seated in the same exact place they were yesterday. I still could not quite put my finger on their accent. After the third or fourth time around, my curiosity got the better of me. I stopped in front of them, stuck out my hand, and introduced myself. They seemed a little shocked at first that anyone was bothering to talk to them, but quickly recovered, and smiled at me as they shook my hand.

"Well, you two are the only brothers I have seen in this place. Where are y'all from?" I said, taking a seat beside them.

"Africa, man. Nigeria and Ghana. You're the American rockstar, eh?" said one of them who had introduced himself as Tony.

"Yeah, that's me. I heard you guys speaking yesterday but couldn't place the accent. What in the hell are you doing in this shit hole? You're a long way from home," I said.

"Charlie, man," Tony said, and gave out a big laugh. This delighted me, because I had never actually heard anyone use the slang "Charlie" for cocaine before. It seemed antiquated, almost square, as I had only ever read about it in high school health class, or one of those ridiculous "How to tell if your kid is on drugs" pamphlets. He went on to explain to me that a lot of the coke in Europe was arriving via West African countries now, as their rather porous ports were much easier for South American ships to slip into than the tightly regulated European ones. He also told me that cocaine use had exploded in Africa as well, and that crack had become a big problem. I asked him if the quality of cocaine in Europe was improving, as it didn't have as far to travel, and he said it definitely was. I laughed, saying at least that was a good thing, as Euro coke was the worst stepped-on crap I'd ever put up my nose back in the day. We had quite a pleasant chat for a bit, mostly about the cocaine business, then I walked on. In retrospect, I realized that it's definitely not normal for most people to sit around laughing and discussing new international drug smuggling routes like they would a recently opened highway bypass that shaves thirty minutes off their commute to the office. But the casual effortlessness with which I fell into the conversation reminded me that I was not a "normal person" when it came to drugs, I had not lived the life of the average everyday normal citizen, and I was definitely not in a normal place.

After a few more laps around the yard, I sat down to have a smoke. I was chatting with Jacob and Ganbold when I heard a voice ask me in a thick Irish brogue if I had a lighter. John was the first and only inmate I met during my entire time in Pankrác whose native tongue was English, although as an Irishman from County Cork, referring to the language he spoke that I somewhat understood as "English" was playing a little loose with the term's definition. I have always had a soft spot for the Irish, as half of my mother's side of the family hail from the Emerald Isle, and I very much look forward to my band's trips there when a tour is routed through Belfast and Dublin. A well-educated businessman, John was both exceedingly funny and very friendly, which came as no surprise to me as I have always found the Irish to be a witty and warm-hearted people.

John's good nature shined through that day as, without prompting, he told me tons of things that would be useful to me in Pankrác. He had the whole place dialed in, and explained how I could order English publications, bargain a bit with the trusties for better food, and told me which guards on our floor were cool and which were jerks. When I asked why he was in prison, he told me he wasn't sure, as he hadn't been charged with anything yet.

"The bloody Czechs can't decide whether they want to call it tax evasion or embezzling public funds. I wish they would just make up their minds and get on with it," he shrugged.

"How long have you been in here?" I asked.

"Six months now, mate," he said with an impish grin. "I've offered them a million Euros in bail, but they aren't interested."

Six months without even being charged? Good grief! This news didn't give me hope for a speedy resolution of my bail issue, but it did put things in perspective for me. The right to an expedient trial obviously didn't exist in the Czech Republic, or if it did it was being soundly ignored in John's case. We talked a little more, and John told me he would bring me a few English newspapers and magazines to read the next day at walk, then we went inside.

The next day was shower day, and I was relieved to find that the shower on our new tier was brighter, cleaner, and had more shower heads than the dingy mildew factory we had been forced to use downstairs. Jacob brought me a real, full-sized towel to the shower, and a pair of shorts along with a few extra t-shirts. He told me not to wear the shorts or t-shirts outside of my cell yet, as he had to try to clear it with the guards before I was allowed to wear any clothes other than my prison uniform. We got done showering, ate lunch, and went to walk, where Jacob and I continued our daily talk about our addictions and the repercussions they had had on our lives. He had been excited by my letter, saying that he had experienced some of the very same feelings about his heroin use I had described in my drinking story, and was gaining hope from the fact that he was not alone in having gone through the brutal emotional and physical isolation that addiction and alcoholism produces.

In the end, alcoholism and drug addiction are almost always horribly lonesome repeat journeys to drink at the wells of despair, and the alcoholic or drug addict often feels as if they are the only person on earth who has experienced and understands their particular pain. They become what I have heard brilliantly described as *terminally unique* (hence the title of a lamb of god song I wrote about a dear friend wallowing in the depths of opiate addiction). This is, of course, an illusion; a merciless trick that the substance-fueled and monstrously inflated ego plays on the drunk or junkie. No one is unique in their addiction, whatever the particulars of their situation may be. A drunk is a drunk, and a junkie is a junkie. Remaining terminally unique for too long leads to insanity or death, or both. It's a tired old tune almost as old as humanity itself, yet as the centuries march on, drunks and addicts the world over endlessly sing its self-pitying refrain. I was happy to hear that Jacob was starting to realize that he was not *special*. Being *special* gets you nothing but pain. I know this from personal experience.

At walk I also talked to John a bit more. It was nice to have a conversation with someone who spoke English so effortlessly, although I had to quickly retrain my ear to decipher some of his dialect (this always happens to me in Ireland, Scotland, Wales, and even parts of Northern England—by day two of a tour run through those places, I can usually understand most of what people are saying). As promised, John brought me an English newspaper, as well as a copy of *Wired* magazine, which I always enjoy skimming through. As he handed me the newspaper, he shook his head and said, "You've got some right nutters back in your country, don't ya, mate?" Back in my cell, I decided to take a gander at the newspaper first in order to find out what looniness was happening back in my corner of the outside world. I almost wish I hadn't.

Other than rumors from prisoners about my court case, I had been without any sort of news source for over a month. While the newspaper was a little over a week old, I was looking forward to looking through a fairly recent window to the outside world, perhaps even a bit of news from home. But the headlining story didn't make me nostalgic for America—some freak had walked into a midnight screening of the latest Batman movie in Aurora,

Colorado, dressed in full tactical gear and body armor, and had opened fire with a shotgun, assault rifle, and handgun, killing twelve people and injuring seventy others before being arrested without any resistance behind the theater. *Well, it's good to know that civilization is still collapsing on schedule*, I thought bitterly. I folded the paper and put it away, thinking about how screwed up the world continued to be.

That evening after lights out I heard a pair of male and female inmates calling to each other in Czech across the prison courtyard outside our cell. Ganbold told me that they were boyfriend and girlfriend, both locked up in the same prison, yelling out a recap of their respective days in Pankrác, along with a little sweet talk. As I lay in bed listening to the two lovers talk, I felt a great swell of longing for my wife. I couldn't understand a word they said, but their tone was unmistakable and familiar to my ear, and re-minded me of the silly and sweet way Cindy and I spoke to each other. *It's probably going to be a long while before I get to see her again*, I thought, and went to sleep with a deep sadness in my heart.

The next day after breakfast as I was measuring our new cell with a ruler my wife had brought me (nine-and-a-half-feet tall arched ceilings, seven-feet wide by thirteen-feet long), a guard came by with an envelope for me. In it was a printed letter from a man named Jonathan Crane. The letter explained that he was a journalist for the *Prague Post*, an English publication in Prague, and was coming to Pankrác later that day for a story he had to cover. Jonathan asked me if it would be possible to sit down for an interview with me while he was in the prison, as the *Post* had been covering my ordeal and he thought I might like the chance to speak for myself to the English speaking press. The only prob-lem was that I would have to give prison officials written notice that he was allowed to speak to me before they would allow an interview. I was excited by the possibility of finally having my voice heard in a forum other than *Blesk*, but I couldn't read or write Czech. After lunch on the way to walk I told the trusty of my predicament, and he kindly agreed to write the note to the prison officials for me and give it to the guard in our tier office. Immediately after walk, a guard came to get me out of my cell, and the trusty told me I was wanted in the office. I grabbed the letter from Jonathan to show the guard in case he had any questions, and walked down the hall to the office.

The guard sitting at a desk smiled at me when I held up the letter and began to explain its contents.

"You won't be needing that," he said.

"Why? Did he already come? Did I miss him?" I asked, my heart sinking. The trusty wouldn't have had time to write the note for me.

"No. You are leaving in thirty minutes. Pack your things—you are going home, Randy," he said, looking pleased for me.

I stood there in disbelief for a second. A great rush of something indescribable washed over my entire being. It was almost like the way my focus had become so hyper-concentrated as time had slowed when I had been arrested, except now everything seemed to move in fast forward. Reality had taken on a surreal quality again, except that this time it was shiny and bright instead of the dingy gloam that had defined my first few days incarcerated. I stammered out a thank you to the man, and returned to my cell.

"I AM GOING HOME!" I hooted to Dorj and Ganbold as soon as I was in the cell.

The next thirty minutes were a blur of movement as I went through my things, distributing almost everything I had accumulated in prison evenly to the two of them, with instructions to give a few various specialty items to certain prisoners. Drawing pens and paper for art supplies to Rene. English books to John. Coffee for the Quiet Gypsy. Tobacco for Jacob. I believe Dorj and Ganbold were almost as happy for me as I was for myself, giving me hugs and laughing, helping me make sure I hadn't forgotten anything. The only damper on the whole excitement came when I thought about Jacob. I paused for a minute and began to worry about him—we had just started to get to know each other, he seemed to be setting off on the right path, and I had great hopes my relatively meager experience with sobriety would be of some small service in helping him to beat his addiction. I said a quick prayer for him, then returned to packing. I took a couple of packs of cigarettes for myself, all my paperwork, letters I had received, drawings Rene had made for me, and all the writing I had done in Pankrác. That was about it. I was almost done packing when I remembered the spoon of teaching.

I had decided long before the day of my release that when I left Pankrác, the spoon would be leaving with me. It had been my sole utensil, the only thing I had been allowed to keep the entire time since the day I had arrived there. I had used it daily to eat with, as a tool for various hammering and scraping and prying jobs, as a drawing aid, and as a teaching implement. I had earned that spoon with my time, and by God it was going with me. I buried it in my papers, hoping the guards wouldn't search me too thoroughly—*What is the penalty for stealing a spoon* from *prison*, I wondered (the spoon now sits in my office). Soon a guard came to get me, and after another round of bear hugs from Dorj and Ganbold, I was on my way.

"Goodbye, Doctor Khun! Goodbye, Doctor Love! I will miss you! I hope you go home soon!" I yelled.

"Goodbye, Doctor Pankrác! Goodbye! You are a good doctor! Do not forget us! Go home, Doctor Pankrác! Go home!" they yelled. It was the last time I would ever see them, and as bad as it was being locked up with them in such a terrible place, sometimes I do miss them, and think fondly of them often.

Even Dorj.

The news of my release had spread through the tier, and men came to their doors, yelling goodbye to me through the open hatches and wishing me luck. I saw Jacob's face peering out, and I ran over to his cell, clasping his hands as I told him to remember that he didn't have to die if he didn't want to. He thanked me, and we said goodbye. I hope he is well wherever he is. The guard took me by the prison laundry, where I dropped off my dirty sheets and clothes, and changed into the clothes I had been arrested in. In an office next to the laundry, an envelope was produced containing everything that had been in my pockets when I was arrested, which a clerk went through with painful slowness, checking off each item on a list as he returned it to me. Then I was taken downstairs, out of the main prison building, and into an office set inside the thick outer prison wall. I signed some papers written in Czech (I had no idea of what they said), was handed some release papers (also in Czech), and was told to hold onto them as they were very important. I turned and walked towards a waiting room at the front of the office and there was Tomas and a woman who worked for Martin's law firm. I grabbed them both and gave them a huge bear hug, then we walked out of Pankrác into the sunny Prague afternoon.

I was free.

While there was no ex-KGB private detective waiting in a fast black car to spirit me over the border (sadly, Martin had deemed this unnecessary), Tomas did tell me that he was taking me to Martin's apartment to hide out until my flight out of Prague had been arranged. The judgment of the appeal court had come down that morning, rejecting the prosecutor's second complaint, and Tomas had waited outside the court all morning in order to get the necessary papers for my release to the prison as soon as possible. As far as we knew, Musik was not aware that I had been released, but if he found out, he could request a brand-new warrant for my arrest. Therefore, I was to lay low in Martin's crib until the time came to leave. As I rode shotgun through Old Town Prague in Tomas's car, my ebullience was tinged with paranoia. I slunk low in my seat every time I saw a policeman or anyone I thought looked like a cop. Musik could be anywhere—I had no idea of what he looked like, but I'm sure my face would be familiar to him. It would be just my luck to pass him coming out of some pub after his lunch break. It wasn't until I was in Martin's spacious apartment that I began to relax a bit. I took a long, gloriously hot shower in a clean bathroom and shaved my face with a fresh razor Martin loaned me, then sat on his rooftop balcony and drank a delicious cup of real coffee his wife made me.

That evening after sunset Martin and his lovely wife Eva and I walked a few short blocks through the narrow and winding cobblestone streets of Old Town to a very nice restaurant they ate at often. I wanted a steak, and although it was not on the menu, Martin knew the staff well and they produced one for me. Sitting there in the clothes I had been arrested in, I felt conspicuous and out of place surrounded by the tables full of well dressed diners, but the food was delicious. After dinner, we returned to the apartment and I turned on Martin's laptop, searching for any news that I had been released. Luckily none appeared, but endless news stories about my arrest and incarceration appeared when I Googled my name. I began to read a few of these, but quickly became overwhelmed and turned the computer off. Martin and Eva went to bed, and I lay down to crash in a spare bedroom, but sleep eluded me. It was so odd to be able to turn a lamp on and off as I wished; to not hear the snores of Ganbold, the whispers of Dorj, the screeching of Ukrainians in the dark, the snap of the cell door hatch as it slid open and lights flashing on as a guard performed his periodic checks throughout the night. I got up and sat in the darkness on the balcony smoking until almost 4:00 a.m., returned to the bedroom to write a quick five sentence entry in my journal noting my freedom, and finally fell into a light sleep.

The next morning Martin drove me to the airport, instructing me to go directly to my gate once I was through security and not lollygag in the terminals. Rumor of my release had made its way to the ears of the press (the previous evening Martin's cellphone had been constantly ringing, mostly calls from reporters at *Blesk*), although no one could confirm it yet. Martin told me that he had arranged for a brief television interview with a news crew he had a good relationship with who agreed not to air it until my plane had left the ground. This made me nervous, as I did not trust the press, especially not the Czech press, who had not exactly been kind to me. But I trusted Martin and agreed to do it. As we walked from the terminal's parking garage, I saw a camera man and a reporter in a white t-shirt standing outside the airport entrance. I did an almost seven minute interview with the reporter, who mostly asked me how I was feeling and what prison was like. At the end he asked me, "You will return to Prague?"

"Of course, if it is necessary. I'm no flight risk. I'm an international touring artist, I have to clear my name, so yes, I will come back here if I'm called to court," I stated with conviction.

I said goodbye to Martin, then walked to the check in counter and presented my passport. The woman looked up my name, then asked me why I had been in Prague so long.

"Weeeeelll . . . I was in prison," I said, handing her my release papers.

"Um, hold on for one second, please," she said, and called over a supervisor. After a few nerve-wracking moments she smiled and handed me my ticket. I went through security without any incident, then made my way to my gate. I still had over an hour to kill before my plane took off, and as I passed a newsstand I saw a Czech magazine with my face on the cover. I pulled the bill of my Surf City, NC Surf Shop baseball cap low across my brow—it was no fedora, but it was my favorite hat, reminding me of the sands of Wrightsville Beach where I had spent so much of my youth, and I was especially glad to have it on this day. Soon I arrived at my gate. It was at the very end of the terminal, and felt like a trap to me, an exposed dead end. My leaving Prague was entirely legal, but I still felt like a hunted man. I expected to see a swat team (just like the one that had arrested me) come marching my way at any moment, and this was, in fact, a very real possibility. I decided the gate was too exposed, so I went into a bar with a smoking section out of sight of the terminal hallway, ordered a smoked sausage and a nonalcoholic beer. I sat smoking and staring out of the window at planes as they landed and took off until my flight number popped up on a screen in the lounge. I slugged back my beer, and went back to my gate.

For an excruciating half hour I sat there, nervously texting with my friend London May, telling him I was free but not to let anyone know until it was announced I was on the ground in America. Finally, at 12:38 p.m. the call went out for first class passengers to board; my band had been kind enough to book me in first class after my ordeal. This was a treat, since despite what many people seem to think, lamb of god always flies coach. I sat in my seat, holding my breath as passengers slowly filed past me boarding the plane, sending a text to my wife to let her know I had made it onto the freedom bird. At last the plane's door shut, and soon we began to taxi down the runway. It wasn't until the second that the plane's wheels left the ground that I emitted a great exhale of relief. I had been incarcerated for thirty-seven days, thirty-four of which I had spent behind Pankrác's ancient walls. I was finally going home.

But I knew this wasn't over. I was positive I would be called to court, and weeks ago in prison, I had already made the decision to return when that call came. I had to.

I could not turn my back on what my heavy heart told me was the right thing to do.

part 3

THE TRIAL

chapter sixteen

The longest walk you will ever take is the one you take with your dead child in your arms.

My first wife and I found out she was pregnant not too long before my thirtieth birthday. Our child wasn't planned, but I would never call our baby a mistake. When she told me, I grinned and said, "Well, it looks like we're going to be parents," and got on with the business of working hard at my roofing job and saving money. My band had just gotten signed to our first label, and had accepted an offer for our first real tour opening for a well-known national act, but I called that off. We weren't making any money yet, and I had responsibilities to meet. I was going to be a father, and I would put the needs of my small family before my own desires. This was the way I had been raised, and I had born witness to my own father doing the very same thing, traveling hours to work every day, five, six, and sometimes seven days a week, in order to provide for my brothers and me. As a child I did not understand or appreciate his efforts, but as a man I was grateful for the lessons he taught me by example.

During the first ultrasound to check our baby's health, the doctor noticed something troubling. Eventually we learned that one of the chambers of our child's tiny heart wasn't developing properly. The doctor assured us that it wasn't a genetic trait our child was inheriting, but a fairly common birth defect; just a random bit of bad luck in the biological game of dice humans play every time two people's chromosomes meet and combine to create a third life. He also told us that the heart defect was easily operated on after birth, and would not affect our child's life too much, aside from preventing extremely strenuous exercise.

"Your baby will never be a marathon runner, but the child will be healthy in every other way," he assured us.

Although I stay in pretty good shape, and have always been very active physically, I've never run a marathon myself. And I didn't give a damn if the child never tried out for the Olympics; I just wanted my baby to arrive safe and sound. I didn't worry about the news of the birth defect too much, as our doctor seemed confident that all would be well after a serious but fairly standard operation. We both worked hard as my wife's stomach grew bigger, and in the evenings after a long day of roofing, I loved to put my ear to her stomach and talk to my child. We were very content in our rented apartment in the working class Oregon Hill neighborhood of Richmond. We read books on pregnancy, started preparing a room as a nursery, and began attending birthing classes. We were so happy in that excited, scared way that only young, first-time parents feel as they watch their baby grow larger and larger in the mother's belly.

One hot summer day I was sweating on a roof in Orange, Virginia, when my boss called up for me to climb down. He told me that my wife had gone into labor. She was fine, he said, but it was time for me to go to the hospital. My guitarist Mark and I worked together at that time, and he came down from the roof to wish me luck. I will never forget the broad smile on his work-tanned face as he clapped me on my shoulder as brothers do.

"You're gonna be a *daddy*, man!" he beamed, then I was in a pickup truck for the hour-long drive back to Richmond.

At the hospital I was rushed to my wife's side. Our baby was coming early, as my wife was only a little over seven months pregnant. We had planned on a natural childbirth, but due to her premature labor, a Caesarean section was necessary. I held her hand as the anesthetist administered the epidural. In short order we were in an operating room. I crouched by her face, holding her hand, telling her everything was going to be okay. A nurse kept yelling at me as I unconsciously and repeatedly pulled my surgical mask down from my face so that my wife could see me when I spoke to her. It was an intense experience, but it didn't bother me or freak me out. All I could think of was my wife's safety, and our soon to be born baby.

"Okay, guys, are you ready for your baby to be born?" the female doctor yelled at us in a happy voice.

We were, and then I saw the doctor holding the small thing that was our child.

"It's a girl! What are you going to call her?" the doctor asked.

With my wife still on the table, we named our daughter Sarah Fisher Blythe. Sarah after my mother's mother and Fisher after the lazy afternoons we spent together on the James River, casting for blue gill and smallmouth bass. As the doctors began sewing my wife up, I walked over to the incubator where my daughter lay. Her hair was full and dark like her mother's, and she was the most beautiful thing I had ever seen. The doctor let me briefly touch her tiny hand, then she was whisked away. There was work to be done, as our daughter had to be stabilized so that she could live in an incubator for a while, so she could grow enough for her heart to be operated on. After they had put my wife back together again, we were given a private room, and we both fell asleep; she in her hospital bed, me in a chair beside her.

At first nurses came by fairly regularly to let us know that the doctors were working on our daughter, and everything was going okay. But the visits began to slow, and the news was noncommittal when it came. I tried to remain positive, but there was a sinking feeling in my guts. Finally, almost seven hours after our daughter had come into the world, a young male intern walked into the room carrying a clipboard. I could see by the pained look on his face the news was not good.

We were taken to the pediatric wing of the hospital, and we saw our child.

Our tiny daughter was on a small operating table, tubes running out of her poor naked little body, and a doctor was keeping her alive by hand, pumping her chest with his fingertips. He looked up at me with great sorrow in his eyes.

"She's not responding," he said.

I nodded.

"Let her go," I said.

The doctors began to pull the tubes out of her tiny frame, like unplugging a broken electrical appliance.

And my wife and I watched our daughter die.

Soon we were alone in a small room down the hall with the still body of our child.

After a while a young chaplain came into the room and asked us if we wanted to pray with him. I believe I told him he could pray if it would make him feel any better. He tried to talk to us, but all I wanted was for him to leave. He was trying to be of service, but he was nervous, and his presence was a great irritant to me. He watched us hold our baby for a while, then suddenly blurted, "Look, give me the baby. I'll carry her back," and took a step towards my wife. I quickly stepped in the way. I felt a great wave of protective violence surge within me, my instincts screaming for me to smash this kind but bumbling man in the face. I restrained myself with great effort, trying to stop my hands from shaking.

"NO!" I barked. "This is *our baby*. *I* am *her father*. I will carry her back. You can leave now."

The chaplain quickly left, and I could tell I had frightened the man. He was only trying to do his job, but he was young and nervous, and could not possibly understand how to speak to a couple like my wife and me. That soft and awful skill only comes through years of bearing witness to tragedies like ours, and he was obviously lean on the heartbreaking experience required of a counselor in such terrible moments. My wife and I sat for a while longer, then I looked at her. It was time to say goodbye.

The walk down the empty hall back to the operating room was just a few hundred feet, but as I put one foot in front of the other, carrying my dead child tightly in my arms, it seemed to stretch on for miles and miles. *I am her father. I am a man. This is my duty. I will carry her back. I will carry her back, no one else,* I thought over and over during that surreal, endless fluorescent-bulb lit nightmare trek. When I reached the operating room, the doctors and nurses looked at me with heartbroken eyes. I could tell this hurt them greatly—they had tried their best, but our little girl was just not strong enough yet. I stood in front of them, and tried to compose myself.

"Thank you all for trying to save our daughter's life," I said in a choked voice, and handed my dead baby to a nurse. I saw tears well up in the doctors' and nurses' eyes. As much as this had been a nightmarish experience for me, it must have been unimaginably painful for the woman who had carried our baby, so I turned and walked out of that room to go to take care of my wife the best I could.

———

A few months later, after the pain of our loss got to be too much, our marriage fell apart on Christmas Eve. My brother Mark came to fetch me, and literally carried me weeping from our house back to my family. I fell deeper and deeper into the bottle for the next decade, and I never dealt with the awful sadness that sat buried inside me. Finally I got sober, and began to face my past. The pain is always there, but it has grown softer over the years. Today I live a happy and free life, but there is not a day that goes by that I do not think of my baby girl.

———

$\mathcal{L}$osing my child is the worst thing that has ever happened to me. Even the pain of decades of active alcoholism, and the fear and uncertainty I faced during my trip to prison look trivial, even laughable, when compared to the way I felt when I watched my daughter die. It was absolute hell, the worst hell I could imagine, and only a parent who has lost a child can understand this. It is not something I wish to discuss with anyone I am not very close with, with the exception of a newly grieving parent. As an elder member of that sad tribe, I can feel their pain on a visceral level, and even if I don't know them, I can listen well with an open, understanding heart. I can't make the hurt go away, but I can extend my hand and let them know that they can survive this.

I could not extend my hand to the family of Daniel, for I was accused of killing their child. They had done nothing wrong, yet suffered in confusion. No reason for their son's death other than hearsay had been given them, unlike the cold light of reason that science provided me when my daughter died. Daniel's family never once attacked me, bad-mouthed me in the press, or lashed out at me in anyway, neither in public nor in private. They just wanted some answers. I knew the way they suffered. I could *feel it* when I thought of my own child's passing. In prison, I asked myself a question: What kind of man would I be if I did not do my best to help them find those answers, through whatever means necessary, no matter the cost?

No kind of man at all, I silently answered, speaking my heart's truth.

I am a man, I thought.

I would go back if called.

chapter seventeen

The words "Welcome home, sir" had never sounded sweeter than they did coming from the US customs agents at New York's JFK airport, as he handed back my passport on August 3, 2012. Beyond a cheap duffle bag half-full of prison ephemera, I didn't have any luggage to recheck for my flight to Richmond, so I made my way directly to the terminal's exit to stand on American soil (or at least New York City concrete), for the first time in months. As I moved with the crowd past the last security checkpoint, I heard a female voice call my name. I turned and saw an attractive dark haired young woman standing by the exit.

"Randy, I just wanted you to know I'm glad you're home" she said, and gave me a hug.

Lia was a lamb of god fan from New York City who had read on the Internet that I had been released from prison. The details of my flight had not been made public, but Lia had smartly figured that I would probably fly directly from Prague to New York or Washington, D.C., and from there catch a connecting flight home to Richmond. As she lived in New York and had the afternoon off, she had checked all the flights from Prague to JFK, and had decided to come and take a chance that she would see me in arrivals. After waiting a few fruitless hours she was about to leave, but decided to take a chance on one more flight. Lia was not a stalker or a weirdo; she just felt that someone should be there to welcome me back to America, and after doing so told me she would be on her way. I was deeply touched by her warm gesture, and asked her if she would stay and have a coffee with me. I called my wife (who would have been in New York to greet me but for a delayed flight from Richmond) to let her know I had landed safely, then sat and chatted with Lia over coffee until it was time for me to go for my flight home.

After going back through security, I found a spare outlet near my departure gate, plugged in my cell phone to give it a little juice, and looked at my email inbox for the first time since I had been released. It was, of course, completely flooded with messages from approximately three million different people, the basic premise of around 95 percent of the emails being "Dude, *what the fuck* is going on? Bro, are you okay?!?" Just looking at this digital river of concern warmed my heart, but it also very quickly began to make me feel overwhelmed. I was just about to turn off my phone when I noticed one email subject heading that kept on popping up again and again. It was a single word: gratitude.

My friend Tommy, a singer from New York City, had assembled several other musicians and men who worked in the music business, all of whom were sober alcoholics or drug addicts like myself, and had begun a daily email gratitude list. Some of these men I knew, some I did not, but all had begun emailing each other lists of things in their lives they were grateful for. These lists were forwarded to me in an attempt to provide moral support as well as help me maintain a proper attitude while in prison. Tommy had no idea of whether or not I could receive email in Pankrác, but had started and sent this chain of positive energy my way regardless. Humbled, I read several of the lists, then pulled out my journal and typed out the gratitude list I had written during my first few days in prison, and sent it to all the men in the email chain. That digital gratitude list carries on to this day, and has become an important part of my life and my sobriety. When I become disgruntled, I will sometimes stop and write a gratitude list, to remind myself of the reality of my situation, which in truth ain't so bad. I have become friends with the guys I did not know on the list, and my friendship with the ones I already knew has deepened. We watch out for each other on the road in person, via phone calls, or emails. We listen to each other's problems, and will offer helpful advice (if we come from a place of useful experience). So shout out to the men of the S.F.G.—I love you guys! (S.F.G. is the name of our small group, and it stands for many different things, but my favorite personal meaning is *Sober, Free, Grateful*—for me, none are possible without the others.)

Soon it was time to board my plane for the forty-five minute flight to Richmond, and I climbed aboard, ready to go home. I was excited to see my friends and family, but mostly I just wanted to sit in my house for a bit and be alone with my wife and Henry the cat. However, there would be a brief bit of sanctioned intrusion to get past before I could truly relax. I had sent a message via management to Don Argott (the director of the documentary about my band's fans that had now taken such a dramatic turn) letting him know that I was okay with him shooting my return to Richmond, but that he should not film the first few moments when I saw my family. It was sure to be an emotional moment, and although I was a public person and was used to being filmed in all sorts of intense situations, my family were not members of my band. They did not sign up for questions and film crews and crazy people bothering them because I scream for a living, and I prefer that they be left alone. If people bother my family, I become quite irate—it's not pretty. But I had no worries about Don respecting my wishes, as he had become a true friend, and had proven this before, during the filming of the documentary. He had gone to Prague when Cindy had come over, and with her permission had done a small amount of filming. But soon Don stopped filming her, as he felt it was more important to be there for her as a friend, not someone shoving a camera in her face during an already stressful time. He would continue to be respectful of my needs and privacy through the rest of my legal ordeal, and I was and am always happy to have him around, camera attached or not.

The second I felt the wheels of the small commuter plane touch the runway at the Richmond airport, I felt a great sense of relief. I was home. After deboarding, I stopped by the bathroom in the small terminal, washed my face, and brushed my teeth. I looked in the mirror, and what I saw looked pretty rough. I was running on very little sleep, and due to delays it was well past midnight—according to my European calibrated body clock it was actually approaching 8:00 a.m. I took a moment to compose myself, then walked down the hall. At the terminal's exit I saw my wife, my family, my band, some friends, and a few well-wishers. They held signs to welcome me home, and a great cheer went up as I walked out of the same narrow glass-walled corridor I had done so many times at the end of a tour. The first person I went to was my grandmother, who I had worried so much about while I was in prison. There she was, a tiny country woman, ninety-two years old and still tough as nails, standing on her own two feet way past midnight and her bed time to welcome her eldest grandson home. I felt a great swell of love for this lady who had helped to raise me, and I have never been happier to hug her, tell her that I loved her, and then scold her for being up so late. She told me that nothing could have kept her from being there to see me safely home, and I knew that old woman well enough to believe her. Then I kissed my wife, and hugged all my family and friends. The most emotional person there was my guitarist, Willie, who cried as he hugged me and told me how much he had missed me. I believe he and I are the most alike in the band in that sense; neither of us are particularly reserved men in nature, and we rarely bother trying to hold back intense emotions. It was good to see everyone, but I felt completely wiped out and unable to communicate well. Luckily everyone was already expecting me to be in less than tip-top shape, so I said goodnight and was soon driving my truck home, my wife by my side.

I spent the next six months in and out of Richmond, visiting family and friends, as well as touring the United States. The last thing I wanted to do was climb up on a stage and entertain people, but my legal bills were piling up very quickly, and my band's bank accounts were being drained at an equally alarming rate. Beyond merely trying to get me out of prison (and keep me from returning), we all had families to feed, mortgage payments to make, and regular bills to stay on top of just like everyone else. We also employ a road crew, a publicist, a management company, and a booking agent, amongst others—these people had all lost money during my time in prison, money they were counting on to feed *their* families when we had been forced to cancel our last tour. Lamb of god, like any successful band, is a *business*, a business with several moving parts beyond its five hairy members. All of these parts need to remain lubricated with money or else the machine ceases to function. I know this doesn't sit well with a large number of naïve people who cling to romantic notions of what being in a touring rock band is like, but it's reality—there's a reason why it's called the *music business*, not the *music everything-is-free-for-band-dudes party*. And like any business that hemorrhages large amounts of money with no foreseeable returns coming in, our business was in trouble. Our friends and fans had come to our rescue though, throwing benefit concerts, making and selling "Free Randy Blythe" t-shirts then donating the profits to a legal defense fund that had been set up for me, as well as bidding on items in an online auction my band had set up to help defray the mounting costs of my court case. These kind people kept us afloat; throughout this time of great expenditure, there was never a time when we missed payroll and we never went bankrupt. Lamb of god remained financially solvent because of these friends and fans, and I am forever grateful to them for their selfless actions during my time of need. I count myself very lucky, for I have no idea how someone without such a generous extended family would have avoided going completely broke had they been in my shoes. But despite the fact that we weren't filing for Chapter 11, we still needed to make some money, and touring was our only option.

Although lamb of god already had a very strict security policy, we had talks long before touring started about making sure it was enforced with draconian severity, resulting in immediate ejection from the show of anyone who could not abide by it. If you got on stage, you were out the door—no exceptions, no refunds given, no questions asked, and no explanations accepted (that policy stands to this day). Beyond my recent situation, there was a very good reason for this. Eight years earlier in a club in Columbus, Ohio, things had changed in the metal world forever. After December 8, 2004, audience members jumping on stage had gone from being accepted by some bands as part of the show (but more commonly as a mildly dangerous annoyance by most groups) to a potentially deadly threat. Several people had died violently that night, and one of the survivors of that evening's horrifying events would be on our upcoming tour. This man was a friend of mine, and some of his words would help me greatly in the months to come.

Lamb of god was headlining the tour, and one of the opening acts was the rowdy supergroup, Hellyeah. Hellyeah's drummer was a Texan named Vinnie Paul Abbott. Vinnie Paul and his brother, guitarist "Dimebag" Darrell Abbott, had been the founders of the now legendary metal band, Pantera. After over twenty years, achieving great success, and gathering a rabid fan base, eventually Pantera fell apart like so many bands do—the members stopped getting along. After the group's dissolution, the Abbott brothers wasted no time forming a new band, Damageplan, recording a new record and hitting the road to support it. On November 3, 2004 in San Antonio, Texas, Damageplan crossed paths with lamb of god while we were both out on tour, and Vinnie and Dimebag showed us great hospitality. It had been an awesome night, and the next day I was already looking forward to running into the Abbott brothers again somewhere down the road, as all touring bands eventually do.

Just over a month later, on the morning of December 9, 2004, I was asleep in my bunk, our bus parked in Brighton Beach, England. I felt a hand come through my bunk curtain and shake me awake. It was my guitarist Mark.

"Randy, wake up. My wife just called me—someone shot Dime, man! Someone fucking killed Dime," he said.

"What? Dude, what the fuck are you talking about?" I said. It just didn't make any sense. It still doesn't.

The night before, December 8, Damageplan had been booked to play a small club in Columbus, Ohio, a venue lamb of god had also performed in a few times. One minute and fifteen seconds into the first song of their set, a deranged Pantera fan who had been discharged early from the Marines due to mental illness, rushed the stage and shot Dimebag several times at point blank range in the head, executioner-style, with a 9mm Beretta handgun. He was killed instantly. Dime never saw a thing, as he had his eyes closed and was doing what he loved best—playing guitar. Big, kind-hearted Jeff Thompson, Damageplan's security who had introduced himself to me as "Mayhem" just a month earlier in Texas, tackled the gunman, and as a result was killed by a bullet to the heart. Club employee Erin Halk was killed as well during a valiant charge to subdue the assassin. Finally, audience member Nathan Bray selflessly lost his life at the young age of twenty-three years old while attempting to perform CPR first on Dime, then on Mayhem. Seven other people were shot and wounded in the chaos, including Vinnie Paul's drum tech Kat, who took three bullets while trying to wrestle the Beretta from the psychotic fan before being taken hostage. When Columbus police officer James Niggemeyer arrived and ended the rampage, killing the gunman with a well-placed blast from a 12 gauge Remington shotgun, the assassin had 35 rounds of ammunition remaining. Ironically, in 1980, John Lennon had been killed by a disgruntled

Beatles fan on the exact same date twenty-four years earlier. A disgruntled *fan . . .* and the root of the word *fan* is *fanatic.*

There are many theories floating around as to why the gunman, a Pantera *fanatic,* killed Dimebag. Some say he was upset over the band's break up, and blamed Dime. There is talk that the fan had become convinced in his twisted psyche that he had written some of Pantera's music, and felt ripped off. I don't know, and don't see much point in speculating, for in the end there are only questions, questions that will never be answered. No one will ever know the exact details of his particular descent into madness; what peculiar delusional knife repeatedly stabbed into his warped mind so sharply that he felt the overwhelming need to publicly execute his hero. Dimebag did nothing wrong; in fact, he was widely known as one of the most down-to-earth guys in the business, an overly generous man who always took time for his fans. And I do not think knowing his mind will solve anything—that is for mental health specialists to analyze, not musicians to figure out. What musicians in our scene did figure out immediately was that no longer would anybody be allowed onstage beyond band, crew, and approved guests.

To fans of other genres of music, this may seem like a given—people pay money to see *a band* appear onstage, not the band's *fans.* Front row attendees at a jazz festival are generally not worried about getting kicked in the face because some pumped up concert goer can't control himself and goes flying off the stage and into the audience while Sonny Rollins rips the sax during "St. Thomas." However, diving off stage is, or rather *was,* commonplace at metal shows, with some bands even encouraging it. But these days, most anyone stage diving has to sneak their way onstage with great swiftness, leap off immediately before security gets their hands on them, then try to disappear into the crowd before they get thrown out of the show (and depending on who's doing the throwing, it can be a very unpleasant experience being ejected from a show). While this still happens from time to time, before December 8, 2004 no one really gave it too much thought. After Dime's murder though, the immediate and overwhelming attitude of most bands towards audience members onstage switched to a very firm *fuck that*.

And yes, those of us in metal bands know that the waste of flesh who killed Dimebag was a highly disturbed anomaly. Yes, we know 99.99 percent of fans who manage to get onstage don't mean us any harm, are just excited, and are trying to have a good time. No, we don't think the audience is generally out to get us.

But you never know.

After all, no one, not in Damageplan, their crew, or in our scene in general, would have ever dreamed that a fan would come to a show with murder in his heart and plenty of ammunition in his gun. Something like that just didn't happen at metal shows, in *our community*, especially not to an overly-nice guy as beloved as Dimebag. But the indisputable fact of the matter is that it did happen, Dime is dead, he's never coming back, and none of us in bands want to be the next one to be attacked and maybe die onstage while we're just trying to do our jobs. Dime wasn't a stranger or a news story to me—he was a dude who knew who I was, showed me respect as a musician, not to mention one hell of a good time—and I've heard the awful story of that nightmarish evening directly from the horse's mouth, from the ones who managed to survive it. I've seen the sadness in my friends' eyes as they remember those that died that night, and it's fucking awful to witness their pain. I can't imagine what it must be like to see someone coming onstage with a loaded gun, then opening fire and killing those you love. Personally, that's not what I signed up for when I joined a band—getting shot just wasn't part of the deal, and I like to do everything I can to keep the odds on my side as much as possible when it comes to my survival. That means stay the fuck off the stage if you aren't band, crew, or guests. To anyone who has problems with that policy or refuses to understand why it is in place: please, stay at home and save your money instead of coming to our show. I neither need nor want the price of a ticket from some moron who can't get it through their head that they are not welcome on stage at a lamb of god show, especially in light of not only what happened to Dime, but what happened in Prague in 2010.

Incredibly, during that first tour after I had been released from prison, a few audience members still attempted to take the stage. Considering what I had recently been through, I had no idea how anyone coming to see us at that time could be so self-centered and/or clueless, but a handful still succeeded in making jackasses out of themselves. Those that weren't immediately wrestled off stage and ejected from the venue by our crew or side stage security were caught and thrown out by other club security soon after landing on the dance floor. But for the overwhelmingly greater part, the tour went very well, although it was extremely emotionally exhausting for me. Every single day of the month and a half tour, before and after gigs, our fans would express their support for me, telling me how glad they were I was out of prison, then they would ask if I was going to be called back for trial. I had no answer for them until a month into the tour, when the Czech State Attorney formally indicted me on November 30, 2012, and a beginning trial date of February 4, 2013 was set. I was actually relieved when the news came, because after four months of constantly saying, "I don't know," I finally had some sort of definitive answer to give the endless people who asked me what was going on with my case. Yes, there would be a trial. Yes, I would go back for it. The vast majority of people told me in no uncertain terms that they would not go back if they were in my position, and thought I was crazy for doing so. But my mind had been made up long before I had ever left prison. I appreciated their concern, but it was time to honor my word.

Towards the end of the run, on December 6, the tour was in Houston, Texas. I was sitting on the loading dock behind the venue enjoying the warm Texas afternoon when Vinnie Paul walked over and sat down beside me.

"Hey brother, what's up? I got something to ask you if you got a second," he said in his usual friendly voice.

"Of course man. What's up?"

"In two days it will be December 8, the anniversary of us losing Dime. We'll be in Kansas City that night. Do you think your guys would mind if we went overtime a little during our set so the whole tour can come up and do a shot onstage for him?" he said.

"Dude, *of course* it's cool. Take all the time you need, I don't give a fuck. I know my guys won't either. I'll sort it out, no problem," I said.

"Thanks brother, I really appreciate it," Vinnie said. It was at that point that I decided to finally ask Vinnie for a favor, not in return or as a tit-for-tat sort of thing, but because the time seemed appropriate. I had been thinking about what I had to ask him for quite a long while, since well before the tour started, but it just never seemed like the right time until that moment. Even then I was very uncomfortable asking my friend for what I did, but I was in trouble, a whole lot of trouble, and I needed his help badly.

"Bro, I really hate to ask this of you, but I need you to do me a big favor if you can," I said.

"Of course man, whatever you need. What is it?" Vinnie said. I felt slightly sick to my stomach as I spoke the next words.

"You know I'm going to trial in February. These judges who will be running the trial, they are not going to understand our world at all. They won't know a thing about metal shows, or what goes on at them. They grew up in Communist-era Czechoslovakia, where there was no metal scene. I have to somehow make them understand what a metal show is like, what happens during one, because they are going to be looking at a video of that show that night in 2010, and they are going to think we are nothing but a bunch of violent freaks. I also need them to understand why no one is allowed on stage. Man, I know this won't be easy for you, and I'm asking a lot, but I'm in deep shit and don't know what else to do. If you could, would you write a letter to the court explaining why bands don't allow audience members on stage anymore? You know, after what happened to Dime?" I said.

"Of course, man. Of course I can do that for you. I'll start on it this evening," Vinnie said without a second's hesitation.

I thanked Vinnie for agreeing to help me out, and two nights later in Kansas City, the entire tour, bands and crews, gathered onstage and did a shot for Dime (Hellyeah's crew brought me a shot glass full of water so I wouldn't be left out). And before I returned to the Czech Republic, I had a copy of Vinnie's letter, which was later translated into Czech and read in court during my trial. The man had done me a great favor, and it was one that could not have been easy for him to do—that is one measure of a friend. True friends will help you even when it is not the most pleasant thing for them to do, because they really do care. Vinnie's letter was brutal and to the point, and it still brings tears to my eyes if I read it. In the letter he described how he had witnessed his brother's murder right before his eyes, then went on to explain how that incident had changed things for performers. He wrote of the necessity for increased security at gigs, spoke highly of our friendship and my character, and closed the letter asking the judges to take into consideration what had happened on December 8, 2004 when reviewing the facts of my case. I was extremely grateful to Vinnie for writing that letter, and always will be. (I love ya, Big Vin!)

After the tour was over, I spent the holidays with my family, then began to pack my bags for my trip to the Czech Republic. As soon as I had been indicted, plans had been made for an early return to Prague to prepare for my trial, and the time of that return was fast approaching. A few days before I was due to leave the United States, I felt a great, formless fear that had been welling up inside of me for months finally take shape and burst to the surface of my consciousness. I realized that somewhere amongst my things, I probably had a journal with an entry dated May 24, 2010, the day of our show in Prague. I had felt this fear flitting around the corner of my mind for quite some time now, but it hadn't shown its face yet. Or maybe it had, and I was repressing it, afraid of what I would find when I faced it. I don't know. I do know that I was standing in my backyard when I was possessed with a simultaneously overwhelming and extremely frightening urge to find this journal, for I was certain it existed. I had even detailed how I had done some writing on that day during my interrogation by the Czech police. I knew if I found a written record of what had happened on May 24, 2010, it might jar my memory; and if that memory was one of me intentionally harming the deceased young man, I would have to plead guilty once I arrived in Prague. And even though I was 99 percent certain I hadn't been drinking that day, if I had somehow been mistaken and the entry contained a reference to me being drunk onstage, I would have to plead guilty as well, or at the very least tell the court I had been intoxicated and honestly didn't know what my actions had been. The thought of both of those things occurring scared the shit out of me, but I had no choice. I had sworn to myself I would do the right thing, and I would. I had to take responsibility for my actions, no matter the consequence, even if I didn't remember performing those actions. So I went into my study, found the box I kept all of my old lyric notebooks and journals in, and dug around until I found one with entries from that time period. Sure enough, there were a few paragraphs of writing under the date of our show. I took a deep breath, sat down and read what I had written two and a half years previously.

As I read the journal, I felt both immense relief and deep sadness. The first half of the entry detailed how sick and tired I was of being on the road, of the loud party atmosphere that surrounded it, and (most tellingly) of my own drinking. I had written it early in the day, drinking coffee and sitting in the doorway of the club as it rained, just as I had told the police. The first half of the entry concluded with a note that I was about to head into Old Town Prague with our drummer and merch guy, exactly as I had recalled during my interrogation. Overall, despite my exhaustion from the tour and with myself, the first few paragraphs were fairly upbeat; I was clearheaded, looking forward to going home, and maybe even putting a stop to my increasingly painful drinking. I got the feeling reading it that I knew my boozing days were coming to an end (as indeed they would roughly four months later). But the rest of that day's writing was significantly darker in tone.

I had taken pen to paper again several hours after the show, right before we were about to pull away from Prague and head to Poland. I wrote of how I had just come off stage that evening when I had received the phone call from our publicist Maria informing me that Paul Gray had died. I wrote about how I hadn't even felt like drinking at all that day, until after the show when I got the sad news my friend was gone. I wrote of taking a few shots in his honor a few hours after the show was over, and about how sour they had tasted in my mouth. I wrote about how awful the show had been, how crappy the club was, about how there was no security. I angrily detailed how there had been kids onstage throughout the show, and about how they flatly refused to take the hint that we didn't want them onstage. In very foul language, I wrote about a young blond man who kept on jumping on stage again and again, until I finally put him down on the stage, my hand around his throat. I wrote of how I had watched him fly from the stage a few times during poorly executed stage dives. Finally, I wrote of how glad I was that that terrible, terrible day was finally over. I wrote it all sounding very, very disgusted with the crowd, the show, and life itself. It was not a pleasant journal entry.

Reading the entry, I was relieved that not only had I not been drunk that day, but hadn't had a drink at all until well after the show. Looking over the small, tight, block letter handwriting that spelled out my emotions of sorrow, disgust, and anger at the senseless death of my friend Paul, sadness came again into my heart as I thought for the hundredth time of how I would never get to see him again. But reading the journal did not jar my memory in the slightest. I did not suddenly recall pushing anyone from the stage. The journal had not solved any mysteries for me.

On January 19, 2013, my wife drove me to Washington DC's Dulles airport. I met Jeff Cohen there, and we flew to Frankfurt, Germany, from there catching a connecting flight to Prague. In two and a half weeks, my trial would begin.

It was time to get ready.

chapter eighteen

could write another entire book about the month I spent in Prague preparing for court then going to trial, but it would not be a volume recounting the exhaustive preparations my lawyers and I made, nor would it be a detailed, blow-by-blow record of the actual court proceedings. This sort of writing is beyond both my interest and my grasp, as I am not a fan of courtroom dramas, nor did I understand much of what occurred as it happened—to a degree, I still do not. The process of getting ready for the trial, then the six days I spent in the Prague Municipal Court building were exhausting, boring, frustrating, terrifying, and (for the most part) very, very confusing. In fact, if I had to use just one word to encapsulate the entire experience of my legal ordeal, it would be just that: *confusing*. It was like watching a very scary movie being made about my life, except that the scriptwriter had penned all the expository dialogue necessary for plot comprehension in the incomprehensible Czech tongue. Listening to judges, witnesses, and attorneys speak in the courtroom, every single English word I heard was layered over a simultaneous and rapidly moving foundation of Czech, since all of my information was first filtered through a translator's brain. Over and over I would interrupt the translator to ask, "Wait, what did he just say?" following an unsatisfactory explanation of some potentially crucial statement made. Meanwhile, as the translator re-explained things to me, the judge or witness or attorney had already moved on to the next topic. Things got lost in the mix all the time. It was immensely difficult to follow along without constantly asking for clarification from my translator, and I was only able to catch the general gist of the trial proceedings as they occurred—at the end of each day, my Czech attorneys would explain to me what in the hell had just happened in there. In order to write a legal thriller based on my trial, I would need a complete transcript of the entire thing translated into English, hundreds of pages long. I do not have one of those, so that sort of book is off the table (thank God). But I could easily fill pages and pages with my perception of Prague itself, formed as I researched its history and learned my way around during hours of solo wanderings through the city's labyrinthine heart. The time I spent wandering the city's snow covered streets, alleyways, riverbank, and innumerable squares was pure magic. I fell completely in love with the city; for it is, indeed, a magical place.

Exiting the plane after Jeff and I had landed in the Czech Republic, I looked to the end of the creepily familiar glass-walled jetway, half-expecting to see a phalanx of machine gun–toting masked men waiting for me. Thankfully my arrival into the country seemed to have gone unnoticed by the authorities this time, and we gathered our luggage from the baggage pick-up area without incident, then hopped into a pre-arranged sedan driven by a pleasant faced Czech man who spoke passable English. Leaving the airport, I noticed that everything was covered in a blanket of fresh snow, and as we made our way towards Prague proper I saw heavily bundled people on cross country skis zipping along through the fields that ran beside the highway. Winter was in full effect in the Czech Republic, and it wore a much different face than the relatively mild months of cold I spent as a native of the Virginia and North Carolina lowlands. Stepping out of the car to pick up our apartment keys from a rental agency situated on the Vltava River just outside Old Town, I could see my breath thick as pipe smoke in the air, and I was glad that I had dressed for the frigid climate accordingly. I was well insulated in a scarf, long underwear, Adidas tactical boots, ski gloves, a woolen knit cap festooned with penguins from Phillip Island, Australia, and a heavy German army parka I had acquired in Berlin on one particularly frigid tour. Except for the gray penguin cap, everything I had on was black. Not that this was out of the ordinary for me, but I always felt less conspicuous in black, better able to fade into the shadows. This was a feeling I highly desired at the time—I wished to remain unnoticed by both authorities and press until the trial started. Then I would have no choice in the matter.

After collecting the apartment keys, we jumped back into the car, and riding through the impossibly narrow streets towards the center of the city, the magic atmosphere that hangs over Prague began to take hold.

"Jesus Christ, this is crazy. Look at this place—I feel like we're in a James Bond movie or something," Jeff said as we made our way down the winding, high-walled cobblestone streets. Looking around at the famous city so vastly different than my own, I had to agree. The roadways were clogged with local pedestrians hurrying to reach their destinations, as well as large numbers of slow-moving tourists. The locals seemed to sense our vehicle approaching from behind, seamlessly stepping out of the way without breaking stride; the tourists often required a honk of the very European-sounding car horn. They stood awkwardly in the middle of the street as tourists do in every destination city across the globe, consulting guidebook maps wet with snow, and gawking at various pieces of the ubiquitous historical architecture that make up the body of Prague. Prague is a year-round tourist destination, for her grandeur is protean and not diminished with the passing of any one season. Like a classically beautiful woman, picking her outfit from an immaculately appointed wardrobe according to the weather, Prague wears the seasons equally well. Recognizing a few landmarks from my one walk through the city a few years previously, I could clearly remember how lovely the town had been in the early summer, and it was just as breathtaking in the middle of winter. It is a testament to Prague's magnificence that even though my reason for being in the city was one of the worst possible, and despite the constant bone-chilling cold and slate gray skies (I remember seeing the sun come out a total of three times), I never once tired of walking her streets during my entire month-long return. During that time, I came to realize a person could easily spend a few lifetimes within the city limits and still not learn all her secrets. Prague has served as muse to countless artists, musicians, and writers over the centuries, and I would heed her gothic call, attempting to capture some of her mystery through the lens of my camera on my nightly sojourns through her frost coated byways.

The claustrophobic streets of one of the great capitals of Europe surrounding us were not the only thing that made Jeff's Bond movie comment ring true. The last time I had ridden through the streets of Prague, I had been on the way to the airport, fleeing the country before the prosecuting attorney discovered my release and had me thrown back in prison. Now I was back, once again attempting to move through the city unnoticed, and the furtive nature of my return gave the whole trip an air of espionage. I felt like a hunted man on a dangerous mission, one with a high probability of a disastrous outcome—and of course, when I thought about the nature of our trip and the stakes at hand, I was. I wanted to remain invisible, lost in the city's million or so souls, but soon people would, in fact, be hunting me—not long after we arrived in Prague, Martin would inform me that people from the newspapers had started to call him after hearing rumors that I had been sighted on the city's streets. He told the press that I would not be in the Czech Republic until my trial began, but it is the business of reporters to dig and to snoop; and if they are any good at their jobs they remain skeptical and open-eyed at all times. I did my best to maintain a low profile as I went about town, but every second I spent outside during the daylight hours held anxiety for me. The last thing I needed were reporters yelling questions in broken English as they followed me to my apartment, taking photos of where I lived, and generally drawing attention to my whereabouts. I didn't think the prosecutor would have me jailed again now that I had returned for trial, but I couldn't be certain. Plus, the added stress of paparazzi during a time when I needed to remain absolutely focused was something I hoped to avoid altogether. Better to be safe than sorry, so when I walked around the city in the daytime, I kept my scarf wrapped around my face and my cap pulled down low—luckily, even during the warmest part of the day, the weather warranted both most of the time.

I did most of my wanderings at night though, when the streets were less crowded, and the few people walking them would be more inclined to steer clear of a grim-looking six-foot-tall man dressed in black. Many people are afraid of the streets at night. I am not; I actually feel safer in the city after dark, able to maneuver easier without the crowds (and disappear quickly if need be). Plus, I do not look or move like a rich and clueless tourist wandering lost somewhere he shouldn't be at night—I look and move like the guy the tourist should be worried about running into, so people generally avoid me at night. This made for some very peaceful walks, which greatly helped to clear my head after a long and confusing day of going over the myriad aspects of my case. In most any city, what often looks banal under the light of the sun takes on a dark majesty at night, but in Prague, this effect is amplified a thousandfold. It's like the city's architects had drawn their plans with intent to maximize the city's otherworldly nocturnal ambience. Prague would make the perfect setting for a vampire novel, and there are many legends of them in the Czech Republic; even a few medieval-era "vampire cemeteries" have been discovered, filled with corpses dismembered and weighted with stones to prevent the (unlucky) suspected vampires from rising from their graves. Although I didn't happen upon any undead in my travels, the spooky atmosphere of the city at night heightened the enjoyment of my walks, and I treasured the solitude these journeys provided. No one recognized me in the night, even after my trial had begun, and I was relaxed most of the time as I strolled the dark streets.

However, I was recognized within my first hour of being in the Czech Republic, instantly setting the tone for all my daytime paranoia that was to follow. As we pulled to the end of a narrow side street named Karlova, two blocks west of Old Town Square, our driver announced that we had arrived. As we removed our bags from the car, he turned to me and said, "You are Randy, yes? I wish you good luck with the court." This immediately freaked me out, but I thanked him as Jeff slipped him a very healthy tip in the hopes of ensuring our anonymity in the city. The man seemed sincere, and I was touched by his kind words despite the case of the jitters they gave me. Although I was pretty wound up over getting recognized so quickly, I soon calmed down for the most part—I should have guessed I couldn't expect to get away with going totally unnoticed in a country where my face was on the front pages of newspapers throughout the land just a few months prior. Still, the encounter had put me firmly on edge, as I had no idea of what public opinion was concerning my case. I could only hope that the people would pay attention to the fact that I had returned and was a man of my word, not whatever drivel *Blesk* would print once they discovered I was in the Czech Republic.

It is an odd and horrible feeling to be a well-known foreigner living in a country as you await trial, charged with causing the death of one of its citizens. For the most part, the general population only knows of you in one capacity—as the accused killer of a native son. You are an unfinished news story, and a very unpleasant one at that. A simple trip to the grocery store or coffee shop is riddled with unease and paranoia. Every person that looks your way in the check-out line, however innocuous their glance may be, feels like judge and juror. The court of public opinion has no physical seat, and the only way to avoid feeling the sting of its judgment is to remain out of view. I suppose I could have remained secluded in our apartment the entire time until my trial began, but it is not in my nature to submit to agoraphobic fear and hide from the world, so I came and went as I pleased. I did not have a single problem with any Czech citizen, even the few that did recognize me when my scarf happened to be pulled down from my face, but it was a constant test of my nerves every time I left the apartment. As in prison, I did not know who would have already decided I was a guilty man, take exception to my presence, and decide to express their displeasure, in a physical manner or otherwise. I wouldn't hide, but I was prepared for anything to happen every time I went out in public. It was a long and heavy month.

Our apartment was a modest two-bedroom affair, five stories up on the top floor of a building that was in all likelihood older than our home nation. It had two bathrooms (convenient during the trial, when both Jeff and I needed to shower and shave before walking to court), as well as an open floor plan with a kitchenette–dining room and living room area. Jeff is an excellent cook, and most nights he would make us a delicious dinner from the strangely labeled items we purchased from a nearby grocery store. Our first trip to the grocery store was fairly comedic; a whole lot of "What in the hell is this?" type of shopping. But we managed to get the essentials, and ate many good meals thanks to Jeff's efforts in the kitchen.

The next day we took a taxi across town to begin preparing for trial at the offices of Tomas Grivna, a young and extraordinarily bright professor of law at Prague's Charles University. We had retained Tomas to be the main mouthpiece of our legal team in court in addition to Martin Radvan, Vladimír Jablonsky, and Tomas Morysek, as well as Michal Sykora, a young lawyer employed by Grivna's firm. Including Jeff Cohen, this meant there was a total of six lawyers working on my case, all with six different brains and six different ways of looking at things. Jeff was not a criminal lawyer, nor a member of the Czech bar association, and as such was excluded from "officially" representing me during trial. But he was a long-term employee of my band, was intimately familiar with us and our business, and had in-depth knowledge of the nature of the unique music scene we were a part of. Because of this, the court had decided he would be allowed to sit with my legal team during the trial, acting as a sort of liaison between myself and my Czech lawyers, as well as an advisor to my team concerning any technical matters on the music business end of things. Jeff would also play a very large part of the pre-trial preparations that began that day, and was with me every moment of every day as I talked to one or all five of my Czech lawyers. Six lawyers . . . I do not mind pointing out that this was a very, very expensive undertaking, and once again, I am filled with gratitude towards all who helped in any way to defray my legal costs. I truly do not have any idea of what a person lacking the huge support network available to me would have done had they been placed in my circumstances.

Including my own, there had been a total of thirty people's testimonies given to the police at various times after an investigation had begun into the events of May 24, 2010. These included concert attendees, club managers, security staff, promoters, and members of my band and crew. The earliest of these testimonies were given on October 6, 2010, well over four months after our show in Prague. Some witnesses had been interviewed more than once, and these interviews were spaced out by months, or even over a year apart. Each one of these testimonies would have to be individually reviewed, scrutinized for discrepancies, and viewed in relation to all of the others. It was a massive undertaking, and for Jeff and me, made all the more difficult as we were reading translations of the majority of the witness statements. Our translator, Rudy Leška, had done a fantastic job of rendering the Czech testimonies into concise, comprehensible English, but there are many nuances involved in word choice and colloquial meaning that simply get lost when something said is restated in a different language, no matter how skilled the translator. Countless times Jeff or I would make note of a specific word or phrase, then ask my Czech attorneys for clarification of its meaning, only to find it conveyed a slightly different yet very significant implication from what a native English speaker would have meant using the same terms. In reviewing all these testimonies, no detail was too minute to analyze. It gives me a headache just remembering the hours and hours I spent reading the widely varying versions given by witnesses of the events, looking for differences (not to mention trying to pronounce, remember, and keep straight all the odd-sounding foreign names). Luckily, Jeff would shoulder a great amount of the work involved in wrestling this massive pile of information into a manageable form, collecting all the available data that was pertinent to my defense into an easily reviewable spreadsheet. Aside from reading the testimonies, my job was to prepare my opening statement.

Unlike America, in a Czech criminal court, the defendant opens up the proceedings after the charges have been read, relaying his version of the events that have brought him to court, then offering an argument in support of his innocence. Then the judges (there are three, one "professional judge" and two "lay judges", who are similar in capacity to jurors in the States) ask the defendant questions, followed by the prosecuting attorney asking the defendant questions, then finally the defense attorney asks questions of his client. After the defendant is done, any witnesses relevant to the proceedings are brought in, and the process begins again. Also unlike America, the witnesses may be cross-examined by the defendant after all the judges and attorneys have asked their questions. The defendant may refute what the witnesses have said, or even just flat out call them a liar. I asked Grivna how long my opening statement should be, and he told me forty-five minutes to an hour. *An hour?* I didn't think I had an hour's worth of things to say, but I began writing out my statement, restating what I remembered of the events of May 24, 2010 exactly as I had during my interrogation by the police.

For the next two and a half weeks, everyday was much the same—we woke up early and made our way to Tomas Grivna's or Martin Radvan's offices. Once there, I read and reread testimonies, asked my lawyers questions, answered questions from my lawyers, and worked on my opening statement while my legal team built my defense. Jeff and my Czech attorneys tore into the available evidence—the thirty widely varying testimonies, a crappy cell phone video of half our show that didn't contain any footage whatsoever of the incident that had resulted in me being incarcerated (much less any footage of the deceased young man), and some police photos of the crime scene, i.e., the stage area of the club. The photos had been taken *months* after the night in question—the club no longer even existed as a business, the stage shown was a mobile one of adjustable height, and there was no guarantee that the stage configuration and shoddy barricade depicted in the photos had been the same the night in question, or for that matter that there had even been a barricade present at all. Some of the testimonies were worrisome to me, but as hard physical evidence, I found the video and photos laughable—they would be presented in court by the prosecuting attorney, to what effect I am still unsure of to this day. Jeff and my Czech attorneys spent hours and hours dissecting all of the evidence, arguing fine points amongst themselves and asking me questions from time to time. I read and wrote and read and wrote and read and wrote until it was time to call it quits for the day, and I could go for a walk to clear my head.

The days were draining, but the early mornings, late afternoons, and nights I spent walking through Prague were rejuvenating. All around me a great throng of humanity pulsed through one of the most beautiful urban settings I had ever seen, for I was quartered in the hallowed *Staré Mesto* district; Old Town Prague. I am a great lover of history, and since the ninth century on the very same cobblestone streets beneath my feet, the Czech people had erected homes, businesses, and government buildings, fought battles, created works of art, suffered under the yoke of different conquerors, raised families, and gone about the business of life in an unbroken stream from medieval times until the present. For over a thousand years life had been *happening* in *Staré Mesto*, and as in any place inhabited for such a lengthy time, a specific culture had developed within it. All foreign culture holds great interest for me, and there was an inexhaustible trove of it to be learned about in my immediate vicinity. I spent every spare second I had wandering *Staré Mesto* and neighborhoods far beyond, taking in the sights and shooting photographs.

And all the wandering and photographing I did served me well, in more ways than one. On one hand it had certainly occupied my free time, the time when I wasn't in my lawyer's offices, the time I would have probably spent consumed in worry over a fate that was currently beyond my control. But also, without consciously seeking it out, my activities had brought me some empathy and respect for the people of the Czech Republic, a people that (had I succumbed to the paranoia and xenophobia that was always trying to burst free and completely dominate my mind) I could have viewed *en masse* as my enemy. I was in a strange country. I could not speak the language. I did not know what opinion that country's people held of me, other than that of its press (which had made me out to be a monster) and that of an ill-mannered representative of that country's legal system (who I knew was about to do his best to put me back in prison). I could have cursed the whole Czech Republic and its dreadful 123-year-old prison and its archaic legal system and its loutish prosecuting attorney and its goddamned freezing cold climate. *Fuck 'em. Fuck 'em all*, right?

Wrong. Very wrong. To have developed that attitude would have been to give into the knee-jerk reactionist mentality that has kept humans at war with each other since the dawn of civilization. This is a small, weak-minded, and fear driven manner of thinking and living life. I have never wanted to have anything but a broad mind and a life free of fear, for therein lies the path to growth. The people of the Czech Republic were no more my enemy than I was theirs, despite what their press had made me out to be (in general, I do not trust the press, period), despite their awful prison (no prison is a nice place to be), despite their strange legal system (I have never heard of a perfect one), and despite their rude prosecuting attorney (I'm sure they exist everywhere). The press and the prison and the legal system and, yes, even the prosecuting attorney, were not the people of the Czech Republic. I saw the people of the Czech Republic every day as I walked through Prague, exploring and shooting photos and filming. Not a single soul mistreated me, and I saw that they were just like people anywhere else. I saw that they were just like people back home.

————

One evening after the trial was underway, I decided to go for a stroll in Wenceslas Square. As I headed towards a coffee shop, I saw an elderly man notice me walking his way. As I got closer and closer, the man continued to stare at me. I walked past him, then turned around after I heard him call my name in a heavy Czech accent.

"Randy. It is good you have come back," he said, then gave me a short nod before turning and walking away into the cold night.

The old man had wanted me to know that he respected me for proving I was a man of my word.

That was the only time anyone said anything about my case to me on the streets of Prague.

————

After my trial had begun, I tried not to read too much of the endless discussion about my case on the Internet, because when I did I would become irate at the comments made by some fans of my band. "Fuck the Czech Republic!" I read more than once. This sort of uneducated commentary, while made with good intent, was just as simple-minded as "Fuck Randy, I hope he goes to prison!" My situation was a complex one, a tragic matter that I had to get to the bottom of for myself—I wanted to know what had happened just as much as anyone else involved. Reading the words of well-meaning fans who cursed the entire country I was in was not helping matters, so one day after court I posted a photo to address the issue. In the photograph, taken in front of the astrological clock in Old Town Square, is a small girl, perhaps two or three years old. The child has her tiny hand outstretched, trying to reach out and touch a giant soap bubble hanging in the air above her head. Her mother stands opposite, watching her baby daughter trying to touch the transparent sphere. Underneath the photo I wrote:

I have heard of some people talking smack about the Czech Republic, saying "Fuck the Czech Republic," etc. This is not how it should be. This is a very sad case, not something to rage at people you do not know over. I am not angry with the Czechs at all. A fan of my band is dead—what do I have to be angry about? I am an innocent man, but I am also a very sad man right now. To not be sad in this instance would be inhuman. But mad at the Czech people? Why would I be mad at them? Here, look at this picture—a mother watches her baby. The child reaches out for something new, laughing and chasing a pretty picture in the air. It is the same here as everywhere else. Do you see? Life is beautiful. I hope to see y'all soon.

As is often the case with my creative endeavors, it wasn't until after I had taken the photo that its meaning was made apparent. Only after I had a bit of time to look at it, analyze it, and finally explain it in writing did I figure out why I had been compelled to create the image in the first place, and what the picture was really *about* in the context of my life. Looking at the photo and what I wrote, I realized that that was what all the walking and exploring and photography had been about: I was trying to *understand* my life as it was, to make some sense of the grim situation I had found myself in. The only way to do that without turning into an overwhelming knot of despair, anger, and nihilistic fear (none of which would have helped me in the least) was to try to find and appreciate the beauty around me during those dark days. This is what creating art in any of its forms does for me.

It helps me to understand my life; right here, right now.

A few days before the trial was scheduled to begin, I pre-sented my opening statement to my legal team. My Czech lawyers seemed to be pleased with what I had written, but advised me to be less emotional in my delivery, as it might make the judges uncomfortable. Less emotional? I am a very expressive person, and I was dealing with very emotional stuff, but I had already done my best to speak in an even, restrained tone—I knew from experience that the Czechs were by nature a reserved breed, not given to public outbursts of passion or excitable speech (the average Czech would have a rough go of it living in Italy, I believe). I didn't think I had been overly-emotional during my presentation in the slightest, but my lawyers thought otherwise, so I tried again, remembering that the word *robot* had originated in the very city I sat in. My lawyers told me I had done better, but said I still might want to tone it down some. *Tone it down? If I show any less emotion, they're gonna think I'm fucking dead*, I thought, but I just sighed and said I would give it my best shot in court. Then, in order to give me practice, my Czech lawyers began asking me questions, just as the judges would. *Explain what a typical lamb of god concert is like. Explain what "stage diving" means. Do you remember ever seeing the deceased? Why do you not wear glasses when you are on stage? What could you see from the stage? Explain what "moshing" means. Did you drink any alcohol or take any drugs before the concert? Who is usually responsible for removing stage divers from the stage?*

On and on they asked me questions, all fairly straight forward, all of which I answered truthfully and with as little emotion as possible. It wasn't the nerve-wracking experience I had expected, and I remember thinking I had done pretty well. Then, everything changed as Jeff took on the role of the prosecuting attorney.

Jeff Cohen has worked for my band longer than any other person we have employed. He is a good man, with a great sense of humor, and I consider him a close friend. I had never once thought of him as a scary or intimidating person. Jeff is a really nice guy.

But he scared the shit out of me that day.

Jeff is an entertainment lawyer. He deals with band contracts, record labels, publishing companies. He's great with all that convoluted music biz crap—the stuff that requires an in-depth knowledge of a massive and arcane legal lexicon, the stuff that makes me want to tear my hair out anytime I get within fifty feet or so of a record label letterheaded document that requires my signature. I would recommend him without hesitation to any band on the planet in need of an entertainment lawyer. I believe he chose wisely when he picked his particular area of law, because he loves it, and he excels at his chosen profession.

But he would have made one cold-blooded killer of a prosecuting attorney.

As he began peppering me with questions about the show that took place May 24, 2010, Jeff abruptly turned into a different person; a person I did not know and hoped to never to meet again. His normally kind face changed, taking on an arrogant, aggressive, and merciless expression. He hit me hard and he hit me fast, twisting the words in my answers around against me until I began to feel *guilty*. He would ask the same question phrased in a slightly different manner, playing with my emotions. I felt like a mouse being toyed with by a very, very smart cat. I was literally shaking by the time he was done, trying not to stutter as I began to question myself, my answers, and my memories under the brunt of his verbal assault. This is what a good prosecuting attorney does.

Then it was over, and Jeff returned to being the Jeff I knew and loved just as abruptly as he had sprouted fangs and bat wings, transforming into the Dracula of prosecuting attorneys. *Jesus Christ, that sucked,* I thought as he told me I had done a good job, *I hope I don't have to do that again.* But the process would be repeated a few times, up until the very last day before trial. By that time I was calm and confident in my answers, no matter what Jeff threw at me. I didn't know what would happen to me, but I felt I had done my best to prepare. The rest was in the judge's hands.

All I could do was tell the truth.

chapter nineteen

I woke up before sunrise on February 4, 2013. As the sky outside our apartment turned from black to a dim gray, I meditated on the floor of the darkened living room. Then I prayed, asking God to give me the strength to carry myself with dignity, no matter what the day brought. Then I showered, shaved, and got dressed. I felt calm as Jeff and I walked to court.

The Prague Municipal Court was a massive yellow four-story building. Built in 1883 in the Neo-Renaissance style, the building took up most of a city block. There was already a line outside, and as we walked up I saw people notice me and begin talking amongst themselves. I saw two cameramen unpacking their gear, preparing to send it through the x-ray machine before they walked through the metal detector just inside the entrance of the building. Jeff and I got in line, went through the screening process, and watched the camera men race to get their gear turned on and in place. As we retrieved our bags from the x-ray machine and began walking up the stairs that led to the second floor court room, the cameramen walked backwards in front of me, shining lights in my face and filming us. Upstairs there were many, many more cameras, and they all immediately turned my way as Jeff and I walked into the waiting room area and over to the rest of my waiting legal team. The reporters and cameramen rushed over to us, shouting questions, but one of my lawyers spoke to them in Czech, telling them that we would have no comments until a final verdict was delivered. They stopped asking questions, but the cameramen remained, filming and shining their lights on us. This would be their standard operating procedure every day that I appeared in court. I was used to having my picture taken, but as the bailiff announced that it was time to enter the courtroom, the cameramen crowded into the narrow hallway that led to the large wooden door of courtroom 101 so tightly that their lenses and lights were inches from my face. It was a tight squeeze, and as some of the cameramen bumped into me, jostling to get a shot, I began to understand why some celebrities flip out and assault paparazzi—it's an incredibly invasive feeling to have twenty or so people shoving cameras in your face all at the same time. I've chastised fans before for filming me without asking; it's inexcusably rude and pushy and it makes you feel like a monkey in a zoo. Just because I am in a band does not make me a monkey in a zoo—I am a human being—and I have absolutely no qualms about sternly reminding people of that fact. God forbid I ever become famous enough to have to deal with paparazzi exercising their legal right to shove cameras in my face on a regular basis as I go about my day-to-day business—I'll be in court a lot more, and my bank account will be a lot thinner on account of all the shattered cameras I'll be paying for after I exercise my right as a human being to maintain my privacy and break their shit.

But at that moment I couldn't afford to break any of these obnoxious cameramen's equipment, neither in the financial sense nor in the damage it would do to my already shaky public image. So I calmly ran the video gauntlet, holding my temper as several of them stepped on my toes and one klutz bumped the side of my head with his lens. I walked into the high-ceilinged courtroom and took my place on the right side of the room with my attorneys, sitting in a row behind a long, low solid-fronted wooden table. On the opposite side of the courtroom sat the prosecuting attorney, beside him a neatly dressed man in his early forties, Daniel's uncle, the family's representative in court. The rear part of the courtroom was a gallery for any who wished to witness the trial, and on that first day it rapidly filled to capacity (trials are open to the public in the Czech Republic, and seating is on a first come, first served basis). At the front of the room was the tall judge's bench. The presiding judge, a round-faced bespectacled man in his late forties, sat in the center, and on either side of him were the lay judges. To his right sat an elegant looking woman who appeared to be in her early sixties, to his left a solid looking goateed man in his forties. Placed on the floor in the center of the room, fifteen feet from the front of the judge's bench, was a slender metal stand where anyone called to testify would stand. The proceedings began with the judge reading in Czech the charge laid against me—the entire trial, according to law, was conducted in the Czech language, whether or not any of the parties involved could speak English (several could). Everything I said would be translated into Czech, and anything anyone else said would be translated into English for me, with varying levels of accuracy. For the majority of my trial, my translator would be my tiny friend from my visit with the shrinks in the city jail. But on this very important first day (the day I had to do the most talking, the day I opened up the whole thing with my version of what had happened, the day I needed my words to be heard as clearly as possible), my Czech mouthpiece was a slender red headed woman, whom immediately before court I was told by one of my lawyers "isn't the best translator." *Great.*

After the judge had read the charges, the prosecuting attorney stood up and said a few things, (from what I could tell from the halting translation provided) confirming to the judge that he was the one who had filed the charges against me or something along those lines. Taller than me, heavyset, and bearded, Vladimir Muzik, to employ a cliché, was a bear of a man. There's really no other accurate way to describe him: the dude looked like a bear.

A great-big-bearded-black-robe-wearing-hung-over bear.

This contrasted greatly with the mental image of Muzik I had formed during the weeks leading up to trial. In my mind's eye, I had seen a slick, well-groomed, muscular, ex-KGB-agent-sort-of-dude with penetrating icy gray eyes who would lean forward as he questioned me in his thickly Russian-accented English, using every Cold War mind control weapon in his arsenal to trick me into saying something that would incriminate myself, possibly allowing him to raise a new charge even more severe than the one already laid against me. I knew Muzik had been a former police interrogator, so I didn't feel totally foolish in expecting someone who resembled my worst Iron Curtain cop fantasies, but the dude (to be perfectly frank) looked sloppy. His face was red and puffy, there were bags under his eyes, and he looked slightly queasy as he rose to speak. Unless Muzik was currently suffering from a terrible combination of the flu and a week's worth of insomnia, he likely had a hangover that morning. *Damn*, I thought, *that guy needs to eat something greasy and have a cup of coffee.*

After Muzik was done speaking, I was called to the center of the courtroom, and I gave my opening statement.

"*Doubry den*," I began, using the Czech phrase for good day, "My name is David Randall Blythe, known to most around the world as Randy. I sing for the international touring heavy metal band, lamb of god. I have returned to the Czech Republic to defend myself against the charge laid against me, that of manslaughter involving the death of a fan, one Mr. Daniel _, just as I vowed I would numerous times, publicly and to the press, both here, in my home country, and abroad . . . "

I went on to repeat what I had told the police during my first interrogation, recounting what I could recall of our show in 2010, placing emphasis on the fact that the stage had been small and crowded and that from the beginning of the show, audience members had taken the stage with ease, as there appeared to be no barricade or interference from security. I explained that this had been an unacceptable situation, and strictly against lamb of god's long standing policy, a policy written into the requisite signed contact we had with every single promoter of every single show we played, including the one we performed that evening at Club Abaton. I listed the reasons for this policy: 1) first and foremost, to ensure the safety of myself, my band, and our road crew. Someone could run into us, knocking us into a guitar headstock or cymbal stand, which could easily puncture an eyeball or knock out teeth. Or they could knock us from the stage, as has almost happened to me on more than one occasion. Or they could knock over any of the heavy equipment on stage, pushing it onto one of us or one of our techs standing behind our back line causing bodily injury (as happened in 2007 to our drum tech Mikey B when a PA stack fell on him, smashing his collar bone and ankle—he was lucky he wasn't crushed), or even death. In short, the stage can be a dangerous place for band members, especially when someone who doesn't belong goes running across it at top speed while we are concentrating on doing our jobs; 2) to ensure the safety of our fans, as any of the above things could happen to a fan on the stage just as easily as it could one of us, in fact easier because we as a band are used to the placement of our equipment—there are plenty of things to trip over on stage. Historically, we have had a great relationship with our fans, and do not wish to see them hurt, even if it is of their own doing. And we certainly don't wish to be held liable for the results of poor choices made by others; 3) for the protection of our equipment. It's very expensive, it's set up specifically for each individual player, and it can be pretty hard to replace on tour, especially when we are overseas. We are professionals, we don't play on cheap gear, and we don't want our stuff getting broken; 4) our audience doesn't pay their hard earned money to see a bunch of strangers jumping around on-stage, interrupting our ability to do our jobs, then leaping into the audience and landing on their heads. They pay money to see lamb of god. Plus, once again, if we allowed strangers on the stage, we could be held legally liable to any damage they may do to audience members in the crowd below. No way, Jose. And finally, 5) I explained what had happened to Dimebag, and how that had resulted in tightened security across the board in our scene. Like it or not, things changed after he was killed. No one belongs on our stage but us and our crew, period. Anyone else, I view as a potential threat.

Then I went on to explain my various encounters with the young blond-headed man who repeatedly took the stage, a young man we now knew to be named Milan. I went into detail about everything I remembered about subduing this young man, exactly as I had during my police interrogation. I stressed the fact that I did not punch, kick, or strangle the young man, despite what some witnesses had reported. I told the judges that I merely knelt on top of him, screaming in his face that he should not be on stage. This was entirely true, for I neither struck him in any manner nor choked him in the slightest. I told the judges what had happened that evening between Milan and me to the best of my memory, as any memories I had of any sort of physical altercation with anyone all involved him and him alone, and what I said was the truth.

But I did not say some other things; things I wanted to say in order to make crystal clear the point that I never attempted to intentionally hurt Milan, or anyone else that night (which was, of course, the very nature of the crime I had been charged with). I did not say that I had experienced violence on more than one occasion in my life, and that if I had wanted to hurt the young man, I would have and very easily could have. I did not say that if I had wanted to hurt him, or anyone else for that matter, I wouldn't roll around on the floor scolding them like a mother dog does a naughty puppy, nor would I push them (from the stage, or anywhere else). I did not say that I am not a tough guy, that I detest violence, and try to avoid it, but that I do not get into shoving matches like a fifth grade schoolboy. I did not say that when I am driven to the point where I feel that hurting someone is the only valid solution to a dangerous situation, I punch them in the face as hard as I can, as fast as I can, and as many times as I can. I did not say that I was, in fact, a model of restraint that evening, since I refrained from loosening a few of the teeth in Milan's blond head as I very easily could have, even though he repeatedly endangered myself, my band, and himself, interrupting our ability to do our job and steadfastly refusing to take the less than subtle hint that he was not welcome on stage. I did not say that in my opinion (an opinion very firmly rooted in brutal, reality-based experience, not hypothetical situations), that I felt had I been a bit more brutal with the young man, then maybe none of this would have happened in the first place, as people tend to strenuously avoid getting anywhere near someone they feel might haul off and punch them in the face for encroaching on their space. I did not say that I had made a critical error in judgment by allowing Milan to drunkenly flail all over the stage without meting out some slightly painful repercussions, since in my hard-earned personal experience, such repercussions are the only thing pointed enough to penetrate into an alcohol-soaked brain, providing a little clarity.

I did not say any of these things, even though I wanted to, and they were just as true as the things I did say. I *couldn't* say them, even though they made perfect sense when viewed in the context of my job and the situation presented to me on that horrible evening in 2010. I couldn't say them because then I would have sounded like a man prone to employ violent solutions to any problems that my job may present, a job so vastly different in circumstance and nature that it is beyond the comprehension of someone employed to sit on their ass behind a wooden desk. I could not expect the judge to understand my job in the slightest, or feel any real empathy for my situation—after all, drunken lunatics who happen to be rabid fans of a judge's verdicts very rarely repeatedly come hauling ass across a court room and scramble onto his bench. The judge probably had never felt the impact of a juiced up judicial junkie smashing at full speed into his honor as he's looking the other way while trying to concentrate on questioning a witness. The judge had never witnessed a completely plastered law-lover stomp all over his carefully prepared pile of evidence, then leap wildly into the air, landing on the prosecuting attorney with a boot to the head. And even if this sort of wildly unlikely scenario were to ever occur in his honor's courtroom, in all probability the bailiffs (who were, after all, employed for the sole purpose of maintaining order in the court) would immediately remove the litigation loving lush from the premises. Or at the very least they would sternly send him back to the public seating gallery, and keep their eyes on him from thereon out, just to sure he didn't run amuck on top of the bench again, kicking over the judge's law books and smashing his expensive teak gavel. Yes, surely the bailiffs wouldn't just stand there watching with their thumbs up their butts, leaving the judge with his ass hanging out in the wind until he finally had to handle the problem himself, since the people getting paid to handle such situations didn't seem inclined in the slightest to do their jobs. The judge would simply never understand what my job was like, since it was unlikely he would ever imagine a scenario in which he showed up to the courtroom and was doing his thing, judging it up and all that, while simultaneously having to try to rid himself of a dangerous, repetitive, and highly intoxicated kinetic interruption—how could he? He was a judge raised during the highly repressive Communist-era of Czechoslovakia, not a professional wrestler. There was no way he was going be able to effectively place himself in my shoes and realize that I had actually displayed great restraint under extremely trying circumstances, so I just said, "I never tried to hurt Milan in any way, nor anyone else," which was the truth.

Then I described the rest of that day, just as I had in my interrogation, and finished my opening statement by expressing what a shock this whole thing had been to me when I was arrested at the airport. I expressed my dismay and utter disbelief that in this era of lightning-fast electronic communication, for two years not one single person could be bothered to get in touch with me or my band to let us know that someone had been injured, much less died. I expressed the fact that the death of a fan was tragic to me and my band members under any circumstances; but for me to be implicated in that death was mentally and emotionally devastating. I expressed my sincere desire to do the right and honorable thing, saying that I did not wish to avoid any responsibility that I may have had in the matter, hence my presence in the courtroom that day. I expressed my sympathy for the friends and family of the deceased, but maintained that I was an innocent man who never attempted to harm anyone, and as such did not wish to suffer the consequences for a malicious act that I simply did not commit.

This whole process took perhaps an hour, as my translator was rather slow. I could only hope that she was able to convey my statement with some modicum of clarity. During this hour, something about the prosecuting attorney kept bugging me, causing me to pause in speaking from time to time. Something about his posture just didn't seem right to me. I kept my gaze firmly in front of me, looking the judges directly in their eyes, but in my peripheral vision, it almost looked like . . . *No, he couldn't be. No fucking way*, I thought, and concentrated on the job at hand. But as I finished my statement and the judge began to ask me a series of questions, I stole a quick glance over to my left, and my suspicions were confirmed. *Unreal*, I thought, *Un-fucking-real*.

Vladimir Muzik, the prosecuting attorney, the man who had done his best to keep me in prison despite my paying bail twice, the man who wanted me returned to prison for five to ten years, the man responsible for attempting to prove my guilt as pertaining to this very serious matter in this court of law . . . was asleep.

Fast asleep.

Mr. Muzik's blatant courtroom napping during my testimony confirmed two things for me: 1) He was almost certainly hungover, and needed to sleep it off, and 2) He was not concerned in the least with anything I or anyone else had to say during this trial, as he was there to obtain a guilty verdict, and nothing less. He probably didn't actually *care* if I was guilty or not, he just wanted a win. Might as well take a nap, eh?

Muzik would fall asleep on several other occasions during the trial, on an almost daily basis. This infuriated me to no end—I was insulted, not only for myself, but for Daniel's family, some of whom were present in the courtroom. This man was supposedly there to obtain justice for a *lethal crime* committed against a member of their family, and he couldn't even be bothered to *stay awake*. After watching him nod out for the third day in a row, I took a chance and did something illegal in the courtroom. I took some surreptitious pictures of sleeping beauty with my cellphone—photos were prohibited in the courtroom unless the judge specifically allowed them, but why the hell not? If an attorney employed by the state could catch forty winks while court was in session, then I could take a few pictures of Rip Van Winkle. Muzik's tendency to slumber in court was even reported in some of the newspaper articles about the case. I was completely astonished everyday when the judge made no effort to admonish the prosecutor for snoozing in his courtroom, much less any attempt to wake him up. Perhaps the phrase "contempt of court" had no entry in the Czech legal code?

The judge questioned me for perhaps twenty minutes, asking various things about the show and the nature of my business. He wanted an explanation of stage diving, he wanted to know if we normally had security, he asked if I had made any effort to contact or meet with the family (I had written them a letter a few months before, expressing my condolences while letting them know that I expected no sympathy from them. I assured them that I would not hide in America, swearing to return for trial if I was called to do so. I also let them know that if they ever felt the need to meet with me, I would do so at any place and time of their choosing, even if it was in prison after I was found guilty.), he asked if I had any memory whatsoever of seeing Daniel (I answered that I did not, for that was the truth). Basically I relayed the fact that the only person that I had any memory of physical contact with was Milan, and that if there had been any other incidents, then I did not remember them. This was the truth. Then it was the prosecuting attorney's turn to ask questions (he had managed to wake up by this point), and I braced myself. He was going to hit me, and hit me hard. He was going to try to grind me down, break my will, destroy my story, discredit my character. But I was ready to go toe to toe, and I was prepared for the long haul. *Bring it, you bastard—let's do this*, I thought as he rose in his chair to cross-examine me.

Muzik asked me a total of three questions. They were so banal, so un-ex-KGB-agent-using-mind-control-tricks-esque that I only remember one: he asked me about my drinking and drug use. I truthfully told him that although I had not yet embraced sobriety as a way of life on the night of the show in Prague, that I had drank no alcohol nor done any drugs before the gig that evening. And that was it. Three questions. It took about seven or eight minutes total. Then, as Tomas Grivna asked me some questions, Muzik went back to sleep.

Un-fucking-real.

As I sat down after everyone had finished questioning me, Jeff leaned over and whispered in my ear, "Did you see the prosecutor? He was *asleep*. Unbelievable!" I was glad to hear that someone other than myself had noticed this, as it was so bizarre I was half-convinced that my mind was playing tricks on me—perhaps I had experienced a stress-induced acid flashback or something like that? Lamb of god's manager at the time, Larry Mazer, took the witness stand, followed shortly by our drummer, Chris Adler, to answer a few brief questions from the judge. Larry looked pretty stressed out (as any band manager in his position understandably would be), while Chris looked so nervous you would have thought he was the one on trial. (I didn't blame him though—it was an extremely intimidating thing to stand there in front of the judges; plus, Chris had not spent the last two weeks in preparation, facing the blistering interrogative wrath of Jeff "Satan Incarnate" Cohen.) Stress and nervousness aside, they both did well. Both explained calmly and coherently that my on-stage persona, which had been described by some witnesses as "extremely aggressive," was just a part of our show. The judge asked Chris a question or two about the concert, but Chris hadn't really seen anything during the show, as he was stuck behind his drum kit. This was the precise reason my lawyers and I had decided that he would be the one from my band to come to trial—he hadn't seen anything, not even my tussle with Milan, and wouldn't have much to say. All we needed were a couple of people who knew me to come and say I wasn't the violent lunatic I had been described to be by a few of the witnesses. Reading the statements of these particular witnesses, my onstage persona had seemed so shockingly evil to their innocent little eyeballs that apparently none of them had ever been to a metal show before—I guess prior to that night, they had only attended sugary-sweet pop concerts where the virginally wholesome audience held hands as the well-groomed teen idol frontman warbled out saccharine love songs and threw roses to the adoring girls in the front row.

What a crock of shit.

After Chris and Larry, the father of the deceased young man was called to the witness stand. The judge was very gentle with him, only asking him a few brief questions about his son. I was grateful for this, as I could see the pain running through the poor man's entire being as he spoke, a mere ten or so feet away from his son's accused killer. He did not want to be there, and I felt a new sort of sadness well up in me, an awful emotion I had never known before—at that moment, I realized that my presence was the human face of the source of the worst possible pain a parent can know. I have never wanted to simply vanish from this plane of existence so badly before.

One question the judge asked Daniel's father was if I had made any attempt to meet with the family at any point before the trial. He answered no. I do not believe that Daniel's father said this out of malice. I believe that he must have gotten confused, understandably overwhelmed by the emotions he had to have felt seeing me sitting there so nearby. Perhaps he thought the judge was asking if we had actually met in person, which we had not. I had sent the family the letter through Martin a few months prior, and had been told by Martin that they had received it and had appreciated the fact that I had made the gesture, but did not wish to meet with me at that time. This was understandable, and I certainly was not going to press the issue. After the judge was done, he asked me (as was my legal right) if I had any questions for the witness. I did not have the heart to ask him to clarify whether or not I had written his family a letter. He had had enough questions that day, and didn't need to see my face any further; so instead I just told him I was extremely sorry for his loss. He gave me a brief nod, then left. That was the only time I have ever seen him.

Also during that first day in court, the video obtained by the police was shown in its entirety, as well as two other videos I had compiled. The first was in two parts, beginning by showing both musicians and audience members stage diving to illustrate the actual act for the judges' understanding; then moving on to footage of several well known musicians shoving audience members who had managed to evade security from the stage. This was to illustrate the fact that I wasn't some sort of oddity in not wanting people on stage, because I'm not. I'm not a singular and foul-tempered monster, alone in a sea of warmed-hearted rockers who welcome all who want to join them onstage with open arms. The last thing most bands want is fans on stage, period. The people who take the stage and don't manage to jump before security or crew gets to them often still leave in a flying manner—just the facts, kids, so think twice about it the next time you get the jones to climb over that barricade at *any* show you are attending—it might not turn out so well for you. In fact, it might be the last thing you ever do.

The second video showed clips from the tail end of several lamb of god shows, including the show we played in Poland the very next night after our Prague gig. In these clips, you see me encouraging the audience to give themselves a round of applause. I say, "Make some noise for yourselves! C'mon!" as I raise my hands and clap, sometimes making a large scooping gesture meant to convey *more*, as in *make some more noise*. Over and over, from different angles and different shows, the video showed slightly differing variations of the same thing: me saying "Make some noise! C'mon!" and waving my arms in the air, encouraging the audience to get louder. In my criminal charge, it was written that I gave unclear instructions to the audience, which led to Daniel climbing onstage that evening, as he decided I was inviting him up there. This was based solely on the *opinion* of his friends (in their testimonies they said "Daniel must have thought he was inviting people on stage"), yet it was presented as fact on my very real criminal charges. I found it ludicrous that mere conjecture could be incorporated into a manslaughter charge, but upon looking over videos of several concerts, I saw how someone who did not speak English very well could perhaps take my gestures and words as an invitation to get onstage. *Maybe.* So I put the video together to clarify these "unclear instructions," which I had been questioned about extensively during my interrogation. I had been asked several times if I made a habit of inviting fans onstage—I do not, and I do not give "unclear instructions" to the audience pertaining to their possible presence on my stage (one particularly ridiculous witness, in describing my unclear instructions, had said that I had held up two fingers while saying "No more than two may come on stage"—while that is just stupid, as I would never say such a thing, those set of instructions seemed rather precise to me).

And according to the testimony of one of the three friends he attended the show with, "Daniel's English wasn't that good" so maybe he *did* misunderstand me. However, according to the testimony of another of those three friends, Daniel's English was excellent; in fact he said in his testimony, "My English is far from perfect, but Daniel was the best in our class, his English was excellent." This would set the tone for the rest of my court case—no one could seem to agree on anything, especially the three friends.

The next day in court, eight witnesses delivered testimonies, including the useless security guard who stood to the side of the stage that day and did nothing but shove Milan from the stage once, then yell at him from the floor another time. I found out from a reliable source that he had not wanted to testify at all, as he was afraid I would put a hit out on him if he showed up in court—I had no idea my reputation had gotten so gangster. He did look extremely nervous when he saw me, and this amused me to no end, along with his assertion in his testimony that I was obviously drugged, as I "ran all over the stage like mad" and kept dumping water over my head during the show. (In fact, several witnesses said they thought I must have been on drugs during their interrogations, since I was moving all over the stage very quickly, I was sweaty, and I kept dumping water over my head. To my mind, this indicated that I was doing my job in a normal manner, I got hot as I always do, and as usual I was trying to cool down; but maybe these people knew something about drugs that I didn't. I mean, I've done plenty of drugs in my day, but none of them have ever caused me to repeatedly douse myself with H_2O. Or maybe I just wasn't doing the right drugs—I don't know, but regardless, the whole high-on-drugs=water-on-the-head thing was pretty funny to me.) When questioned, the security guard refused to take any responsibility for not doing his job, saying that I was too quick and he was too old for this type of music, although I'm sure he had no problem accepting payment for his "services" that night.

Another witness that day was a self-styled "journalist" (translation: writes online metal show reviews for some obscure website—if he qualifies as a journalist because he does that, then I'm a pro surfer because I can catch a knee-high wave without looking too foolish) who had testified that I was punching people out, hammering them like a pro boxer from the beginning of our set: "Once they got up there, Randy immediately attacked them. He attacked them with his fists, beating them to the ground there on stage, then throwing them back into the audience. These incidents happened about three times towards the beginning of the show. These people definitely weren't drunk or attacking him . . . but I have never seen the level of aggression that Randy Blythe displayed there." This "journalist" made me out to be a pretty gnarly hard-assed dude, whooping ass and taking names, Bruce Lee–style, from the very start. While this flattered my fragile male ego, there was a slight problem with his elaborate tale of my savage flying fists of fury— we had all watched the video of the show in court the day before. This video showed the whole first half of the gig. Except for a few brief seconds, you can see me the whole time. I'm not punching anyone to the ground, nor throwing anyone into the audience. I'm pretty quick, but I'm not the Flash, able to beat multiple people up in the span of the two or three seconds I was off camera—this guy was full of shit.

Of the six others that testified that day, only the three friends who had come to the show with Daniel really mattered. These three young men all had already been interrogated by the police twice, once in 2010 when the investigation had begun after Daniel had passed away, then again in 2012. Their stories were full of inconsistencies to begin with, but got worse with their second interrogation. The fact that their stories still didn't match up in 2012 surprised me; after all, the police *had* given them transcripts of their first testimony, allowing them plenty of time to get their shit straight. Yes, that's right, the cops interrogated them then gave them notes to study before questioning them again. They even admitted to discussing the differences in testimony in court. Amazing. And as they took the stand, one after the other in the courtroom on that day in 2013, they still couldn't get their stories to line up, neither individually nor as a unit.

I won't bother to list out all of the numerous conflicting things these three young men said over the course of three years and three different questionings by the authorities. It only aggravates and depresses me to think about it, so I will only say that my defense team basically eviscerated them, and it wasn't too hard of a task to accomplish. Hell, I'm no lawyer and I could have done it—I had definitely read and reread their testimonies enough to tear them apart on the stand by myself. And I do not know why they said some of the things they did; why they felt the need to lie about what they saw that night and about me and my actions. I do not know why they changed their stories, why their descriptions of me and my actions got worse with each telling, for they did. Perhaps they were just scared. Perhaps they were angry over losing their friend and wanted to point a finger at someone. Perhaps they thought they were doing the right thing by Daniel's family by trying to make me look as bad as possible so that I would be sent to prison. Perhaps they were even hiding something, holding some bit of information back, something that . . . well, speculation is pointless at this point. I do not know much about them, their character, their reasoning, and I probably never will. I simply do not know.

But there was one particular inconsistency from one of these three witnesses that does deserve mention, because this young man actually displayed a bit of conscience, and I would like to give him credit for it. I could tell that one of them in particular was severely uncomfortable being near me in the courtroom. Something was bothering him, and he studiously avoided looking my way as he took the witness stand. As he nervously answered the judge's questions, giving stumbling replies to queries about my aggressiveness and whether or not he thought I had been intoxicated on the evening of the show, I consulted my notes. After the judge, the prosecutor, and my lawyer were done with him, the judge asked me if I had questions for the witness. I did not consult with my attorneys first, and I did not listen to the logical part of my head, the part that was shrieking, *Do not do this, you idiot! Let the lawyers handle this! This dumb idea of yours could turn out very badly.* I stared at the miserable-looking boy standing before me with downcast eyes, and I decided to take a chance on what my gut told me: here was a young man who knew right from wrong.

During his first interrogation on October 6, 2010, the police asked this witness if he could confirm with certainty that I was the one who threw Daniel from the stage, and if it had been this action of mine that had led to his fatal injury. The young man replied:

"Yes, I am absolutely certain, I know the singer very well, as well as the other members of the band. There are four others: William Adler, guitarist, Mark Morton, guitarist, Chris Adler, drummer, and John Campbell, bassist. As I said, I was their fan and I know them all. I know the singer very well. He acts similarly at all concerts, I can't say if there were any signs of alcohol consumption or not. As I said, it is perfectly normal at concerts like this and it's part of the show that members of the audience who climb on stage are thrown back into the crowd. In my opinion, the singer had no intention to harm Daniel in any way."

But during his second interrogation, on September 14, 2012, he said:

"I have never seen anyone push a fan down in such an aggressive way. And I think that in Blythe's case, it was caused by alcohol . . . Because I saw them in the backstage when they were coming up, they were drinking Jim Beam, and I think he was drunk, seeing how aggressive he was . . . You simply could tell, for example by his movements, and of course what happened, a sober person doesn't do this . . . I think he had to be drunk, he certainly wasn't stumbling, but it was obvious; also from the energy he poured into it, he had to have something in his bloodstream . . . "

I put my notes down, and stood up in my chair. I looked straight at this dark-haired young man as he managed to briefly raise eyes to meet my gaze, and in a voice as calm as I could muster, I said, "Do you think I had any intention to harm Daniel in any way that evening?"

The boy's eyes shot back towards the ground, and he closed them as he bowed his head. He looked ashamed. There was a long, deafening pause. I could see the massive internal struggle written on his face as he did battle within himself, grappling with the decision whether to say what he believed to be true and right, or to tell a lie. All around me the courtroom had become a vacuum of silence, and I could see all three judges, the prosecutor, my attorneys, and the people in the gallery, all leaning forward in their seats as they waited for his answer. It felt like being in a movie, so dramatic was the tension hanging in the air. After a solid ten seconds of silence, the young man raised his head, opened his eyes, and said in a soft voice:

"No. No, I do not think you meant to harm him that night. Not on purpose."

I actually heard the entire courtroom exhale. I thanked the young man, told the judge I had no further questions, and sat down. The female judge shot me an amused-looking glance from beneath a raised eyebrow, as if to say, *Well, that was a foolish idea, you big dummy—but somehow it actually worked. Lucky you.* And I did not have to ask the young man any further questions. I did not have to ask him why he had suddenly become so sure that I was drunk when before he was not. I did not have to ask him why he changed his story about me behaving in any way other than what he very clearly had known from the start was my normal manner. I did not have to needle him about any of the other inconsistencies in any of his testimonies, including the one given that very day. I did not have to break him down any further, and

I did not want to. All I had to do was follow my instincts; the instincts that told me that the young man before me was at his core a decent person, and when it really and truly mattered and he was called to task for his words, that his inherit human decency would prevail.

And I was right.

———

On the third day of court, a few more witnesses who had been at the show testified, saying that there had been nothing out of the ordinary about my behavior on the evening of the show, that I acted in the manner standard for the frontman of a heavy metal band. They also said that I had made it clear that I did not wish for fans to come on stage; in fact *all* of the witnesses who had attended the show that evening said the same exact thing in one way or another—it was obvious from my words and actions throughout that evening that audience members were not welcome on stage. The promoter of the show, Tomas Fiala, also testified that day. After being asked if in our contract with him lamb of god had specific security and barricade requirements, he answered that we did. When asked if those requirements were not met, he answered honestly that they were not. When asked why a barricade with a solid metal face had not been placed properly as our signed contract with him specified (at least five feet from the stage with room for security to stand between it and the stage to prevent concert goers access), he said that we as a band had not complained to him before or after the show about it. Useless.

After reviewing the video tape and all the available testimonies, my lawyers and I had come to the conclusion that there had, in fact, been a barricade at the show that evening. It was perhaps five or six inches taller in height than the stage, as I caught a glimpse of it sticking up when reviewing the video. But I only saw it for a second, when an audience member turned briefly and removed their arms from the top of it. The fans had leaned on top of it all across its entire length, their arms hanging over and onto the stage. And if it was in the fact the same barricade I had seen in the police photos, then it had no solid face. It was just a long metal rectangle, with a single horizontal bar running across its middle. I never saw it, because it was crammed with audience members hanging over it, shoved flush with the stage.

It was, in effect, a ladder for the fans.

Our tour manager had held a security meeting before the show began, as he does at every show. He had explained our requirements. The club employees understood what was said. The promoter understood what was said. We were not the only band on the bill that evening, and I do not know whether or not the barricade had initially been placed properly and the fans had simply pushed it up to the stage while security did nothing about it. My tour manager, who is also our front of house soundman, did not sit behind his console during the opening act, making sure that the barricade stayed in place properly. That is not his job—he did his job. That is the job of the promoter, the club manager, and security, to make sure our contractual requirements are fulfilled. And I never saw the stage before I set foot on it. I did not go and do a barricade inspection, as that is not my job. Once again, that is the job of the promoter, the club manager, and security.

Several of these people admitted in their testimonies that they had not done their jobs, but couldn't seem to give any real reason when asked why. No one seemed inclined to be accountable for their actions, or in this case, their *lack* of actions.

But one person who testified that day *did* hold himself accountable for his actions, and in doing so, did me a great service. Milan had cut his hair since our last encounter, and was dressed neatly in a suit jacket and tie as he took the witness stand. He looked to have grown up quite a bit in the three years since I had wrestled him to the stage, but as soon as I saw his face I recognized him.

When asked by the judge to explain what had happened between him and me that evening, he spoke calmly, confidently, and without stumbling over his words in the slightest, as other witnesses had. He spoke of how he had been extremely intoxicated that evening. He told how he had taken the stage several times, and of how he had hit the floor hard on different occasions when no one had caught him after he left the stage. He spoke of how his actions had been ill advised, as he had known that he was not welcome on stage. He spoke with regret over his drunken stupidity. He spoke of how I had neither struck nor strangled him on stage. And he told how he considered my actions that evening to be appropriate, given the highly inebriated state he had been in.

The man that other witnesses had described me as punching, kicking, choking, and physically brutalizing in an extreme manner had suited up and showed up. He told the truth, and took responsibility for his own actions that evening. Aside from myself, he seemed to be the only one truly willing to do so. During a brief recess that day, I ran into him as I stood outside on the sidewalk smoking a cigarette. As he walked out of the large wooden front doors of the court building, I caught his eye and simply said, "Thank you." He gave me a tiny nod accompanied by a small, sad smile, and replied, "You're welcome. Good luck." As he walked away down the sidewalk and out of my life without looking back, I thought of all the stupid, reprehensible things I had done while drunk. I could not be mad at the man at all, for that is what he was—a man, not a drunken, irresponsible boy anymore. He had done his best to make right his mistakes that evening years ago. I will always be grateful to him for it.

————

After the recess was over, the judge called me to the witness stand again. He informed me that I did not have to answer his questions, and had the right to remain silent. I said

I was prepared to answer any questions he may have for me, so the judge went through parts of my testimony again, asking if I was sure it had been Milan that I had pushed away from me, as I had stated during my interrogation and opening statement. I replied: "To the best of my knowledge, it was Milan who was coming up on the stage every time." This was the truth, for I had no memory of pushing anyone else that evening.

But now that all is said and done, in all honesty, I do not have a clear memory of pushing anyone from the stage *period* that evening. I do not know if the very hazy memories I do have are entirely false, conjured as the result of me reading and rereading my charges over and over again in prison. Or if I confused some of the times when Milan jumped from the stage with me pushing him. Or if I perceived the security guard running and pushing him from the stage from behind both of us as an action of my own, as I never saw the guard at all until I watched video of the incident later. Or if I can't clearly remember pushing anyone simply because I never did, or I did have some sort of real memory of pushing someone and just thought *It must have been Milan.* I do not know. But after discussing all of these things in advance with my attorneys, I knew I could not say to the judge "I do not know"—it would not have looked good. So I told the truth, and said my only real memories of anyone being onstage that night were of Milan. To this day, those are the only memories I have that I can say are real.

Finally that day, a medical expert read an in-depth report on the cause of Daniel's death. He had died of pneumonia as a result of a blow to the brainstem. Hearing the exact details of what had killed the young man almost brought tears to my eyes, as had the pictures of the young man shown to me by the judge earlier that day. "Do you remember seeing this person on the evening of your show in Prague?" he had asked as I looked at several photos of who I then knew to be Daniel. I had looked long and hard at the photos, but I could not place his face at all in my mind. The photos and the medical report choked me up, but for some reason, the tears refused to flow.

The fourth day of court, a witness testified on my behalf. This young man had been following reports of the trial in the newspapers, and did not like the way some of the witnesses had described my behavior as being aggressive. When I asked him a question, he began to reply in English, for he had understood what I said, but the judge quickly barked at him, sternly instructing him to speak Czech. Another witness who was supposed to appear that day had called in sick, so the judge temporarily adjourned the trial for a month's time. He then informed me that I did not have to return for the rest of the court dates, as my presence was no longer needed in the courtroom, and I could be tried *in absentia*. I told the judge in front of the entire courtroom that I would definitely be returning for the rest of the trial. I had promised Daniel's family that I would be present, and that would not change. A representative of the family had told my wife and drummer after court one day that the family was not interested in mounting a campaign against me, nor were they out to get me. They just wanted to know what had happened to their family member, and their actions proved this so—no member of his family ever attacked me, in the press, in the courtroom, or in private. The least I could do was honor my word and be there for the entire trial.

The next day, Jeff, my wife, and family (who had flown over for the trial), and myself all returned to America for a month. I hung out with my wife and friends. I turned forty-two years old. Then I returned to Prague to finish it.

On the fifth day of my trial, the court heard from two different qualified criminal mental health experts, both of whom had tested me. The first was the female shrink from the jail house; according to her analysis of the test results I was not mentally ill, but I had problems controlling my emotions in stressful situations. Furthermore, I exhibited some of the traits associated with something called *dissocial* (or *antisocial*) *personality disorder*. This disorder may be characterized by: a lack of empathy for others, no sense of remorse for harmful actions committed, a general lack of morality, impulsive and aggressive behavior, and a pervasive pattern of disregard for the rights of others—in short, someone with this disorder doesn't care to play nice or abide by society's rules. This woman said that my history of speeding tickets (by the way, I've had maybe three or four during my twenty-year-plus driving career, none of them reckless—more than one of my friends have accused me of driving like a little old lady), coupled with my taking-a-leak-in-an-alley incident so long ago, was indicative of the fact that I was not willing to take responsibility for my own actions, and that sometimes I overstepped the boundaries of societal norms.

I'm sure I'm about to sound pretty callous here, hell, maybe even *criminal*, but I feel the need to tell the truth, so here it is: I hold absolutely *no remorse whatsoever* for getting busted taking a leak in an alley, nor do I feel the tiniest shred of guilt over getting caught a few times on the highway going ten or fifteen miles over the speed limit. I didn't feel bad about it then, and I don't now. *Not at all*. It's just not a big deal to me, and if that makes me some sort of cold-blooded psychopath unfit for normal society, then so be it. For sure, I was none too happy about getting sixty-five community service hours for taking a whiz, and I *definitely* wasn't jazzed about getting arrested a few times after I refused to do those community service hours. Without question, I was *absolutely* bummed out as I stroked the check to pay the fine imposed when I foolishly stopped paying close enough attention to the speed limit a few times in my twenties and thirties. But I'm not going to have a guilt-induced nervous break down over this piddling stuff, in fact I don't give two flying fucks about it. I mean Jesus H. Christ, I had to pee and I went a little bit over the speed limit—it's not like I went on an old lady mugging spree, or chopped up my neighbors with an axe. If after hearing me speak merely about peeing and driving a little fast, that shrink had somehow deduced that I lacked empathy for others, didn't want to be held accountable for my actions, and had an impoverished sense of morality, then I shudder to think what kind of crap she would have come up with if I had told her about some stuff I really *have* felt remorse over. Or, heaven forbid, I had admitted to that one late night in the early nineties when I had been forced to take a poop behind a dumpster in a Chicago alley after eating bad Mexican food earlier. None of the surrounding businesses were open for me to beg a bathroom, so I had to do what I had to do. Had the shrink known about that particular smelly emergency, she probably would have made a motion to have me declared criminally insane.

Not willing to take responsibility for my own actions? She could stand there with a straight face in that courtroom and actually say that? My own government didn't deem it worth their time to cooperate in any way whatsoever with the Czech authorities in an investigation into my alleged crime—I could have decided to just stay in America and not have to face five to ten years of my life possibly being flushed down an ancient prison shitter. But I had returned anyway, because (as I had very publicly stated) I felt an ethical obligation to do so. I paid a very expensive bail, twice, and had made good on my word to honor the conditions of that bail and return for trial if called. Furthermore, I had traveled at great expense to come to court, not once, but twice; the second time even after being informed that my presence was no longer required. I had done everything *exactly* as I had said I would do, and I thought maybe that my actions might speak to her a little louder about my character and personality type than the two or three pages of test results she clutched in her mousey paw. But when questioned about the results, she indignantly maintained that they were accurate, and that the tests she had given me were of the latest modern standard. She looked slightly insulted when my attorney had asked her if the circumstances under which she had tested me could have possibly affected my results, as if it was an affront to her hallowed profession to have the infallibility of her 1920s ink blots questioned.

Luckily, the second qualified criminal mental health expert (a woman I had been tested by during my trial preparations) testified that even in jail, when aggressive/anti-social behavior might be understandable, I had tested within normal ranges on various stress tests during my initial days of incarceration. While she said that I could exhibit asocial tendencies under stress, she added, "Every one of us could in their lifetime get into a situation in which we act without mercy, but this is not a personality trait of his." This woman obviously had a better head on her shoulders than the first, and seemed to think I was a pretty normal person. But then again, I don't think I had told her about my dark and wildly immoral history of peeing in places I shouldn't . . .

The witness who had been too ill to appear in court the first time showed up that day. She was a teenage girl, accompanied by her doctor father (the very person, by the way, who had written the note to get her out of court the first time) who ushered her in with a protective hand on her shoulder. She was dressed in the goth style, all baggy black clothes and gigantic black boots with lots of chrome buckles, and had a cheap looking inverted cross necklace hanging around her neck. Daddy's dark little princess smiled a lot and giggled from time to time as the judge questioned her. During her initial interrogation, she claimed to have seen me push Daniel from the stage before he even had time to stand up, which contrasted with the version of events given by every other witness who testified against me. She didn't bring any earth shattering new evidence into court that day, so her appearance was not a lengthy one, and the judge soon dismissed her. Then he adjourned court for the day, announcing that a verdict was likely to be handed down the next day.

———

That evening I lay in my bed, trying to get to sleep, but slumber eluded me. Restless in body and mind, I finally got up, walked outside onto the balcony of the apartment and lit a cigarette. As I stood there smoking in the cold night air, I could hear a piano being played somewhere nearby. The melody was slow and sweet and a little sad sounding, and it fit my mood perfectly. I leaned on the balcony's railing, looking up at the starless night sky, smoking and trying to identify the tune, but I couldn't place it. The pianist would abruptly stop from time to time, then a moment later pick back up from where they had left off. I was looking around, trying to find the source of this beautiful and unfamiliar music, when I saw movement in a window directly across the apartment's courtyard, one floor below mine in the next building over. A wrinkled pair of male hands moved with confidence across black and white keys, illuminated by a single lamp resting atop a small piano. The hands would stop from time to time, grab a piece of paper propped up on the piano's small wooden music stand, and with a pencil make small marks on the tightly compressed horizontal printed rows running across the piece of paper. I then knew why I could not identify the mysterious song—it had never been played before. The song was being composed before me.

What a gift! I thought as I finished my cigarette, then went back into the apartment. I cracked my bedroom window a bit so that I could still hear the piano, then went back to bed, lulled to sleep by the sound of new music entering the world.

Such moments as this, those fleeting and ineffable seconds of grace that the universe occasionally provides as we move through this strange thing called life, cannot be bought for any sum.

I woke up the next morning and the sun was shining brightly in a clear blue sky. As Jeff and I walked to court the next morning, we talked about how surreal our whole experience had been thus far. We had spent a month living in Prague, both working hard in preparation for my trial, and wandering the streets of one of the most beautiful cities on earth. Both aspects of our time in that ancient city seemed equally significant, and this oddly harmonious dichotomy had made for a profound experience, one neither of us would ever forget.

On the final day of my trial, the judge called to the witness stand the only expert in the highly specialized field of biomechanics in the entire Czech Republic who was legally qualified to testify in a court of law. During our review of the testimonies that described me pushing the deceased from the stage, my attorneys and I had noticed that some of these testimonies, specifically the second testimonies given by Daniel's three friends in 2012, described things that seemed to us as being physically impossible. During their initial testimonies in 2010, some of these witnesses had described me as turning towards and then pushing Daniel with either one or both hands squarely in the chest, causing him to fall backwards from the four-foot-tall stage, striking the back of his head on the concrete floor below. This made perfect sense, as medical records showed that the injury leading to his death had been an impact to the back of his cranium. But by 2012, some of the stories had changed. Suddenly I had run from fifteen or twenty feet away, sprinting at top speed across the narrow and crowded stage, then striking a completely unprepared Daniel, unaware, from behind as he looked out waving at the audience (and according to some testimonies, I had simultaneously pushed a mysterious second person as well, an unknown boy whose identity has never been ascertained). According to these testimonies, this caused the deceased to be launched from the stage, flying completely over the row of people standing directly in front of the stage, somehow do a 180-degree flip while in midair, then land on the back of his head.

I am not a scientist. I am not a physics expert, able to illustrate through mathematical formulas the effects of impact, inertia, and gravity on a body in motion. But I have been a skateboarder for over thirty years, and I have fallen many, many times after hitting an unseen rock or crack in the pavement beneath my wheels as I sped along. I have busted my ass at high velocities and from great heights as I attempted to fly off the edge of various elevated concrete surfaces while trying what is known as an acid drop, or attempting to clear the coping of a half pipe ramp. Although physically feasible under these circumstances, given the heights I have fallen and my already advanced speed, I have been lucky enough to have never done a flip in midair during these disasters—I have just landed with a painful and sometimes bone-breaking thud below, like an anorexic sack of potatoes thrown from the back of a tiny wooden truck with urethane wheels. I am also a front man who has jumped, tripped, and just plain fallen off of stages of various heights (occasionally knocking myself completely unconscious), many times over the twenty plus years as a musician. The only time I have ever done a flip in midair during these departures from the stage was when I intentionally tried to do so, running and compressing my legs before take off in order to build the momentum and spring necessary to execute such an acrobatic maneuver. I know what falling and flipping from an elevated position (and its sometimes unfortunate consequences) is like on a very visceral level. I had never experienced anything that matched the description given in the oddly altered 2012 testimonies.

The forced acrobatics described in these second testimonies were physical impossibilities cooked up by boys with obviously less-than-stellar critical-thinking skills. They were trying to make me appear as a vicious and cold-blooded man who would make haste to attack someone without mercy from behind. So we provided the testimonies to the biomechanics expert weeks before the trial ever started, and after a series of several experiments which recreated the fall in various ways (some of these experiments, gruesomely enough, involved the use of fresh human cadavers to measure the force of impact on a human skull), the expert confirmed what I, a person who had somersaulted off of many, many stages myself, had known all along—in order for the deceased to fly and flip through the air over the front row of fans from a height of just four feet, he would have had to have jumped. And despite the prosecuting attorney's objection, the judge allowed the biomechanics expert to present his precisely illustrated scientific findings in the courtroom that day.

After the biomechanics expert had presented his results, he and the prosecuting attorney had a brief but heated exchange. The visibly angered prosecutor loudly claimed that the expert's findings were not valid, that he had not taken into account the various circumstances surrounding the fall at the show, and that he had discounted other testimonies describing the fall in different ways. The biomechanics expert coldly replied in a contemptuous voice that he had recreated the fall exactly as had been described several different ways, and as there were no magical circumstances capable of suspending the laws of physics, that his conclusions were correct. His test results were not subjective, dependent on the highly unknown variables of human perception and bias (as is the case with psychological tests), but were rooted in irrefutable scientific fact. They went back and forth for a bit, the irritated expert making the prosecutor look a bit foolish with his bull-headed insistence on dismissing the laws of physical reality. The judge seemed to agree with each of them on different points, but in the end allowed the expert's testimony to stand. Then the judge read aloud various letters of character reference we had translated into Czech, which were to be entered into the court record. (These letters had already been reviewed by the judges, but according to Czech law, any and everything pertaining to the trial in document form had to be audibly read into the court record.) Amongst the letters the judge read was the one written by Vinnie Paul detailing the murder of his brother onstage, and as I heard Vinnie and Dimebag's names pronounced in the judge's Czech accent, the urge to cry returned. But once again, the tears would not fall—it was as if all the sadness I had known over the years was trapped inside me and unable to escape. My tears were locked up as I had been in prison, waiting for release at the end of this strange nightmare I was living in. The judge finished reading the letters, then adjourned the court for an hour-and-a-half lunch break, announcing that he would deliver a verdict when we reconvened.

My legal team and I walked to a nearby Southeast Asian restaurant we had eaten lunch at every day of the trial. The chef, an attractive British woman of Malaysian descent, came out to wish me luck at the end of our meal. She and her staff had been very kind to us throughout the trial, making sure our large table was served quickly in the limited time available to us. I thanked her for the family-style meals, which had been truly delicious. I was happy to have eaten a good lunch before facing judgment, for I didn't know if my next meal would be in Pankrác.

In the courtroom, the prosecutor stood and presented his final argument, saying that after taking into consideration the various charitable works I had provided documentation of, he saw some decency in me, and as such would not ask the judge for the maximum penalty. It was his generous recommendation that I be given instead a mere five years of hard time (there was no time off for good behavior allowed in a charge as serious as mine). He said that even a kindergartener would know better than to do what I had done, therefore there had to have been some intent on my part to harm the deceased young man. The prosecutor's closing statement was brief, taking up perhaps ten minutes.

In contrast, my defense attorney, Tomas Grivna, spoke for around forty-five minutes. He systematically tore apart the evidence laid against me, discrediting testimony after testimony. It was fairly brutal, and the judge later told him he had perhaps done "too good of a job."

Then Daniel's uncle, the family's legal representative, stood and spoke for the first and only time during the entire trial. He told the judge that the family would not be substantiating the monetary claim previously laid against me, as no amount of money would ever bring their child back. He said that after hearing all of the evidence presented, that they had come to the conclusion that the blame for Daniel's death did not lay solely on my shoulders, and blamed the promoter and security for not fulfilling their contractual obligations. But he also said that he wished me to know how seriously the family had been affected by Daniel's death. Daniel had died on his father's birthday. He would never be able to celebrate the day he had been born again. Daniel's mother had been unable to return to work, remaining so torn by grief she had been forced to seek psychiatric help. Their child's death had destroyed their family, and he wanted to make sure I understood that.

I understood it all too well. My daughter's death had destroyed my own.

Then I stood and spoke for the last time in that courtroom. I expressed my sorrow over Daniel's death. I said that if ultimately I was found guilty of the charge against me, I would do my time without complaint, like a man. I maintained my innocence, saying that if I had thought I was guilty, then I would have pleaded so. And I said that after hearing all of the evidence, the only explanation for this whole horrible ordeal I could come up with was that there had been a tragic accident.

That was the truth.

The judge then delivered the verdict. He read a bunch of legal stuff, which my small friend translated almost simultaneously. I did not hear the words "guilty" or "not guilty" come from her mouth. Instead at some point she said "and the charge has been removed." I did not understand what this meant, and asked her to clarify as the judge droned on. "It means you are not guilty," she said. "What about a lesser crime? Are they charging me with a lesser crime?" I asked. "No. I think you are through," she said. I was still unsure what was going on until Jeff leaned over and whispered, "Total exoneration." I looked across the courtroom to Don Argott, who had been allowed to film the delivery of the verdict along with members of the press. I saw him silently mouth the words *What is going on? What happened?* I slightly raised my thumb upward in reply. I saw my family sitting in the gallery, tears on my mother's face. I kept my expression as neutral as I possibly could, for I had decided long before this day that no matter what verdict was handed down, I would do my best to show no emotion. I would not smile, nor would I cry. I would remain stoic, and face my judgment like a man of character and dignity.

I do not know how I appeared to others as they watched me face judgment, for I neither smiled nor cried. I did not feel like doing either. I suppose some of the strange emotions sweeping through me could be characterized as feelings of relief, but there was no joy in my heart. That heart contained far too much sadness, swirling like a thick fog through the slowly dawning realization that I was a free man, for me to feel any happiness. A great coat of sorrow had been painted over my entire being, and I did not know what I was feeling, other than shell-shocked. I have never known anything like it before or since, and hope never to again.

After the judge had finished speaking, the prosecutor immediately stood, announced that he would appeal the verdict, and then court was adjourned. I had asked my attorney to speak to the judge earlier and ensure that Daniel's family would be allowed to leave out a back door and avoid the press, and I walked out of the main courtroom door slowly. I took my time leaving, as I wanted to keep the press distracted for a bit as an extra-precautionary measure for the family. They had been through more than enough, and did not need to deal with flashing cameras and reporters shouting questions. As I walked into the blinding camera lights, strolling silently through a forest of microphones thrust towards my face, I took a small camera of my own fitted with a fisheye lens and proceeded to shoot pictures of all the TV and newspaper people who had filmed so much of me. I had decided to do this days before, as I thought I might capture a unique image. I also hoped to make some of them uncomfortable, as I found them unforgivably rude and intrusive, not just to myself, but to Daniel's family as well. My idea worked on both counts—the photos have a nightmarish and claustrophobic quality to them, and as I shot them, I noticed several of these press men looking nervously away. They were visibly uneasy having the tables turned on them. They did not want me to photograph them. *You don't like that, now do you?* I thought, *Too bad.* I snapped a few photos, told the shouting reporters that I had no comments for them, then Jeff and I walked out of that courtroom building, never to return.

———

The court had found me not guilty of manslaughter, and as such, not criminally liable for Daniel's death. I was declared innocent because of the extenuating circumstances that evening— my nearsightedness, the repeated appearances of Milan (who looked similar enough to Daniel that some witnesses with perfectly fine vision had confused the two), and the absence of any sort of effective security or a properly placed barricade. In fact, the judge maintained that there had been negligence across the board from the people putting on and working the show with regard to security issues that evening. However, the judge also said that the court had proven that I had thrown Daniel from the stage, and as such I held the moral responsibility for his death. I felt that this rather wishy-washy judgment was a cop-out on the part of the court, a weak attempt to pacify the prosecuting attorney. Either I was guilty or not guilty, right?

However, I do agree 100 percent that I do hold the moral responsibility for his death. I must claim it, and live with it the rest of my life. I must hold myself accountable for my actions, for I believe that had Daniel never seen my face that night, he would still be alive today.

But not because of anything the court said—the court didn't prove a damn thing. The investigation into my crime was pathetic, and the evidence arrayed against me was a joke. Everything said against me was based on hearsay, mostly from three boys who couldn't get their stories straight if their lives depended on it. The prosecutor was literally *asleep at times*. The trial was a total fiasco.

The court proved *nothing*.

But what the court said happened is not what's important to me. What the judges and attorneys believed is not important. What anyone else on this planet (with the exception of Daniel's family) believes about the situation is ultimately not important to me at all. I do not care what anyone else believes happened, nor what opinion they may have about me and my actions. Why?

Because I can look myself in the eye in the mirror every day and honestly say to myself: *You did the right thing in a really tough spot. You did not break or run away. You are a man of your word.* No one, *no one*, can ever take that from me, just like the court could not have taken it from me even if they had sent me to prison. The comfort provided by the irrefutable certainty of one's internal rectitude is a luxury afforded only to those who prove themselves able of acting with honor in the face of great adversity; for one must be tested to find out what one is really made of. It is never available to the ever-growing multitude of yapping dogs in our soft and castrated society who constantly criticize what they could never muster the courage to be.

No, what others think happened is not important at all. It is what I believe happened that is important.

So, what do I believe?

I believe that at the end of the show that evening, Daniel used the barricade as a ladder and climbed onto the stage.

I do not know exactly why he climbed onto the stage. Perhaps he had misheard my words, and thought I was inviting him up—heavy metal concerts are loud, raucous, and at times confusing affairs. I speak in a Southern drawl into a microphone that amplifies my voice and sometimes distorts it, depending on the acoustics of a venue, the loudness of the PA, and the position of the person listening. English was not Daniel's native language. He easily could have misunderstood me. Maybe he thought I wanted him on stage.

Or maybe he was just an excited teenager, happy to be so close to his favorite band, and merely wanted to get closer. I do not think Daniel had any intent to harm me at all; from what I have been told of him, he was a gentle and kind boy. He was just nineteen years old. At age nineteen I was a freshman in college, living away from home for the first time. I was, to put it mildly, a wildly irresponsible young man. I made many, many mistakes during my nineteenth year on earth; several of which could have resulted in my death. I cannot be mad at Daniel for climbing on that stage, even if he knew he shouldn't have. He was just a boy, and boys make mistakes.

Whatever his reasoning, I believe Daniel did climb on the stage that night. I believe I turned, saw him, stepped forward, and pushed him in his chest. I believe that he fell backward from the stage as the result of my push, that no one caught him, and that he struck his head on the concrete floor.

I believed he died a month later from that injury.

I believe that I accidentally killed him.

And accident or not, I believe that I hold the moral responsibility for the death of another human being, a young nineteen-year-old fan of my band from the Czech Republic named Daniel. Accident or not, I believe that I made a critical error in judgment that cost another human being his life.

But my error did not lie in removing unwanted people from the stage that night—the situation was dangerous, out of control, and I addressed it the best I could under the circumstances. I absolutely have the right to protect my person, and after I was released on bail, I talked to many, many musicians who told me that after hearing about my arrest, they had thanked their lucky stars it wasn't them in prison. All of them had done the exact same thing I had been accused of: pushed an uninvited person off of their stage. Many said they had done far worse. Sooner or later, what happened in Prague was going to happen somewhere to someone, and more than likely it was going to be someone I knew, given the nature of the crowds most of my friends play to. It was only a matter of time—I just happened to be the one who caught the bullet.

And whether an audience member likes it or not, they have absolutely no right whatsoever to come onto a stage uninvited. The price of a ticket entitles them to watch the show—*that's it*. If they do elect to disregard that obvious fact, they should be prepared to deal with the consequences of endangering the musicians, other audience members, and themselves. Musicians on stage concentrating on doing their jobs cannot be expected to play bouncer, or stop to evaluate each person that comes uninvited onto the stage to ascertain if they are a potential threat—that is what security is for. Security is supposed to prevent people from coming onstage. Security is supposed to deal with people who do manage to get on stage. I was unfortunate enough to not have a real barricade or any security placed properly to do what they were supposed to do that evening, and my crew was stuck behind a mountain of equipment crammed onto a tiny stage. However, in an extremely unreasonable situation, I acted in an entirely reasonable manner to protect myself and my bandmates. I acted without malice. I did not beat anyone up. I didn't throw a single punch. If placed in the same completely out of control situation again though, I will not be so reasonable.

Not at all.

But I will never allow myself to be placed in that situation again, because I will never ever repeat the critical error in judgment I made that night. That error, *my error*, cost another human being their life, just as surely as if I had held them down and force-fed them deadly poison.

I should have stopped the show.

Daniel wasn't the only fan onstage that night. Milan wasn't the only fan onstage that night. There were several others, the first of whom is seen in the video the police showed in court running across the stage at just over three minutes into our set, before our first song was even finished. Someone jumping onstage was not a singular incident, and it started as soon as the show began. It was obvious that no one was making any real attempt to stop these fans, aside from myself. I should have turned to my band, told them, "We're outta here," and walked off that stage.

I should have stopped the show.

Because I didn't, a young man is dead.

And that is *my fault.*

Lamb of god had never been to the Czech Republic before. We wanted to make a good impression on our first visit there. I did not know what would happen if we just walked off the stage. I did not know if they would trash the club. Or riot. Or destroy our gear or bus. All of these things are very real possibilities that have happened to bands before. Neither I nor my bandmates spoke their language, and some of them were obviously disinclined to act as if they understood the very clear message I repeatedly put across through both words and actions: *Stay off the stage. You are not welcome here.* If they would not take the hint that they were not wanted on stage, then what would happen if I shut it down? I had no idea. I didn't know what would go down if I simply walked off stage and refused to return. It could have been very, very bad.

But none of that sort of speculation really matters at all in the face of this very real fact: a young man would not have lost his life if I had stopped the show. The fans would have been angry, for sure. They would have booed and hissed and the drunker of them would have most assuredly thrown things at us and our crew. They definitely would have complained to the club employees and tried to get their money back. Without question they would have taken to the Internet in hordes and written about what a bunch of spoiled American rockstars we were. And who knows? Maybe they would have gotten violent, and we would have had to fight multiple people—I personally know bands who have had to fight their audience when a show went wrong. Drunken metal heads are not known for their restraint at times, and it's not like there was anywhere for my band and crew to go hide—security was a joke, and the only thing separating the audience from the tiny backstage area were a few sheets hung from a flimsy pipe and drape rig on the side of the stage.

But I would rather have dealt with that—any of it, all of it— than have to live with the knowledge that a young fan of my band is dead because I did not simply walk off stage and call it quits for the night.

Because that is exactly what happened. That was my error, my mistake, and I will never forget or deny it. I failed in my responsibility as a human being by allowing an obviously out of control situation that was dangerous to both myself and others to continue happening, a situation I could have put a stop to. I was the last link in a disastrous chain of events that could have prevented what occurred from happening, but I failed. So in my eyes, I am morally responsible for that young man's death.

That is the truth, and it grieves me to no end.

———

Jeff and I walked from court to the apartment. While Jeff changed out of his suit, I put on a pot of coffee, and waited for Daniel's mother and uncle to arrive. His uncle had told me earlier that day that they wished to meet with me privately before they left Prague and returned to their home village, and I readily agreed. Jeff asked me if I wanted him to stay during the visit, but I declined. This was something I had to do alone. Jeff went downstairs to wait for them, and they arrived shortly thereafter. He brought them upstairs to our apartment, and then he left, leaving the three of us alone. As I shook Daniel's mother's hand, the tears finally came.

I will never discuss in detail what was said between the three of us that day, for to do so would be a betrayal of the trust of these people who never once smeared my name. I will only say that they were very kind to me that day as we sat and talked. They told me what I had long ago guessed from their silence during the media frenzy surrounding my arrest: they did not hold a vendetta against me. They did not wish to see me suffer anymore than I already had, for that would not bring Daniel back. These were not cold-hearted people. They had just wanted to know what had happened to their son. That was it. We both had come to court searching for the truth. Not to hear the opinions of judges and arguments of lawyers, but to try to find that truth for ourselves the best that we could. And after hearing all of the evidence, we had both come to the same sad conclusion. Yet here they were, talking to me openly and without hate in their hearts.

They were two of the strongest people I have ever met.

As they were leaving, Daniel's uncle turned to me and reiterated something he and Daniel's mother had brought up earlier.

"Remember—you can be a spokesperson for safer shows. You have that power. Good luck, man. Go live your life."

I promised them I would, and then they left. I staggered back into the apartment and fell completely apart. I do not know how long I cried, or even what happened for the next few hours. My body was trying to purge all the grief I had held inside for so long, and it seemed to be endless.

The next thing I can remember is going out to eat with my family and entire legal team, who brought their families as well. That evening, for the first and only time in my entire life, I saw my father take a shot of liquor. It would have been bad form not to—everyone else drank one. It was a toast to my freedom.

I drank water.

How strange life can be.

———

The following day Jeff and I took a train to see the Sedlec Ossuary, the famous "bone church" in the village of Kutná Hora. I walked through the basement of the church, elaborately decorated with bones from the skeletons of over 40,000 people. I took pictures inside the ossuary for a good while, then that evening Jeff and I went out to dinner in a Czech restaurant. We ordered an enormous meal for two, a massive pile of wild game meat and vegetables served in a long wooden tray, and we ate it all. As we waddled out of the restaurant, we saw several copies of that day's paper hanging on a rack by the front door. On the front page was a large picture of my face and bold Czech lettering spelling my name and something else. I hoped it said "Not guilty."

The next day we left Prague for America.

Five months passed, and on June 5, 2013, the prosecuting attorney's appeal was heard by three judges of the Prague High Court. The court upheld my acquittal.

Two months later, on August 19, 2013, I was on a plane in France with lamb of god, about to fly home after a summer European festival run. Right before the plane's doors were shut, Chris Adler looked up from his phone in the seat across the aisle from me. He had just received an email from Jeff Cohen. The second and final possible appeal to the verdict of my case, one to the Czech Supreme Court, had either not been made within the required two month time period, or it had been denied. I do not know which.

"Jeff says you're done, dude. It's over," Chris said.

The plane doors shut, and we fastened our seat belts. Before too long, we were in the air, flying towards home.

I was, and I remain,

a free man.

epilogue

$\mathcal{L}$amb of god finished the tour supporting our *Resolution* album at the end of January of 2014. The tour had begun in our hometown of Richmond, VA almost exactly two years previously, and we finished it in Johannesburg, South Africa. During that two-year period, we played shows on every continent on earth except for Antarctica. Stuck in the middle of this tour was a very stressful year and two months, from the day I was arrested at the Prague airport until the day I sat on the runway at Charles de Gaulle airport in Paris and learned that the specter of my return to prison had finally vanished.

It had been a brutal fourteen months.

After the tour ended, I returned to Richmond. After a week or so at home, I kissed my beloved wife goodbye and moved south into a cheap and slightly run-down beach house I had rented. The small house sat on a barrier island where I had spent some time as a very young child, and I knew that the sound of the waves would soothe me while I relived the troubling events in this book as I wrote. I spent too many hours at local thrift stores (as well as the nearest epicenter of all evil, Walmart), buying all the basic necessities I came to realize one needs in a new home; the things a married man such as myself tends to take for granted: throw rugs; can openers; rods for toilet-paper holders; pot holders; bath towels. Then, alone on an island wedged along the seacoast of my childhood, I sat down to finish this book. I had begun writing it while still on the road with lamb of god, but a heavy metal tour is most definitely not conducive to the quiet and solitary atmosphere I have found I require to do serious writing. I needed peace in order to delve deep inside my head and wring this story out, and I was unable to get much work done on the road. It wasn't until I had walked the deserted beach for a while, a good week or so of allowing myself to just breathe the salty winter air and forget about my band and touring for a bit, that I was able to start implementing the daily stringent self-discipline that writing a book requires.

Besides, I had not wanted to write it in the first place anyway.

Months before even my first appeal had occurred, lamb of god's booking agent, Tim Borror, had started bugging me about calling a literary agent who was interested in talking to me. I blew Tim off for a bit, because I knew any agent would only want to talk to me about one thing: the story of what had happened in Prague. I ignored Tim's emails and voice messages as long as I could, until guilt got the better of me and I gave him a call, taking the agent's contact info. I phoned the agent, Marc Gerald, and told him how I already had a photography book in the works and a publisher lined up. I told him how I had realized even as I was arrested that I would tell this story one day, but that I didn't think I was ready yet. I told him I just wanted to relax and forget about it all for a bit. I told him that I believed my story had some value, that it might even be able to help someone one day, but that the memories were still too painful, still too fresh.

"Yes, but Randy—the memories are going fade," Marc said softly.

And with that sentence, spoken in his kind voice, he convinced me to write this book. I had my journal from my time in prison, but even so, my recall would suffer more and more as each day passed. He was right—it was time to put down the memories I still retained on paper, and try to make some sense of what I had gone through.

A few weeks after I sat down by the ocean to write the majority of this book, I agreed to do a few publicity interviews with major press outlets about Don Argott's documentary, *As the Palaces Burn*. The film would be in theaters soon, and although I did not want to do the interviews (as I knew all of the questions would be about my experience in Prague, something I was already writing about for hours every day), I agreed, for the movie is not about just me. It is about lamb of god, and being in lamb of god (or any band) is like being in a marriage—if the marriage is to survive, each partner must do his or her part to keep it afloat, even when they don't feel like it.

I was standing in my kitchen, on the phone with a writer for a well-known New York paper and answering questions about my experience in Prague in a rather matter-of-fact manner when I heard her pause on the other end.

"Randy . . . " she said, trying to formulate her words, "I'm having a hard time . . . getting something out of you. You seem rather . . . *cavalier* about what you went through, as if it hasn't really affected you. Like it was no big deal, just something you went through and now you've moved on."

"You mean you are not eliciting the emotional response you are looking for," I replied.

"Sorta. Randy, I guess what I want to know is how has this experience changed you?" she said.

I told her I was still processing the whole thing, but that I supposed I was a sadder person in some ways—but that was about it. And while what I went through definitely *was* a big deal to me, it hadn't changed me or my values at all. I had already changed long before I was arrested that day in 2012.

Most of the people who interview me about Prague seem to be looking for some big "Aha!" moment in the tale of my arrest, incarceration, and trial. They want to nail down a Hollywood-esque scene for their story, an emotional climax where I experience a sudden and blinding flash of insight, finally realizing one of life's big lessons before moving forward into the gauze-filtered, softly lit warmth of grace and redemption. I do not blame them for trying to find this nonexistent *denouement* in the story of my ordeal in Prague—they are writers, just like myself. Almost without exception, all of us are searching for the emotional highlight of any story we write as (subconsciously or not) we endlessly attempt to shove every tale into the accepted, formulaic, and monomythic box laid out in Joseph Campbell's famous work, *The Hero with a Thousand Faces.* The essence of Campbell's universal hero's journey goes something like this: A hero leaves his everyday life and goes on an extraordinary journey. On this journey, he encounters a difficult obstacle or powerful foe, fighting a great battle against the forces arrayed against him. He wins the battle, then returns as a changed man from his mysterious adventure to his mundane home, bearing a great gift or bit of hard-earned wisdom which he graciously imparts upon his people.

It's great stuff, and this basic structure can be found in virtually every best selling novel and Hollywood blockbuster. To explain it another way: exposition, rising conflict, climax, falling conflict, resolution. Storytelling 101. It sells a lot of movie screenplays and novel manuscripts. It makes for wonderfully warm and fuzzy feelings as you watch the credits roll and walk out of the theater. We all need those from time to time. It's called escape.

But life isn't a movie, or a book (not even this one).

Life is life; and until the very second you die, there is no lasting escape from it. In life, sometimes horrible things just happen. Sometimes there is no new lesson to be learned, only tragedy to be endured the best one can. And sometimes the best a person can do is hang on as hard as they can, keep putting one foot forward in front of the other, and try to do what they know to be the right thing until they reach the end of that particular sad leg of their journey.

Sometimes, life just sucks. I try to deal with it the best I can.

———

I was talking to my wife about these interviews, telling her about the writers looking for that big, flashy, important moment in my story, and how this frustrated me.

"Honey, what was important to you was to remain the man you had already become," Cindy said.

A few months ago, I was talking with my father, and the subject of Prague came up.

"I did not try to convince you what to do one way or the other," he said. "I did not feel it was my place to give you my opinion on whether or not you should return for trial. But I know what kind of man you are, and I know your morals. I knew it would have hurt you badly to not go back. It would have been worse than prison for you."

For as long as I can remember, I have always known it was important to do the right thing according to the dictates of my conscience, no matter what problem I found myself faced with. This moral imperative sits deep within the core of my being, for I was raised by parents with a very strong sense of right and wrong. The value and necessity of personal responsibility had been instilled in me by those parents, but somewhere along the way I had allowed myself to get lost in a haze of alcohol. When I woke up one morning in Brisbane, Australia and realized that no matter how far I tried to run into a bottle, I would always carry my problems with me . . . I gave up the race. I began to face my problems, to try as hard as I could to live in a manner I could be proud of, and to take responsibility for my own actions and life.

There is no escape.

So I simply stopped running.

That was the change in me, *that* was the big "aha!" moment in my life. It wasn't cinematic, it wasn't glamorous, and it didn't happen in a prison cell or courtroom. It occurred as I sat alone and hungover, looking at a bunch of empty beer bottles on a hotel balcony.

This type of moment can happen for anyone. Anywhere and at anytime.

Everything I have done since then has just been me trying my best to follow the correct standard operating procedure, including returning to Prague for trial. I simply committed to what my heart told me was the correct course of action, fumbling my way through what I knew was the right thing to do, even though I was very, very scared to do so. And I'm still putting one foot in front of the other, doing the best I can. That's all I or anyone can do.

I am not perfect by a long shot, and by no means have I done everything correctly since I have gotten sober. I am learning how to become a better person, but sometimes this is a slow and very painful process. I am just another human being, no better or worse than anyone else on this planet, and as such I still make mistakes. I always will. But I own my mistakes now, and try not to repeat them when I can.

If I could go back in time to that day in Prague, I would walk into that club, take one look at the place, and shake my head. I would go to my band and crew and say to them, "There is absolutely no way we are doing a gig in this dump tonight," then we would get back on our bus and ride to Poland without playing a note, and a young man from the Czech Republic would still be alive today. Of course, if I could go back in time, I would do all sorts of amazing things. I would prevent the rise of Hitler. I would warn the people of New York City that the World Trade Center was about to go down in flames. I would not be such a self-centered jerk as many times as I have been. I would do many, many things very differently.

But that line of magical thinking is useless to pursue, for me and for anyone else who wishes to live their life the best they can. I lived in my head for far too long, and that did both myself and others nothing but harm. Today I am a reality-based man, and reality tells me that I exist in the here and the now—not anywhere else but exactly where I am, not three years ago, not yesterday, not tomorrow, not five minutes from now, but *right here, right now.* And my heart tells me I must try as hard as I possibly can to live the best I can, in this eternal here and now.

This morning when I woke up, I felt the first chill of fall on the slight wind blowing into my open bedroom window from the ocean. I made a pot of coffee, poured myself a cup, and walked down to the beach. The sun hung low but bright in the sky as I shielded my eyes and looked out at the sea. Its surface was hushed, flat, and glassy. Only the tiniest of waves were breaking, and they crumbled directly onto the shore, wetting the edge of the sand just long enough to hold the sun's reflection for a second's time before shapelessly disappearing from whence they came. I thought of how I would finish writing this book today, and I thought about a young man named Daniel, and I felt the sadness pass though me just as it does everyday, as slow and as soft as the breeze flowing all around me from the Atlantic. I thought of how I would go for a swim after the writing was finally done. I stared at the almost perfectly still ocean for a moment, then turned and walked back to the faded wooden porch of my small house by the sea, to sit and write this.

Now the work is done, a thing of the past just like the events that birthed it. The wind is blowing harder now, and I can hear the sound of the ocean waves breaking on the beach a block away much louder than this morning. The surface of the sea is probably no longer calm, and sounds as if it is boiling and white-capped and choppy. The waves may be rough.

No matter. I will still go down to the beach for a swim in just a second; for the ocean is the ocean, vast and uncontrollable. I cannot dictate her fickle moods.

I can only swim in her waters as safely and as strongly as I am able, until the winter comes and it is too cold to do so. To not immerse myself in her majesty while I can as the last bit of summer's warmth fades away would be a shame.

For she is beautiful, and she is the only one I have.

—*D. Randall Blythe*
October 1, 2014
Cape Fear, NC

acknowledgements

*T*he following people made this book possible:

Tim Borror for bugging me to talk with Marc Gerald. Marc Gerald for convincing me to write this book and then selling it to Ben Schafer. Ben Schafer at Da Capo Press for buying it and then editing it. You three are the front line. Salute.

Random House for picking up the UK rights. My UK editor, Adja Vucicevic. To Jack Fogg, the Englishman with the greatest name ever—I hope we can work together all the way through a project one day. Kirsten Sprinks for all the help getting the word out in Merry Olde—Roger Brilliant thanks you.

P.R. Brown and Marco Pavia for design and proofs. Sean O'Hern at Commercial Taphouse, 111 N. Robinson St, Richmond, VA for pouring the beer I didn't drink for the Chapter Four photo—if I could still drink like a normal person, it would be at the Taphouse.

To my friend and editor at www.thetalkhouse.com, Michael Azerrad, for reading with a critical editorial eye. To Greg "Eagle Eyes" Puciato of the almighty Dillinger Escape Plan and The Black Queen for doing the same—if the music thing doesn't work acknowledgements

out, I will get you a gig as a copy editor. To the hometown homie Kevin Powers for advance reading and encouragement from a *real* writer. Jeff Cohen for proof reading, long walks in Prague, and keeping me out of prison—love ya, bro. Brad Warner for punk rawk, posture correction, and advance reading.

To Pen Rollings, Paul Aneshensel, and Emory Flournoy at Uptown Color in Richmond, VA for coming to my rescue with all the journal scans. Y'all rule—Pen, keep riffing—one day, I will be rich enough to pay for a Breadwinner/Sliang Laos reunion show.

To the fine Gentlemen of the Tuning Room Group for carrying me through the beginning of my new life—I will see y'all on the road. To the S.F.G.'s for constant gratitude, companionship across the globe, and being my lifeline during my long exile on Shaka Brah Island—I love each and every one of you, you are my brothers. To Rabbi Michael "Stick" Shefrin and my father, the Reverend Wayne T. Blythe, for reading my Q&A with God from the first draft of this beast—it's still there, it just didn't make it into this book—next time, I will hit 'em with a *mazel tov* cocktail. Matt Frain for endless talks in the funny voice—I learn from you constantly, and I am proud of the man you have become. Bill Griggs and Stephen McMasters for teaching me the right stuff.

Pete Adams for real talk and fly fishing when I needed it most. Jamey Jasta for being the truth. Vinnie Paul Abbott for being a true friend when the chips were way down. Don Argott for late night Misfits jam sessions and being there for me in Prague. Y'all are good people.

Cory Brennan (let's go surfing soon), Justin Arcangel, and everyone else at 5B Artist Management for steering the lamb of god ship and helping me out with this book, especially Bob "The Quiet Genius" Johnsen—you rule, bro. Maria Ferrero for loaning me Uncle Vincent's Rolleiflex and being an all-around bad-ass; kisses.

To anyone who made or sported a "Free Randy" shirt, contributed to my legal defense fund, bought something at our auction, or just spread the word and thought good thoughts for me—I honestly don't know what would have happened to me if it hadn't been for you people. This book, to a massive degree, was written for you. Thank you—I am truly humbled. Special thanks to those that wrote me while I was locked up—I needed it.

To all the musicians who spoke up in my defense—there are far too many of you to name. Know that I am honored to walk amongst you men and women. I salute you—see ya on the road.

lamba gawd—Doug Flutie threw the fütball. Flutie threw the fütball, and threw the fütball, and threw the fütball. Flutie was pooped.

To Martin Radvan, Vladimír Jablonsky, Tomá Morysek, Michal Sykora, and, of course, Tomá Grivna for representing me in court. Thank you for helping me to remain a free man. Rudy Leška for superlative translation services and manuscript review.

To the people of Richmond, VA—thank you for all the thoughts and prayers, and the overwhelming and warm welcome home. I'm proud to call RVA home.

This book was written to the rhythm of the ocean tides, so shout outs are in order for my Cape Fear coastal family: T-Roy, Birds, and Shiny Bones—I love y'all. David & Norma Edralin for surfing, sandwiches, and ribs—Team Greensboro will rip forever! Chad Nicoll for having the greatest attitude at any surf session—it's a pleasure to ride waves with you. Scooter at Surf Unlimited, OI—one day I will start a surf rock band and take you on a coastal-only tour. To head-high glassy hurricane swells and the bottlenose dolphins who ride them with me—you keep me sane. Left is right.

I would like to thank the following bands for writing the songs I sang everyday while I was locked up—you kept my brain from falling to pieces: Bad Brains for "Attitude", Black Flag for "Rise Above", and Misfits for "London Dungeon". You have been the soundtrack to my life since I was a kid.

My family for standing by me and not disowning me, even after all the grief I have put you through. This is never what I wanted my first book to be about, but I think the story needed to be told. I love you so much, and I promise I'll write a happier book next time.

Salad the cat for keeping me company while I wrote.

Last and most importantly, to my wife, for everything. I love you so much, honey.